NUCLEAR WEAPONS

A new nuclear arms race is underway between Russia and the United States, one that focuses on the technology of delivery of nuclear warheads. This book describes how and why this race is happening, who still possesses nuclear weapons, and what constraints apply to those weapons under international law. A global nuclear ban treaty entered into force in January 2021, but the nuclear powers kept distant. The last remaining treaty restraining the arsenals of the two nuclear superpowers will expire in less than five years' time and the risk is that other States will turn to nuclear arms for their defence, further fracturing the non-proliferation regime installed after the Cuban missile crisis.

Stuart Casey-Maslen is an Honorary Professor at the University of Pretoria, South Africa. He was the legal advisor to the Austria delegation in the diplomatic conference that negotiated the United Nations Treaty on the Prohibition of Nuclear Weapons in 2017. He has written or edited ten major works on different aspects of weapons law.

Nuclear Weapons

LAW, POLICY, AND PRACTICE

STUART CASEY-MASLEN
University of Pretoria

CAMBRIDGE
UNIVERSITY PRESS

CAMBRIDGE
UNIVERSITY PRESS

University Printing House, Cambridge CB2 8BS, United Kingdom

One Liberty Plaza, 20th Floor, New York, NY 10006, USA

477 Williamstown Road, Port Melbourne, VIC 3207, Australia

314–321, 3rd Floor, Plot 3, Splendor Forum, Jasola District Centre,
New Delhi – 110025, India

103 Penang Road, #05–06/07, Visioncrest Commercial, Singapore 238467

Cambridge University Press is part of the University of Cambridge.

It furthers the University's mission by disseminating knowledge in the pursuit of education, learning, and research at the highest international levels of excellence.

www.cambridge.org
Information on this title: www.cambridge.org/9781316510858
DOI: 10.1017/9781009039864

First published 2021

Printed in the United Kingdom by TJ Books Limited, Padstow Cornwall

A catalogue record for this publication is available from the British Library.

Library of Congress Cataloging-in-Publication Data
NAMES: Casey-Maslen, Stuart, author.
TITLE: Nuclear weapons : law, policy, and practice / Stuart Casey-Maslen, University of Pretoria.
DESCRIPTION: Cambridge, United Kingdom ; New York, NY : Cambridge University Press, 2022. | Includes bibliographical references and index.
IDENTIFIERS: LCCN 2021038923 | ISBN 9781316510858 (hardback) | ISBN 9781009018661 (paperback) | ISBN 9781009039864 (ebook)
SUBJECTS: LCSH: Nuclear weapons (International law)
CLASSIFICATION: LCC KZ5665 .C37 2022 | DDC 341.7/34–dc23
LC record available at https://lccn.loc.gov/2021038923

ISBN 978-1-316-51085-8 Hardback
ISBN 978-1-009-01866-1 Paperback

Contents

Cases and Materials *page* x
Table of Cases xiv

Introduction 1
The Layout of the Book 3

1 **The Development of Nuclear Weapons** 7
The Theory and Early Development of Nuclear Weapons 7
The Energetic Effects of Nuclear Fission and Nuclear Fusion 7
The Manhattan Project 11
Nazi Germany and the Bomb 16
Japanese Research into an Atomic Bomb 22
The Development of Nuclear Weapons after the Second World War 23
The Soviet Nuclear Weapons Programme 23
Thermonuclear (Hydrogen) Bombs 26
The Soviet–US Arms Race 27
From Bombers to Land-Based Missiles to SLBMs 29
The United Kingdom's Nuclear Weapons Programme 35
France's Nuclear Weapons Programme 38
China's Nuclear Weapons Programme 39
The Development of Nuclear Weapons by Other States 40
Israel's Nuclear Weapons Programme 40
India's Nuclear Weapons Programme 42
Pakistan's Nuclear Weapons Programme 43
South Africa's Nuclear Weapons Programme 45
North Korea's Nuclear Weapons Programme 45
New Technologies 47

2 **Use of Nuclear Weapons** 52
The Use of Nuclear Weapons in 1945 52
Hiroshima 55
Nagasaki 56

Use of Nuclear Explosive Devices for Peaceful Purposes 57
The US Plowshare Program 57
The Soviet 'Nuclear Explosions for the National Economy' Programme 58
The 1976 Peaceful Nuclear Explosions Treaty 59
Envisaged Use of Nuclear Weapons against a Nuclear Power 60
The Cuban Missile Crisis 60
Envisaged Use by the United States in the Yom Kippur War 61
The 'Petrov' Incident 62
Envisaged Use against Non-nuclear Forces 62
The Korean War 62
Wars in Indochina 63
Dien Bien Phu 63
The Vietnam War 63
'Broken Arrow' Incidents 64

3 **The Treaty on the Non-proliferation of Nuclear Weapons** 67

The Rationale for the NPT 67
The Negotiation of the Treaty 69
Entry into Force and Universalisation of the NPT 72
The (Non-)Definition of Nuclear Weapons in the NPT 73
The Obligations of the Nuclear-Weapon States Parties 74
The Prohibition on the Transfer of Nuclear Weapons 74
The Prohibition on the Transfer of Control over Nuclear Weapons 77
The Prohibition on Assisting the Acquisition of Nuclear Weapons 78
Peaceful Nuclear Explosions 79
The Obligations of the Non-Nuclear-Weapon States Parties 80
The Prohibition on Acquisition 80
A Prohibition on Development? 80
A Limited Prohibition on Assisting Another Non-nuclear-Weapon State to Acquire Nuclear Explosive Devices 81
Domestic Implementation and Reporting 82
Verification: The IAEA Safeguards Agreements 82
The Comprehensive Safeguards Agreement 83
The IAEA Additional Protocol 84
Small Quantities Protocol 84
The Peaceful Use of Nuclear Energy 85
The Duty to Pursue Nuclear Disarmament 86
NPT Review Conferences 94
Concluding Remarks 96

4 **The Testing of Nuclear Weapons** 98

Nuclear Testing by the NPT Nuclear-Weapon States 99
Nuclear Testing by the United States 99
Nuclear Testing by the Soviet Union 101

Nuclear Testing by the United Kingdom 103
Nuclear Testing by France 103
Nuclear Testing by China 104
The International Legal Regimes for Nuclear Testing 104
The 1959 Antarctic Treaty 105
The 1963 Partial Test-Ban Treaty 107
The 1966 Outer Space Treaty 110
The 1974 Threshold Test-Ban Treaty 111
The 1996 Comprehensive Nuclear-Test-Ban Treaty 112
The Negotiation of the Treaty 112
The Content of the Treaty 113
The 2017 Treaty on the Prohibition of Nuclear Weapons 114
Explosive Nuclear Testing under Customary International Law 115

5 **Agreements between Russia and the United States** 118

The 2010 New Strategic Arms Reduction Treaty (New START) 119
The Negotiation of New START 119
The Content of New START 122
The 1987 Intermediate-Range Nuclear Forces (INF) Treaty 126
The Strategic Arms Limitation Talks (SALT) 129
The 1972 Anti-Ballistic Missile Treaty 130
The 1972 Strategic Arms Limitation Treaty (SALT I) 132
The 1979 Strategic Arms Limitation Treaty (SALT II) 133
The Strategic Arms Reduction Treaties (START) 135
START I 135
START II 136
START III 137
The SORT Treaty 138
Concluding Remarks 139

6 **Treaties Prohibiting Nuclear Weapons** 141

The Regional Nuclear Prohibition Treaties 142
The 1959 Antarctic Treaty 142
The 1966 Outer Space Treaty 142
The 1967 Tlatelolco Treaty 144
The 1970 Sea-Bed Treaty 147
The 1985 Treaty of Rarotonga 148
The 1995 Bangkok Treaty 150
The 1996 Pelindaba Treaty 151
The 2006 Treaty of Semipalatinsk 153
The Nuclear-Weapon-Free 'Status' of Mongolia 154
The Conferences of Nuclear-Weapon-Free Zones and Mongolia 155
The Proposal for a Nuclear-Weapon-Free Zone in the Middle East 155
The Treaty on the Prohibition of Nuclear Weapons 156
The Negotiation of the TPNW 157

The Prohibitions in the TPNW 159
Positive Obligations of States Parties 162
The Declaration of Nuclear Status 163
National Implementation Measures 164
The Duty to Promote the Universalisation of the TPNW 165
Victim Assistance 166
Environmental Remediation of Irradiated Land 167
Disarmament Obligations 169
The Obligations of International Cooperation and Assistance 170
Verification of Compliance 171
Safeguards Agreements 171
The First Meeting of States Parties 172
The Impact of the TPNW 172

7 **Verification** 174

Verification of Testing 175
Verification of the Treaty Prohibitions of Explosive Nuclear Testing 175
Project Vela 175
Verification of the CTBT 177
The International Monitoring System 177
On-Site Inspections under the CTBT 179
Verification of the Prohibition of Testing under the TPNW 179
Preventing the Proliferation of Nuclear Weapons 180
The Development of IAEA Safeguards 180
The IAEA Safeguards 181
The Comprehensive Safeguards Agreement 181
IAEA Safeguards and Iran's Nuclear Weapons Programme 182
IAEA Safeguards and Iraq's Nuclear Weapons Programme 184
IAEA Safeguards and Libya's Nuclear Weapons Programme 185
IAEA Safeguards and the Risk of Proliferation in Saudi Arabia 186
The IAEA Additional Protocol 186
Iran and the Additional Protocol 187
Verification of Destruction of Nuclear Weapons 188
The INF Treaty's Verification Regime 189
Verification of Compliance with the TPNW 191
Verification of Deployed and Non-deployed Weapons 192
Verification under New START 193
Reporting and Missile Identification 194
Telemetric Data 194
Inspections 195
The Open Skies Treaty 195
Concluding Remarks 196

8 **Use and Testing of Nuclear Weapons under International Law** 198

International Law Governing the Use of Nuclear Weapons 199

Jus ad bellum 199
Necessity *ad bellum* 201
Proportionality *ad bellum* 201
International Humanitarian Law 202
The Principle of Distinction 203
Belligerent Reprisals 206
The Principle of Proportionality 208
The Superfluous Injury Principle 208
International Human Rights Law 210
The Law of Neutrality 211
International Environmental Law 211
Responsibility under International Law for Unlawful Use or Testing of Nuclear Weapons 212
State Responsibility 212
Individual Criminal Responsibility 216
Use of Nuclear Weapons as a Crime of Aggression 217
Use of Nuclear Weapons as a War Crime 220
Use of Nuclear Weapons as a Crime against Humanity 223
Use of Nuclear Weapons as an Act of Genocide 224

Concluding Remarks on the Future of Nuclear Arms Control and Disarmament 226

Select Bibliography 229

Index 235

Cases and Materials

TREATIES AND LEGISLATION

Treaties

1868 Declaration Renouncing the Use, in Time of War, of Explosive Projectiles Under 400 Grammes Weight; adopted and signed at St Petersburg, 11 December 1868; entered into force the same day. 208
1899 Regulations concerning the Laws and Customs of War on Land annexed to Convention (II) with Respect to the Laws and Customs of War on Land; adopted at The Hague, 29 July 1899; entered into force 4 September 1900. 209
1945 Charter of the United Nations; signed at San Francisco, 26 June 1945; entered into force 24 October 1945. 71, 116, 117, 143, 147, 148, 149, 199, 200, 217, 218
1948 Convention on the Prevention and Punishment of the Crime of Genocide (Genocide Convention); adopted at Paris, 9 December 1948; entered into force 12 January 1951. 224
1959 Antarctic Treaty; adopted at Washington DC, 1 December 1959; entered into force 23 June 1962. 5, 73, 104, 105–07
1963 Treaty Banning Nuclear Weapon Tests in the Atmosphere, in Outer Space and Under Water; concluded at Moscow, 25 July 1963 (Partial Test-Ban Treaty); opened for signature at London, Moscow, and Washington, DC, 8 August 1963; entered into force 10 October 1963. 5, 38, 41, 59, 73, 104, 107–10, 111, 112, 113, 115, 143, 159, 175, 176
1966 Covenant on Civil and Political Rights; adopted at New York, 16 December 1966; entered into force 23 March 1976. 210
1966 Treaty on Principles Governing the Activities of States in the Exploration and Use of Outer Space, including the Moon and Other Celestial Bodies (Outer Space Treaty); concluded under UN General Assembly Resolution 2222 (XXI), adopted without a vote on 19 December 1966; entered into force 10 October 1967. 110–11
1967 Treaty for the Prohibition of Nuclear Weapons in Latin America and the Caribbean; opened for signature at Tlatelolco, Mexico, 14 February 1967; entered into force 22 April 1969. 73, 79, 144–47, 160

1968 Treaty on the Non-proliferation of Nuclear Weapons (NPT); opened for signature at London, Moscow, and Washington, DC, 1 July 1968; entered into force 5 March 1970. 1, 3, 6, 37, 42, 45, 46, 59, **67–97**, 141, 146, 156, 158, 159, 188, 198

1969 Vienna Convention on the Law of Treaties; adopted at Vienna, 23 May 1969; entered into force 27 January 1980. 90, 92, 93, 116, 158

1970 Treaty on the Prohibition of the Emplacement of Nuclear Weapons and Other Weapons of Mass Destruction on the Sea-Bed and the Ocean Floor and in the Subsoil Thereof (Sea-Bed Treaty); adopted at New York 7 December 1970; entered into force, 18 May 1972. 147–48

1971 Convention on the Prohibition of the Development, Production and Stockpiling of Bacteriological (Biological) and Toxin Weapons and on Their Destruction (Biological Weapons Convention); adopted at New York, 16 December 1971; entered into force 26 March 1975. 159, 161

1972 Treaty between the United States of America and the Union of Soviet Socialist Republics on the Limitation of Anti-Ballistic Missile Systems (ABM Treaty); adopted at Moscow, 26 May 1972; entered into force 3 October 1972; expired 13 June 2002. 47, 118, 119, **130–32**, 135, 138

1972 Interim Agreement between the United States of America and the Union of Soviet Socialist Republics on Certain Measures with respect to the Limitation of Strategic Offensive Arms (SALT I); adopted at Moscow, 26 May 1972; entered into force 3 October 1972; expired 3 October 1977. 119, 130, **132**, 133

1974 Treaty between the United States of America and the Union of Soviet Socialist Republics on the Limitation of Underground Nuclear Weapon Tests (and Protocol Thereto); signed at Moscow, 3 July 1974; entered into force 11 December 1990. 104, 111

1976 Treaty between the United States of America and the Union of Soviet Socialist Republics on Underground Nuclear Explosions for Peaceful Purposes (and Protocol Thereto); signed at Moscow and Washington DC on 28 May 1976; entered into force 11 December 1990. 59, 118

1977 Protocol Additional to the Geneva Conventions of 12 August 1949, and relating to the Protection of Victims of International Armed Conflicts (1977 Additional Protocol I); adopted at Geneva, 8 June 1977; entered into force 7 December 1978. 205, 207, 208

1979 Treaty between the United States of America and the Union of Soviet Socialist Republics on the Limitation of Strategic Offensive Arms (SALT II); adopted and signed at Vienna, 18 June 1979; never entered into force. 133–35

1982 Convention on the Law of the Sea (UNCLOS); adopted at Montego Bay, 10 December 1982; entered into force 16 November 1994. 161

1986 Vienna Convention on the Law of Treaties between States and International Organizations or between International Organizations; adopted at Vienna, 21 March 1986; not yet in force. 169, 180

1987 Treaty between the United States of America and the Union of Soviet Socialist Republics on the Elimination of Their Intermediate-Range and Shorter-Range Missiles (INF Treaty); signed at Washington DC, 8 December 1987; entered into force 1 June 1988; expired (de facto), 2 August 2019. 2, 30, 31, 35, 50, 118, 121, 124, **126–29**, 139, 188, **189–91**, 226

1991 Treaty between the United States of America and the Union of Soviet Socialist Republics on the Reduction and Limitation of Strategic Offensive Arms (START I); signed at Moscow, 31 July 1991; entry into force, 5 December 1994. 35, 119, 120, **135**, 188, 192
1992 Convention on the Prohibition of the Development, Production, Stockpiling and Use of Chemical Weapons and on Their Destruction (Chemical Weapons Convention); adopted at Geneva, 3 September 1992; entered into force 29 April 1997. 68, 112, 159, 162
1992 Treaty on Open Skies; signed, 24 March 1992; entered into force 1 January 2002. 195–96
1993 Treaty between the United States of America and the Union of Soviet Socialist Republics on Strategic Offensive Reductions (START II); signed at Moscow, 3 January 1993; no entry into force. 32, 132, 135, **136**, 137, 227
1995 Treaty on the Southeast Asia Nuclear Weapon-Free Zone (Bangkok Treaty); adopted at Bangkok, 15 December 1995; entered into force 28 March 1997. **150–51**, 161
1996 Comprehensive Nuclear-Test-Ban Treaty (CTBT); adopted at New York, 10 September 1996; not yet in force. 3, 38, 42, 60, 80, 89, 98, 99, 104, 110, 112, 153, 158, 159, 166, 175, **177–79**, 198, 226, 227
1996 African Nuclear Weapon-Free Zone Treaty (Pelindaba Treaty); opened for signature at Cairo, 11 April 1996, entered into force 15 July 2009. **151–52**, 153, 160
1997 Memorandum of Understanding Relating to the Treaty between the United States of America and the Union of Soviet Socialist Republics on the Limitation of Anti-Ballistic Missile Systems of May 26, 1972; adopted at New York, 26 September 1997; never entered into force. 131
1998 Rome Statute of the International Criminal Court; adopted at Rome, 17 July 1998; entered into force 1 July 2002. 116, 217, 219
2002 Treaty between the United States of America and the Russian Federation on Strategic Offensive Reductions; signed at Moscow, 24 May 2002; entered into force 1 June 2003; expired, 5 February 2011. 119, 121, **138**
2003 South Pacific Nuclear Free Zone Treaty; concluded at Rarotonga, 6 August 1985; entered into force 11 December 1986. 148–50, 160
2006 Treaty on a Nuclear-Weapon-Free Zone in Central Asia (Treaty of Semipalatinsk); adopted, 8 September 2006; entered into force 21 March 2009. **153**, 160
2009 Agreement between the Kingdom of Saudi Arabia and the International Atomic Energy Agency for the Application of Safeguards in Connection with the Treaty on the Non-proliferation of Nuclear Weapons, IAEA doc. INFCIRC/746 signed at Vienna, 16 June 2005; entered into force 13 January 2009. 85, 186
2010 Treaty between the United States of America and the Russian Federation on Measures for the Further Reduction and Limitation of Strategic Offensive Arms (New START); signed at Prague, 8 April 2010; entered into force 5 February 2011. 2, 3, 37, 118, **119–26**, 138, **192–95**, 227
2017 Treaty on the Prohibition of Nuclear Weapons; adopted at New York, 7 July 2017; entered into force 22 January 2021. 114, 117, 141, 154, **156–73**, **191**, 198, 226

National Legislation

1954 Atomic Energy Act (United States). 16, 36, 73, 78
2000 Law on the nuclear-weapon-free status of Mongolia. 154
2019 Prohibition of Nuclear Weapons Act 2019 (Act 40 of 2019) (Ireland). 165

Table of Cases

INTERNATIONAL COURTS AND TRIBUNALS

Case concerning the differences between New Zealand and France arising from the Rainbow Warrior affair, ruling of 6 July 1986 by the UN Secretary-General, in *Reports of International Arbitral Awards*, Vol. XIX (1986), pp. 199–221. 38

International Court of Justice, Nuclear Tests Case (Australia *v.* France), Judgment, 20 December 1974. 216

International Court of Justice, Case Concerning Military and Paramilitary Activities in and against Nicaragua (Nicaragua v. United States of America), Judgment (Merits), 27 June 1986. 200

International Court of Justice, Case Concerning Oil Platforms (Islamic Republic of Iran *v.* United States of America) Judgment, 6 November 2003. 200, 201, 202

International Court of Justice, Legality of the Threat or Use of Nuclear Weapons, Advisory Opinion, 8 July 1996. 88, 93, 188, 198, 199, 200, 202, 203, 204, 205, 208, 209, 210, 211, 212

International Court of Justice, Obligations Concerning Negotiations Relating to Cessation of the Nuclear Arms Race and to Nuclear Disarmament (Marshall Islands *v.* United Kingdom), Judgment (Preliminary Objections), 5 October 2016. 213, 214, 215

International Criminal Court, Prosecutor *v.* Bosco Ntaganda, Judgment (Trial Chamber) (Case No. ICC-01/04-02/06), 8 July 2019. 222

International Criminal Court (Pre-Trial Chamber), 'Situation in the Republic of Kenya, Decision Pursuant to Article 15 of the Rome Statute on the Authorization of an Investigation into the Situation in the Republic of Kenya', ICC doc. ICC-01/09-19, 31 March 2010. 224

International Criminal Tribunal for the former Yugoslavia (ICTY), Prosecutor *v.* Blaškić, Judgment (Trial Chamber) (Case No. IT-95-14-T), 3 March 2000. 223

ICTY, Prosecutor *v.* Zoran Kupreškić and others, Judgment (Trial Chamber) (Case No. IT-95–16-T), 14 January 2000. 206

ICTY, Prosecutor *v.* Mrkšić, Judgment (Trial Chamber) (Case No. IT95-13/1-T), 27 September 2007. 223

ICTY, Prosecutor *v.* Kunarac, Judgment (Appeals Chamber) (Case Nos. IT-96-23 & IT-96-23/1-A), 12 June 2002. 223
ICTY, Prosecutor *v.* Krstić, Judgment (Appeals Chamber) (Case No. IT-98-33-A), 19 April 2004. 224

NATIONAL COURTS

Tokyo District Court, Shimoda et al. *v.* The State, Decision, 7 December 1963, decision translated in The Japanese Annual of International Law, Vol. 8 (1964), 231. 206
United Kingdom House of Lords, R *v.* Jones (Margaret) [2007] 1 AC 136. 218, 219

Introduction

For the first time in a quarter of a century working with the problems of the arms race and arms control, I am beginning to get scared. These are not my words, but those of William Epstein, a disarmament expert, which he penned forty-five years ago.[1] Epstein's concern arose from an array of adverse circumstances. India had detonated a nuclear explosive device in 1974, becoming what he (wrongly) believed was only the world's sixth nuclear-armed State (in fact, Israel had already produced nuclear weapons). Also in 1974, Britain had resumed explosive nuclear testing for the first time in a decade; the United States was increasing the sophistication of its manoeuvrable re-entry vehicles on its missiles in order to deliver multiple warheads while also engaging in the development of new nuclear-armed cruise missiles; and the Soviet Union was producing multiple independently targetable re-entry vehicles (MIRVs) of its own to equip its intercontinental ballistic missiles (ICBMs).

What is more, in May 1975, the first review conference of the Treaty on the Non-proliferation of Nuclear Weapons (NPT)[2] had just taken place, an event which Epstein cast firmly as a failure. There was, he argued, a 'clear and present danger' of the 'crumbling' of the entire structure of the non-proliferation regime. The reason, he affirmed, was the inaction and obduracy of the five Nuclear-weapon States, since they had – 'at least in substantial part' – failed to live up to their disarmament obligations under the NPT.[3]

Five decades later, a similar set of challenges are confronting the international community. After massive cuts in the level of nuclear arsenals began in the latter years of the Cold War and gathered pace after the fall of the Berlin Wall, a new form of nuclear arms race is underway. Conservatively calculated, since 1940 the world expended the equivalent of more than \$15 trillion (in 2020 United States dollars) on nuclear weapons systems and infrastructure.[4] The next thirty years are expected to see the dedication of many trillions

1 W. Epstein, *The Last Chance: Nuclear Proliferation and Arms Control*, The Free Press, New York, 1976, p. xiii.

2 Treaty on the Non-proliferation of Nuclear Weapons; opened for signature at London, Moscow, and Washington, DC, 1 July 1968; entered into force 5 March 1970.

3 Epstein, *The Last Chance: Nuclear Proliferation and Arms Control*, pp. xiv–xv.

4 The United States alone had dedicated \$5.5 trillion to nuclear weapons development, production, and maintenance by 1996 (in 1996 dollar equivalents). 'Introduction', S. I. Schwartz (ed.), *Atomic Audit: The Costs and Consequences of U.S. Nuclear Weapons Since 1940*, The Brookings Institution, Washington, DC, 1998, p. 3.

more to the upgrading of nuclear weapons and their delivery systems. The United States has initiated the development of a US$100 billion land-based ICBM force that is intended to serve until 2075.[5]

In 2019, the United States formally withdrew from the 1987 Intermediate Nuclear Forces (INF) Treaty,[6] citing cheating by Russia, an act that was followed swiftly by Russia's withdrawal. The INF Treaty, now defunct, was the first Cold War disarmament treaty to both reduce arsenals and even to eliminate a category of nuclear weapons. It had successfully removed short- and intermediate-range nuclear missiles from Europe and prevented their insertion elsewhere.

The United States also pulled out of the multilateral Joint Comprehensive Plan of Action (JCPOA), which limited Iran's enrichment of uranium from 2015 for an initial period of ten years. Although there were clear signs that it would return to compliance, should the United States decide to rejoin the political agreement,[7] Iran announced in January 2021 that it had produced 17 kilograms of 20 per cent-enriched uranium within a single month, sharply reducing its nuclear break-out time.[8] In February 2021, Iran's Minister of Intelligence Mahmoud Alavi even declared in an interview with Iranian TV that Iran could produce nuclear weapons 'in self-defence'. This provocative statement was made despite a religious edict in the 1990s by Supreme Leader Ali Khamenei, which had forbidden them.[9] In 2021, Iran's Supreme Leader said that Iran could increase its level of uranium enrichment to 'whatever' the nation needed, including up to 60 per cent purity of uranium-235.[10]

Earlier in February 2021, the incoming Biden administration in the United States formally agreed with Russia to extend the New START Treaty[11] between the two nuclear superpowers for a further five years, restricting the size of each nation's deployed strategic nuclear arsenal. New START would otherwise have expired on 5 February 2021, meaning that, for the first time since 1972, no upper limits whatsoever would have been imposed by treaty on the number of American and Russian nuclear weapons. Precious breathing space had been secured to negotiate a new treaty.[12] In announcing the extension, US Secretary of

5 E. Eaves, 'Why Is America Getting a New $100 Billion Nuclear Weapon?', *Bulletin of the Atomic Scientists*, 8 February 2021, at http://bit.ly/3bfyUPX.

6 Treaty between the United States of America and the Union of Soviet Socialist Republics on the Elimination of Their Intermediate-Range and Shorter-Range Missiles; signed at Washington, DC, 8 December 1987; entered into force 1 June 1988; expired (de facto), 2 August 2019. The Russian Federation was bound as a successor State to the Soviet Union along with, for the purpose of the INF Treaty, Belarus, Kazakhstan, Turkmenistan, Ukraine, and Uzbekistan.

7 E. Yeranian, 'Rouhani: Iran Will Comply with Nuclear Deal If Other Countries Do', *Voice of America*, 10 February 2021, at http://bit.ly/3jFoYTF.

8 Radio Farda, 'Iran Enriched "17 Kilograms" of 20 Percent Enriched Uranium, Exceeding Goals', Radio Free Europe/Radio Liberty, 28 January 2021, available at http://bit.ly/2MDDdfs.

9 Yeranian, 'Rouhani: Iran Will Comply with Nuclear Deal If Other Countries Do'.

10 'Khamenei Says Iran Could Enrich Uranium to 60%', *Voice of America*, 22 February 2021, at http://bit.ly/3qO1XAK.

11 The Treaty between the United States of America and the Russian Federation on Measures for the Further Reduction and Limitation of Strategic Offensive Arms; signed at Prague, 8 April 2010; entered into force 5 February 2011.

12 Later in February 2021, however, Russian Deputy Foreign Minister Sergei Ryabkov said that any possible replacement of New START with a new treaty would be impossible without action by the United States on missile defence. 'If the US is not ready to move on [this] then there are little chances of having a new deal to

State Antony Blinken declared, 'Extending the New START Treaty makes the United States, U.S. allies and partners, and the world safer. An unconstrained nuclear competition would endanger us all.'[13]

But at the global level, the NPT – the 'cornerstone' of the nuclear non-proliferation regime – is under severe pressure, with 'dismal progress' achieved towards nuclear disarmament.[14] Expectations for the next NPT review conference, its tenth, were correspondingly low. The conference had been postponed from 2020 until August 2021 and then until 2022 as a result of the global COVID-19 pandemic.

The fracture in the international community, with most non-nuclear-weapon States deeply frustrated at the refusal of the five nuclear-weapon States to countenance disarmament, was further emphasised by the entry into force of the Treaty on the Prohibition of Nuclear Weapons on 22 January 2021.[15]

The Comprehensive Nuclear-Test-Ban Treaty, concluded in 1996,[16] has still not entered into force, and there is little prospect it will ever do so. In 2020, the United States, a treaty signatory (but not a contracting State), is reported to have even mulled resuming explosive nuclear testing, at the same time as it accused China and Russia of having violated the Treaty's norms.[17]

In February 2021, US Admiral Charles Richard, the head of US Strategic Command, warned that nuclear war between the United States and either China or Russia had become a 'very real possibility'.[18] Was this apparent admission of the failure of strategic deterrence an indirect form of fundraising by the military, or does it represent a sober assessment of the prevailing landscape?

THE LAYOUT OF THE BOOK

This book describes how we arrived at this bleak legal and military environment through the lens of State practice and policy as well as under international law. In particular, it articulates the content, implementation, and impact of key bilateral and multilateral

replace the New START, we should focus on the missile defence problem. Otherwise, arms control will be in question', Minister Ryabkov said at a press conference. E. Mikhaylov, 'Russian Deputy FM: Any Agreement to Replace New START Treaty Requires Discussing US Missile Defence', *Sputnik News*, 11 February 2021, at http://bit.ly/379s4KH.

13 'On the Extension of the New START Treaty with the Russian Federation', press Statement by Antony J. Blinken, Secretary of State, 3 February 2021, at http://bit.ly/3cEegLV.

14 'Who Will Go Nuclear Next?', *The Economist*, 30 January 2021, at http://econ.st/3r8HcPX.

15 Treaty on the Prohibition of Nuclear Weapons; adopted at New York, 7 July 2017; entered into force 22 January 2021.

16 Comprehensive Nuclear-Test-Ban Treaty; adopted at New York, 10 September 1996; not yet in force.

17 J. Hudson and P. Sonne, 'Trump Administration Discussed Conducting First U.S. Nuclear Test in Decades', *Washington Post*, 23 May 2020, at http://wapo.st/2yv76ba. In June 2020, it was reported that the Senate Armed Services Committee had set aside $10 million in its version of the National Defense Authorization Act for fiscal year 2021 to speed up preparations in case the United States decided to resume nuclear testing. Arms Control Association, 'Reaction to White House Nuclear Testing Proposal Strongly Negative', *Issue Briefs*, Vol. 12, No. 4 (16 June 2020), at http://bit.ly/3hMiYHp.

18 B. Hoyle and M. Evans, 'Nuclear War with Russia or China Now a Very Real Possibility, Warns US Admiral', *The Times*, 4 February 2021, at http://bit.ly/2YKJnNy.

treaties. Written as a work of normative reference, the legality of nuclear weapons is portrayed in accordance with the sources of contemporary international law.

Chapter 1 depicts the development of nuclear weapons from the early work of atomic scientists through to the Manhattan Project and its fission bombs. Also sketched are Nazi Germany's and Imperial Japan's abortive atomic research during the Second World War, followed by the Soviet nuclear weapons programme that followed it. The United States' creation of the first hydrogen (thermonuclear) bomb in the 1950s is part of a broader outline of the nuclear arms race in the Cold War. The nuclear weapons programmes of the other nuclear-armed powers throughout history that built their own weapons – in chronological order, the United Kingdom, France, China, Israel, India, Pakistan, South Africa, and latterly the Democratic People's Republic of Korea (North Korea) – are then summarised in turn. A final section describes the current focus of research and development, to the extent they are known publicly, including the influence of artificial intelligence and cyber operations on nuclear weapons development and launch procedures, as well as the technologies being created and deployed to overcome missile defences.

Chapter 2 details the use of nuclear weapons on two occasions in 1945 as a direct result of which several hundred thousand civilians died at Hiroshima and Nagasaki. Subsequent instances are then recounted in which the use of nuclear weapons in hostilities was seriously entertained. Also described briefly are the dozens of detonations of nuclear explosive devices for 'peaceful purposes' and, to test the ability of troops to fight during a nuclear war, the more limited employment of nuclear weapons in military training exercises. The test detonation of more than two thousand nuclear weapons in 1945–2017 is summarised in Chapter 4.

Chapter 3 chronicles the elaboration and content of the Treaty on the Non-proliferation of Nuclear Weapons, an instrument devised to stem the horizontal proliferation of nuclear weapons. As the NPT was being negotiated, beginning in the mid-1960s, it was feared that several dozen States were either already engaged in or seriously contemplating, a nuclear weapons programme. Almost all, though, subsequently renounced their respective efforts. Five nuclear-weapon States – China, France, the Soviet Union, the United Kingdom, and the United States – were effectively recognised as possessor States and given a special status under the Treaty. All other States were designated 'non-nuclear-weapon States', with those joining the Treaty undertaking never to acquire a nuclear explosive device. But implementation of another 'pillar' of the Treaty, according to which the nuclear-weapon States would seek to reach agreement to destroy their nuclear arsenals, has not been achieved. North Korea withdrew from the NPT in controversial circumstances in 2003 and has aggressively pursued a nuclear weapons programme since. The intentions of Iran and Saudi Arabia, both States Parties to the NPT, appear uncertain. India, Israel, and Pakistan never joined and each became a nuclear-armed State.

Chapter 4 describes the explosive testing of nuclear weapons and other nuclear explosive devices between July 1945 and September 2017 (the last time a State – North Korea – conducted a test detonation). The lives of millions around the world have been prematurely curtailed by atmospheric tests, especially those in the 1950s and early 1960s involving nuclear explosive devices whose explosive yield is counted in equivalence to millions of tons of trinitrotoluene (TNT). Some areas of the world will remain uninhabitable for hundreds of years as a result of radioactive contamination from nuclear tests. In the South Pacific, for instance, parts of the Marshall Islands are still more radioactive than sites like Chernobyl and Fukushima after the respective accidents at the nuclear power plants in 1986 and 2011. Against this backdrop, the chapter traces the legal regulation of nuclear testing, from its first prohibition in the south polar region under the 1959 Antarctic Treaty, through the 1963 Partial Test-Ban Treaty that banned atmospheric testing, and to the Comprehensive Nuclear-Test-Ban Treaty that outlaws also underground explosive testing and all peaceful use of nuclear explosive devices. With the CTBT still to enter to force, the extent to which its core provisions reflect customary international law is considered. Reference is also made to the relevance of subcritical testing to nuclear weapons development, activities which are outlawed by the 2017 Treaty on the Prohibition of Nuclear Weapons.

Chapter 5 narrates the content of the principal nuclear arms control and disarmament treaties between the Soviet Union/Russian Federation and the United States. These include, among others, the 1972 Anti-Ballistic Missile (ABM) Treaty and the Strategic Arms Limitation Treaty (SALT I), the INF Treaty, the 1991 START Treaty, and the 2010 New START Treaty that replaced both START I and the 2002 Strategic Offensive Reductions Treaty (SORT). All these bilateral (occasionally plurilateral) treaties are now defunct, apart from New START, which, pursuant to its recent five-year extension, formally expires on 5 February 2026.

Chapter 6 considers the comprehensive nuclear weapon prohibition treaties which exist at both global and regional level. Regional treaties outlaw nuclear weapons in the Americas and the Caribbean, Africa, South-East Asia, the South Pacific, and Central Asia, as well as in Antarctica, on the sea bed, and in outer space. The failure – thus far – to conclude a nuclear-weapon-free zone for the Middle East is briefly explained. At the global level, the United Nations Treaty on the Prohibition of Nuclear Weapons, which entered into force in January 2021, is the first terrestrial treaty to proscribe all development, production, stockpiling, transfer, and use of nuclear weapons and other nuclear explosive devices.

Chapter 7 delineates the nature and specific measures of the treaty-based verification regimes, including within the INF Treaty, the CTBT, and New START, as well as the more generic Open Skies Treaty. Transparency measures and national technical means of verification are supplemented by extensive provision for on-site inspections. Particular attention is also paid to the safeguards over nuclear material established in accordance with the NPT between States and the International Atomic Energy Agency (IAEA).

Chapter 8 recounts how *jus ad bellum*, international humanitarian law, international human rights law, the law of neutrality, and international environmental law apply to and restrict nuclear weapons. Jurisprudence in national and international courts is reviewed, particularly the 1996 Advisory Opinion on the legality of the threat or use of nuclear weapons issued by the International Court of Justice. The chapter further discusses individual and national responsibility for unlawful use or testing of nuclear weapons, including under the jurisdiction of the International Criminal Court.

The concluding chapter includes a brief consideration of future prospects for nuclear arms control and disarmament. It might have been hoped that the devastating economic impact of the COVID-19 global pandemic might lead to renewed action in support of reductions and restrictions on nuclear armaments. On 27 April 2020, as the NPT Review Conference was due to open, its postponement owing to COVID-19 was remarked upon by the German Minister for Foreign Affairs in a press conference: 'More than ever we will need our entire strength for economic recovery and investments in the future. We do not need investments in a new nuclear arms race.' His hopes look set to be dashed. On the front cover of *The Economist*'s 30 January 2021 issue, the headline asked simply: 'Who will go nuclear next?'[19]

[19] At http://econ.st/39BaWiP.

1

The Development of Nuclear Weapons

This chapter summarises the science behind nuclear weapons and describes their practical development. It begins with a description of the early theoretical work of the 'atomic' scientists, which generated an understanding of the possibility of building nuclear explosive devices. It outlines the work of the Manhattan Project, which resulted in the creation of the first fission bombs, while also detailing Nazi Germany's and Imperial Japan's abortive atomic research before and during the Second World War. The Soviet nuclear weapons programme that followed the end of the war and the United States' development of the first fusion (thermonuclear) bomb in the 1950s are then related together with a narrative of the nuclear arms race between the two superpowers during the Cold War.

The narrative then recounts the programmes of the other eight nuclear-armed powers throughout history that built their own weapons, in chronological order of acquisition of nuclear explosive devices: the United Kingdom, France, China, Israel, India, South Africa, Pakistan, and the Democratic People's Republic of Korea (North Korea). The situation in three States that acquired nuclear weapons upon the disintegration of the Soviet Union and then renounced them – Belarus, Kazakhstan, and Ukraine – is then briefly summarised. A final section describes the current focus of research into and development of nuclear weapons and their delivery systems, particularly the technologies created to overcome missile defences, the development of autonomous weapons through the incorporation of artificial intelligence, and the influence of cyber operations on launch policies.

THE THEORY AND EARLY DEVELOPMENT OF NUCLEAR WEAPONS

The Energetic Effects of Nuclear Fission and Nuclear Fusion

Albert Einstein's famous equation of 1905 – a consequence of his special theory of relativity – implies that energy (E) and mass (m) are interchangeable with each other. But $E = mc^2$ does not in and of itself explain the power of a nuclear explosion, which is due to a particular form of energy. Within an atom, the energy released when the nucleons (protons and neutrons[1]) bind together to form the nucleus is called the *binding energy*. This binding energy determines which nuclei are stable and how much energy is released in a nuclear reaction. A heavy nucleus, such as that within an atom of uranium, will release energy when it splits apart (fission),[2] whereas two light nuclei – hydrogen being the obvious example – will release energy when they join together (fusion).[3]

The potential for atomic energy to be harnessed to create hugely powerful bombs had been emotively envisaged by the author H. G. Wells in his 1914 book *The World Set Free*.[4] Wells imagined a small, uranium-based bomb that would be thrown out of an aircraft by hand and that 'would continue to explode indefinitely'. Wells predicted the outbreak of a European war decades later that would reduce cities to radioactive wastelands.[5] As 'more and more of the Carolinum became active', he wrote, 'the bomb spread itself out into a monstrous cavern of fiery energy at the base of what became very speedily a miniature active volcano'. Describing the bomb as the 'crowning triumph of military science', the book expressed the belief that Carolinum – the 'ultimate explosive' – would give the 'decisive touch' to war.[6] The great Hungarian physicist, Leo Szilard, who had read the book, would later write that Wells had showed him 'what the liberation of atomic energy on a large scale would mean'.[7]

Although the first nuclear weapons were fission bombs, the theory of nuclear fusion predated the discovery of nuclear fission by a decade.[8] In his journal article of 1920, 'The Internal Constitution of the Stars', astrophysicist Arthur Eddington theorised that 'the atoms of all elements are built of hydrogen atoms bound together, and presumably have at one time been formed from hydrogen'. He speculated that 'the interior of a star seems as likely a place as any for the evolution to have occurred; whenever it did occur a great amount of energy must have been set free'.[9] Prophetically, he declared: 'If, indeed, the sub-atomic energy in the stars is being freely used to maintain their great furnaces, it seems to bring a little nearer to fulfilment our dream of controlling this latent power for the well-being of the human race – or for its suicide.'[10]

1 A neutron is an elementary particle that can penetrate the atomic nucleus because its electric neutrality means it is not repelled by the nucleus's electric barriers.

2 The English word *atom* is derived from the ancient Greek word ατομον (atomon), which means, ironically in the context of nuclear physics, 'that which cannot be divided'. In fifth century BCE, Leucippus and his pupil Democritus proposed that all matter was composed of these small indivisible particles, 'infinite in number' and in 'constant and eternal motion'. B. Pullman, *The Atom in the History of Human Thought*, Oxford University Press, Oxford, 1998, p. 32.

3 Atomic Archive, 'Einstein's Equation', 2020, at http://bit.ly/35iG3M7; see also M. Pössel, 'From $E=mc^2$ to the Atomic Bomb', Einstein Online, Band 04 (2010), 01–1004, at http://bit.ly/2VKd2pn.

4 The text of the book is available at http://bit.ly/2zTMpGe.

5 T. Powers, *Heisenberg's War: The Secret History of the German Bomb*, Jonathan Cape, London, 1993, p. 51.

6 Section 4 of chapter 2 ('The Last War'), *The World Set Free*.

7 BBC, 'Was HG Wells the First to Think of the Atom Bomb?', 4 July 2015, at http://bbc.in/3c01Gn4.

8 J. Gribbin, 'The Power behind the Sun: It Is 70 Years since the Pioneering Astrophysicist Arthur Eddington Told the Scientific World That the Source of Power That Keeps the Sun Hot Must Be Subatomic Energy', *The New Scientist*, 3 November 1990, at http://bit.ly/3aJLGUL.

9 A. S. Eddington, 'The Internal Constitution of the Stars', *Scientific Monthly*, Vol. 11, No. 4 (October 1920), 297–303, at p. 299.

10 Ibid.

During the last year of the First World War, two years prior to Eddington's article, the British physicist Ernest Rutherford had already engaged in experimentation indicating to him that the atom could be artificially disintegrated. By bombarding nitrogen with alpha particles, at times he had transformed it into oxygen and hydrogen.[11] But the man known as the 'father of nuclear physics' would die in 1937, convinced that the world would 'never be able to exploit the slumbering energy in the atom'.[12] Only a year later, however, nuclear fission would be discovered by German scientists working in Nazi Germany.

The existence of the neutron had already been identified in 1932 by British physicist James Chadwick; he would be awarded the 1935 Nobel Prize in Physics for his work. In an address in Berlin, German physicist Fritz Houtermans remarked that it might be possible to free powerful forces dormant in the particle, though his pronouncement attracted little serious attention at the time.[13] A year later, Szilard realised that a chain reaction might be provoked if an element could be found that would emit two neutrons when it swallowed one neutron. For some reason that remains unexplained, the experiment was never carried out.[14]

In the course of experimentation in 1934, Enrico Fermi, an Italian physicist who had previously studied under Rutherford at Cambridge, became the first person to split the uranium atom.[15] At the time, Fermi believed that by bombarding uranium – the heaviest of all metals – with neutrons, he had created a new element.[16] Referring to that erroneous conclusion, German scientist Ida Noddack wrote in the applied chemistry magazine *Angewandte Chemie* that 'when heavy nuclei are bombarded with neutrons the nuclei in question might break into a number of larger pieces, which would no doubt be isotopes of known elements but not neighbours of the elements subjected to radiation'.[17] Fermi, who fled fascist Italy (accompanied by his Jewish wife), became a naturalised American and would go on to create the world's first nuclear reactor: Chicago Pile-1. Back in 1934, however, he (along with other leading scientists of the day) casually dismissed Dr Noddack's conclusions. But she was right and they were wrong.

In 1935, Frédéric Joliot-Curie went to Stockholm with his wife, Irène, so they could formally receive the Nobel Prize for Chemistry for their discovery of artificial radioactivity. In his acceptance address, Dr Joliot-Curie noted that scientists 'building up or shattering

11 R. Jungk, *Brighter than 1000 Suns*, trans. J. Cluegh (1958), Penguin Books, London, 1980, p. 15.

12 Ibid., p. 19. In an address in 1933, he had described people who were prophesying the release of atomic energy on a large scale as 'talking moonshine'. Ibid., p. 54.

13 Ibid., p. 53.

14 Ibid., p. 54.

15 Uranium had been discovered by chemist Martin Heinrich Klaproth, who had isolated a small sample of the heavy metal from pitchblende ore found in Saxony in 1789. Powers, *Heisenberg's War: The Secret History of the German Bomb*, p. 24. Klaproth dissolved pitchblende in nitric acid and then added potash to obtain a yellow precipitate. Adding excess potash dissolved the yellow precipitate and generated a hitherto-unknown element. He named his discovery after the planet Uranus, which had been discovered eight years earlier by astronomer William Herschel, first as Uranit and then as Uranium. H. Hübner, 'Uran und seine Entdeckungsgeschichte durch Martin Heinrich Klaproth', *Isotopenpraxis Isotopes in Environmental and Health Studies*, Vol. 25, No. 9 (1989), pp. 361–67; F. J. Dahlkamp, *Uranium Ore Deposits*, Springer, Berlin, 1991, p. 5.

16 Jungk, *Brighter than 1000 Suns*, p. 63.

17 I. Noddack, 'Über das Element 93', *Angewandte Chemie*, Vol. 47, No. 37 (15 September 1934), 653–55.

elements at will' would be capable of bringing about 'transmutations of an explosive type'. 'If', he continued, these succeed in spreading, an 'enormous liberation of usable energy can be imagined'. But should 'the contagion' spread to 'all the elements of our planet', he cautioned, 'the consequences of unloosing such a cataclysm can only be viewed with apprehension'.[18]

The discovery of nuclear fission is formally attributed to two German chemists working in tandem in December 1938: Otto Hahn and his assistant Fritz Strassmann. Thus, although foreign physical laboratories had far greater resources, 'it was a German chemist working with the most primitive of equipment who had made the discovery that was to throw the word of physics into pandemonium'.[19] Their discovery – that the bombardment of uranium with slow neutrons would yield barium as a result of decay, an element not much over half its atomic weight[20] – came only a year before the outbreak of the Second World War. As a chemist, however, Hahn was initially reluctant to propose a revolutionary discovery in the realm of physics.[21]

In Sweden, Austrian physicist Lise Meitner and her nephew Otto Frisch correctly interpreted the results of the experimentation by Strassmann and Hahn, with Frisch widely credited with devising the term 'fission' to describe what had occurred.[22] Niels Bohr and John Archibald Wheeler wrote an article in the American journal *Physical Review*, observing that it was a rare isotope of uranium,[23] uranium-235 (^{235}U),[24] which fissioned when uranium was bombarded with neutrons.[25] The path to a nuclear explosive device was now open, at least in theory. In early March 1939, Szilard and Walter Zinn, a Canadian-American nuclear physicist to whom Fermi had given laboratory space at Columbia University, conducted the latest in a series of experiments to measure neutron emissions. They realised from a series of flashes produced by fast neutrons emitted in fission that the atom had disintegrated. That night, Szilard recorded, 'there was very little doubt in my mind that the world was headed for grief'.[26]

18 F. Joliot, 'Chemical Evidence of the Transmutation of Elements', Nobel Lecture, 12 December 1935, at http://bit.ly/3bGtwVb.

19 D. Irving, *The German Atomic Bomb*, Simon & Schuster, New York, 1967, p. 26.

20 Atomic weight describes the number of protons in the nucleus of an atom. Uranium has an atomic weight of 92; barium's is 56.

21 Atomic Heritage Foundation, 'Otto Hahn', 2019, at http://bit.ly/3bWLH9p. When he learnt of the bombing of Hiroshima, Hahn was badly affected, as he felt that his discovery of nuclear fission had resulted to the death and suffering of tens of thousands of innocent Japanese people.

22 'Disintegration of Uranium by Neutrons: A New Type of Nuclear Reaction', letter by L. Meitner and O. R. Frisch, *Nature*, Vol. 143 (1939), 239–40.

23 Uranium has the atomic number 92, indicating that its nucleus consists of 92 protons. The mass of natural uranium is 238, meaning that the nucleus has a further 146 neutrons. The higher the atomic number, the heavier the atom.

24 Naturally occurring uranium contains almost 99.3 per cent uranium-238 and only 0.7 per cent uranium-235. See on this issue K. O'Neill, 'Building the Bomb', chapter 1 in Schwartz (ed.), *Atomic Audit: The Costs and Consequences of U.S. Nuclear Weapons since 1940*, p. 35.

25 N. Bohr and J. A. Wheeler, 'The Mechanism of Nuclear Fission', *Physical Review*, Vol. 56 (1 September 1939), 426–50, at http://bit.ly/3c10djh, esp. at pp. 441–42.

26 S. Weart and G. Szilard, *Leo Szilard: His Version of the Facts*, MIT Press, Cambridge, MA, 1978, p. 55.

As late as the summer of 1939, however, Albert Einstein had not considered the possibility of a chain reaction in uranium. Szilard came to see him with the plea that he sign a letter to US President Franklin D. Roosevelt, warning him of the possibility of creating a nuclear explosive device and the danger that Nazi Germany would be the first to do so. The letter, which Einstein did sign, said:

> Some recent work by E. Fermi and L. Szilard, which has been communicated to me in manuscript, leads me to expect that the element uranium may be turned into a new and important source of energy in the immediate future. Certain aspects of this situation which has arisen seem to call for watchfulness and, if necessary, quick action on the part of the Administration.

Although the letter had been signed at the beginning of August 1939, it would only be placed before President Roosevelt two months later in October. Alexander Sachs, an American economist and banker who had the president's ear, struggled initially to persuade him of the importance of the issue. He was able to eventually convince Roosevelt to act by using the example of Napoleon Bonaparte's rejection of the idea of ships being powered by steam rather than sail (the development of which would have enabled him to defeat Britain at sea).[27] Roosevelt replied to Einstein's letter, saying that 'I found this data of such import that I have convened a Board consisting of the head of the Bureau of Standards and a chosen representative of the Army and Navy to thoroughly investigate the possibilities of your suggestion regarding the element of uranium.'[28] Even then, a further two years would go by before the United States would begin to conduct meaningful research into atomic weapons.

The Manhattan Project

The Manhattan Project – officially code-named the Manhattan Engineer District[29] – was formally established on 13 August 1942. The project's name stemmed from the fact that preliminary research was conducted at Columbia University in Manhattan.[30] The British were by then already actively engaged in preparatory research into an atomic bomb. In the spring of 1940, the so-called MAUD Committee had been set up by the British government to study the possibility of developing a nuclear weapon.[31] In 1941, James Chadwick wrote the final draft of the MAUD Report, which helped to prompt the US government's decision to initiate serious research efforts towards its creation of an atomic bomb. The

27 Jungk, *Brighter than 1000 Suns*, pp. 106–7.

28 Text available at 'Manhattan Project and Atomic Energy Act, United States', blog entry, *Building the World*, 2020, at http://bit.ly/2zjzRHW.

29 M. Roussel, 'Manhattan Engineer District Established', National WWII Museum, New Orleans, 13 August 2012, at http://bit.ly/35Inj9d.

30 'Manhattan Project and Atomic Energy Act, United States' blog entry, *Building the World*, n.d., accessed 24 June 2021 at https://bit.ly/2Stiq1y.

31 The selection of the term MAUD was apparently chosen in the mistaken belief that its incorporation towards the end of a telegram by Niels Bohr to Otto Frisch, while Bohr was still in German-occupied Denmark, was a cryptic reference to something atomic. In fact, it was the first name of the former governess of Bohr's children.

report precipitately dismissed the feasibility of plutonium production for such a weapon,[32] as well as thermal diffusion, the electromagnetic method, and the centrifuge as a means of isolating the 235 isotope of uranium. Instead, it recommended that gaseous diffusion be undertaken on a massive scale to generate sufficient uranium-235. The British firmly believed that uranium research could lead to the production of a bomb in time to affect the outcome of the war against the Nazis.[33]

Leslie Groves was a 'mere' colonel in the US Army Corps of Engineers at the time of his appointment to head the Manhattan Project, but he had already been entrusted with overseeing the construction of the Pentagon in August 1941.[34] In September 1942, when he was appointed as director of the Manhattan Project, he was given the rank of Temporary Brigadier General, and charged with overseeing all scientific, technical, and process development, including construction, production, security, and military intelligence pertaining to enemy activities. In 1945, he was further entrusted with planning the use of the atomic bomb.

Groves was known for his critical and stubborn attitude, his egotism, but also his intelligence, all of which combined to fuel an unfettered drive to succeed. Colonel Kenneth D. Nichols, who worked as an engineer for the Manhattan Project, described Groves as the biggest 'S.O.B.' he ever worked for but also said that if he had to do his part of the project again and was allowed to pick his boss, he would pick Groves.[35] Groves also clearly enjoyed the complete trust of the authorities, as funding for the Manhattan Project was directed through his personal bank account, both with a view to maintaining secrecy and in order to avoid the need for Congressional approval.[36]

Robert Oppenheimer was in many ways a surprising choice to head the scientific effort to develop a nuclear weapon. Hard-working and gifted, though not brilliant, he had been an enthusiastic communist sympathiser in the 1930s (although he would go on to marry a relative of General Wilhelm Keitel, Chief of the High Command of the German Armed Forces). In mid-1943, a report by the US Army's counter-intelligence branch (G-2) warned that Oppenheimer might be passing confidential information to the Soviets. In July, after receiving the report, Groves had to order that security clearance be granted 'irrespective of the information which you have concerning Mr Oppenheimer'.[37] But only a month later, Oppenheimer was informing a security officer at Los Alamos of an indirect approach by the Soviets to a scientist at the facility. Oppenheimer refused to name the target of the approach – it was, in fact, him – but his action served only to heighten concern about where his ultimate loyalties lay.[38] Subsequently, he would divulge the name of the man

32 Plutonium exists naturally in only minute quantities. About two billion years ago, a high concentration of uranium ore formed a 'natural' underground reactor, producing plutonium which has long since decayed into other elements. M. Eisenbud and T. Gesell, *Environmental Radioactivity from Natural, Industrial and Military Sources: From Natural, Industrial and Military Sources*, 4th ed., Academic Press, San Diego, 1997, p. 198; see O'Neill, 'Building the Bomb', p. 35.

33 US Department of Energy, 'The MAUD Report (1941)', at http://bit.ly/2W1ZAgY.

34 R. Hull, 'Saluting the Engineer Who Oversaw Pentagon Construction and the Manhattan Project', ASCE News, 1 September 2015, at http://bit.ly/2WytUyP.

35 Atomic Heritage Foundation, 'Leslie R. Groves', 2019, at http://bit.ly/2zcVvgH.

36 O'Neill, 'Building the Bomb', p. 40.

37 Jungk, *Brighter than 1000 Suns*, pp. 131–33.

38 Ibid., pp. 134, 138.

who had casually passed on the Soviet interest in procuring information from the project. But in so doing, he exaggerated the nature of the contact from Haakon Chevalier, a lecturer in romance languages at the University of California.[39]

The main laboratory for the Manhattan Project would be built at a remote spot in New Mexico, at Los Alamos. Oppenheimer had been educated at a boarding school there as a child and had good memories of the area. The isolation of the locale also appealed to Groves, though he grossly underestimated how many people would need to be quartered there. Expecting around one hundred scientists and their families, within a year 3,500 people were living at Los Alamos, while a further 12 months later, that number had risen to 6,000.[40] The site was purchased in November 1942 on the order of the Assistant Secretary of War, John J. McCloy. McCloy, a lawyer by profession, would argue in 1945 that the United States should issue a warning before dropping the atomic bomb, to give the Japanese the chance to surrender, but he was overruled. In 1961, he would become President John F. Kennedy's chief disarmament adviser and negotiator.[41]

The Manhattan Project employed both highly enriched uranium and reprocessed plutonium from spent reactor fuel for its nuclear weapons. On 18 September 1942, the United States bought 1,250 tons of uranium ore from Union Minière du Haut-Katanga, a company that extracted uranium ore in the Belgian Congo; additional purchases would ensue.[42] What would become known after the Second World War as Oak Ridge, in the state of Tennessee, would be the site of what was then the world's largest factory, the Clinton Engineering Works. This is where the uranium-235 would be extracted.[43] A secret city would come to be built on the 59,000 acres of land purchased along the Clinch River, 20 miles west of Knoxville, where 70,000 people would be housed.

The world's first self-sustaining chain reaction occurred on 2 December 1942 at a building erected on a squash court under Stagg Field at the University of Chicago.[44] The first chain reaction was too weak to power even a single light bulb, but its 'complex legacy' includes 'the peaceful uses of nuclear energy, the terrible power of nuclear weapons, and a new era of other scientific and technological advances'.[45] Chicago Pile Number One (CP-1) consisted of 40,000 graphite blocks enclosing 19,000 pieces of uranium metal and uranium oxide fuel. The scientists of the Metallurgical Laboratory[46]

39 Ibid., pp. 138–44.

40 Ibid., p. 123.

41 'John J. McCloy, Lawyer and Diplomat, Is Dead at 93', *New York Times*, 12 March 1989, p. 44.

42 P. Ham, *Hiroshima Nagasaki*, Transworld Publishers, London, 2013, p. 137.

43 Ibid., p. 148.

44 R. Braithwaite, *Armageddon and Paranoia: The Nuclear Confrontation, Profile Books*, London, 2019, p. 54.

45 S. Koppes, 'How the First Chain Reaction Changed Science. Legacy of 1942 Breakthrough on Campus Includes Advances in Many Fields', University of Chicago, 2020, at http://bit.ly/2LYYIUn.

46 A few weeks after the end of the war, the scientific staff of the 'Met Lab' founded the Atomic Scientists of Chicago, publishing the first issue of the *Bulletin of the Atomic Scientists of Chicago* on 10 December 1945. The Bulletin's Doomsday Clock stands 'as a symbol of humanity's vulnerability to man-made catastrophe, with an agenda that expanded from nuclear weapons to include climate change and biological weapons'. Koppes, 'How the First Chain Reaction Changed Science. Legacy of 1942 breakthrough on Campus Includes Advances in Many Fields.'

had arranged the graphite in layers within a 24-foot-square wooden framework. They had to do so 30 times before they found an effective arrangement.[47]

The plutonium was produced at a nuclear reactor at the Hanford Reservation facility in Washington state.[48] Almost all the spent fuel from a nuclear reactor is composed of uranium with less than 1 per cent plutonium and smaller quantities of other radioactive waste.[49] The scientists needed an area of 225 square miles, with a good source of water, for safety and security reasons. B-Reactor at Hanford would produce the plutonium for both the Trinity test in mid-July 1945 and the 'Fat Man' bomb detonated over Nagasaki the following month.[50] The first uranium slug was placed in pile 100-B of B-Reactor on 13 September 1944. Initially, problems were encountered with the pile, which failed to maintain a chain reaction as a result of 'xenon poisoning'. Xenon, a fission product, was produced as the pile operated; it captured neutrons faster than the pile could produce them, causing a gradual shutdown.[51]

The 'Trinity' test of 16 July 1945, using plutonium from Hanford, was the first man-made nuclear explosion in history. Jungk had postulated that what he termed this 'blasphemous' title was either a reflection of the name of a turquoise mine near Los Alamos or a nod to the fact that three bombs had been prepared by the Manhattan Project.[52] Subsequently, it was revealed that it was a reference to a holy sonnet by John Donne,[53] a writer Oppenheimer greatly appreciated.[54] The device used in the Trinity test contained a plutonium core since

47 Ibid.

48 During the Manhattan Project, microgram quantities of plutonium were first extracted from reactor fuel in 1942 using the bismuth-phosphate precipitation process; this was then scaled up significantly at the Hanford facility. After the end of the Second World War, a process referred to as PUREX (Plutonium Uranium Recovery by Extraction) was employed in the Savannah River F Canyon facility; it has since become a standard method of solvent extraction for plutonium. M. F. Simpson and J. D. Law, 'Nuclear Fuel Reprocessing', Idaho National Laboratory, Idaho Falls, February 2010, at http://bit.ly/2SBDFuT; and T. Todd, 'Introduction to Nuclear Fuel Cycle Separations', Introduction to Nuclear Fuel Cycle Chemistry, CRESP Short Course, Crystal City VA, 4 August 2009, at http://bit.ly/2ynhlON.

49 The process of making plutonium is extremely 'inefficient' in that a massive amount of liquid and solid waste is generated while only a small amount of plutonium is produced. Clean-up of the Hanford site continues today, including for solid transuranic (TRU) waste – debris that is contaminated with plutonium or other materials that may remain radioactive for hundreds of thousands of years. TRU waste is packaged and is shipped to the Waste Isolation Pilot Plant in New Mexico where it will be permanently and safely buried. The liquid waste that had been poured onto the ground or held in ponds or trenches has long since evaporated or soaked into the soil, creating underground 'plumes' of contaminants that join with water beneath the surface. Many of the plumes are moving, at varying speeds, towards the Columbia River. US Department of Energy, Office of River Protection (Richland Operations Office), 'About Hanford Cleanup', last updated 19 April 2020, at http://bit.ly/3frDyMe.

50 By the end of the Cold War, Hanford is said to have produced sufficient plutonium for more than 60,000 nuclear warheads. Braithwaite, *Armageddon and Paranoia: The Nuclear Confrontation*, p. 57.

51 Atomic Heritage Foundation, 'Hanford, WA', 2019, at http://bit.ly/2A8if2d.

52 Jungk, *Brighter than 1000 Suns*, p. 180.

53 The sonnet's four opening lines are as follows:

> 'Batter my heart, three-person'd God, for you
> As yet but knock, breathe, shine, and seek to mend;
> That I may rise and stand, o'erthrow me, and bend
> Your force to break, blow, burn, and make me new.'

54 Atomic Heritage Foundation, 'Trinity Test – 1945', 18 June 2014, at http://bit.ly/2xGrpBV.

the scientists were confident of the success of the uranium fission device without a need for testing. Nicknamed the 'Gadget', the device was detonated from a tower 30 metres above the New Mexico desert, with an explosive yield of somewhere between 15 kilotons (kt) of TNT and 25 kt.[55] The scientists had bet among themselves on what the equivalent explosive yield would be: Oppenheimer had opted for 300 tons of TNT; Teller for 45,000 tons.[56] Groves, who had famously warned that for a few thousandths of a second, the light would be 'as bright as a thousand suns', found the gambling distasteful.[57]

As the test was ongoing, Oppenheimer recalled to himself passages from the *Bhagavad Gitā*, a 700-verse sacred Hindu text, part of the epic *Mahabharata*, written at some point in time between the fifth century BCE and the second century BCE. His most famous recollection is of the line 'I am become Death, the shatterer of worlds', uttered by Sri Krishna, the Lord of the fate of mortals. But as the Gadget exploded, his first thought was of another passage:

> If the radiance of a thousand suns
> were to burst into the sky,
> that would be like
> the splendour of the Mighty One.[58]

The bright, early morning flash in the New Mexico desert would still attract some attention from people as far as 200 kilometres away. But an employee of the Manhattan Project press agency had a prepared story: a munitions depot had detonated; no lives had been lost.[59]

The critical mass necessary to sustain a chain reaction in Little Boy, whereby neutrons would be released in an uncontrolled and exponential manner from their nuclei, comprised two hemispheres of uranium that would be fired into each other at the moment of release.[60] The process was designed by Louis Slotin, a Canadian physicist and chemist. The experimentation involved him manipulating two screwdrivers to bring the hemispheres together, but separating them just as the critical point was reached. He would later be killed in a similar operation in preparation for a thermonuclear weapon test, known among the experts as 'tickling the dragon's tail'.[61]

55 For differing estimates, see ibid. (citing 15–20 kt); F. A. Khan, 'Estimating the Photo-Fission Yield of the Trinity Test', *Scientific Reports* (*Nature*), Vol. 10, Art. no. 4200 (2020), at http://go.nature.com/3egLoZ1 (citing 21 kt, the official figure). US Department of Energy, 'The Trinity Test', at http://bit.ly/2zjlcNm. In 2016, scientists used the decay of Zirconium and the creation of molybdenum in the Trinity nuclear debris samples to claim a yield of 22.1 ± 2.7 kt. S. K. Hanson, A. D. Pollington, C. R. Waidmann, W. S. Kinman, A. M. Wende, J. L. Miller, J. A. Berger, W. J. Oldham, and H. D. Selby, 'Measurements of Extinct Fission Products in Nuclear Bomb Debris: Determination of the Yield of the Trinity Nuclear Test 70 y Later', *Proceedings of the National Academy of Sciences of the United States of America*, Vol. 113, No.29 (19 July 2016), 8104–8, at http://bit.ly/2TEq1aV.

56 Ham, *Hiroshima Nagasaki*, pp. 254–55.

57 Ibid., pp. 255, 320.

58 Jungk, *Brighter than 1000 Suns*, p. 183.

59 Ibid., pp. 184–85.

60 The bomb, which contained 60 kg of uranium, was 3 metres in length.

61 In a fission-fusion thermonuclear weapon, the explosion of a core of deuterium through the fusion of hydrogen atoms is achieved by a fission detonation that raises the temperature in the core to something

Groves was fanatical about security throughout the life of the Manhattan Project. His concern was justified – for, despite his best efforts, information leaked out. Klaus Fuchs, who came to Los Alamos in 1944 as part of a British team of atomic scientists, operated as a spy for the Soviets for many years. He would later save his own neck by putting much of the blame for 'this diabolical conspiracy to destroy a God-fearing nation'[62] on Julius and Ethel Rosenberg; they would both be executed for their crimes. But there were also simply errors, which enraged Groves. On 9 October 1943, the *New York Times* carried a story announcing that Niels Bohr had reached London with 'a New Atomic Blast Invention'. The story, which had been taken from an Associated Press wire release the previous day, reported that the plans for a new invention involving atomic explosions 'were described as of the greatest importance to the Allied war effort'.[63]

The Manhattan Project formally closed at the end of 1946, handing over nine plutonium bombs to the Atomic Energy Commission, which had been created under the Department of Energy under the 1946 Atomic Energy Act.[64] Also known as the McMahon Act (after the freshman senator who had sponsored it), the law determined how the nuclear technology developed with several of its Second World War allies would be managed. To their rage and distress – and despite a commitment from President Roosevelt – the British were excluded. The Act was later amended, but only in 1958, to allow the United States to share information with close allies. In August 1964, President Lyndon Johnson signed into law the Private Ownership of Special Nuclear Materials Act, bringing to an end the eighteen-year government monopoly over nuclear material stipulated by the McMahon Act.

Nazi Germany and the Bomb

As Jungk characterises it, in signing the letter to President Roosevelt, Einstein 'acted on the assumption that the United States would never use such a bomb for any object other than self-defence against a similar weapon and even then only if its own safety were imperilled to an extreme degree'.[65] After the Second World War, Einstein famously declared: 'If I had known that the Germans would not succeed in constructing the atom bomb, I would never have lifted a finger.'[66]

close to the surface of the sun. Less than a year after the end of the Second World War, Slotin was preparing the fissile sphere for the second thermonuclear test on Bikini Atoll in the Marshall Islands when his screwdriver slipped. The half-shell of beryllium, called the tamper, completely covered the core for just an instant, causing a blue flash of radioactivity. Slotin prised the sphere apart with his hands, but he realised that the dose of radiation he had received would likely be fatal. He died nine days later from radiation sickness, aged thirty-five. Jungk, *Brighter than 1000 Suns*, pp. 177–79. Thereafter, the plutonium core became known as the 'demon core'. A. Wellerstein, 'The Demon Core and the Strange Death of Louis Slotin', *The New Yorker*, 21 May 2016, at http://bit.ly/3aNhXdt.

62 The remarks of Judge Irving Kaufman in 1951 are available in 'Judge Kaufman's Statement upon Sentencing the Rosenbergs for Atomic Espionage', *Digital History*, ID 1118, 2019, at https://bit.ly/2XHphml.

63 Powers, *Heisenberg's War: The Secret History of the German Bomb*, pp. 239–40.

64 The text of the Act is available at Atomic Archive, 'Atomic Energy Act of 1946', at http://bit.ly/35DcZ2d.

65 Jungk, *Brighter than 1000 Suns*, p. 87.

66 'Atom: Einstein. The Man Who Started It All', *Newsweek*, 10 March 1947; see, e.g., T. Lipscombe, 'Einstein Feared a Nazi Atom Bomb – But Immigrants Made Sure the U.S. Got There First', *Time*, 2 August 2019, at http://bit.ly/3cVYx7O.

Yet, at the end of the 1930s, there were good reasons to fear Germany would succeed in developing a nuclear explosive device.[67] When war broke out in 1939, Germany was the only world power that had a military office exclusively devoted to the study of military applications of nuclear fission.[68] Within academia, many of the world's greatest physicists were working and studying in Germany in the 1930s. Indeed, Einstein's letter of 2 August 1939 to President Roosevelt had specifically noted that 'the son of the German Under-Secretary of State, von Weizsäcker, is attached to the Kaiser-Wilhelm Institute in Berlin where some of the American work on uranium is now being repeated.'

In addition to his own abilities, Carl Friedrich von Weizsäcker was a protégé of Werner Heisenberg, who conducted research at both the Kaiser-Wilhelm Institute[69] and the University of Strasbourg during the Second World War.[70] Despite later dismissals of his abilities (discussed below), Heisenberg was a brilliant theoretical physicist, possibly the world's greatest atomic physicist at the time,[71] and one of the pioneers of quantum mechanics. In the winter of 1939–40, he had already theorised the differences between a uranium pile, in which the chain reaction is controlled, and a uranium bomb, in which the 'avalanche of neutrons is allowed to accelerate to the point of explosion'.[72] And by late 1939, Heisenberg was reporting that enriched uranium could be used for large-scale energy production, demonstrating his understanding of what was needed for a successful military programme. Heisenberg had written that enriched uranium was 'the only method of producing explosives several orders of magnitude more powerful than the strongest explosives yet known'.[73]

In 1940, a small laboratory code-named 'The Virus House' (a title chosen to ward off the curious) was built to house the creation of the world's first subcritical uranium pile; work began on this endeavour in December.[74] By the end of June 1940, Germany had captured Europe's largest heavy-water factory (in Norway); it had a cyclotron[75] nearing completion; and although Germany had lost numerous world-leading physicists, it still had the greatest chemical engineering industry in the world.[76]

Also during June, von Weizsäcker, who was by then leading a group of scientists in Nazi Germany on atomic energy research, had realised that some of the neutrons released by

67 Mission Alsos would be established as part of the Manhattan Project to obtain intelligence related to German nuclear activities. The name was ill chosen as it was a Greek translation of Groves; General Groves was said to be furious when he discovered this, but feared that a change of nomenclature would only draw attention to the project. Atomic Heritage Foundation, 'Alsos Mission', 6 June 2014, at http://bit.ly/2KJDHfQ.

68 Irving, *The German Atomic Bomb*, p. 42.

69 This subsequently became the Max Planck Institute for Physics, first in Göttingen and then, in 1955 and since, in Munich.

70 Atomic Heritage Foundation, 'Carl Friedrich von Weizsäcker', 2019, at http://bit.ly/3d7Asen.

71 M. Grimsley, 'What If Werner Heisenberg Had Been a Nazi?', *HistoryNet*, 2020, at http://bit.ly/2xr8eMi.

72 Jungk, *Brighter than 1000 Suns*, p. 91.

73 Cited by ibid., p. 53.

74 Irving, *The German Atomic Bomb*, pp. 56, 79.

75 The cyclotron, invented by Ernest Lawrence in 1932, was a critical tool in the development of an atomic bomb, serving to irradiate and thereby enrich uranium. See Braithwaite, *Armageddon and Paranoia: The Nuclear Confrontation*, pp. 33, 54; 'Lawrence and the Bomb', American Institute of Physics, 2020, at http://bit.ly/3goX8ZV.

76 Irving, *The German Atomic Bomb*, p. 72.

the fission of ^{235}U would be captured by ^{238}U, transforming it into ^{239}U. But this isotope would be unstable and would soon decay, first into neptunium-239 and then, through further beta decay, into a new element. He called it eka-rhenium, given its similarity to rhenium (Re), atomic number 75 in the periodic table. In fact, it was plutonium-239, and unlike the 235 isotope of uranium, it could be separated by conventional chemistry. When Heisenberg read his student's paper on the results of the experimentation, completed in July 1940, he realised the additional potential it offered for a nuclear explosive device.[77]

Set against those advantages, Germany's scientific endeavour was undermined by the rabid anti-Semitism propagated by the Nazi regime. This had three consequences. First, after being subjected to abuse and persecution by Nazi supporters or sympathisers, leading Jewish scientists working in Germany (and in Austria following the *Anschluss*)[78] fled the country. Attacks against them emanated even from within the 'Aryan' scientific community; among the most virulent of the anti-Semitic scientists were Philipp Lenard and Johannes Stark,[79] both Nobel Prize winners.[80] Second, the scientific discoveries of Jewish scientists were roundly dismissed – Lenard and Stark led the charge against Einstein's theory of relativity as 'Jewish world bluff'.[81] Ideology trumped 'decadent' science, making it harder to work effectively in nuclear physics.[82] Third, the brain drain caused by Nazi racism gave its enemies a huge advantage, establishing the United States as a 'scientific superpower'.[83]

Even so, it is claimed that, given the necessary time, the Germans 'would and could have produced an atomic bomb'.[84] Jungk offers four reasons to explain why Germany did not manage to build a nuclear explosive device. The first three of these are generally (though not universally) accepted; the fourth is fiercely disputed. The first, and arguably the most severe impediment, was, as described previously, the loss of many great scientists, especially those Jews who fled Germany in fear for their lives. The second obstacle was the poor organisation by the Nazis of research in the interests of war. The third was the insufficiencies in the technical equipment available and needed for so complex an endeavour. The fourth factor, Jungk claimed, was the 'actual personal attitudes of the German experts in atomic research', which 'counted against success'.[85] This controversial claim is discussed below.

77 Powers, *Heisenberg's War: The Secret History of the German Bomb*, p. 21.

78 On 13 July 1938, Lise Meitner, an Austrian national, fled to the Netherlands without a passport, ultimately reaching Stockholm. She had been formally denied the right to leave Germany. R. L. Sime, 'Lise Meitner's Escape from Germany', *American Journal of Physics*, Vol. 58, No. 3 (March 1990), 262–67.

79 See, e.g., P. Ball, *Serving the Reich: The Struggle for the Soul of Physics under Hitler*, University of Chicago Press, Chicago, 2014.

80 Lenard had won the Nobel Prize for Physics in 1905 for his work on cathode rays (the 'radiation' emitted from hot metals), while Stark had been awarded the Nobel Prize in Physics in 1919 for his discovery of the effect of electric fields on the energies of photons emitted from atoms as electrons jump between their quantum orbits.

81 Jungk, *Brighter than 1000 Suns*, p. 40.

82 D. Irving, *The German Atomic Bomb*, Simon & Schuster, New York, 1967, p. 177.

83 Lipscombe, 'Einstein Feared a Nazi Atom Bomb – But Immigrants Made Sure the U.S. Got There First'.

84 Irving, *The German Atomic Bomb*, p. 296.

85 Jungk, *Brighter than* 1000 Suns, p. 88.

But one might also qualify the failure, not in terms of a deliberate decision by principled scientists to prevent Hitler from getting a hold of a nuclear explosive device, but because of a more mundane reason: human error. Initially, at least, Heisenberg did not reject the possibility of an atom bomb as a matter of principle, but rather on the grounds that its creation was impracticable in the circumstances.[86] Germany had sought to procure heavy water for use as a moderator in its nuclear reactors. Owing to an experimental error by Professor Walther Bothe in 1941, it was wrongly believed that graphite could not meet this purpose.[87] Heavy water, which contains greater amounts of deuterium than ordinary water, absorbs fewer neutrons than hydrogen, but was much harder to procure than graphite. When war broke out, only the Norwegian Hydro-Electric Company was producing heavy water on a commercial scale within Europe, at its plant in Vemork.[88] Germany's installation of a puppet government in Norway in June 1940 meant their access, initially restricted, was opened.[89] But sabotage at Europe's biggest production facility, in Norway, badly affected its supply. In February 1944, the Norwegian resistance used a timed explosive device to sink the *Hydro*, a ferry carrying the last 600 kilograms en route towards Germany.[90]

A lack of uranium was certainly not the reason for Germany's failure to develop the bomb. At the time of the German invasion in May 1940, France had the largest stocks of uranium oxide in the world (as well as all the stock of heavy water in Europe).[91] There were, though, other supplies of uranium ore in Europe, notably in Belgium, which were seized by the invading German forces in 1940.[92] And in taking Czechoslovakia, the Nazis had also obtained an abundant source of natural uranium from the mines at Joachimstal.[93] In 1945, Operation Alsos III discovered an inventory of close to 1,100 tons of uranium ore in an area near the town of Stassfurt in Saxony in Germany. Groves wrote to General George Marshall, the Chief of Staff of the US Armed Forces, to inform him that the capture of the material, which was the bulk of uranium supplies available in Europe, 'would seem to remove definitely any possibility of the Germans making any use of an atomic bomb in this

86 That said, the Uranium Society (*Uranverein*) in which he participated had cautioned that the issue 'must be thoroughly investigated in order to make sure that the Americans will not be able to develop atom bombs either'. Jungk, *Brighter than 1000 Suns*, p. 92.

87 Irving, *The German Atomic Bomb*, pp. 84–86.

88 Ibid., p. 53.

89 On 9 April 1940, Germany launched an invasion of Norway, capturing several strategic points along the Norwegian coast. During the preliminary phase of the invasion, Norwegian fascist forces under Vidkun Quisling acted as a 'fifth column' for the German invaders, seizing Norway's nerve centres, spreading false rumours, and occupying military bases. After two months of desperate resistance, the last surviving Norwegian and British defenders of Norway were overwhelmed by the Germans and the authorities surrendered. 'This Day in History: June 10 (1940), Norway Surrenders to Germany', *History*, at http://bit.ly/3gmvFs3.

90 Powers, *Heisenberg's War: The Secret History of the German Bomb*, pp. 212–13.

91 Jungk, *Brighter than 1000 Suns*, p. 103.

92 In April 1939, Britain had tried to buy up the entire Belgian store of uranium, which had been extracted from company mines in the Belgian Congo, to deny it Germany. The refusal of the president of Union Minière to agree to this led to him being warned that in his company's hands lay something that might mean a catastrophe for both countries should it fall into enemy hands. Irving, *The German Atomic Bomb*, pp. 37–38.

93 Powers, *Heisenberg's War: The Secret History of the German Bomb*, p. 15.

war'.[94] Already in March of the previous year, Sir John Anderson, the head of the British atomic bomb project that followed the MAUD Committee, the 'Tube Alloys Directorate', had told Winston Churchill that 'fortunately all the evidence we have goes to show that the Germans are not working seriously on the project'.[95]

Throughout 1940 and 1941, German military research into atomic energy was focused on two priorities: how to make a chain-reacting pile and how to isolate uranium-235.[96] While commentators tend to dismiss the early research as lacking urgency – the result of Germany's stunning military successes across continental Europe – the same claim could not be made by 1942. This included 'one of the most far-sighted [developments] of the uranium research program in Germany: an ultracentrifuge to enrich the uranium-235 isotope'.[97]

In April 1942, General Friedrich Fromm told Albert Speer, who had been made Reichsminister for Armaments and Munitions following Fritz Todt's death in a plane crash that February, that Germany's only hope of winning the war was to develop a devastating new weapon: the atomic bomb.[98] Speer brought a large contingent of senior military officials to a meeting with Germany's nuclear physicists on 4 June 1942.[99] This meeting would prove to be the beginning of the end for any serious prospects of a Nazi atomic bomb.

At the meeting, Speer asked Heisenberg directly 'how nuclear physics could be applied to the manufacturing of atomic bombs'. Heisenberg replied that theoretically it was possible, but that two years at least would be necessary 'even provided that the programme received maximum support'.[100] General Erhard Milch, the Chief of Staff of the *Luftwaffe*, asked how large a bomb must be to reduce a city the size of London to ruins. Heisenberg replied that it would need to be 'about as big as a pineapple'. He was then asked how long the Americans would need to develop an atomic bomb; in 1945 came the prescient reply.[101]

But perhaps the key moment of the meeting came when Speer asked how much money the scientists would need to work on a nuclear reactor and a bomb. When von Weizsäcker responded 40,000 Reichsmarks (equivalent to around US$100,000 at the time), Speer thought the desultory amount the scientists were seeking meant that the project was simply not serious.[102] Speaking in 1967 to the German magazine *Der Spiegel*, Speer said that he and his military colleagues got the impression that the development was very much at the beginning and that the physicists did not want to put much effort into it.[103] He left the

94 Atomic Heritage Foundation, 'Alsos Mission'. Germany had sought to develop the technology needed for a thermonuclear weapon, using a silver sphere filled with heavy hydrogen around which was packed ordinary explosive, but experimentation was conducted on too small a scale to have ever generated a radioactive response. Irving, *The German Atomic Bomb*, pp. 216–17.

95 Irving, The German Atomic Bomb, pp. 224–25.

96 Powers, *Heisenberg's War: The Secret History of the German Bomb*, p. 98.

97 Irving, *The German Atomic Bomb*, p. 90.

98 A. Speer, *Inside the Third Reich*, Weidenfeld & Nicholson, London, 2003, pp. 314–15.

99 Powers, *Heisenberg's War: The Secret History of the German Bomb*, pp. 144, 145.

100 Ibid., p. 147.

101 Ibid., p. 148.

102 Ibid., pp. 148–49.

103 *Der Spiegel*, 3 July 1967, cited by Powers, *Heisenberg's War: The Secret History of the German Bomb*, p. 150.

meeting feeling that there was little mileage – '*nicht viel Musik*' – in the possibility of an atomic weapon.[104] He did, though, report back to Hitler 'briefly' on the conference and the support they were providing to the project.[105]

Why then did Germany not succeed in developing a nuclear explosive device? Claims by both Jungk and Powers that Heisenberg was a nationalist but not a Nazi,[106] and that he secretly feared what Hitler would do with an atomic bomb in his hands,[107] are fiercely rejected by most commentators. In his 2001 work *Heisenberg and the Nazi Atomic Bomb Project, 1939–1945: A Study in German Culture*, Paul Lawrence Rose effectively writes off Heisenberg as a mediocre scientist who never overcame critical misconceptions about nuclear fission.[108] A fellow American historian, Mark Grimsley, is a little more forgiving, terming him a genius (though 'not genius enough'), but still dismisses the notion that Heisenberg deliberately led research away from the path towards a nuclear bomb.[109] Irving also rejected the notion that scruples were at play: scientists' natural curiosity would have been too powerful, he argued. His explanation for the failure is more anodyne: that while Germany had an outstanding theoretical physicist in Heisenberg, it lacked top experimental physicists.[110]

It is certainly true that scientists on all sides committed fundamental errors and made material miscalculations with respect to the harnessing of atomic energy throughout the 1930s and early 1940s. The great Ernest Rutherford famously believed that the possibility of developing a nuclear explosive device was 'moonshine'. In 1939, the French physicist Francis Perrin believed that a nine-foot-diameter sphere of uranium oxide weighing 12 tons (if tamped) would be needed to achieve critical mass.[111] He had not yet appreciated, as Niels Bohr had, that uranium-235 was far more likely to capture neutrons, vastly reducing the amount needed for a self-sustaining chain reaction. All the same, Bohr's claim in 1943 that Heisenberg thought a bomb and a reactor were 'the same thing' is simply not credible.[112] Speer certainly had the impression that Heisenberg's heart was not in the project.

Powers notes the extreme sensitivity of the atomic scientists in the United States after Hiroshima and Nagasaki to accusations that they had failed humanity – and therefore to any suggestion that atomic scientists in Nazi Germany were somehow morally superior.[113] Von Weizsäcker's work towards developing an atomic bomb for Nazi Germany spurred him to help found his country's post-war peace movement. When he died in 2007, an

104 'Übers Plutonium kann man was machen', *Der Spiegel*, 26 December 1988, at http://bit.ly/2z1nOPo.
105 Speer, *Inside the Third Reich*, p. 316 note 25.
106 See, e.g., Powers, *Heisenberg's War: The Secret History of the German Bomb*, pp. 328, 426.
107 Ibid., p. 444: Heisenberg was overheard by a secret microphone while in detention saying that he had not been '100 per cent anxious' to build a bomb for Hitler.
108 P. L. Rose, *Heisenberg and the Nazi Atomic Bomb Project, 1939–1945: A Study in German Culture*, University of California Press, Berkeley, 2001.
109 M. Grimsley, 'What If Werner Heisenberg Had Been a Nazi?', *HistoryNet*, 2020, at http://bit.ly/2xr8eMi.
110 Irving, *The German Atomic Bomb*, pp. 296, 299.
111 C. Reed, 'Francis Perrin's 1939 Analysis of Uranium Criticality', American Physical Society (APS), paper presented at the APS Meeting on 1 April 2012.
112 Powers, *Heisenberg's War: The Secret History of the German Bomb*, p. 430.
113 Ibid., p. 436.

obituary in the *New York Times* recorded that 'in 1945, he and Dr Heisenberg were among 10 top German physicists detained by the British at Farm Hall, near Cambridge. Intelligence officers secretly taped the detainees as Dr von Weizsäcker led the scientists in concocting a story that they lacked "passion" for building the bomb.'[114]

Japanese Research into an Atomic Bomb

A leading figure in Japan's abortive nuclear weapon programme was Dr Yoshio Nishina. A close associate of Niels Bohr, he had also studied under Rutherford.[115] Preliminary research began in 1940, with Nishina chosen to lead a programme called Ni-Go that was initiated under the Imperial Japanese Army the following year.[116] A Japanese naval programme, F-Go (F denoting fission), began in Kyoto in 1942 under the auspices of Bunsaku Arakatsu, a physicist who had studied in Europe in the 1920s under Einstein.[117]

In contrast to the situation in Nazi Germany, a key challenge for both Japanese programmes was the obtention of sufficient quantities of uranium-235. While Nishina's team concentrated on thermal diffusion, Arakatsu employed centrifuges in which the heavier 238 isotope of uranium is spun to the outside while the lighter 235 isotope is collected on an inner wall. It is generally believed, however, that the military effort did not receive sufficient resources to ensure their success. Japanese efforts to develop a nuclear explosive device are said to have been effectively over by March 1943, with a colloquium of scientists concluding they would need ten years for the endeavour.[118]

Nishina would still be asked by the Deputy Chief of the Japanese General Staff late in the war whether he could construct an atomic bomb within six months, as Japan might be able to hold out that long. He replied that in the conditions at the time six years 'would not be long enough. In any case we have no uranium.'[119] Yet, after Japan surrendered on 15 August 1945, the occupying US Army found five Japanese cyclotrons that were still intact.[120] Some of the parts were blown up in situ while others were tipped into Tokyo Bay in November 1945.[121]

Robert Wilcox suggests that sufficient mining of uranium and advanced nuclear research were both conducted by Japan in what would become the Democratic People's Republic of Korea.[122] More likely, the shortage of ^{235}U was an obstacle that the Japanese atomic programmes could not overcome in the circumstances. On 19 May 1945, a Nazi

114 D. Martin, 'Carl F. von Weizsäcker, German Physicist and Thinker, Dies at 94', *New York Times*, 2 May 2007, at http://nyti.ms/3b4QiVO.

115 D. Shapley, 'Nuclear Weapons History: Japan's Wartime Bomb Projects Revealed', *Science*, Vol. 199, No.4325 (13 January 1978), 152–57, at p. 152; R. K. Wilcox, *Japan's Secret War*, 3rd rev. ed., Permuted Press, New York, 2019, p. 53.

116 Atomic Heritage Foundation, 'Japanese Atomic Bomb Project', 25 May 2016, at http://bit.ly/2TU293a.

117 R. Benke, 'New Details Emerge About Japan's Wartime A-Bomb Program', *Los Angeles Times*, 1 June 1997, at http://lat.ms/2ZAfqBm; Atomic Heritage Foundation, 'Bunsaku Arakatsu', 2019, at http://bit.ly/2XKfJav.

118 Ham, *Hiroshima Nagasaki*, p. 154.

119 Jungk, *Brighter than 1000 Suns*, p. 193.

120 Wilcox, *Japan's Secret War*, 3rd rev. ed., p. 172.

121 Ibid.; Braithwaite, *Armageddon and Paranoia: The Nuclear Confrontation*, p. 45.

122 Wilcox, *Japan's Secret War*, 3rd rev. ed.

U-boat that surrendered to US naval forces in the North Atlantic contained 560 kg of uranium oxide in ten cases which were said to have been destined for the Japanese army; two Japanese officers were aboard, accompanying the cargo.[123]

At the same time, one may legitimately enquire as to why, if the Japanese effort to create a nuclear explosive device were truly at an end, this delivery was still being made; it is also remarkable from the German side given that the Nazis had already suffered a crushing military defeat. That said, if Japan had been considerably closer to developing a nuclear explosive device than is generally appreciated, there would surely have been no incentive on the part of the Americans to conceal that fact. Quite the opposite: it might have provided greater justification for its decision to use the atomic bombs less than three months later. It is now pure conjecture, but Japan might have been preparing for a final throw of the dice by using a dirty bomb – if not a nuclear explosive device – against the expected American invasion of the Japanese homeland.[124]

THE DEVELOPMENT OF NUCLEAR WEAPONS AFTER THE SECOND WORLD WAR

The Soviets were already engaged in a nuclear weapons programme before the end of the Second World War, but their efforts were massively ramped up after the United States dropped an atomic bomb first over Hiroshima and then, three days later, over Nagasaki. A couple of years after the end of the war, the United Kingdom restarted its nuclear weapons programme, followed by France, China, and later several other countries. As of 2021, nine States were still nuclear-armed: China, the Democratic People's Republic of Korea (DPR Korea), France, India, Israel, Pakistan, the Russian Federation, the United Kingdom, and the United States.

The Soviet Nuclear Weapons Programme

In May 1945, the Red Army was at 'the pinnacle of its power, standing victorious in the smouldering ruins of Berlin'.[125] But then, in the words of the British ambassador to Moscow, 'Plump came the atomic bomb' and the Soviet army's three hundred divisions were 'shorn of much of their value'.[126] Enraged at the shattering of his dreams of European

[123] The nuclear material, which is believed to have gone to Oak Ridge, may even have found its way into one of the two bombs dropped on Japan. Whether there was sufficient time to incorporate the material effectively is uncertain. W. J. Broad, 'Captured Cargo, Captivating Mystery', *New York Times*, 31 December 1995, at http://nyti.ms/3ey1P1Q.

[124] Two military invasions were planned by the US armed forces as part of its Operation Downfall: Operation Olympic on 1 November 1945 and Operation Coronet, which would begin on 1 March 1946. In the first invasion, combat troops would be landed by amphibious assault after a massive naval and aerial bombardment. Fourteen combat divisions of American soldiers and marines would land on heavily fortified and defended Kyushu, southernmost of the Japanese home islands. The second invasion (Operation Coronet) would send twenty-two more American combat divisions against one million Japanese defenders to assault the main island of Honshu and the Tokyo Plain in a final effort to obtain unconditional surrender. M. Thomson, 'Operation Downfall – The Invasion of Japan', *Naval Historical Society of Australia*, 1 September 1999, at http://bit.ly/2MeM9Ev.

[125] S. J. Zaloga, *The Kremlin's Nuclear Sword: The Rise and Fall of Russia's Strategic Nuclear Forces, 1945–2000*, Smithsonian Books, Washington, DC, 2002, p. 1.

[126] Cited at ibid.

expansion, Stalin ordered a massive acceleration of the Soviet nuclear weapons project under Lavrentiy Beria, the head of the People's Commissariat for Internal Affairs (NKVD); no expense was now to be spared.[127]

But although the Soviet nuclear programme only began in earnest after the Hiroshima bombing, the potential for human creation of explosive atomic energy was already known by Soviet physicists before the Second World War broke out. Already in 1939, several had sought to reproduce the fission experiment that Hahn and Strassmann had conducted in Berlin earlier in the year with a view to identify the conditions, if any, under which a nuclear chain reaction would take place.[128]

Within days of Britain's secret decision in 1941 to begin research towards the creation of an atomic bomb, an informant in the British civil service, John Cairncross, who served as Secretary to the Chairman of the government's Scientific Advisory Committee, is said to have notified the Soviets.[129] On 4 November 1941, Beria received a coded telegram from the Soviet Embassy in London reporting that theoretical work on a uranium bomb was being undertaken in England.[130] At the time, Beria – but not yet Stalin – was persuaded of the authenticity of the report. Cairncross is considered by some the first atomic spy.[131]

Early in 1942, frustrated at the lack of action by the authorities, a young Soviet nuclear physicist, Georgy Nikolayevich Flyorov (also sometimes transliterated from Cyrillic as Flerov), wrote directly to Stalin urging him to start a nuclear weapons programme.[132] Flyorov proposed that a meeting be called to discuss nuclear research, boldly warning that when the West developed a bomb 'the results will be so huge that there will be no time to decide who was guilty of the fact that we abandoned this work here in the Union'. It is unclear if Stalin ever saw the letter.[133] But in May 1942, after confirmation of the British research by Klaus Fuchs, the German emigré who would pass many secrets from the Manhattan Project to the Soviets, Beria went again to Stalin. After the Soviet leader met with leading scientists to discuss the feasibility of an atomic bomb, Stalin ordered the initiation of the Soviet nuclear weapons programme.[134]

The programme was under the scientific control of Igor Kurchatov, then Flyorov's boss, and the scientific research was conducted primarily at the 'Laboratory No. 2' within the Soviet Academy of Sciences in Moscow.[135] In 1944, Kurchatov had written to Beria begging for uranium; this was the project's most urgent need, so that they could create

127 Ibid., p. 2.

128 Atomic Heritage Foundation, 'Soviet Atomic Program – 1946', 2019, at http://bit.ly/2KMs9bM.

129 M. S. Holmes, 'Spies Who Spilled Atomic Bomb Secrets', *Smithsonian Magazine*, 19 April 2009, at http://bit.ly/3aPaydK.

130 Zaloga, *The Kremlin's Nuclear Sword: The Rise and Fall of Russia's Strategic Nuclear Forces*, 1945–2000, p. 5.

131 Holmes, 'Spies Who Spilled Atomic Bomb Secrets'.

132 D. Holloway, *Stalin and the Bomb: the Soviet Union and Atomic Energy*, 1939–1956, Yale University Press, New Haven, 1996, p. 421.

133 Atomic Heritage Foundation, 'Georgy Flerov', 2019, at http://bit.ly/2WwicVr.

134 Zaloga, *The Kremlin's Nuclear Sword: The Rise and Fall of Russia's Strategic Nuclear Forces*, 1945–2000, p. 6.

135 In 1947, the organisation was renamed the delightfully anodyne 'Laboratory for Measuring Instruments', and in 1955, it became the Kurchatov Institute in honour of the 'Father of the Soviet atomic bomb'.

a reactor or at least an experimental pile.[136] When Truman told Stalin at Yalta of a new and extremely powerful weapon that the United States had developed, he feigned total ignorance, utterly fooling the president as well as Churchill and then US presidential advisor James Byrnes, both of whom were standing within earshot. This was, in Ham's words, the first poker-faced gambit of the nuclear age.[137]

As Soviet forces moved westwards in 1944 and early 1945, they seized key German supplies, and by the end of the year, they had their hands on 100 tons of uranium oxide.[138] Kurchatov began building a nuclear reactor in the summer of 1946 at Ozersk, code-named City 40, on the outskirts of Moscow;[139] by December, the reactor had gone critical, some four years after Fermi's pile at Chicago.[140] Soviet espionage had learnt that a plutonium implosion device was easier to construct than a gun design, which demanded highly enriched uranium;[141] this knowledge saved the programme considerable time. Plutonium could be obtained through the use of the experimental reactor at City 40.[142]

By 1947, a site for testing had been selected in Kazakhstan, 160 kilometres west of the town of Semipalatinsk. On 29 August 1949, a 22 kt device was detonated in an operation later code-named First Lightning.[143] The device would itself be termed RDS-1, an abbreviation variously said to stand for the words *Reaktivnyy Dvigatel Stalina* (meaning 'Stalin's Rocket Engine'), *Reaktivnyy Dvigatel Spetsialnyy* ('Special Rocket Engine'), or even *Rossiya Delayet Sama* (Russia Does It Herself!).[144] If it were the latter, the nomenclature would be tinged with irony, given that the RDS-1 was a copy of the US atomic bomb dropped on Nagasaki; the requisite technical data had been provided to the Soviets by Fuchs.[145]

The successful detonation in First Lightning came as both a surprise and a shock to the United States. Stalin did not announce the achievement publicly, but US atmospheric sampling detected trace elements resulting from the explosion. By then, Stalin had already authorised funding for the twenty atomic bombs he sought before the end of 1950, which were to be produced at the Avangard plant at Saransk, a city in the Volga basin more than 600 kilometres east of Moscow. In fact, production and associated testing were largely a failure. In September 1951, however, a home-grown implosion device (RDS-2) was successfully test detonated at Semipalatinsk; Operation Second Lightning had succeeded in achieving an explosive yield equivalent to 38 kt.[146]

136 T. B. Cochran, R. S. Norris, and O. A. Bukharin, *Making the Russian Bomb: From Stalin to Yeltsin*, Westview Press, Boulder, CO, 1995, p. 10.

137 Ham, *Hiroshima Nagasaki*, p. 280. See also Braithwaite, *Armageddon and Paranoia: The Nuclear Confrontation*, p. 20.

138 Zaloga, *The Kremlin's Nuclear Sword: The Rise and Fall of Russia's Strategic Nuclear Forces, 1945–2000*, p. 7.

139 S. Goetschel, '"The Graveyard of the Earth": Inside City 40, Russia's Deadly Nuclear Secret', *The Guardian*, 20 July 2016, at http://bit.ly/2yGln4K.

140 Braithwaite, *Armageddon and Paranoia: The Nuclear Confrontation*, pp. 90–91.

141 Plutonium is too impure to easily chain-react under a gun blast. Ham, *Hiroshima Nagasaki*, p. 253.

142 Zaloga, *The Kremlin's Nuclear Sword: The Rise and Fall of Russia's Strategic Nuclear Forces, 1945–2000*, p. 7.

143 The United States called it Joe-1, in reference to Stalin.

144 'First Soviet Nuclear Test: RDS-1 vs. Joe-1, Stalin's Rocket Engine, and First Lightning', blog entry, *Russian Strategic Nuclear Forces*, May 2017, at http://bit.ly/3eBF65b.

145 Cochran, Norris, and Bukharin, *Making the Russian Bomb: From Stalin to Yeltsin*, p. 17.

146 Zaloga, *The Kremlin's Nuclear Sword: The Rise and Fall of Russia's Strategic Nuclear Forces, 1945–2000*, pp. 10–11.

A month later, the first Soviet atomic bomb (RDS-3) was dropped over the test site. It detonated with an explosive yield equivalent to 42 kt.[147] Despite massive funding, however, by the time of Stalin's death in 1953, the Soviet Union had fewer than a dozen atomic bombs ready for use, while the United States already had 1,350 in its nuclear arsenal.[148]

Thermonuclear (Hydrogen) Bombs

Fusion reactions are what occur in the Sun to give the star its energy. In its core, the Sun fuses more than 500 million metric tons of hydrogen each second.[149] In reproducing a tiny fraction of that level of fusion, a thermonuclear device releases energy equivalent to millions of tons of TNT. It is thus typically hundreds of times – though the order of magnitude is sometimes in the thousands – more powerful than is a fission weapon.

Sir Marcus Laurence Elwin 'Mark' Oliphant had discovered the elements helium-3 and tritium. He also found that the nuclei of heavy hydrogen could be forced to react with one another and to fuse together. It was this discovery of fusion that led the way to the hydrogen bomb.[150] It is Edward Teller, though, who is widely referred to as the 'father of the hydrogen bomb'. His single-mindedness overcame the many technical obstacles, including the exceptionally high temperatures needed to provoke a thermonuclear explosion. In defence of his research, he argued: 'It won't be until the bombs get so big that they can annihilate everything that people will really become terrified and begin to take a reasonable line in politics.'[151]

The first hydrogen device test-detonated was 'Ivy Mike'. Exploded by the United States over Enewetak atoll in the Marshall Islands at the beginning of November 1952, the device contained 65 tons of heavy hydrogen.[152] The bomb, which weighed 82 tons, was housed in a refrigeration system that itself took six weeks to assemble.[153] The top of the mushroom cloud following the detonation stabilised at a height of 41 kilometres, spreading out to a diameter of more than 160 kilometres. Its awesome effects would, though, be dwarfed by the device detonated over Bikini atoll eighteen months later in Operation Bravo; the fallout from the 15 megaton (MT) detonation spread traces of radioactive material as far as Australia, Europe, and the United States.[154]

Some of the atomic scientists, even those who had worked actively to develop fission bombs, objected. Oppenheimer and Fermi had both opposed the development of the hydrogen bomb, with a committee of scientists led by Oppenheimer arguing that a 'super' bomb, as it had earlier been termed, might become a 'weapon of genocide' and should never be produced.[155] Szilard warned publicly that the explosion of 500 tons of heavy

[147] Ibid., p. 12.
[148] Ibid., pp. 12, 21.
[149] H. A. Bethe, 'The Hydrogen Bomb', *Bulletin of the Atomic Scientists*, Vol. 6, No.4 (April 1950), 99–104.
[150] J. Glorfeld, 'Science History: The Man Who Went from Bomb-Maker to Pacifist', *Cosmos*, 15 October 2018, at http://bit.ly/2SmqBJC.
[151] Jungk, *Brighter than 1000 Suns*, p. 246.
[152] Ibid., p. 271.
[153] T. Downing, 1983: *The World at the Brink*, Little, Brown, London, 2018, p. 7.
[154] G. DeGroot, *The Bomb: A Life*, Jonathan Cape, London, 2004, pp. 196–98.
[155] Braithwaite, *Armageddon and Paranoia: The Nuclear Confrontation*, p. 65.

hydrogen would be sufficient to extinguish all life on earth.[156] But Teller dismissed the scientists' objections to thermonuclear weapons; he appears to have considered the development of the hydrogen bomb as almost a sacred duty.

Andrei Sakharov led the Soviet effort to develop a thermonuclear weapon, resulting in him being widely considered in turn as the 'Father of the Soviet H-Bomb'. Although the United States had only test-detonated its first thermonuclear device in 1952, less than twelve months later, on 12 August 1953, RDS-6s was the first Soviet hydrogen bomb to be exploded. While the detonation yielded the relatively modest explosive equivalent of some 400 kt, the presence of lithium in the radioactive cloud demonstrated to the United States that the Soviets had managed to build a hydrogen device that was far smaller in physical size than theirs.[157] This detonation is said to have prompted the United States to seek to halt the horizontal proliferation of nuclear armaments to other nation-states.[158] Then, in November 1955, the Soviet Union detonated its first megaton-range bomb, the RDS-37. In his memoirs, Sakharov would point to that test as a turning point in his journey from nuclear weapons designer to prominent dissident.[159]

Sakharov's fears would be greatly amplified six years later. On 30 October 1961, the Soviet Union detonated the RDS-220 (nicknamed 'Tsar Bomba' by the West) at an altitude of 4 kilometres above Novaya Zemlya island in the Arctic sea. The 8-metre-long, 57 MT device, whose blast wave broke windowpanes in Finland and Norway, remains the most powerful nuclear weapon explosion in human history.[160] In fact, in order to limit fallout, Soviet engineers had reduced the yield down by around half from the 100 megatons that Premier Nikita Khrushchev had demanded.[161] For the first time in history, humans had developed the ability to extinguish their own species. US military strategist Herman Kahn, reputedly one of the inspirations for Dr Strangelove in the eponymous 1964 film directed by Stanley Kubrick, was now talking of 'megadeath': a unit for measuring the millions of deaths that would result from thermonuclear blasts in cities. Estimates for the human toll in the Soviet Union and China within the first few hours of a US nuclear attack ranged from 360 million to 450 million.[162]

The Soviet–US Arms Race

As Zaloga wrote in 2002, 'The terrible heart of the Cold War was the nuclear arms race.'[163] Funding equating to many trillions of US dollars was devoted to the research,

[156] Jungk, *Brighter than 1000 Suns*, p. 258.

[157] Downing, *1983: The World at the Brink*, p. 7.

[158] J. Woodliffe, 'Nuclear Weapons and Non-proliferation: The Legal Aspects', chapter 5 in I. Pogany (ed.), *Nuclear Weapons and International Law*, Avebury, Aldershot, 1987, p. 85.

[159] Atomic Heritage Foundation, 'Soviet Hydrogen Bomb Program', 8 August 2014, at http://bit.ly/2Wt5pTF; A. Wellerstein, 'Sakharov's Turning Point: The First Soviet H-Bomb Test', The Nuclear Secrecy Blog, 31 January 2014, at http://bit.ly/3fmS8EQ.

[160] Atomic Heritage Foundation, 'Andrei D. Sakharov', 2019, at http://bit.ly/2WtSD79; S. Dowling, 'The Monster Atomic Bomb That Was Too Big to Use', BBC, 6 August 2017, at http://bbc.in/2W3JeV2.

[161] Preparatory Commission for the CTBTO, '30 October 1961 – The Tsar Bomba', at http://bit.ly/2YIdWox.

[162] Downing, *1983: The World at the Brink*, p. 8.

[163] Zaloga, *The Kremlin's Nuclear Sword: The Rise and Fall of Russia's Strategic Nuclear Forces*, 1945–2000, p. v.

development, and production of nuclear weapons.[164] In 1950, the United States had fewer than 300 nuclear weapons. By the end of the decade, it had 16,000 nuclear warheads, while in 1967 it reached its peak of more than 32,000.[165] In September of that year, Robert McNamara was speaking of the 'mad momentum of the arms race'.[166] In the 1960s, which saw the 'greatest accumulation in killing power on all human history', the world went from 50 intercontinental ballistic missiles (ICBMs) and 32 submarine-launched ballistic missiles (SLBMs) to 2,000 ICBMs and nearly 1,000 SLBMs, along with tens of thousands of tactical nuclear weapons.[167] Between 1945 and 1990, the United States produced more than 70,000 nuclear warheads and bombs.[168] They developed 65 different types of nuclear weapons for use in 116 delivery systems, ranging from so-called tactical 'battlefield' weapons to strategic bombs and missiles. Land mines, artillery shells, anti-submarine depth charges, gravity bombs, and cruise missiles were all employed as nuclear weapons or as a means to deliver other nuclear explosive devices.[169]

On the smallest end of the nuclear spectrum, the M28/M29 'Davy Crockett' was a variable yield nuclear weapon, formally known as the Battle Group Atomic Delivery System (BGADS). It had a range of 2 kilometres, with an explosive yield ranging from 10 tons to 1 kt of TNT. Two live warheads were fired in testing the system: 'Little Feller I' was detonated in mid-July 1962 in the presence of the Attorney General, Robert F. Kennedy, and then presidential military advisor General Maxwell D. Taylor. This would prove to be the last atmospheric nuclear test at the Nevada Test Range.[170] Highly inaccurate, the weapon was retired from service in 1971 after a total of 2,100 had been produced; the US Army had calculated at one point that they would need more than 100,000 Davy Crocketts.[171]

US expenditure on nuclear arms was partially motivated by a desire to protect Western Europe against Soviet expansionism and its overwhelming superiority in conventional forces. This propelled the United States into a 'one-sided strategic arms race' even before the first Soviet nuclear test in August 1949.[172] In the early years of the arms race, US expenditure on nuclear weapons was considered separately from the defence budget, giving the military little incentive to rein in costs or to consider the relative need for and

[164] See generally, e.g., Schwartz (ed.), *Atomic Audit: The Costs and Consequences of U.S. Nuclear Weapons since 1940*.

[165] T. B. Cochran, W. M. Arkin, and M. M. Hoenig, *Nuclear Weapons Databook, Vol. I: U.S. Nuclear Forces and Capabilities*, National Resources Defense Council, Cambridge MA, 1984, at https://bit.ly/3rpM5nW, p. 12.

[166] W. Epstein, *The Last Chance: Nuclear Proliferation and Arms Control*, The Free Press, New York, 1976, p. 26.

[167] Ibid., p. 28.

[168] O'Neill, 'Building the Bomb', p. 33; and B. G. Blair, J. E. Pike, and S. I. Schwartz, 'Targeting and Controlling the Bomb', chapter 3 in Schwartz (ed.), *Atomic Audit: The Costs and Consequences of U.S. Nuclear Weapons since 1940*, pp. 203–4.

[169] O'Neill, 'Building the Bomb', p. 42.

[170] E. French and M. Seelinger, 'The M28/M29 Davy Crockett Nuclear Weapon', US Army National Museum, 2020, at http://bit.ly/2TWgeNl.

[171] D. Porter, 'Back to the Drawing Board: the Davy Crockett "Tactical" Nuke', *Military History Matters*, 20 January 2020, at http://bit.ly/3ezIoWn.

[172] D. A. Rosenberg, 'American Atomic Strategy and the Hydrogen Bomb Decision', *Journal of American History*, Vol. 66, No.1 (1 June 1979), 62–87, at p. 86; see also 'Introduction', Schwartz (ed.), *Atomic Audit: The Costs and Consequences of U.S. Nuclear Weapons since 1940*, p. 14.

effectiveness of non-conventional capabilities. Indeed, throughout the Cold War, costs were typically underestimated while Soviet threats and progress were systematically overstated.

From Bombers to Land-Based Missiles to SLBMs

In 1945, the heavy bomber was the only means by which nuclear weapons could be delivered to their target.[173] Although Soviet fighters performed well in combat during the Korean War – not a single aircraft was shot down by US bombers – the vulnerability of bombers to attack was clear to all. Attention quickly turned in both the Soviet Union and the United States to the delivery of nuclear weapons by missile warhead. Initially, the Soviets focused on air-launched missiles, basing their design on the Nazi V-1 'doodlebugs'. While not particularly successful, they had opened the path towards the second arm of the superpowers' nuclear triad.

In mid-1957, the Soviets successfully flight-tested their first operational ICBM, the R-7, which the North Atlantic Treaty Organization (NATO) referred to as the SS-6.[174] The R-7's engines achieved thrust far in excess of anything the United States could then produce.[175] Then in October, using the R-7 rocket, the Soviet Union again stunned the United States by launching Sputnik, the world's first artificial satellite, into outer space. This led to the development of a US project, A119, to detonate a nuclear bomb on the surface of the moon, seemingly with a view to impressing the Soviets with US nuclear technology.[176] In Congress, Democrats attacked the Eisenhower administration for allowing a 'missile gap' to arise, with Senator John F. Kennedy exploiting the issue to help defeat Vice-President Richard Nixon in the US presidential election of November 1960.[177] In reality, with the R-7 needing twenty hours to be fuelled for launch, the gap was rather in reliable intelligence.[178] This would later be closed, at least to some extent, by reconnaissance from the U-2 spy plane.[179]

After becoming president, and learning that in fact the United States had a huge numerical advantage in missiles even when SLBMs were taken into account, Kennedy nonetheless authorised a sizeable increase in US strategic nuclear forces.[180] This provoked a predictable response, with the Soviet decision to secretly base R-12[181] ballistic

173 Zaloga, *The Kremlin's Nuclear Sword: The Rise and Fall of Russia's Strategic Nuclear Forces*, 1945–2000, p. 12.

174 G. Thielmann, 'The Missile Gap Myth and Its Progeny', *Arms Control Today*, May 2011, at http://bit.ly/3dlpWQD.

175 Federation of American Scientists, 'R-7/SS-6 Sapwood', 29 July 2000, at http://bit.ly/3fiA6Ds.

176 A. Barnett, 'US Planned One Big Nuclear Blast for Mankind', *The Guardian*, 14 May 2000, at http://bit.ly/2Yo5EBs.

177 'What Missile Gap?', *The Atlantic*, September 2013, at https://bit.ly/3dmtnqg; and 'Introduction', Schwartz (ed.), *Atomic Audit: The Costs and Consequences of U.S. Nuclear Weapons since 1940*, p. 16.

178 Braithwaite claims that the Central Intelligence Agency's (CIA's) first major Soviet source – Piotr Popov, an officer in Soviet military intelligence – was only recruited in 1953. Braithwaite, *Armageddon and Paranoia: The Nuclear Confrontation*, p. 65.

179 See, e.g., Remarks by Gene Poteat, President of the Association of Former Intelligence Officers, '50th Anniversary: The Missile Gap Controversy Panel', John F. Kennedy Presidential Library and Museum, Washington, DC, 26 September 2011, at http://bit.ly/2WARBGw.

180 'Introduction', Schwartz (ed.), *Atomic Audit: The Costs and Consequences of U.S. Nuclear Weapons since 1940*, p. 16. Kennedy did, though, restrict the right to authorise use of nuclear weapons to the president; he had been astonished to discover that Eisenhower had granted US Air Force commanders authority to make the decision in case of urgent operational need when unable to get through to the president to seek confirmation. Downing, *1983: The World at the Brink*, p. 10.

181 SS-4 in Soviet designation.

missiles in Cuba triggered in part by the overall strategic imbalance existing at the time.[182] The R-12, which was equipped with a thermonuclear warhead, was a ground-launched intermediate-range ballistic missile (IRBM) capable of hitting targets two thousand kilometres away.[183] The prelude to the Cuban missile crisis had begun.

Although the world breathed a collective sigh of relief as first Khrushchev and then Kennedy backed away from nuclear war in October 1962, neither superpower contemplated an end to the arms race. Action begat reaction. When in the mid-1960s, the Soviets built anti-ballistic missiles to intercept incoming US ICBMs, the United States responded by developed MIRVed weapons: missiles with multiple independently targetable re-entry vehicles.[184] With each missile capable of containing ten MIRV warheads, any missile defence system would be overwhelmed.

Neither superpower could hope to win a major nuclear exchange. Robert McNamara, Secretary of Defense under President Kennedy and later President Lyndon B. Johnson, devised the term 'assured destruction' to describe the policy whereby neither superpower would dare to attack the other since this would invite the attacker's own devastation. Someone else added the qualifier 'mutual', and the term MAD was born. A concept that President Ronald Reagan would later describe as 'the craziest thing I ever heard of' became one of the central tenets underpinning the Cold War.[185]

The United States gradually reduced its reliance on thermonuclear weapons as the accuracy of its ballistic missiles increased. But the gap in explosive yield between atomic and hydrogen bombs narrowed. The yield of plutonium or highly enriched uranium (HEU) fission weapons can be 'boosted' by releasing into the core a mix of tritium and deuterium – isolated from heavy water – shortly before detonation. The energy caused by the fission explosion causes tritium atoms to fuse with deuterium and release neutrons, causing more of the plutonium or HEU to fission than would otherwise be the case. By 1983, a year when the risk of nuclear warfare erupting between the two superpowers was exceptionally high,[186] 85 per cent of the weapons in the US stockpile (totalling more than 23,000 warheads at the time)[187] required tritium to ensure their full operation.[188]

[182] Thielmann, 'The Missile Gap Myth and Its Progeny'.

[183] The last of the 149 missiles was eliminated at the Lesnaya Missile Elimination Facility on 22 May 1990 as part of the implementation of the 1986 Intermediate Nuclear Forces (INF) Treaty. Federation of American Scientists, 'R-12/SS-4 Sandal', last updated 18 July 2000, at http://bit.ly/2WBcnFY.

[184] It would not be until the mid-1970s that the Soviets would operationally deploy MIRVed ICBMs, first in their SS-17s and shortly thereafter in the SS-19. Braithwaite, *Armageddon and Paranoia: The Nuclear Confrontation*, p. 121. The SS-17 was the first Soviet ICBM to contain multiple independently targetable warheads (four). Federation of American Scientists, 'UR-100MR/SS-17 Spanker', 29 July 2000, at http://bit.ly/2ZKvwbX. The SS-19, a version of which continues to be deployed by the Russian Federation today, contained six MIRVs each warhead having around half a megaton in yield. Missile Threat, 'SS-19 "Stiletto"', 15 June 2018, at http://bit.ly/2XdGxRi.

[185] Downing, *1983: The World at the Brink*, pp. 12, 93.

[186] See generally Downing, *1983: The World at the Brink*.

[187] R. S. Norris and H. M. Kristensen, 'Global Nuclear Weapons Inventories, 1945–2010', *Bulletin of the Atomic Scientists*, Vol. 66, No.4 (2010), 77–83, at http://bit.ly/3dmXxJX, at p. 81.

[188] K. O'Neill, 'Building the Bomb', chapter 1 in Schwartz (ed.), *Atomic Audit: The Costs and Consequences of U.S. Nuclear Weapons since 1940*, p. 38.

The policy of strategic deterrence operated on the basis that neither superpower would dare to attack the other because of the consequences it would suffer from a devastating counterstrike. But that only held true if a first strike could not be a knock-out blow. In the early 1980s, the Soviets – and specifically their new leader Yuri Andropov – became convinced that the United States was contemplating a massive 'decapitation' strike, seeking to destroy the overwhelming number of Soviet nuclear weapons before they could be launched.[189] Andropov is said by one commentator to have suffered from a 'Hungarian complex', having witnessed members of the secret police being hung from lamp posts during the uprising in Budapest in October to November of 1956.[190] Andropov, who was the Soviet ambassador to Hungary at the time, is said to have become paranoid as a result of his experiences, 'haunted by the speed with which an apparently stable communist one-party society could collapse'.[191]

By the end of the 1970s, with President Jimmy Carter seeking re-election, his Republican opponent, Ronald Reagan, attacked him on the basis of a perceived failure to invest sufficiently in defence, particularly the nuclear arsenal. At rally after rally, Reagan claimed, 'We are in an arms race, but only one side is racing',[192] famously describing *détente* as 'a satanic device to blunt America's sword'.[193] Following his election, President Reagan made good on his promise to massively ramp up defence spending, succeeding to double it within five years in the biggest peacetime build-up of military spending in US history.[194]

Reagan restarted the development of enhanced radiation weapons (more commonly known as neutron bombs), which President Carter had deferred owing to protests, particularly from US allies in Europe.[195] Funds were also devoted to accelerating the development of the Pershing II IRBM,[196] whose single, variable-yield warhead had an explosive force equivalent to up to 80 kt, as well as the Tomahawk Cruise missiles that were also planned to be stationed in Europe. In 1987, just a few years after their deployment, the United States and the Soviet Union would conclude the Intermediate-Nuclear Forces (INF) Treaty, which would require their destruction, with the Soviets undertaking to destroy the RSD-10 (SS-20) IRBMs that had been stationed in Eastern Europe since the late 1970s.

189 Downing, *1983: The World at the Brink*, p. 15.
190 Ibid., p. 44.
191 Ibid.
192 F. FitzGerald, *Way Out There in the Blue: Reagan, Star Wars, and the End of the Cold War*, Touchstone, New York, 2001, p. 110.
193 G. Barass, *The Great Cold War: A Journey through the Hall of Mirrors*, Stanford Security Studies, Stanford University Press, 2009, p. 263.
194 Downing, *1983: The World at the Brink*, p. 52.
195 In these weapons, which were developed following calculations by Samuel Cohen of the RAND Corporation, greater initial radiation is generated instead of explosive yield in a hydrogen bomb by using a casing that does not so effectively prevent the emission of neutrons. See, e.g., J. T. Correll, 'The Neutron Bomb', *Air Force Magazine*, 30 October 2017, at http://bit.ly/36KwbeL. The decision by President Jimmy Carter to cancel the US neutron bomb programme in 1978 was described by Cohen as a 'shameful' error. Braithwaite, *Armageddon and Paranoia: The Nuclear Confrontation*, p. 292.
196 Smithsonian National Air and Space Museum, 'Pershing II', 2020, at http://s.si.edu/3cZFx8L.

The Mod 2 version of the Soviet SS-20, the most widely deployed variant, was equipped with three MIRVed 150 kt warheads. The missile was designed to be fired from mobile launchers.[197] The SS-20, which was deployed out from forty-eight bases in the Soviet Union, could reach any target in Europe, but not – at least without modification – the continental United States.[198] The decision to deploy the SS-20 was, though, 'ill thought through', backfiring on the Kremlin.[199] Greeted with alarm in the West, it served as ammunition for the military hawks in the Reagan administration. The Soviet leadership did not perceive the deployment of Pershing IIs and cruise missiles as a predictable reaction, instead deeming it American belligerence.[200] In a speech to Soviet leaders in January 1983, Andropov claimed that those US missiles were intended for a 'future war', which, he said, the United States somehow believed it could win.[201]

In a rare example of a failure by his administration to push greater defence spending through a willing Congress, President Reagan did not manage to secure approval for a full rollout of the MX (Missile Experimental) ICBM. Originally developed in 1971, progress later stalled, although in 1979 the programme had been rejuvenated by Carter. Costs, environmental implications, and disputes as to where the missiles should be located led to plans for one hundred silo-based missiles being scaled back to fifty in 1984. The MX, which had been renamed the LGM-118 'Peacekeeper' in 1982, was first deployed in 1986 at Warren Air Force base in Cheyenne, Wyoming. It was the most sophisticated ICBM fielded by the United States during the Cold War. With the missile capable of containing up to twelve MIRVs,[202] each equipped with a W87 nuclear warhead of between 300 kt and 475 kt, it was primarily a counterstrike weapon.

In 2002, it was announced that the Peacekeeper would be phased out of service by the end of 2005, in line with the START II Treaty (the 'De-MIRV-ing Agreement').[203] The two superpowers had signed START II in Moscow in 1993, though ultimately the treaty did not enter into force.[204] But by the early 2000s, the average cost per operational Peacekeeper missile had ballooned to US$400 million – twenty times the budgeted estimate of $20 million – and the programme was scrapped.[205]

Huge expenditure allied to aggressive rhetoric pushed tensions between the superpowers to historic highs in the early 1980s. On 8 March 1983, in a speech to the National Association of Evangelicals in Orlando, President Reagan famously described

197 Missile Threat, 'SS-20 "Saber" (RSD-10)', 2020, at http://bit.ly/3efQDH6.

198 J. Pike, C. Vick, M. Jacubowski, and P. Garrett, 'RT-21M/SS-20 SABER,' RT-21M/SS-20 SABRE – Russian/Soviet Nuclear Forces', updated 18 July 2000, Federation of American Scientists, at http://bit.ly/2WYiHZO.

199 Downing, 1983: *The World at the Brink*, p. 75.

200 Ibid., p. 78.

201 Ibid., p. 88.

202 The restrictions imposed by the 1991 Strategic Arms Reduction Treaty (START I), however, capped the number of permissible warheads at ten. Art. V(12)(a), Treaty between the United States of America and the Union of Soviet Socialist Republics on the Reduction and Limitation of Strategic Offensive Arms; signed at Moscow, 31 July 1991; entry into force 5 December 1994 (hereinafter, 1991 START I Treaty).

203 Treaty between the United States of America and the Union of Soviet Socialist Republics on Strategic Offensive Reductions (START II); signed at Moscow, 3 January 1993; no entry into force.

204 Missile Threat, 'LGM-118 Peacekeeper (MX)', 2020, at http://bit.ly/3e9ut9a; 'The Peacekeeper (MX) ICBM. LGM-118A', *Nuclear Weapon Archive*, last updated 10 October 1997, at http://bit.ly/2LWiT5u.

205 'The Peacekeeper (MX) ICBM. LGM-118A', *Nuclear Weapon Archive*.

the Soviet Union as an 'evil empire' and 'the focus of evil in the modern world'. 'In your discussions of the nuclear freeze proposals', Reagan said, 'I urge you to beware the temptation of pride, the temptation of blithely declaring yourselves above it all, and label both sides equally at fault, to ignore the facts of history and the aggressive impulses of an evil empire, to simply call the arms race a giant misunderstanding and, thereby, remove yourself from the struggle between right and wrong and good and evil.'[206]

One of the most dangerous periods of the Cold War ensued. Angered by persistent US Air Force incursions into Soviet airspace, Andropov issued an order to shoot down any unauthorised aircraft penetrating the territory of the USSR. On 1 September 1983, this would have tragic consequences for a scheduled civilian Korean Air flight from New York City to Seoul via Anchorage, Alaska, the circumstances of which have never been satisfactorily explained. What is not contested is that, for whatever reason, flight KAL 007 strayed hundreds of miles off course and into sensitive areas of Soviet airspace. After apparently ignoring warning shots from combat aircraft, the Boeing 747 aircraft was shot out of the skies by a Su-15 fighter. President Reagan called the attack a 'crime against humanity' with 'absolutely no justification, legal or moral'. In stark contrast, Andropov accused the United States of a 'sophisticated provocation masterminded by the US special services with the use of a South Korean plane'.[207]

But the moment of most acute risk, albeit unbeknownst to the United States, came two months later, in early November 1983, when NATO conducted a military exercise named Able Archer 83.[208] This was not a traditional war game in which forces are deployed in the field, but an exercise to test command-and-control procedures. The invented scenario for the exercise was a coup in Moscow leading to the institution of a new, harder line leadership in the Kremlin. A few months into the exercise scenario, Soviet forces had invaded first Finland and then Norway, followed by Greece and Germany. Soviet forces would use chemical weapons against NATO forces, which responded in kind before active consideration would begin of nuclear options.

Although messages passed among the NATO forces participating in Able Archer 83 were preceded by the words 'Exercise ... Exercise ... Exercise ... ', the Soviets were concerned this was an elaborate deceptive pretext for the launching of a massive nuclear strike against them. When a new code was introduced for the request to use nuclear weapons, Soviet intelligence officers believed their worst fears were being realised. To add to the credibility of the threat, they saw President Reagan and the First Lady stepping on board Air Force One, ostensibly for a tour of Japan and the Far East, but potentially with the capability to issue orders to US forces to launch a nuclear attack.

Soviet aircraft in East Germany and Poland were loaded with bombs, 70 SS-20 IRBMs were put on high alert, and nuclear-armed submarines were sent under the Arctic ice,

[206] A. Glass, 'Reagan Brands Soviet Union "Evil Empire", March 8, 1983', *Politico*, 8 March 2018, at http://politi.co/2A2CP3N.

[207] T. Patterson, 'The Downing of Flight 007: 30 Years Later, a Cold War Tragedy Still Seems Surreal', *CNN*, 31 August 2013, at http://cnn.it/3gizWwA; P. Grier, 'The Death of Korean Air Lines Flight 007', *Air Force Magazine*, 1 January 2013, at http://bit.ly/2TChhC9.

[208] See, generally, Downing, *1983: The World at the Brink*, chapter 14.

where they would be undetected by American radar and sonar systems. A heightened level of activity was duly detected by the United States but not considered unusual – a major failure of US intelligence.[209] Indeed, intelligence papers released in February 2021 demonstrated how seriously the Soviets had taken the situation, with one hundred nuclear-armed bombers made ready to take to the skies on thirty-minute alert. A senior US intelligence officer wrote later that a lack of intelligence of Soviet intentions and apprehensions during Able Archer could have led to 'a potentially disastrous situation'.[210]

When Mikhail Gorbachev came to power as General Secretary of the Communist Party of the Soviet Union in 1985, following the death of Premier Konstantin Chernenko, US strategists initially wrote him off as just another Soviet apparatchik. Their appreciation of his abilities and intentions was, though, exceptionally poor, for he was anything but. Eloquent, thoughtful, and bold, he had seen the extent of the problems with the Soviet system, and he knew that economic collapse was a real possibility. The blast at the nuclear reactor at Chernobyl in April 1986 laid bare the inadequacies of the huge Soviet bureaucracy; only the heroic efforts of many thousands of ordinary men and women who lined up to 'serve the Soviet Union' had prevented continental Europe from being transmogrified into a radioactive wasteland.

In stark contrast to the growing problems in the Soviet Union, within the United States Edward Teller had been telling Ronald Reagan since 1967 (when Reagan was Governor of California) of the technology that could underpin a space-based anti-ballistic missile system. Teller had vaingloriously asserted that directed-energy weapons, to be powered by nuclear explosions in space, could be employed to defend against a nuclear attack. He characterised the new nuclear weapons as a 'third generation' (after fission and thermonuclear bombs).[211]

In early 1981, after coming into the Oval Office, Reagan signed National Security Decision Directive 12, which included the creation of a 'vigorous research and development program on ballistic missile defense systems'. Reagan publicly announced the Strategic Defense Initiative – baptised 'Star Wars', following critical remarks in the media by Democratic Senator Ted Kennedy – a fortnight after his 'evil empire' speech of March 1983. The announcement caught many of his own administration off guard, and despite claims that this was the beginning of the end of the arms race, the Soviets felt more threatened than ever. So too ironically did many of the US's NATO allies, fearing that the United States would no longer feel motivated to defend Western Europe.[212]

In fact, despite Teller's claims, the technology did not work. Nor did the other myriad of projects the Strategic Defense Initiative spawned in the United States. US Secretary of

[209] Atomic Heritage Foundation, 'Nuclear Close Calls: Able Archer 83', 15 June 2018, at http://bit.ly/2Zz05V0.

[210] M. Evans, 'Soviet Union Was Ready to Scramble 100 Nuclear Bombers in 1983, Files Reveal', *The Times*, 20 February 2021, at http://bit.ly/3azyfK6,

[211] K. Tsipis, 'Third-Generation Nuclear Weapons' in H. G. Brauch (ed.), *Military Technology, Armaments Dynamics and Disarmament: ABC Weapons, Military Use of Nuclear Energy and of Outer Space and Implications for International Law*, Palgrave Macmillan, London, 1989, pp. 67–91, at 67; Downing, 1983: *The World at the Brink*, p. 97; Atomic Heritage Foundation, 'Strategic Defense Initiative (SDI)', 18 July 2018, at http://bit.ly/36riVeR.

[212] Atomic Heritage Foundation, 'Strategic Defense Initiative (SDI)'.

State George Shultz recalled saying at the time, 'The Soviets will assume that we are on the verge of some special technical innovation. Maybe that is the greatest benefit.'[213] The Soviets were certainly spooked and, despite the huge cost, felt constrained to embark on a programme of their own for a space-based anti-ballistic missile system. The 'high point' of the effort, such as it was, came on 15 May 1987 when they launched a rocket from the Baikonur Cosmodrome launch site in southern Kazakhstan to deploy the Polyus spacecraft. Polyus was equipped with a laser system, Skif, and a missile system, Kaskad. The system was designed to shoot down US weapons in space, but the craft failed to reach orbit, breaking apart.[214]

SDI became a key negotiating point in a series of summits between Reagan and Gorbachev: in Geneva (1985), in Reykjavik (1986), in Washington (1987), and in Moscow (1988). While the INF Treaty and ultimately START I represented successful outcomes of the talks, the bold proposal to eliminate all Soviet and US nuclear weapons by 2000 foundered on the rock of Star Wars, with Reagan refusing to shut down the programme. Whether total nuclear disarmament could ever have survived intact in the US Congress is now moot,[215] but the discussions between the two leaders in Reykjavik are certainly the closest the two superpowers ever came to even a political agreement to destroy all nuclear weapons. As Gorbachev later recalled, Reykjavik was 'the site of a truly Shakespearean drama. ... Success was a mere step away, but SDI proved an insurmountable stumbling-block.'[216]

The United Kingdom's Nuclear Weapons Programme

The United Kingdom had begun research into the possibility of developing a nuclear explosive device very early in the Second World War. The work of the MAUD Committee had spurred, in 1941, the creation of the Tube Alloys Project, the first British programme to develop a nuclear explosive device. The MAUD Committee reported in July 1942 that firing two subcritical pieces of uranium at each other in the barrel of a gun would generate a nuclear explosion.[217] But given the huge cost of extracting ^{235}U for such an endeavour, and with the Manhattan Project in the United States moving ahead far more quickly, by the end of 1943 work in Great Britain towards the creation of a nuclear explosive device had come to a virtual standstill.[218]

According to an informal political accord of 1944 – termed the Hyde Park Agreement in reference to the US presidential estate in New York state where Roosevelt and Churchill met to hammer out its terms – the United States committed to sharing all its nuclear weapon information with the United Kingdom.[219] After the Second World War, however,

213 G. P. Shultz, *Turmoil and Triumph: Diplomacy, Power, and the Victory of the American Ideal*, Charles Scriber's Sons, New York, 1993, p. 251.

214 Atomic Heritage Foundation, 'Strategic Defense Initiative (SDI)'.

215 Braithwaite describes the two men as 'naïve' in seeking the elimination of nuclear weapons. Braithwaite, *Armageddon and Paranoia: The Nuclear Confrontation*, p. 370.

216 M. Gorbachev, *Memoirs*, Doubleday, New York, 1995, p. 418.

217 Braithwaite, *Armageddon and Paranoia: The Nuclear Confrontation*, p. 50.

218 D. Irving, *The German Atomic Bomb*, Simon & Schuster, New York, 1967, p. 185.

219 Ham, *Hiroshima Nagasaki*, p. 15.

the United States reneged on its pledge, deciding that it preferred a monopoly to the duopoly foreseen in the Agreement. The passage of the McMahon Act in 1946, which stipulated that the United States would not share information concerning atomic weapons with anyone, was a legislative hammer blow to the British.[220] The so-called Special Relationship (ironically a phrase coined by Churchill while speaking in Missouri that year) looked more chimera than political reality.[221]

In January 1947, as a result of the McMahon Act and the subsequent forlorn discussions between Ernest Bevin, the British Secretary of State for Foreign Affairs and the (now) US Secretary of State, James Byrnes, Prime Minister Clement Attlee decided that the United Kingdom would initiate its own atomic weapons programme.[222] Led by Nobel Prize-winning physicist Sir John Crockcroft, Britain's first nuclear reactor went critical on 3 July 1948. Sites for the production and processing of plutonium and for the generation of HEU were also constructed.[223]

The first British test detonation of a nuclear explosive device was in October 1952 at the Monte Bello Islands, seventy kilometres off the Western Australian coast. Operation Hurricane involved the detonation of a fission device placed in a British frigate just below the waterline. Initially, the United Kingdom nuclear force was planned to consist of home-grown IRBMs: Blue Streak. Work on the project started in 1955, but five years later, with costs mounting and fears that the housing of missiles in vulnerable silos near population centres would cause public anxiety, Blue Streak was cancelled in favour of the US air-launched ballistic missile, Skybolt.[224] By then, following the United Kingdom's testing of its first thermonuclear weapon in May 1957, US cooperation with the British had resumed.[225]

In 1962, however, US Secretary of Defense Robert McNamara decided in controversial circumstances to scrap Skybolt, leaving the government of Harold Macmillan without a nuclear deterrent.[226] The submarine-based Polaris system, already in service with the US navy since 1960,[227] was identified as the most viable replacement, and Macmillan persuaded Kennedy and his administration to allow the United Kingdom to buy it.[228] In 1969,

220 'The Cabinet Papers', *The National Archives*, at http://bit.ly/2ZOorXV.

221 Churchill's 1946 speech represented little more than an indirect, albeit eloquent entreaty for US funding for postwar Europe. See, e.g., O. B. Waxman, 'The "Special Relationship" between the U.S. and U.K. Is Unlike Any Other Alliance. Here's How It Got That Way', *Time*, 13 July 2018, at http://bit.ly/2XoW5I6.

222 Braithwaite, *Armageddon and Paranoia: The Nuclear Confrontation*, p. 192; 'The Cabinet Papers', The National Archives.

223 Atomic Archive, 'Cold War: A Brief History. Britain Goes Nuclear', 2020, at http://bit.ly/3ct3zYS.

224 Glossary entry for Blue Streak in 'The Cabinet Papers', *The National Archives*, at http://bit.ly/36NC37g.

225 Braithwaite, *Armageddon and Paranoia: The Nuclear Confrontation*, p. 197.

226 For a discussion of the transatlantic politics at play, see K. Young, 'The Skybolt Crisis of 1962: Muddle or Mischief?', *Journal of Strategic Studies*, Vol. 27, No. 4 (2004), 614–35; and 'GAM-87 Skybolt', *Global Security*, entry last updated 11 September 2017, at http://bit.ly/2ZQ2tDR.

227 Epstein, *The Last Chance: Nuclear Proliferation and Arms Control*, p. 20. The United States had possessed nuclear-powered submarines since 1954. The first nuclear-armed submarine, the USS *George Washington*, was designed to carry 16 Polaris thermonuclear ballistic missiles. Braithwaite, *Armageddon and Paranoia: The Nuclear Confrontation*, p. 254; Federation of American Scientists, 'SSBN-598 George Washington-Class FBM Submarines', last updated 13 November 1997, at http://bit.ly/2M9OAZo.

228 Braithwaite, *Armageddon and Paranoia: The Nuclear Confrontation*, pp. 201–2.

the British 'continuous at-sea' deterrent, with British warheads fitted in US Polaris missiles, took over from the Royal Air Force's nuclear bombers.[229]

But Polaris, which was likely to miss its target by more than one kilometre, was too inaccurate to be aimed at Soviet missile sites. Accordingly, since its potential for use as a 'counterforce' weapon was minimal, it was considered to serve only as a second strike weapon to hit cities (so-called countervalue targets).[230] Needing a long-term replacement for Polaris, the United Kingdom once again turned its eyes westwards across the Atlantic. The US Navy had begun work on the Trident ICBM in 1972 under President Richard Nixon, but the first variant was inaccurate and its payload capacity was deemed too limited. The Reagan administration's huge boost to defence spending included the rapid development and deployment of the Trident II D5 missile, which the United Kingdom selected as its replacement. A single Trident II missile can carry up to twelve MIRVed warheads, though the 2010 New START treaty restricts the number that may lawfully be carried by the United States to eight.[231] A study in 2013 by the Scottish Campaign for Nuclear Disarmament concluded that a British attack on Moscow and the surrounding area using forty Trident II warheads would kill more than five million civilians in and around the city within the first few months of the strike.[232]

In February 2020, it was disclosed that the United Kingdom had secretly committed to developing a new generation of nuclear warheads to replace those in Trident II, which will again be based on US technology. The decision was revealed by officials from the US Department of Defense, whose unauthorised disclosure pre-empted an official announcement by the British government.[233] Admiral Charles Richard, commander of US Strategic Command, and Alan Shaffer, US Deputy Undersecretary of Defense for Acquisition and Sustainment, separately revealed that the United Kingdom was pursuing the development of its own version of the US W93 warhead. The compatibility of the United States' action with its obligations under the Treaty on the Non-proliferation of Nuclear Weapons (NPT)[234] is considered in Chapter 3. As of this writing, the W93 was being assessed for its ability to replace the US Navy's W76 warhead.[235]

The United Kingdom was already engaged in building a new generation of submarines for its nuclear deterrent, a decision authorised by the British parliament in 2016.[236] The Dreadnought Class submarines will be the UK's next generation of nuclear deterrent under the Successor programme, replacing the current four Vanguard Class submarines.

229 'Skybolt and Polaris Missiles', in 'The Cabinet Papers', *The National Archives*, at http://bit.ly/3clm7df.

230 E. Schlosser, *Command and Control*, Penguin, New York City, 2014.

231 Missile Threat, 'Trident D-5', last updated 15 June 2018, at http://bit.ly/2TTTxtk.

232 John Ainslie, *If Britain Fired Trident: The Humanitarian Consequences of a Nuclear Attack by a Trident Submarine on Moscow*, report, Scottish CND, Glasgow, February 2013, at http://bit.ly/36JRkWp.

233 J. Doward, 'Pentagon Reveals Deal with Britain to Replace Trident', *The Guardian*, 22 February 2020, at http://bit.ly/3dio3Vs.

234 Treaty on the Non-proliferation of Nuclear Weapons; opened for signature at London, Moscow, and Washington, DC, 1 July 1968; entered into force 5 March 1970.

235 A. Chuter, 'Britain Confirms New Nuclear Warhead Project after US Officials Spill the Beans', *Defense News*, 25 February 2020, at https://bit.ly/3cy8cRt.

236 C. Mills, 'Replacing the UK's Nuclear Deterrent: Progress of the Dreadnought Class', House of Commons Library, 11 February 2020, at http://bit.ly/3cKzOTD.

Expected to enter service in the 2030s, they will be the largest submarines ever operated by the Royal Navy.[237]

France's Nuclear Weapons Programme

President John F. Kennedy had also offered the Polaris missile system to France, but President Charles de Gaulle decided not to accept, concerned that US commitment to extended deterrence would not be respected if ever it were truly put to the test.[238] Following the French military (and political) humiliation at Dien Bien Phu, the government of Pierre Mendès France had already decided to develop a French independent nuclear deterrent.[239] In 1960, France test detonated its first fission bomb, becoming the world's fourth nuclear-armed State, followed eight years later by an explosive test of its first thermonuclear device.[240]

Concerned not to tie its hands (and excluded from the negotiating process), France refused to adhere to the 1963 Partial Test-Ban Treaty, although it did later sign and ratify the 1996 Comprehensive Nuclear-Test-Ban Treaty (CTBT)[241] after halting its nuclear testing in the South Pacific. A decade earlier, French agents operating in New Zealand had sunk the Greenpeace ship, *Rainbow Warrior*, hoping to stop the organisation's protests against French nuclear testing. The bombing operation on 10 July 1985 by the Direction générale de la sécurité extérieure (the French foreign intelligence service), code-named *Opération Satanique*, killed Fernando Pereira, a photographer on board the ship. Added to the human tragedy was the political disaster. In 1987, after sustained international pressure, France paid US$8.2 million in damages to Greenpeace and significant sums in compensation to the Pereira family.[242]

After France ratified the CTBT in 1998, it closed its nuclear test site in the Pacific. It also ceased the production of plutonium and enriched uranium for nuclear weapons and dismantled its production facilities.[243] Since the end of the Cold War, France is the only nuclear weapons power that has eliminated its fissile material production facilities.[244]

Today, France's nuclear arsenal contains around three hundred warheads, a number that has remained stable over the past decade.[245] Nearly all the warheads are deployed or are available for operational deployment at short notice; a small number of warheads are

[237] British Forces Broadcasting Service (BFBS), 'We Give You: Dreadnought Class Trident Nuclear Submarines', *Forces.net*, 20 March 2020, at http://bit.ly/3crY9NI.

[238] Braithwaite, *Armageddon and Paranoia: The Nuclear Confrontation*, p. 210.

[239] Ibid.

[240] Ibid., p. 211.

[241] Comprehensive Nuclear-Test-Ban Treaty; adopted at New York, 10 September 1996; not yet in force.

[242] K. Willsher, 'French Spy Who Sank Greenpeace Ship Apologises for Lethal Bombing', *The Guardian*, 6 September 2015, at http://bit.ly/3cgjoUe; see also *Case concerning the differences between New Zealand and France arising from the Rainbow Warrior affair*, ruling of 6 July 1986 by the UN Secretary-General, in Reports of *International Arbitral Awards*, Vol. 19 (1986), pp. 199–221, at http://bit.ly/2AjOxaz.

[243] J. Marcus, 'France's Enduring Nuclear Deterrent', *BBC*, 28 March 2012, at http://bit.ly/3dMO4fW.

[244] Federation of American Scientists, 'Nuclear Weapons: France', undated but accessed 1 June 2020 at http://bit.ly/2Y5fmay.

[245] This is a considerable reduction on the peak in 1991–92, when France had around 540 warheads.

undergoing maintenance. In contrast to the UK's exclusively naval deterrence, France also has some fifty air-launched nuclear missiles.[246]

Although France is a member of NATO, its nuclear forces are not part of the Alliance's integrated military command structure. In 2020, however, French President Emmanuel Macron offered to open discussions with other European nations concerned by the unpredictability of the Trump administration, inviting them to potentially share in the protection afforded by France's nuclear force. At the same time, President Macron called on European Union (EU) Member States to play a more direct role in halting a new nuclear arms race, saying they 'cannot remain spectators' faced with the threat to the continent's collective security.[247]

China's Nuclear Weapons Programme

In 1964, China became the world's fifth nuclear-armed State, with its atmospheric testing of a uranium fission weapon.[248] Operation '59-6' was carried out at the Lop Nur test site in the Gobi desert of Xinjiang province, Western China, close to the ancient Silk Route. An implosion device, using uranium-235 rather than plutonium, was mounted from the top of a steel tower, producing an explosive yield equivalent to 22 kt. China had initiated its nuclear weapons programme in the 1950s, with research on nuclear weapon design conducted at the Institute of Physics and Atomic Energy in Beijing and a uranium enrichment plant built in Lanzhou.[249]

China's nuclear programme benefitted for most of the 1950s from significant help from the Soviet Union, which contributed advisors and technical equipment.[250] The bitter split between Mao Tse Tung and Nikita Khrushchev, however, which led to severe strains in the relations between the two nations, saw a definitive end to bilateral nuclear cooperation by the end of the decade. Thenceforward China would plough its own nuclear furrow. On 17 June 1967, just three years after Operation 59-6, China test-detonated its first hydrogen bomb.[251]

Today, despite the secrecy regarding its nuclear deterrent, China is known to possess a nuclear triad of bombs, SLBMs, and ICBMs, totalling an estimated 270 operational warheads, with another 78 introduced as of late 2020. In terms of size, its total arsenal has now surpassed that of France.[252] China's JL-2 SLBM is believed to have a range of 7,200

[246] H. M. Kristensen and M. Korda, 'French Nuclear Forces, 2019', *Bulletin of the Atomic Scientists*, Vol. 75, No. 1 (2019), 51–55.

[247] France 24, 'Macron Unveils Nuclear Doctrine, Warns EU "Cannot Remain Spectators" in Arms Race', 7 February 2020, at http://bit.ly/2McsCEX.

[248] See, e.g., M. S. Minor, 'China's Nuclear Development Program', *Asian Survey*, Vol. 16, No.6 (June 1976), University of California Press, 571–79, available at http://bit.ly/2MqBhna.

[249] CTBTO, '16 October 1964 – First Chinese Nuclear Test', undated but accessed 1 June 2020 at http://bit.ly/2MssQYv.

[250] Center for Arms Control and Non-proliferation, 'Fact Sheet: China's Nuclear Arsenal', 2 April 2020, at http://bit.ly/2MqhSCQ.

[251] Ibid.

[252] H. M. Kristensen and M. Korda, 'Chinese Nuclear Forces, 2020', *Bulletin of the Atomic Scientists*, Vol. 76, No.6 (November–December 2020), 443–57, at https://bit.ly/30ASV8f.

kilometres, which gives China the ability to target Alaska, Guam, Hawaii, India, and Russia from Chinese waters. But to be able to hit the southern 48 states on the continental United States, China's Jin-class submarines would need to travel deep into the Pacific Ocean, making them vulnerable to detection from US maritime patrols.[253]

On 8 May 2020, Hu Xijin, editor-in-chief of the *Global Times*, called on the regime in Beijing to expand its stockpile to 1,000 nuclear weapons. These should, he said, include 100 DF-41s, a newly developed ICBM capable of hitting targets anywhere in the continental United States.[254] The payload of the hypersonic DF-41 (CSS-X-20 in Chinese classification) is probably either a single 1 MT warhead or up to 10 MIRVed warheads with selectable yields of 20 kt, 90 kt, or 150 kt on each.[255] Once operational, its range may even attain 15,000 km, with a 'likely' top speed for the missile of Mach 25 (19,000 mph).[256]

THE DEVELOPMENT OF NUCLEAR WEAPONS BY OTHER STATES

Israel's Nuclear Weapons Programme

Israel's possession of nuclear weapons is an open secret. Never publicly acknowledged by its government,[257] it is uncontested that Israel became the sixth nuclear-armed State in the 1960s, probably at some point in the first few months of 1967. Israel began its nuclear weapons programme from the inception of the State of Israel in 1948. In exchange for Israeli participation in the Suez Crisis of 1956, France provided nuclear expertise and constructed a reactor complex for Israel at Dimona capable of large-scale plutonium production and reprocessing. France also received heavy water from Israel for its own nuclear weapons programme, which Israel in turn had procured from the United States.[258]

On 2 December 1960, the US Department of State announced that Israel had a secret nuclear installation; a media report two weeks later repeated the news to the world.[259] On 21 December, Israeli Prime Minister David Ben-Gurion announced that Israel was building a 24 MW nuclear reactor 'for peaceful purposes'. The year before, Norwegian heavy water, sold to the United Kingdom but surplus to its requirements, had been

[253] Center for Arms Control and Non-proliferation, 'Fact Sheet: China's Nuclear Arsenal', 2 April 2020.

[254] 'Three's a Crowd: Donald Trump wants China to Join a Nuclear-Weapons Pact', *The Economist*, May 2020, at http://econ.st/2zQogxH.

[255] In contrast, Kristensen and Korda believe that the MIRVed missiles are assigned 'a low number of warheads (perhaps three each), and that part of the missile payload capability is intended for decoys and penetration aids'. Kristensen and Korda, 'Chinese Nuclear Forces, 2019'.

[256] Missile Threat, 'DF-41 (Dong Feng-41/CSS-X-20)', last updated 8 October 2019, at http://bit.ly/2AFuNhu.

[257] When the former speaker of the Knesset, Avraham Burg, broke the taboo in 2013, confirming Israeli possession of both nuclear and chemical weapons and describing the official non-disclosure policy as 'outdated and childish', one right-wing group formally called for a police investigation for treason. J. Borger, 'The Truth about Israel's Secret Nuclear Arsenal', *The Guardian*, 15 January 2014, at http://bit.ly/30aMxwb.

[258] W. D. Farr, 'The Third Temple's Holy of Holies: Israel's Nuclear Weapons', The Counterproliferation Papers, Future Warfare Series No. 2, USAF Counterproliferation Center, Air War College, Air University, Maxwell Air Force Base, Alabama, September 1999, available at http://bit.ly/30d8ACe.

[259] A. Cohen, 'Most Favored Nation', *Bulletin of the Atomic Scientists*, Vol. 51, No.1 (January–February 1995), 44–53.

supplied to Israel. In 1963 or 1964, Israel purchased about 100 tons of yellowcake from Argentina.[260]

Israel is said, by a number of authorities, to have assembled its first nuclear explosive devices – of a rudimentary nature – in late May 1967, in the run-up to the Six-Day War.[261] This was despite assertions by successive governments that Israel would 'not be the first country to introduce nuclear weapons into the Middle East'.[262] The following year, Richard Helms, Director of the US Central Intelligence Agency (CIA), told President Lyndon Johnson that Israel had managed to build nuclear weapons and that its air force had conducted sorties to practise dropping them. In the Yom Kippur War of 1973, on the brink of military defeat, Israel prepared to use nuclear weapons against Egypt and Syria.[263] On the night of 8 October, Prime Minister Golda Meir gave the go-ahead for the assembly of a dozen 20 kt bombs.[264] Only a stunning reversal of fortunes on the battlefield by Israeli conventional forces prevented their use.

On 22 September 1979, a US satellite, Vela 5B,[265] detected the double-flash typical of a nuclear weapon test off the coast of South Africa. This is widely believed to have been a test detonation of an Israeli nuclear explosive device.[266] At the time, both Israel and South Africa were already party to the 1963 Partial Test-Ban Treaty that outlawed all atmospheric nuclear tests.

In 1986, Mordechai Vanunu, a former technician at the Dimona reactor, was the source for a story on Israel's nuclear arsenal, which was published in the *Sunday Times*. He reported in detail on Israel's nuclear programme, which had developed two hundred bombs and ballistic missiles, some with boosted warheads. Vanunu was subsequently kidnapped by Israeli agents, returned to Israel, and sentenced to eighteen years' imprisonment for treason.

As of April 2020, Hans M. Kristensen and Matt Korda estimated Israel's nuclear arsenal at ninety warheads, all of which were being held in reserve.[267] Most of the weapons are in the form of air-dropped bombs and ground-launched missiles, but there may also be

260 Borger, 'The Truth about Israel's Secret Nuclear Arsenal'.

261 Nuclear Threat Initiative, 'Israel', last updated July 2017, at http://bit.ly/2AGtCyB, citing A. Cohen, 'Crossing the Threshold: The Untold Nuclear Dimension of the 1967 Arab-Israeli War and Its Contemporary Lessons', *Arms Control Today*, Vol. 37 (June 2007); A. Cohen, 'Nuclear Arms in Crisis under Secrecy: Israel and the 1967 and 1973 Wars', in P. R. Lavoy, S. D. Sagan, and J. J. Wirtz (eds.), *Planning the Unthinkable: How Powers Will Use Nuclear, Biological and Chemical Weapons*, Cornell University Press, Ithaca, 2000, pp. 112–13; W. E. Burrows and R. Windrem, *Critical Mass: The Dangerous Race for Superweapons in a Fragmenting World*, Simon & Schuster, New York, 1994, p. 280.

262 Epstein, *The Last Chance: Nuclear Proliferation and Arms Control*, p. 237.

263 There were also CIA reports that the Soviet Union had dispatched a ship to Egypt with nuclear weapons on board, raising the spectre of a nuclear exchange in the Middle East. T. Naftali, 'CIA Reveals Its Secret Briefings to Presidents Nixon and Ford', *CNN*, 26 August 2016, at http://cnn.it/3d5lHbZ.

264 Farr, 'The Third Temple's Holy of Holies: Israel's Nuclear Weapons'.

265 For further information on the United States' Project Vela, which was devised to verify compliance with the 1963 Partial Test Ban Treaty; see Chapters 4 and 7.

266 See C. M. Wright and L.-E. De Geer, 'The 22 September 1979 Vela Incident: The Detected Double-Flash', *Science & Global Security*, Vol. 25, No.3 (2017), 95–124, at https://bit.ly/2NpYw4U.

267 H. M. Kristensen and M. Korda, 'Status of World Nuclear Forces', update of April 2020, Federation of American Scientists, at http://bit.ly/2B71Qcf; see also H. M. Kristensen and R. S. Norris, 'Israeli Nuclear Weapons, 2014', *Bulletin of the Atomic Scientists*, Vol. 70, No. 6 (2014), pp. 97–115.

a third arm of Israel's nuclear arsenal. Although Israel does not have nuclear-powered submarines (allegedly because of the prohibitive cost), their diesel-electric submarines, procured from Germany, are believed to be capable of launching nuclear cruise missiles.[268]

India's Nuclear Weapons Programme

India test-detonated its first nuclear explosive device in May 1974, thereby becoming the sixth nuclear-armed State.[269] Officially known as Pokhran I, the test is better known as 'Smiling Buddha'. Announced at the time by the government as a peaceful nuclear explosion, Raj Ramanna, the head of India's nuclear programme, later admitted that the Pokhran test 'was a bomb'.[270] India did not, however, go on to develop a significant nuclear arsenal until two decades thereafter.

Although tension with Pakistan would become a contributing factor to India's nuclear weapons programme, it is considered to be an armed conflict with China that first prompted India to build an atomic bomb. In October 1962, the two nations fought a border war in the Himalayas; the month-long conflict ended in victory for China and humiliation for India.[271] Tensions over the border continue to this day.[272] India has refused to adhere to the NPT, accusing the nuclear powers of 'atomic collusion' and criticising (in the past) the fact that the NPT did not differentiate between military and peaceful nuclear explosions.[273]

In 1996, India opposed the adoption of the CTBT in the Conference on Disarmament, leading to Australia submitting the text of the treaty to the UN General Assembly where it was formally concluded. There, India would vote against the resolution that adopted the Treaty. Four decades earlier, in 1954, Indian Prime Minister Jawaharlal Nehru had championed a nuclear test ban, calling for a 'standstill' agreement. In 1993, India was even among the States that had co-sponsored the call for a test ban treaty. But when States Parties to the NPT agreed to that treaty's indefinite extension in 1995 without any firm commitment by the five permanent members of the UN Security Council (equating to the nuclear-weapon States in the NPT) to nuclear disarmament, India felt the only way to obligate them to a time-bound elimination of nuclear weapons was through the CTBT.[274]

Two years later, India formally became a nuclear-armed State. Over the course of three days in May 1998, Operation Shakti – also known as Pokhran II – saw India test five nuclear

[268] NTI, 'Israel Submarine Capabilities', 16 October 2019, at http://bit.ly/3cv1SKo; and S. Roblin, 'Learn about Israel's Secret Nuclear Submarine Fleet. Which They "Officially" Don't Have', *The National Interest*, 15 January 2020, at https://bit.ly/2Y5STKj.

[269] Center for Arms Control and Non-proliferation, 'India's Nuclear Capabilities', Fact Sheet, 29 August 2019, at http://bit.ly/3cEINFv.

[270] Atomic Heritage Foundation, 'Indian Nuclear Program', 23 August 2018, at http://bit.ly/3dFIZWw.

[271] Ibid.

[272] See, e.g., N. Reynolds and S. Kaushal, 'A Military Analysis of the Sino–Indian Border Clashes', Commentary, RUSI, 2 June 2020, at http://bit.ly/2UdzuGs.

[273] Atomic Heritage Foundation, 'Indian Nuclear Program', 23 August 2018.

[274] R. Neog, 'CTBT at 20: Why India Won't Sign the Treaty', *South Asian Voices*, 23 September 2016, at http://bit.ly/3gSB9uG.

devices (though not all of them detonated). Indian officials claimed that the bombs had a yield equivalent to 45 kt, though independent estimates put the figure at closer to 16 kt.[275] 'India is now a nuclear weapons State', Prime Minister Vajpayee declared following the tests. 'We have the capacity for a big bomb now. Ours will never be weapons of aggression.'[276] In response, on 6 June 1998, the UN Security Council unanimously adopted Resolution 1172, condemning India's nuclear tests on 11 and 13 May 1998 and Pakistan's tests on 28 and 30 May 1998.[277] The Council called upon India and Pakistan 'immediately to stop their nuclear weapon development programmes, to refrain from weaponization or from the deployment of nuclear weapons, to cease development of ballistic missiles capable of delivering nuclear weapons and any further production of fissile material for nuclear weapons'.[278]

Today, however, India possesses a nuclear triad, with an estimated total of 150 warheads, all held in central storage. More warheads are said to be in production.[279] The Agni-V is an ICBM with a range in excess of 5,000 km, capable of hitting any target in China.[280] It was expected to enter into service in the course of 2020,[281] but this was pushed back to an unspecified point in 2021.[282] The Arihant[283] class of nuclear-powered ballistic missile submarines being built for the Indian Navy is intended to reinforce the sea-based element of its nuclear deterrent.[284] India maintains a No First Use policy (except in retaliation for use of biological or chemical weapons against it), though comments by Indian officials in August 2019 indicated that the Indian government might be reconsidering this policy.[285]

Pakistan's Nuclear Weapons Programme

Pakistan's development of nuclear weapons was motivated by fear of India's nuclear weapons programme. In 1965, President Zulfikar Ali Bhutto famously declared: 'If India

275 T. C. Reed and D. B. Stillman, *The Nuclear Express: A Political History of the Bomb and Its Proliferation*, Zenith Press, Minneapolis, 2009, p. 241.

276 Atomic Heritage Foundation, 'Indian Nuclear Program'.

277 UN Security Council Resolution 1172, adopted by unanimous vote on 6 June 1998, operative para. 1.

278 UN Security Council Resolution 1172, operative para. 7.

279 Kristensen and Korda, 'Status of World Nuclear Forces', update of April 2020.

280 China does not believe that the common story of India's nuclear programme is complete – that India developed nuclear weapons in response to China's own nuclear programme – without also including India's own aspiration to become a great power as a major motivation. X. Yang, 'China's Perceptions of India as a Nuclear Weapons Power', *Regional Insight*, Carnegie Endowment for International Peace, 30 June 2016, at http://bit.ly/2MtNo4v.

281 'Indian-Made Agni-V ICBM Intercontinental Ballistic Missile Could Enter in Service in 2020', *Army Recognition*, 3 January 2020, at http://bit.ly/2Uavzu4.

282 'India Plans Deployment of Nuclear-Capable Agni-V This Year', *New Indian Express*, 4 January 2021, at http://bit.ly/2MHlVyo.

283 *Arihant* means 'Slayer of Enemies' in Sanskrit.

284 M. Pubby, 'India's Rs 1.2 Lakh Crore Nuclear Submarine Project Closer to Realisation. Nuclear Attack Submarines Will Give India a Significant Strike and Area Denial Capability in the Region', *Economic Times*, 21 February 2020, at http://bit.ly/3gYt47B; and see 'India's Nuclear Submarine Programme to Reach Another Major Milestone with Commissioning of Second SSBN, Arighat, Early Next Year', *Swarajya*, 18 December 2020, at http://bit.ly/2MMx68t.

285 Center for Arms Control and Non-proliferation, 'India's Nuclear Capabilities', 29 August 2019.

builds the bomb, we will eat grass or leaves, even go hungry – but we will get one of our own.' Three weeks after India's nuclear weapons tests in May 1998, Pakistan detonated five bombs in a single day and a sixth three days later. But Pakistan's nuclear weapons programme began in earnest following the Indo-Pakistani war of 1971, in which it lost nearly half its territory, with East Pakistan becoming the independent nation of Bangladesh. In 1975, scientist A. Q. Khan returned to Pakistan from studying in Europe and accelerated Pakistan's fledgling nuclear weapons development, leading a process of uranium enrichment. Khan's research laboratory would later provide materials and technical knowledge gained in Pakistan to assist nuclear weapons programmes in Iran, Libya, and North Korea.[286]

Today, Pakistan is thought to have a slight numerical advantage in nuclear warheads over India (estimated at 160 to India's 150), redressing the huge disparity in conventional military forces between the two nations.[287] The precise yields of Pakistan's fission weapons are not known, but estimates are typically between 5 kt and 12 kt for most of the warheads, with those in some of its longer-range ballistic missiles possibly reaching 40 kt. Pakistan's Ababeel medium-range ballistic missile is believed to have MIRV capabilities,[288] intended to penetrate India's ballistic missile defence system.[289]

As is the case with India, none of Pakistan's warheads are thought to be operationally deployed but instead are kept in central storage, mostly in the south of the country. More warheads were similarly believed to be in production as of April 2020.[290] Back in 2018, Pakistan's nuclear arsenal was said to be growing, with the prediction that the country's stockpile could increase to between 220 and 250 warheads by 2025 if the existing trend continued. But speculation that Pakistan might become the world's third-largest nuclear weapon State within a decade, with a stockpile of some 350 warheads, was deemed 'exaggerated', not least 'because that would require a build-up two to three times faster than the growth rate over the past two decades'.[291]

On 9 January 2017, it was announced that Pakistan had successfully test-fired an SLCM for the first time. Babur-3, which opened the door to a nuclear triad, would provide Pakistan with a second strike nuclear capability.[292] In February 2019, during the armed conflict between India and Pakistan, which involved air strikes on each other's territories for the first time by the two nuclear-armed nations, there were fears that the conflict would end in a nuclear confrontation. At that time, Pakistan was said to be still working on preparing SLCMs for operational service in order to 'complete' its nuclear triad.[293]

286 M. Tobin, 'Explained: How India and Pakistan Became Nuclear States', *South China Morning Post*, 7 March 2019, at http://bit.ly/3czR8dP.

287 NTI, 'Pakistan', last updated April 2017, at http://bit.ly/2Y7PqLm.

288 Center for Arms Control and Non-proliferation, 'Pakistan's Nuclear Capabilities', Fact Sheet, 29 August 2019, at http://bit.ly/30c3lCI.

289 V. Sv, 'How India's BMD Program Forced Pakistan to Develop "MIRV Capable" Ababeel Missile', *One India*, 27 June 2019, at http://bit.ly/30hGV3j.

290 Kristensen and Korda, 'Status of World Nuclear Forces', update of April 2020.

291 H. M. Kristensen, R. S. Norris, and J. Diamond, 'Pakistani Nuclear Forces, 2018', *Bulletin of the Atomic Scientists*, Vol. 74, No. 5 (2018), 348–58, at p. 348.

292 K. Arif, 'Pakistan Completes Nuclear Triad', *Foreign Policy News*, 16 January 2017, at http://bit.ly/372eQ1b.

293 Z. Siddiqui, 'Factbox: India and Pakistan – Nuclear Arsenals and Strategies', *Reuters*, 1 March 2019, at http://reut.rs/3710C3s.

South Africa's Nuclear Weapons Programme

South Africa never developed fully fledged nuclear weapons as such, but it did produce nuclear explosive devices during the latter years of Apartheid rule. Possessing one of the world's largest reserves of uranium ore,[294] South Africa is the only nation to have built and then voluntarily dismantled a nuclear arsenal.[295]

In the late 1960s, South Africa's Atomic Energy Corporation (AEC) began to consider the potential for peaceful nuclear explosions in construction projects, similar to the United States' Project Plowshare.[296] In 1971, however, the AEC officially approved investigative work on nuclear weapons.[297] F. W. de Klerk, the last president of the Apartheid regime, explained that the main motivation for South Africa's nuclear weapons programme was the 'expansionist policies' of the Soviet Union in southern Africa, which was then supplying national liberation movements with weapons and training.[298]

In the 1980s, South Africa constructed six gun-type devices and had started building a seventh.[299] But in 1991, with Apartheid finally ending, it abandoned its nuclear weapons programme, adhered to the NPT as a non-nuclear-weapon State, and allowed inspections of its former programme by the International Atomic Energy Agency (IAEA).[300] In an interview in 2017, former president de Klerk said he 'felt that it's meaningless to use such a bomb in what was essentially a bush war – that it was unspeakable to think that we could destroy a city in one of our neighbouring countries in any way whatsoever. From the beginning, in my personal opinion, I regarded it as a rope around our neck.'[301]

North Korea's Nuclear Weapons Programme

The tenth State to build a nuclear weapon was the Democratic People's Republic of Korea (North Korea). In 1959, it signed a civil nuclear agreement with the Soviet Union, and a few years later received Soviet assistance to build a research reactor near the town of

294 South Africa began supplying the United Kingdom and the United States with uranium ore, also known as yellowcake, at the end of the Second World War, providing more than 40,000 tons over the next few decades. Atomic Heritage Foundation, 'South African Nuclear Program', 15 August 2018, at http://bit.ly/2XAIK9B.

295 Four states in history have surrendered their nuclear weapons. The other three – Belarus, Kazakhstan, and Ukraine – did so with nuclear arms that they inherited from the Soviet Union. They agreed to hand over the weapons in exchange for support from the United States and security assurances from Russia. Had Ukraine and Kazakhstan kept the arsenals on their territory, they would have become the world's third- and fourth-largest nuclear powers, respectively. U. Friedman, 'Why One President Gave Up His Country's Nukes', *The Atlantic*, 9 September 2017, at http://bit.ly/3cBoLZC.

296 See Chapter 2 for more on this issue.

297 In 2010, it was revealed that Israel had offered to sell nuclear warheads to the apartheid regime in 1975. Top secret minutes of meetings between senior officials from the two nations show that South Africa's Minister of Defence, P. W. Botha, asked for the warheads and Shimon Peres, then Israel's Minister of Defence and later its president, agreed. Ultimately, the cost proved prohibitive for South Africa. C. McGreal, 'Revealed: How Israel Offered to Sell South Africa Nuclear Weapons', *The Guardian*, 24 May 2010, at http://bit.ly/3dO26hn.

298 Friedman, 'Why One President Gave Up His Country's Nukes'.

299 See also TPNW Article 2 Declaration by South Africa, 18 February 2021, at https://bit.ly/3aEen8W, p. 1.

300 J. W. De-Villiers, R. Jardine, and M. Reiss, 'Why South Africa Gave Up the Bomb', *Foreign Affairs*, Vol. 72, No.5 (November/December 1993), 98–109.

301 Friedman, 'Why One President Gave Up His Country's Nukes'.

Yongbyon. Throughout the 1960s and 1970s, the Republic of Korea (South Korea) hosted US tactical nuclear weapons while also engaging in nuclear weapons research of its own. In the North, Kim Il Sung sought to acquire nuclear weapons, with a view to guaranteeing his regime's survival.[302]

Under pressure from the Soviet Union, North Korea acceded to the NPT in December 1985, but did not conclude and see enter into force a safeguards agreement with the IAEA within eighteen months of becoming a State Party, as Article III of the NPT required. North Korea linked inspections to the withdrawal of US nuclear weapons from South Korea. In September 1991, US President George H. W. Bush announced the unilateral withdrawal of all naval and land-based tactical nuclear weapons deployed abroad, which included the one hundred US nuclear weapons stationed in South Korea.[303] In April 1992, DPR Korea ratified a comprehensive safeguards agreement with the IAEA and the following month allowed its inspectors into the seven sites it had declared as relevant to the NPT.

In February 1993, however, the IAEA demanded to conduct special inspections of two sites believed to store nuclear waste, acting in the belief that North Korea had been violating its obligations under the NPT. The regime refused, and on 12 March 1993, it announced its withdrawal from the NPT in accordance with Article X(1). This provision permits withdrawal if a State Party 'decides that extraordinary events, related to the subject matter of this Treaty, have jeopardized the supreme interests of its country'. On 11 June 1993, however, one day before the expiration of the treaty mandated three months' notice period, North Korea suspended withdrawal and declared it would accept the full and impartial application of IAEA safeguards.[304] On 21 October 1994, the United States and the Democratic People's Republic of Korea concluded the 'Agreed Framework' under which the North Korean authorities undertook to freeze and eventually eliminate their nuclear facilities, including by dismantling three nuclear reactors and transferring eight thousand spent nuclear reactor fuel elements to a third country.

On 29 January 2002, in his State of the Union address, President George W. Bush described North Korea, along with Iraq and Iran, as constituting an 'axis of evil, arming to threaten the peace of the world.' On 22–24 December 2002, North Korea cut all seals and disrupted IAEA surveillance equipment on its nuclear facilities and materials. On 27 December, all IAEA inspectors were ordered out of the country. On 10 January 2003, North Korea announced that it was withdrawing from the NPT, 'effective immediately'. On 9 October 2006, the regime conducted an underground nuclear explosive test at a site near the village of Punggye-ri. Analyses of the test based on seismic data estimated the yield to be below 1 kt, while Russia suggests the yield was between 5 kt and 15 kt.[305]

[302] D. Wertz, M. McGrath, and S. LaFoy, 'North Korea's Nuclear Weapons Program', The National Committee on North Korea, last updated April 2018, at http://bit.ly/3dCQorb.

[303] K. Davenport, 'Chronology of U.S.-North Korean Nuclear and Missile Diplomacy', Fact Sheets & Briefs, Arms Control Association, last updated May 2020, at http://bit.ly/2XAorcd.

[304] Ibid.

[305] Ibid.

As of April 2020, after a total of six nuclear explosive tests (including two between 10 and 20 kt and one of more than 200 kt), Kristensen and Korda estimated that North Korea might have produced sufficient fissile material for around thirty-five warheads, although they caution that it is difficult to assess how many warheads have been assembled or deployed.[306] Two summits between North Korean leader Kim Jong Un and US President Donald Trump (in Singapore in June 2018 and in Hanoi in February 2019) achieved little of substance, although, as of this writing, North Korea has not conducted a nuclear explosion since its thermonuclear test detonation on 2 September 2017. That test led to the adoption on 11 September 2017 of UN Security Council Resolution 2375, in which Council members unanimously expressed their 'gravest concern' at the test, which was in violation of numerous earlier resolutions, and 'at the challenge such a test constitutes' to the NPT and 'the danger it poses to peace and stability in the region and beyond'.

In March 2020, DPR Korea launched a series of short-range missiles – its first missile tests in 2020 – potentially signalling the intent to pursue Kim Jong Un's promise to possess a 'new strategic weapon' in the near future.[307] In January 2021, with the incoming Biden administration clearly in its thoughts, the regime displayed a new submarine-launched ballistic missile. Kim Jong Un was 'inching closer to something genuinely powerful' – a solid-fuel missile capable of reaching most of the mainland United States.[308]

NEW TECHNOLOGIES

The nuclear-armed States have been engaged in what is termed the modernisation of their nuclear arsenals to varying degrees since the end of the Cold War. The largest and most expensive effort is currently in the United States, although Russia's programmes are also significant. As described previously, India and Pakistan are both increasing the size of their nuclear arsenals, while China may be preparing to do so. The situation in Israel and North Korea is unclear as of this writing.

Russia's nuclear development activities responded to the US withdrawal from the 1972 Anti-ballistic Missile (ABM) Treaty in 2002. The 1993 START II Treaty, which would have prohibited MIRVs on ICBMs, never formally entered into force, as a direct response to the US withdrawal from the ABM Treaty. On 1 March 2018, speaking in a televised address weeks before the presidential election, Putin showed video and animations of ICBMs, nuclear-powered cruise missiles, underwater drones, and other weapons that he claimed Russia had developed as a result of the US withdrawal. 'You didn't listen to our country then', he said. 'Listen to us now.'[309]

On the ground, the RS-24 Yars ICBM, which was introduced around 2005, can strike anywhere in the United States with what may be as many as ten MIRVed missiles. The RS-

306 Kristensen and Korda, 'Status of World Nuclear Forces', update of April 2020.

307 J. Masterson, 'North Korea Tests First Missiles of 2020', *Arms Control Today*, April 2020, at http://bit.ly/372Mnbm.

308 M. S. Larsen, 'North Korea's New Sub Missile Is First Step Toward a New ICBM', *Foreign Policy*, 21 January 2021, at http://bit.ly/30EjAkw.

309 A. Roth, 'Putin Threatens US Arms Race with New Missiles Declaration', *The Guardian*, 1 March 2018, at http://bit.ly/30c7Pte.

24, which can be launched from either underground silos or road-mobile launchers, fires the missiles into space. They re-enter the earth's atmosphere at hypersonic speeds – almost five miles per second.[310] On 6 February 2019, Russia conducted a test launch of its RS-24 at Plesetsk spaceport in the Arkhangelsk region. According to a press release from the Russian Ministry of Defence, the missile was armed with multiple warheads and achieved all training objectives. The RS-24 will ultimately replace Russia's SS-18 Satan and SS-19 Stiletto ICBMs.[311]

President Putin claimed that Russia had also developed a plane-launched hypersonic missile, the *Kinzhal* ('dagger'), which could manoeuvre while travelling at more than ten times the speed of sound, making it 'guaranteed to overcome all existing and I think prospective anti-missile systems' and deliver a nuclear strike.[312] In March 2018, the president said that it had completed testing and was already operational.[313] In December 2019, however, Russia's Chief of the General Staff of the Armed Forces, General Valery Gerasimov, remarked that the Kinzhal system was on experimental combat duty, having been test launched 'at training grounds in various climate conditions, including in the Arctic.'[314] By May 2020, Russia's 'Aerospace Forces' (*Vozdushno Kosmicheskikh Sil* – VKS) were preparing to create a MiG-31 K regiment in the Siberian city of Kansk, which would be fully equipped with Kh-47 M2 Kinzhal hypersonic missiles. The training of flight crews was planned to commence in late 2021, with the switch to the new weapons systems complete by 2024.[315]

However, the largest and most costly nuclear modernisation programme has been in the United States. US President Barack Obama had advocated a 'world without nuclear weapons', but despite his pledge to produce no new nuclear arms under his leadership, the United States continued to modernise its existing nuclear arsenals. Nonetheless, at the 2016 presidential debates, Republican candidate Donald Trump claimed that Russia had been 'expanding' their nuclear arsenal, giving them 'a much newer capability' than the United States.[316]

In February 2018, the US Department of Defense released its *Nuclear Posture Review*,[317] declaring that US nuclear capabilities would be expanded to counter an increasing threat

310 A. Lockie, 'How the US's Nuclear Weapons Compare to Russia's', *Business Insider*, 28 September 2016, at http://bit.ly/30d41I3.

311 J. Chin, 'Russia Tests RS-24 Yars ICBM', Missile Threat, Center for Strategic and International Studies, last updated 8 April 2019, at http://bit.ly/2ANrzJa.

312 The value of hypersonic weapons is their ability to evade missile defence systems. They do so by virtue of their manoeuvrability, which is considerably greater than that enjoyed by even ballistic missiles equipped with manoeuvring re-entry vehicles. See, e.g., S. J. Freedberg, 'Pentagon Hypersonics Director Rebuts Critics, Step by Step', Breaking Defense, 2 February 2021, at http://bit.ly/3jqbMCk.

313 Roth, 'Putin threatens US arms race with new missiles declaration'.

314 T. Nilsen, 'Russia's Top General Indirectly Confirms Arctic Deployment of the Unstoppable Kinzhal Missile', *The Barents Observer*, 19 December 2019, at http://bit.ly/2Y2OesK.

315 R. McDermott, 'Russia's Aerospace Forces Prepare Training for Kinzhal Hypersonic Missiles', *Eurasia Daily Monitor*, Vol. 17, No. 67 (May 2020), at http://bit.ly/3cBw6eD.

316 In fact, although Russia has certainly been updating its missiles and warheads more, the idea that Moscow has better capabilities is 'almost certainly not true'. Opinion of Dr Jeffrey Lewis, cited in Lockie, 'How the US's Nuclear Weapons Compare to Russia's'.

317 US Department of Defense, *Nuclear Posture Review 2018*, Washington, DC, February 2018.

from Russia. The Ground-Based Strategic Deterrent (GBSD) programme is slated to replace the US ICBM force, which currently consists of more than four hundred single-warhead Minuteman III missiles deployed in underground silos across several states.[318] According to the manufacturer, Northrop Grumman, GBSD 'represents the modernization of the ground-based leg of the nuclear triad'.[319] Yet with the arrival of President Joe Biden in the White House, the future of the new ICBM force, which scheduled to take over from the Minuteman missiles in 2029 and remain in service until 2075, appeared 'more uncertain'.[320] Speaking at a virtual event organised by the Bulletin of the Atomic Scientists in late February 2021, Thomas Countryman, the former US Assistant Secretary of State for International Security and Nonproliferation, suggested that the decision to commit to the GBSD for the coming fifty years was a 'premature surrender' that would undermine US credibility in nuclear arms control.[321]

Speed has been a major component of modernisation programmes; combined with MIRVed missiles, no missile defence system can hope to be effective against a major attack from multiple warheads travelling a high hypersonic speed. But the development of low-yield nuclear weapons has also characterised Russian and US programmes, a return to the fanciful notion of earlier decades that a limited nuclear conflict could somehow be fought on the battlefield without triggering a massive strategic response.

The B61 Model 12 (B61-12) is the first of five new warhead types which are estimated to cost the United States up to US$1 trillion over three decades. The plan for the B61-12 was to merge four old B61 models into a single version with greatly reduced destructive power. The new bomb would have a 'dial-a-yield' feature whose lowest setting was only 2 per cent of the power of the atomic bomb dropped on Hiroshima. The *Nuclear Posture Review 2018* affirmed the following:

> Russia's belief that limited nuclear first use, potentially including low-yield weapons, can provide such an advantage is based, in part, on Moscow's perception that its greater number and variety of non-strategic nuclear systems provide a coercive advantage in crises and at lower levels of conflict. Recent Russian statements on this evolving nuclear weapons doctrine appear to lower the threshold for Moscow's first-use of nuclear weapons. Russia demonstrates its perception of the advantage these systems provide through numerous exercises and statements. Correcting this mistaken Russian perception is a strategic imperative.[322]

In response, the Review declared that 'in the near-term', the United States would 'modify a small number of existing SLBM warheads to provide a low-yield option', and in the longer term pursue a modern nuclear-armed SLCM. This new capability is intended to

318 Ibid., p. X.

319 Northrop Grumman, 'GBSD', accessed 1 June 2020 at http://bit.ly/3dFjjt1.

320 'Nukes of Hazard: America's ICBMs Are Ageing. Does It Still Need Them?', *The Economist*, 22 February 2021, at http://econ.st/2NVr8Ti.

321 Remarks of Thomas Countryman, 'Why Is America Getting a New $100 Billion Nuclear Weapon?', Virtual Program, Bulletin of the Atomic Scientists, 24 February 2021. The presentation by Mr Countryman is available at http://bit.ly/2MvJx9d.

322 *Nuclear Posture Review 2018*, pp. xi–xii.

provide an 'arms control-compliant response' to Russia's non-compliance with the INF Treaty, its non-strategic nuclear arsenal, and its 'other destabilizing behaviors'.[323]

In April 2020, Russia warned that any US attempt to use a low-yield nuclear weapon against a Russian target would set off a massive nuclear response. The Russian Ministry of Foreign Affairs was reacting to a US Department of State paper claiming that putting low-yield nuclear weapons on ballistic missiles launched from submarines would 'reduce the risk of nuclear war by reinforcing extended deterrence and assurance'. Russia denied considering using such nuclear weapons in a limited war and accused the United States of 'lowering the nuclear threshold'.[324]

Other dangerous developments concerned the use of cyber operations against other nations' nuclear weapons. In September 2018, the Nuclear Threat Initiative (NTI) reported on the results of its Cyber-Nuclear Weapons Study Group, established two years earlier. The Study Group, which included high-level former and retired government officials, military leaders, and experts in nuclear systems and policy, concluded that a successful cyberattack on nuclear weapons or related systems could have catastrophic consequences. Cyber threats to nuclear weapons systems increase the risk of use as a result of false warnings or miscalculation and also increase the risk of unauthorised use of a nuclear weapon.[325] The report ultimately questions whether, in the age of cyberwarfare, nuclear deterrence is becoming dangerously obsolete.[326]

Since the publication of the NTI report, there have been other warnings of the potential dangers of offensive cyber operations. In Brussels, on 18 December 2018, at the EU Non-proliferation and Disarmament Conference, one expert cited increasing calls within China to move its nuclear arsenal to a 'launch on warning' posture.[327] This 'hair-trigger' policy has its roots in the Cold War, where US military strategists feared that a massive first strike by the Soviet Union, involving hundreds or thousands of nuclear weapons, would compromise its ability to retaliate.[328] Such a change in Chinese nuclear posture would exacerbate the risk of an accidental or mistaken launch of nuclear weapons.

In addition to the long-standing nuclear superpower rivalry between Russia and the United States, China has now become an even more important player. If it were to increase its arsenal significantly, going far beyond the defensive nuclear posture it currently adopts, multilateral arms control would become even more challenging. In June 2020, Singapore's prime minister Lee Hsien Loong cautioned China and the United States not to allow their great power rivalry to force Asian countries to choose between them, fearing a new Cold War, played out this time in Asia. Lee argued that US efforts to 'contain' China would risk decades of confrontation that would cause economic

323 Ibid., p. xii.

324 'Russia Threatens Massive Response If US Deploys Low-Yield Nukes on Subs', *VOA News*, 29 April 2020, at http://bit.ly/2Wg1Srz.

325 NTI, *Nuclear Weapons in the New Cyber Age*, September 2018, at http://bit.ly/2WcsY1S, p. 7.

326 Ibid., p. 29.

327 Remarks by Tong Zhao, Fellow at the Carnegie-Tsinghua Center for Global Policy in Beijing, at the European Union Non-proliferation and Disarmament Conference, Brussels, 18 December 2018.

328 Union of Concerned Scientists, 'Nuclear Weapons: Hair-Trigger Alert', at http://bit.ly/2S7IidY.

damage to the whole region. At the same time, he suggested that a US military pullback from east Asia could encourage South Korea and Japan to acquire nuclear weapons.[329]

Also looming on the horizon is the extent to which artificial intelligence (AI) will be incorporated into nuclear weapons systems. Warning systems already act automatically to alert nuclear weapons operators of an attack, which led to the potential for disaster on a number of occasions during the Cold War. The heroic action of Lieutenant-Colonel Petrov to ignore system warnings of a US missile attack one day in 1983 is described in Chapter 2. Even after the Cold War, Russian missiles were programmed to automatically retarget themselves to hit US targets if they were launched without a flight plan.[330]

Rapid advances in AI and increasing degrees of military autonomy could amplify the speed, power, and scale of future attacks in cyberspace. There are three specific ways in which AI and cybersecurity might converge in a military context.[331] First, advances in autonomy and machine learning mean that a much broader range of physical systems is now vulnerable to cyber attacks, including, hacking, spoofing, and data poisoning. Second, cyber attacks that target AI systems can offer attackers access to machine learning algorithms, potentially enabling the cueing of munition strikes. Third, AI systems used in conjunction with existing cyber offence tools might become powerful force multipliers, allowing sophisticated cyber attacks to be executed on a large scale, at faster speeds, simultaneously across multiple military domains, and with greater anonymity than before.[332]

In 2019, US Air Force Institute of Technology associate dean Curtis McGiffin and Louisiana Tech Research Institute researcher Adam Lowther, also affiliated with the Air Force, co-wrote an article entitled 'America Needs a "Dead Hand"', arguing that the United States needs to develop 'an automated strategic response system based on artificial intelligence'. The authors admitted that giving AI the nuclear codes sounds a lot like the 'Doomsday Machine' from the film *Dr Strangelove*. The 'Dead Hand' reference in the title harks back to the Soviet Union's serious flirting with an automated system that would have launched nuclear weapons if certain conditions were met, including the death of a Soviet leader. This time, though, the AI-powered system would not even wait for a first strike against the United States to occur: it would pre-empt it.[333] Others argue that the priority must be to ensure that rapid advancements in AI strengthen command and control over nuclear weapons, 'not repeat the past and relinquish it to an automatic or nearly automatic Doomsday machine'.[334]

329 R. Lloyd Parry, 'New Cold War Risks Nuclear Arms Race in Asia, Singapore PM Warns', *The Times*, 6 June 2020, at http://bit.ly/3eOHyVY.

330 See, e.g., M. Field, 'As the US, China, and Russia Build New Nuclear Weapons Systems, How Will AI Be Built In?', *Bulletin of the Atomic Scientists*, 20 December 2019, at http://bit.ly/2XB4jqG.

331 J. Johnson and E. Krabill, 'AI, Cyberspace, and Nuclear Weapons', commentary, *War on the Rocks*, 31 January 2020, at http://bit.ly/3h1Ifx6.

332 Ibid.

333 'US Military Report Recommends Giving AI Autonomous Authority to Launch Nuclear Weapons', *Fanatical Futurist*, 5 October 2019, at http://bit.ly/378A4u4; see also M. Field, 'Strangelove Redux: US Experts Propose Having AI Control Nuclear Weapons', *Bulletin of the Atomic Scientists*, 30 August 2019, at http://bit.ly/2XBObVK.

334 L. Esposito Murray, 'Pairing AI and Nukes Will Lead to Our Autonomous Doomsday', *Defense News*, 13 November 2018, at http://bit.ly/2MxHHAP.

2

Use of Nuclear Weapons

This chapter describes the use of nuclear weapons and other nuclear explosive devices. To date, the dropping of the two atomic bombs on Japan in August 1945 is the only hostile use of nuclear weapons by one State against another. But in the 1960s to 1980s, around 170 nuclear explosive devices were detonated for alleged 'peaceful purposes'. The overwhelming majority of such explosions were conducted by the Soviet Union.

The chapter also describes situations in which hostile use of nuclear weapons was actively considered. During the Cuban Missile Crisis in 1962, the two nuclear superpowers came perhaps closest to deliberately initiating a nuclear Armageddon. The use of 'tactical' nuclear weapons had already been envisaged by the United States during the Korean War, and the notion would be seriously entertained during the subsequent wars in Indochina. Dozens of so-called broken arrow incidents also occurred during the Cold War, when bombs were accidentally dropped during training or military exercises.

The test detonation of more than two thousand nuclear weapons and other nuclear explosive devices is described in Chapter 4. This includes the instances where, during the Cold War, the aim of the test was to assess the ability of soldiers to fight in areas of radioactive contamination amid a nuclear war.

THE USE OF NUCLEAR WEAPONS IN 1945

In an interview after the Second World War, Leo Szilard said that during 1943 and the first half of 1944, the greatest worry he and his fellow scientists on the Manhattan Project had harboured was that Germany would develop a nuclear explosive device before the Allied invasion of Europe. By 1945, however, when fears of a German nuclear weapon had abated, 'we began to worry about what the Government of the United States might do to other countries'.[1]

Scientists' concerns notwithstanding, in the spring of 1945, with Germany on the brink of total military defeat, a study group within the Manhattan Project was tasked with identifying targets in Japan for the first two nuclear bombs. The group, which comprised

[1] Cited in, e.g., 'Conscience, Arrogation and the Atomic Scientists', *Journal of the Federation of American Scientists*, Vol. 47, No. 4 (July/August 1994), at http://bit.ly/3cZaiKO.

theoretical physicists, mathematicians, meteorologists, and experts in explosives engineering, identified four cumulative criteria for determining where the bombs should be dropped:

- a large concentration of closely built frame buildings and other constructions that would be especially susceptible to destruction by blast and fire;
- a densely built-up area of one mile in radius;
- a target of high military and strategic value; and
- a target that had not been damaged by other air raids.[2]

Four Japanese cities were initially identified based on the criteria: Hiroshima, Kokura, Kyoto, and Niigata. But Kyoto was taken off the list and replaced with Nagasaki. Robert Jungk claimed this was a result of the personal intervention of Edwin Reischauer, a professor at Harvard University born in Tokyo to American educational missionaries. Reischauer, however, denied the claim in unequivocal terms, declaring that there was 'not a word of truth to it'. He said that the only person who deserved credit for saving Kyoto from destruction was Henry L. Stimson, the Secretary of War at the time, 'who had known and admired Kyoto ever since his honeymoon there several decades earlier'.[3]

The arguments for and against the dropping of the atomic bombs are well known,[4] and the debate will not be resolved here. The primary reason given to justify their use was the likelihood that the United States would suffer very many military casualties in a ground offensive on the Japanese homeland. Based on the experiences during the retaking of the island of Iwo Jima and then of Okinawa in the latter stages of the Pacific War, it was feared that thousands, possibly even hundreds of thousands, would die on both sides during a ground invasion of mainland Japan. Even though the true extent of the human tragedy is unknown, casualties suffered during the retaking of Okinawa in April through June 1945 were certainly significant. In a 1989 work edited by military historian John Keegan, the 82-day battle was estimated to have killed more than 20,000 Americans and wounded another 55,000 (though other casualty estimates for the Okinawa campaign are considerably lower), while upwards of 100,000 Japanese perished.[5]

Yet it is also true to say that by late July 1945, food in Japan was running perilously low and fuel was almost exhausted. US military intelligence believed that Japanese surrender would come before the end of the year (not, as Jungk claimed, that it was at most weeks away).[6] A key issue for the Japanese was whether the emperor, Hirohito, would be deposed and put on trial for war crimes (and possibly executed). James Byrnes, who had stepped down from the Supreme Court as an Associate Justice to join the Roosevelt administration,

[2] R. Jungk, *Brighter than 1000 Suns*, trans. J. Cluegh (1958), Penguin Books, London, 1980, p. 163.

[3] E. Reischauer, *My Life between Japan and America*, Harper Collins, New York, 1986, p. 101.

[4] For a reflective review of the literature, see J. S. Walker, 'Recent Literature on Truman's Atomic Bomb Decision: A Search for Middle Ground', *Diplomatic History*, Vol. 29, No.2 (April 2005), 311–34.

[5] J. Keegan (ed.), *The Times Atlas of the Second World War*, Times Books, London, October 1989, p. 169.

[6] Jungk, *Brighter than 1000 Suns*, p. 188. Ultimately, of course, Hirohito did remain, generating enquiry as to why this possibility was not made clearer to the Japanese in the closing days of the war.

had become head of the Office of War Mobilization, supporting the military production effort in the United States. Byrnes, the first to discuss the Manhattan Project with incoming President Harry S. Truman (who knew nothing of the existence of the bomb, even though he was the Vice-President), was adamant that the emperor could not be allowed to remain.[7]

Writing in his memoirs, President Truman accepted full responsibility for the decision to drop the atomic bombs on Japan. Despite terming the nuclear weapon 'the most terrible bomb in the history of the world', it was not a decision that he regretted, at least in public. He had considered but rejected the option of continuing to target Japanese cities using conventional bombs to seek to force an end to the war:

> Despite their heavy losses at Okinawa and the firebombing of Tokyo, the Japanese refused to surrender. The saturation bombing of Japan took much fiercer tolls and wrought far and away more havoc than the atomic bomb. Far and away. The firebombing of Tokyo was one of the most terrible things that ever happened, and they didn't surrender after that although Tokyo was almost completely destroyed.[8]

Indeed, Curtis LeMay, the US Air Force General responsible for the bombing campaign over Japan, proudly boasted at a press conference on 30 May 1945 that firebombing had killed a million Japanese.[9] The obvious problem with this argument is that given the fact that the Japanese had not surrendered after such terrible civilian losses, what would be different with the atomic bomb?

Roosevelt had died in office without deciding which cities would suffer the first atomic bombs. Truman's main decision, once he had resolved that the bomb would indeed be dropped, was thus to determine where this should occur. Stimson advised the creation of a committee of experts to counsel the incoming president on this judgment. The 'Interim Committee', formed by President Truman in May 1945, was never charged with considering whether the bomb should be dropped – only what the targets should be.[10] In fulfilling the Committee's mandate, its members made three main recommendations: that the bomb should be used against Japan as soon as possible, that it should be used against a 'dual' target (meaning a military installation that was also close to houses, presumably those of a civilian nature), and that the bomb should be dropped without prior warning.[11] Truman accepted all three recommendations.

[7] D. McCullough, *Truman*, Simon & Schuster, New York, 1992, p. 352; P. Ham, *Hiroshima Nagasaki*, Transworld Publishers, London, 2013, p. 243.

[8] US Department of the Interior, 'Harry S. Truman's Decision to Use the Atomic Bomb', Harry S. Truman National Historic Site, Manhattan Project National Historical Park, last updated 25 October 2017, at http://bit.ly/3aPv4em.

[9] Ham, *Hiroshima Nagasaki*, p. 81. After the War, LeMay would go on to direct the first nuclear tests at Bikini Atoll in 1946. Atomic Heritage Foundation, 'Curtis LeMay', 2020, at http://bit.ly/2A8sKSQ. Termed the 'Executioner of Tokyo' by one Japanese academic, he is said to have provided the inspiration for the deranged US General, Jack D. Ripper, in Kubrick's *Dr Strangelove*. M. Fujimoto, 'Gen. Curtis LeMay "The Executioner of Tokyo"', *Japan Times*, 13 March 2005, at http://bit.ly/3bZnKNP.

[10] Jungk, *Brighter than 1000 Suns*, pp. 166–67.

[11] Ibid., p. 168.

Hiroshima

The code name for the nuclear bombing was Project Alberta (also referred to as Project A). Mission headquarters were located in Guam, although all bombing operations would be launched from Tinian island in the Marianas. The two atomic bombs – the first a uranium fission device and the second a plutonium implosion bomb – were ready to be deployed within three weeks of the success of the Trinity test in mid-July 1945.[12] By the end of July, training and testing for the first bomb were complete.[13]

If Project Alberta's first target were to be primarily military, the most obvious city to strike would have been Kokura, which was the site of a major arsenal as well as coal and ore docks, a steelworks, and a power plant.[14] Indeed, Kokura was General Groves's preferred target for the second bomb. But for the first, he selected Hiroshima as the primary target.[15] Although soldiers and other military objectives were undoubtedly located within Hiroshima, the fact that the city was 'compact' was perhaps highly significant. As one commentator has remarked: 'If you put a bomb like this in the middle of it, you end up destroying almost the entirety of the city.'[16]

Hiroshima – so named in Japanese the 'City of Wide Islands' in the late sixteenth century[17] – had been deliberately spared Allied bombing by conventional means so that the effects of the atomic bombing would be clearly visible. The city's population, as in other cities across Japan, was blighted by widespread malnutrition, the result of an effective US blockade of food and fuel.[18] There were two fire stations for the city, where a total of 440 professional firefighters were employed in August 1945 – for a city whose population was variously estimated at between 250,000 and 320,000 at the time.[19] A thousand beds were spread across the city's 40 civilian hospitals. Five larger hospitals with 5,000 beds served the Japanese army.[20]

The uranium fission bomb, called Little Boy, was dropped over Hiroshima on 6 August 1945 from the US B-52 bomber *Enola Gay*. It detonated directly over Shima Hospital in the centre of the city at 8:15 in the morning, local time. Every doctor, nurse, and patient in the hospital was killed instantly. Everything within a 500-metre radius of Ground Zero was charred; ground temperatures briefly attained 4,000 degrees Celsius.[21] Tens of thousands of people within a 2-kilometre radius were 'burned, decapitated, disembowelled, crushed and irradiated'. The sudden, precipitate drop in air pressure 'blew their eyes from their sockets and ruptured their eardrums; the shockwave cleaved their bodies apart'.[22] The mushroom cloud reached more than 13 kilometres into the clear morning sky. While the

[12] See, for the details of the test, Chapter 4.
[13] Atomic Heritage Foundation, 'Project Alberta', 2019, at http://bit.ly/3ejW1bY.
[14] Ham, *Hiroshima Nagasaki*, pp. 178–79.
[15] Two others were also on the short list: Niigata and Nagasaki. Ham, *Hiroshima Nagasaki*, pp. 401, 319.
[16] G. Brumfiel, 'Why Did The U.S. Choose Hiroshima?', *NPR*, 6 August 2015, at http://n.pr/2TEZoCK.
[17] Ham, *Hiroshima Nagasaki*, p. 46.
[18] Ibid., p. 47.
[19] Ibid., pp. 168, 175.
[20] Ibid., p. 310.
[21] Ibid., p. 357.
[22] Ibid., p. 358.

captain of the *Enola Gay* had no qualms about the bomb, Robert Lewis, his co-pilot, wrote in the diary he kept during the flight, 'My God, what have we done?'[23]

On the evening (London time) of 6 August, the BBC Home Service declared in anodyne fashion: 'President Truman has announced a tremendous achievement by Allied scientists. They have produced the atomic bomb. One has already been dropped on a Japanese army base. It alone contained as much explosive power as two thousand of our great ten-tonners.'[24] At dawn on 7 August 1945, the Deputy Chief of the Japanese General Staff received a report stating, 'The whole city of Hiroshima was destroyed instantly by a single bomb.'[25] Still, the Japanese did not surrender.

Nagasaki

Nagasaki was not the primary target for the second atomic bomb dropped on 9 August 1945; it was the arsenal at Kokura.[26] But the smoke from the previous night's air strikes on nearby Yamata had obscured the primary target, and with fuel running low, the crew of *Bockscar* decided to fly to their secondary target. But clouds were covering Nagasaki too, and it was only in the last moments that a gap revealed buildings in the north of the city.[27] The plutonium bomb, called Fat Man, detonated 500 metres above Urakami, a densely populated district that was home to most of Nagasaki's 12,000 Catholics, the largest Christian community in Japan.[28] Some of the city's population were until then of the belief that their 'foreign' religious community, with its ties to Britain and America, had helped spare the city from the worst of the US bombing.[29]

Some forty thousand people died instantly as the plutonium bomb exploded with a force equivalent to 21 kt of TNT. Fewer died initially than had done so in Hiroshima three days earlier, partly because the hillsides around the city contained, to a certain degree, the bomb's shockwave. The Mitsubishi Steel and Arms Factory, the most significant military objective in the city, was obliterated by the blast, but the city centre several kilometres to the south was relatively unscathed, which also limited the number of human casualties. However, in addition to absorbing the shockwave, the hills also captured the radioactive dust resulting from the detonation, leading to greater losses subsequently from radiation poisoning.

Nagasaki had just 287 professional firefighters in August 1945,[30] for a city of fewer than 200,000 people.[31] Nine thousand Japanese soldiers were believed to be living there at the time.[32] On 9 August 1945 Eastern Standard Time, the day after the Nagasaki bombing,

23 R. Braithwaite, *Armageddon and Paranoia: The Nuclear Confrontation*, Profile Books, London, 2019, p. 16.
24 Cited by D. Irving, *The German Atomic Bomb*, Simon & Schuster, New York, 1967, pp. 14, 15.
25 Jungk, *Brighter than 1000 Suns*, p. 193.
26 Ham, *Hiroshima Nagasaki*, p. 404.
27 Ibid., pp. 406–7.
28 Ibid., pp. 53, 409.
29 Ibid., p. 62.
30 Ham, *Hiroshima Nagasaki*, p. 168.
31 B. French, S. Funamoto, H. Sugiyama, R. Sakata, J. Cologne, H. M. Cullings, K. Mabuchi, and D. L. Preston, 'Measurement and Impact on Radiation Risk Estimates in the Life Span Study of Atomic Bomb Survivors', *American Journal of Epidemiology*, Vol. 187, No. 8 (August 2018), 1623–29.
32 T. Skylark, *Final Months of the Pacific War*, Georgetown University Press, Washington, DC, 2002, p. 178.

President Truman received a telegram from a Protestant clergyman, who pleaded with him to stop the bombing 'before any further devastation by atomic bomb is visited' upon Japan's people. In his reply, Truman noted, 'The only language they seem to understand is the one we have been using to bombard them. When you have to deal with a beast you have to treat him as a beast.'[33]

A third bomb was due to be ready for use just after the middle of August. But it would not be dropped. On 15 August 1945, Emperor Hirohito spoke to his people over the radio, almost all of whom had never heard him speak before, declaring that the war was over. He uttered the famous words: 'The war situation has developed not necessarily to Japan's advantage.' Referring to a 'grand peace', he acknowledged that they would be 'suffering what is insufferable' but without ever using the words 'defeat' or 'surrender'.[34] He mentioned a 'new and most cruel bomb' that would take 'many innocent lives',[35] placing the bomb front and centre of the justification for giving up the fight. Two days later, however, when he spoke to the soldiers and sailors of the Japanese armed forces, he gave as the reason for laying down their arms as the entry of the Soviet Union into the war against Japan on 8 August, the day before the bombing of Nagasaki. The Soviet invasion of the mainland was a critical issue in Japan's decision to surrender.[36]

USE OF NUCLEAR EXPLOSIVE DEVICES FOR PEACEFUL PURPOSES

The atomic bomb would never again be used again in warfare. But following the end of the Second World War, and despite revulsion at its use against Japan, a large number of nuclear explosive devices – some 170 – were detonated for so-called peaceful purposes. From the 1960s to the end of the 1980s, the Soviet Union and the United States performed a series of 'peaceful nuclear explosions'. Conceptually, industrial applications resulting from the use of nuclear explosives could be divided into two broad categories: large-scale excavation or quarrying and underground engineering.[37] Conducted for economic reasons, the detonations are said to have achieved 'mixed results'.[38]

The US Plowshare Program

On 6 June 1958, the US Atomic Energy Commission publicly announced the establishment of the Plowshare Program, named after the biblical injunction, to ensure peace by beating swords into plowshares. The US program explored the use of fission devices to, among others, dig harbours, cut through mountain passes, and 'perhaps even dig a new

[33] US Department of the Interior, 'Harry S. Truman's Decision to Use the Atomic Bomb'.

[34] T. B. Allen and N. Polmar, 'The Radio Broadcast That Ended World War II', *The New Atlantic*, 7 August 2015, at http://bit.ly/2WZz8EX.

[35] Ham, *Hiroshima Nagasaki*, p. 449.

[36] '1945. August 08. Soviets Declare War on Japan; Invade Manchuria', *History*, 2020, at http://bit.ly/3flExac.

[37] US Department of Energy, 'Plowshare Program', at http://bit.ly/2Xj1xX1, p. 1.

[38] Preparatory Commission for the CTBTO, 'Peaceful Nuclear Explosions', accessed 1 June 2020 at http://bit.ly/3eZpV5E.

Panama Canal'.[39] The programme, which continued through to 1975, involved thirty-five individual detonations between December 1961 and May 1973.[40]

On 6 July 1962, 'Storax Sedan' caused more radioactive fallout contamination than any other nuclear explosion conducted in the United States, releasing some 880,000 curies of iodine-131 into the atmosphere. Radioactivity from the 104 kt explosion, which involved excavation by means of nuclear detonation, was especially high in Illinois, Iowa, Nebraska, and South Dakota, exposing millions of people to fallout. The Sedan device created the largest man-made crater in the United States, displacing more than 12 million tons of earth.[41]

An earlier detonation in 1961 of a nuclear device of some 3 kt for the purpose of salt extraction had created a cavity in a salt bed with a diameter of some 50 metres and a height of around 20 metres. 'Unfortunately', it was later reported, after the initial detonation, 'the experiment went awry – the cavern failed to seal itself as predicted and radioactive vapor escaped through the shaft'.[42] Later in the decade, Project Gasbuggy sought to test the practicality of nuclear devices to 'frack' a well, with a view to stimulating gas production. But the explosions, which began in 1969 with a view to stimulating the extraction of natural gas, were either not commercially viable or generated greater fallout than expected.[43]

Towards the middle of the 1970s, with the Vietnam War having consumed huge government funding, the demise of the project was fast becoming a certainty. When it closed at the end of Financial Year 1975, more than US$770 million had been expended, for little concrete outcome. Plowshare was, in the words of the US Department of Energy, a programme 'that started with great expectations and high hopes' but wherein many engineering projects 'did not progress beyond their planning phase and construction was not started'.[44]

The Soviet 'Nuclear Explosions for the National Economy' Programme

The Soviet Union had its own peacetime nuclear programme, called 'Nuclear Explosions for the National Economy'. By 1989, when the programme effectively ended, at least 124 tests involving the detonation of a reported 135 devices had occurred at sites throughout the USSR (80 in Russia, 39 in Kazakhstan, 2 in Ukraine, 2 in Uzbekistan, and 1 in Turkmenistan). Like Project Plowshare, the programme originally focused on excavation and oil and gas recovery, though interest in other applications soon emerged.[45] A proposal

39 O'Neill, 'Building the Bomb', chapter 1 in S. I. Schwartz (ed.), *Atomic Audit: The Costs and Consequences of U.S. Nuclear Weapons Since 1940*, The Brookings Institution, Washington, DC, 1998, p. 79. The new Panama Canal was to be created through Central America. W. Epstein, *The Last Chance: Nuclear Proliferation and Arms Control*, The Free Press, New York, 1976, p. 175.

40 US Department of Energy, 'Plowshare Program'.

41 Preparatory Commission for the CTBTO, 'The United States' Nuclear Testing Programme', accessed 1 June 2020 at http://bit.ly/2XEFNF9.

42 T. Owens, 'H-Bombs for Peace: The Lasting Legacy of Project Plowshare's Nevada, New Mexico & Colorado Experiments', *Farmington Daily Times*, 12 December 2019, at http://bit.ly/3euAmoW.

43 O'Neill, 'Building the Bomb', p. 79.

44 US Department of Energy, 'Plowshare Program', p. 5.

45 World Nuclear Association, 'Peaceful Nuclear Explosions', updated December 2018, at http://bit.ly/2ZRGqfR.

to create a Pechora–Kama Canal to the River Volga and the Caspian Sea would have required up to 400 cratering explosions over 65 kilometres 'with all the attendant dangers of releasing massive radioactivity'.[46]

The first of the programme detonations was in January 1965 at Shagan, on the edge of the Semipalatinsk Test Site in Kazakhstan. At 140 kt in explosive yield, it was also the largest. Designed to test the suitability of nuclear explosive devices for creating reservoirs, the blast formed a crater 400 metres across and 100 metres deep. Initially, the crater held 6.4 gigalitres of water, with the reservoir as a whole containing some 10 gigalitres, but subsidence later reduced this figure by about one quarter. Around one-fifth of the radioactive products from the test are feared to have escaped the blast zone; some were later detected over Japan. This resulted in complaints from the United States, which thought that the explosion was a weapons test in violation of the 1963 Partial Test Ban Treaty.[47] In the 1990s, radiation dose levels were reported to be 100 times greater than the background levels at the lip of the crater, with water in the crater itself containing 100 times the level of radionuclides than is the standard for drinking water.[48]

More successful was the use of a 30 kt device in 1966 at Urtabulak gas field in Southern Uzbekistan to extinguish a gas-well fire that had been burning for almost three years. The gas fountain had resulted in the loss of more than 12 million cubic metres of gas per day. The device, which had been inserted within a borehole almost 35 metres below the surface and then covered with cement, swiftly extinguished the fire, allowing the well to be finally sealed.[49]

The 1976 Peaceful Nuclear Explosions Treaty

The 1976 Peaceful Nuclear Explosions Treaty, negotiated and signed by the Soviet Union and the United States in May 1976, limited the yield of individual nuclear explosions for peaceful purposes to 150 kt.[50] The Treaty would enter into force only in December 1990, after the Cold War had already ended. An agreed statement between the two parties to accompany the Treaty specifies that a 'peaceful application' of an underground nuclear explosion would not include the developmental testing of any nuclear explosive device. Such an act is treated as the testing of a nuclear weapon. Article V of the 1968 Treaty on the Non-Proliferation of Nuclear Weapons (NPT)[51] allows for peaceful nuclear explosions. At

[46] Epstein, *The Last Chance: Nuclear Proliferation and Arms Control*, p. 176.

[47] Treaty Banning Nuclear Weapon Tests in the Atmosphere, in Outer Space and Under Water; concluded at Moscow, 25 July 1963; opened for signature at London, Moscow, and Washington, DC, 8 August 1963; entered into force 10 October 1963. The Treaty is discussed in Chapter 4, and the national verification system created by the United States is further considered in Chapter 7.

[48] World Nuclear Association, 'Peaceful Nuclear Explosions'.

[49] Ibid.; see also for video of the detonation S. Malm, 'The Raging Gas Inferno That Could Only Be Extinguished with a Nuclear Bomb', *Daily Mail*, 14 September 2017, at http://dailym.ai/2zKA6wo.

[50] Art. III(2), Treaty between the United States of America and the Union of Soviet Socialist Republics on Underground Nuclear Explosions for Peaceful Purposes (and Protocol Thereto); signed at Moscow and Washington, DC, on 28 May 1976; entered into force 11 December 1990. The text of the Treaty is available at http://bit.ly/3cLtjzX.

[51] Treaty on the Non-proliferation of Nuclear Weapons; opened for signature at London, Moscow, and Washington, DC, 1 July 1968; entered into force 5 March 1970. See further on this issue Chapter 3.

the NPT's 2000 Review Conference, however, the States Parties agreed that Article V was to be interpreted in the light of the Comprehensive Nuclear-Test-Ban Treaty (CTBT),[52] once the CTBT enters into force. Article I(1) of the CTBT bans any nuclear detonation other than hostile use, even when it is carried out for ostensibly peaceful purposes.

ENVISAGED USE OF NUCLEAR WEAPONS AGAINST A NUCLEAR POWER

The world has come close to nuclear warfare on numerous occasions. The best known of these are the Cuban Missile Crisis of October 1962 and, as recounted in Chapter 1, during Able Archer 83, the military exercise led by the United States in 1983. Less well known is that, in November 1979, an exercise tape simulating a Soviet nuclear attack was mistakenly put into the US Strategic Air Command's computerised defence system, causing interceptors to launch and the president's 'doomsday plane' to put to the skies. The president was not on board his flying command post, from where nuclear forces can be launched and managed.[53]

The Cuban Missile Crisis

In a speech to the UN General Assembly on 25 September 1961, President John F. Kennedy had cautioned that everyone was living 'under a nuclear sword of Damocles, hanging by the slenderest of threads, capable of being cut at any moment by accident, or by miscalculation, or by madness'.[54] A little over a year later, during the Cuban missile crisis, the world did indeed come perilously close to all-out nuclear war between the two superpowers.

The roots of the crisis can be traced back to the failed Bay of Pigs invasion orchestrated by the US Central Intelligence Agency (CIA) a year earlier. The operation had been authorised by President Eisenhower and approved by Kennedy. To protect their Cuban ally from future attacks, and to strengthen the Soviet hand in future arms control negotiations, Premier Nikita Khrushchev initiated Operation Anadyr,[55] a secret military operation to deploy short- and intermediate-range nuclear missiles in Cuba.

The United States soon learned that missile sites were being prepared in communist Cuba for Soviet weapons. The US military called on the president to authorise air strikes to destroy the sites, but Kennedy decided instead to institute a naval blockade. This proved to be an exceptionally wise decision as – contrary to the reports produced by US intelligence – several of the sites were already operational and were hosting armed nuclear weapons. A US attack might have provoked a nuclear exchange. Instead, negotiating unofficially through his brother, Robert (the Attorney General), President Kennedy agreed that in

52 Comprehensive Nuclear-Test-Ban Treaty; adopted at New York, 10 September 1996; not yet in force.

53 Braithwaite, *Armageddon and Paranoia: The Nuclear Confrontation*, p. 257.

54 Text available at http://bit.ly/3gopRhG.

55 J. H. Hansen, 'Soviet Deception in the Cuban Missile Crisis', Learning from the Past, CIA, last updated 27 June 2008, at http://bit.ly/36RutbK.

return for the removal of Soviet nuclear weapons from Cuba, he would remove US Jupiter missiles from Turkey,[56] which were sited close to the border with the Soviet Union.[57]

But it was a close-run thing. On 27 October 1962, a U-2 spy plane was shot down over Cuba, and then a Soviet submarine in the Caribbean was spotted by the US Navy, which began dropping depth charges over it. The submarine was equipped with a tactical nuclear torpedo on board, and the captain, Valentin Savitsky, was getting ready to fire. He is said to have shouted: 'Maybe the war has already started up there. … We're going to blast them now! We will die, but we will sink them all; we will not become the shame of the fleet.'[58] But the flotilla commander on board, Vasili Arkhipov, only thirty-four years of age, kept his cool amid the blistering heat on the diesel-powered submarine where the air conditioning had broken down, refusing to endorse the order. Instead of firing, the Soviet submarine rose to the surface, where it was met by a US destroyer. The Americans did not board.[59]

Envisaged Use by the United States in the Yom Kippur War

On 24 October 1973, Soviet forces were preparing to enter the Arab-Israeli conflict. With President Richard Nixon heavily intoxicated that evening and under extreme pressure following the 'Saturday Night Massacre' four days earlier,[60] US Secretary of Defense James Schlesinger and the Joint Chiefs of Staff raised the DEFCON (Defense Condition) status of US military forces up from IV to III. At US air bases, B-52 bomber aircraft were loaded with nuclear weapons and lined up nose to tail. Launch commanders in silos made ready the launching of Minuteman-III and Titan-II thermonuclear missiles while nuclear-armed submarines approached the Soviet coast awaiting an order to fire.[61]

According to documents declassified in 2016, the move to DEFCON III followed CIA reports that the Soviet Union had dispatched a ship to Egypt, one of its allies in the region, with nuclear weapons on board.[62] Admiral Elmo Zumwalt later recalled that 'we had to go on nuclear alert without his [President Nixon's] permission. … Nixon obviously had too much to drink. … I was told they were not able to wake him.'[63]

[56] The SM-78 Jupiter was a medium-range, ground-launched, liquid-fuelled ballistic missile. Its development was led by Dr Werner Von Braun, with many of its components constructed by the Chrysler Corporation. The Jupiter was flight tested in 1957, entering operation service in 1959. It was stationed in both Italy and Turkey. Missile Threat, 'SM-78 Jupiter', CSIS Missile Defense Project, last updated 15 June 2018, at http://bit.ly/30KgefT.

[57] T. Downing, *1983: The World at the Brink*, Little, Brown, London, 2018, p. 11.

[58] R. Krulwich, 'You (and Almost Everyone You Know) Owe Your Life to This Man', *National Geographic*, 24 March 2016, at http://on.natgeo.com/3eDAkEd.

[59] Ibid.

[60] On 20 October 1973, President Nixon had 'upended the Justice Department, having let go of his attorney general, deputy attorney general and the special counsel investigating the Watergate scandal'. R. Elving, 'A Brief History of Nixon's "Saturday Night Massacre"', *NPR*, 21 October 2018, at http://n.pr/3h14B1P.

[61] A. Summers, *The Arrogance of Power: The Secret World of Richard Nixon*, Orion Books, London, 2000, pp. 460, 461.

[62] T. Naftali, 'CIA Reveals Its Secret Briefings to Presidents Nixon and Ford', *CNN*, 26 August 2016, at http://cnn.it/3d5lHbZ.

[63] Summers, *The Arrogance of Power: The Secret World of Richard Nixon*, pp. 461–62.

The 'Petrov' Incident

On 26 September 1983, Lieutenant-Colonel Stanislav Petrov, Deputy Chief of the Department of Military Algorithms, was on duty at Serpukhov-15, a command station for the Soviet early warning observation system. The message 'Launch' flashed up three times on one of the monitors in the control room, indicating that three US missiles had been fired against the Soviet Union. The world is fortunate that Colonel Petrov was the responsible person in the station that evening because he had helped to install the system and therefore knew its shortcomings. He decided not to sound the alarm, knowing full well that this might have led to a Soviet missile launch. It is claimed he was subsequently dismissed for the failure to follow established protocol.[64] But his courageous actions prevented what could have been a catastrophe.

ENVISAGED USE AGAINST NON-NUCLEAR FORCES

In the decades following the use of the atomic bomb against non-nuclear-armed Japan in 1945, the United States considered using nuclear weapons on a number of occasions, first during the Korean War against Chinese and North Korean forces and later during the wars in Indochina, against North Vietnamese forces.

The Korean War

In 1949, on the eve of the Korean War, General LeMay had prepared a detailed operational plan for use of America's entire stockpile of 133 atomic bombs to be dropped on 70 cities in the Soviet Union within 30 days.[65] On 9 December 1950, after the Chinese People's Volunteers Force (CPVF) troops had pushed the United Nations (UN) forces under General Douglas MacArthur out of the north, MacArthur sought the authority to use nuclear weapons as a last resort against two non-nuclear armies. Two weeks later, with Chinese forces still pushing hard against his forces MacArthur submitted a list of his targets in both Korea and China, for which he had calculated 34 bombs would be needed.[66]

President Truman refused to countenance their use in 1950. But in April, he did allow nine nuclear bombs to be transferred into US Air Force custody and transported to Okinawa. The president also authorised a second deployment of nuclear-capable B-29 bombers to Okinawa.[67] This would not be the last time that UN forces considered using nuclear weapons in Korea. In December 1952, the Commander of the US Pacific Fleet, Admiral Arthur Radford, specifically suggested to President-elect Dwight D. Eisenhower

[64] Downing, 1983: *The World at the Brink*, p. 199.

[65] Fujimoto, 'Gen. Curtis LeMay "The Executioner of Tokyo"', *Japan Times*. Under President Dwight Eisenhower in the 1950s, LeMay was even given a free hand to order a nuclear strike without presidential authorisation if the president could not be contacted.

[66] S. Weintraub, *MacArthur's War: Korea and the Undoing of an American Hero*, Free Press, New York, 2000, p. 263.

[67] C. A. Posey, 'How the Korean War Almost Went Nuclear', *Air & Space Magazine*, July 2015, at http://bit.ly/3h4sLsf.

on his three-day trip to Korea that nuclear weapons should be used to overturn the military situation.[68]

Wars in Indochina

Dien Bien Phu

The Battle of Dien Bien Phu was the worst disaster suffered by the French armed forces since the Second World War. The battle between the French Far East Expeditionary Corps and Viet Minh (League for the Independence of Vietnam) insurgents, which lasted from 13 March to 7 May 1954, led to the entire 14,000-strong French force being either killed or captured. The crushing French defeat effectively brought an end to the First Indochina War and saw France withdraw from Vietnam. The United States had considered carrying out air strikes to support the besieged French troops.

Operation Vulture, a series of military operations proposed by Admiral Radford (who by then had been promoted to Chairman of the Joint Chiefs of Staff by President Eisenhower), included the option to use three tactical nuclear weapons against Viet Minh forces, a course of action endorsed by Vice-President Richard Nixon and US Air Force General LeMay.[69] Eisenhower, though, was said to have been appalled: 'You boys must be crazy. We can't use those awful things against Asians for the second time in less than ten years. My God … .'[70] There was also an obvious practical challenge: senior US Air Force commanders became convinced that the French had not thought through the consequences of air strikes, both conventional and nuclear. There was no way to separate the French fortress from the bombs that would fall from B-29s and certainly not from the blast radius of nuclear weapons.[71]

The Vietnam War

The use of nuclear weapons was envisaged by successive US presidents during the two decades of US intervention in Vietnam.[72] Operation Fracture Jaw was a US military plan by which General William C. Westmoreland sought to ensure the availability of nuclear weapons in South Vietnam in February 1968, where they could be used on short notice against North Vietnamese troops, specifically in the defence of US forces at Khe Sanh in

68 S. Tucker, *U.S. Leadership in Wartime: Clashes, Controversy, and Compromise*, Vol. 1, ABC-CLIO, Santa Barbara, CA, 2009, p. 726.

69 R. Grant, 'Dien Bien Phu', *Air Force Magazine*, Vol. 87, No. 8 (August 2004), at http://bit.ly/35t5tXE; Summers, *The Arrogance of Power: The Secret World of Richard Nixon*, pp. 165, 166.

70 Summers, *The Arrogance of Power: The Secret World of Richard Nixon*, p. 166. In stark contrast, Grant suggests that Eisenhower 'never showed his hand'. His long-time aide, Army General Andrew J. Goodpaster, recalled in a 1967 interview that the president simply 'never told anybody whether he would or not'. Grant, 'Dien Bien Phu'.

71 Grant, 'Dien Bien Phu'.

72 See, e.g., M. Beschloss, *Presidents of War: The Epic Story, from 1807 to Modern Times*, Broadway Books, New York, October 2019; and 'Nixon White House Considered Nuclear Options against North Vietnam, Declassified Documents Reveal' in W. Burr and J. Kimball (eds.), *Nuclear Weapons, the Vietnam War, and the 'Nuclear Taboo'*, reproduced in *National Security Archive Electronic Briefing Book No. 195*, at http://bit.ly/2YsCpxH.

the Qung Trị province. The plan was so secret that, initially, US President Lyndon B. Johnson had not even been informed about it. But when he did learn what Westmoreland was planning, he shut down the operation.[73]

During President Nixon's tenure, Operation Duck Hook rehashed earlier plans to cut off North Vietnamese supply lines to the Viet Cong in the south, but also comprised the possible use of nuclear weapons to try to block the Ho Chi Minh Trail.[74] An associated report on planning for Operation Duck Hook in early October 1969 explained that the action, whose basic objective was to coerce Hanoi 'to negotiate a compromise settlement through a series of military blows', would walk a fine line between inflicting 'unacceptable damage to their society' and bringing about 'the total destruction of the country or the regime, which would invite major outside intervention [by the Soviet Union or China]'.[75] Preparations included parading nuclear-armed bombers on full alert to attract the attention of spies, especially from the Soviet Union.[76]

The use of nuclear weapons was again given serious consideration by President Nixon during the planning for Operation Linebacker, the bombing campaign against the Democratic Republic of Vietnam (North Vietnam), conducted by US Air Force and US Navy forces from 9 May to 23 October 1972. Nixon had told Kissinger he was interested in using 'a nuclear bomb' to 'reduce' civilian casualties (when compared to plans to destroy North Vietnam's dike system through conventional bombing), while still inflicting a powerful 'psychological' blow on the North Vietnamese Government and the Soviets. Ultimately, Nixon did not order the use of nuclear weapons, settling instead on 'merely' an implied threat of their use.[77]

'BROKEN ARROW' INCIDENTS

Since 1950, there have been thirty-two recorded instances of nuclear weapon incidents, known as 'broken arrows', involving either Soviet/Russian or US nuclear forces. A *broken arrow* is a collective term for a range of unexpected events involving nuclear weapons that result in either accidental launching, firing, detonating, theft, or loss.[78] One of the most serious accidents involved a B-52 bomber flying over North Carolina in January 1951. The aircraft fell apart and the two 24 MT thermonuclear bombs it was carrying fell to earth. Five of the six safety devices on one of the two

[73] D. E. Sanger, 'U.S. General Considered Nuclear Response in Vietnam War, Cables Show', *New York Times*, 6 October 2018, at http://nyti.ms/3bXTmnQ.

[74] R. Reeves, *President Nixon, Alone in the White House*, Simon & Schuster, New York, 2001, p. 97; see generally also T. C. Robison, *Operation Duck Hook*, XLIBRIS, United States, 2012.

[75] 'Nixon White House Considered Nuclear Options against North Vietnam, Declassified Documents Reveal', in *National Security Archive Electronic Briefing Book No. 195*.

[76] Reeves, *President Nixon, Alone in the White House*, p. 136.

[77] Ibid., citing Executive Office Building Conversation No. 332-35, Nixon and Kissinger, 25 April 1972, White House Tapes, Nixon Presidential Materials Project (NPMP); Memcon, National Security Council (NSC) Meeting, 8 May 1972, Box 998, Haig Memcons [January–December 1972], A. M. Haig Chronological Files, NSC Files, NPMP.

[78] 'Broken Arrows: Nuclear Weapons Accidents', *Atomic Archive*, 2020, at http://bit.ly/3gg6VBr.

bombs had failed; only the sixth safety feature prevented a humanitarian catastrophe. The other 24 MT bomb was never found.[79]

It is alleged that, in the course of the Cold War, possibly as many as fifty nuclear explosive devices went astray and were never recovered[80] (the US Department of Defense has acknowledged that it lost only eleven).[81] Many of these bombs disappeared in plane crashes over the ocean in the early days of the Cold War, since the bombers carrying them lacked the range to cross the Atlantic on a single tank of fuel. Some of the aircraft collided with their refuelling tanker planes, while others simply missed the tankers and, after running out of fuel, plunged into the sea.[82]

On 17 January 1966, during refuelling operations a B-52 carrying four nuclear weapons collided with a Boeing KC-135 Stratotanker (a military refuelling aircraft) and crashed near Palomares, a village in Andalucía in Spain on the Mediterranean Sea. Following the incident, one of the weapons was safely recovered on the ground and another was recovered from the sea two months later. But when the other two weapons hit the ground, the high explosive they contained detonated, releasing three kilograms of radioactive plutonium that spread out over two square kilometres of land.[83]

Shortly after the accident, the United States shipped 1,700 tonnes (approximately 1,200 cubic metres) of contaminated earth to South Carolina, after which the incident was largely forgotten. Concern was rekindled by tests in the 1990s in Palomares, which revealed high levels of americium, a decay product of plutonium. Further tests showed that 50,000 cubic metres of earth were still contaminated.[84] In October 2015, then US Secretary of State John Kerry and Spanish Foreign Minister José Manuel García-Margallo signed an agreement, subject to parliamentary ratification by both nations, to clean up the site and 'store the contaminated earth at a suitable location in the United States'.[85] But the work remains to be performed. In October 2020, a senator from an electoral coalition questioned in parliament why the United States had never fulfilled its promise to rid Palomares of plutonium-239 contamination. 'What steps has the Spanish government taken to persuade the US government to meet its obligations?', the senator asked.[86]

In February 2020, US Air Force veterans drafted in to tackle the clean-up in the aftermath of the disaster in Palomares won the right to sue collectively for health benefits. By then, however, many had already lost battles with cancer or other

79 Downing, 1983: *The World at the Brink*, p. 190.

80 B. Maack, 'A Nuclear Needle in a Haystack: The Cold War's Missing Atom Bombs', *Der Spiegel*, 14 November 2008, at http://bit.ly/2XhXzxE.

81 Ibid; and Braithwaite, *Armageddon and Paranoia: The Nuclear Confrontation*, p. 259.

82 Maack, 'A Nuclear Needle in a Haystack: The Cold War's Missing Atom Bombs'.

83 M. Gonzalez, 'Trump Presidency Will Force Renegotiation of Palomares Nuclear Clean-Up', *El País*, 27 January 2017, at http://bit.ly/2Ak8iMH.

84 S. Burgen, 'US to Clean Up Spanish Radioactive Site 49 Years after Plane Crash', *The Guardian*, 19 October 2015, at http://bit.ly/2DomXz4.

85 See ibid.

86 L. Hall, 'Palomares Still Waiting for Comprehensive Clean Up Following B-52G Incident', *Euroweekly*, 23 October 2020, at http://bit.ly/2MJZw3h.

ailments.[87] The *New York Times* reported that as one of the first cases granted class-action status by the Court of Appeals for Veterans Claims, the *Skaar* lawsuit, 'represents a major step forward for veterans with long-term health issues linked to toxic exposure in the service'. In a statement issued in February 2020, however, the US Air Force maintained its assessment that the troops deployed to Palomares had not suffered harmful exposure to radiation.[88]

87 D. Philipps, 'Legal Win Is Too Late for Many Who Got Cancer after Nuclear Clean-Up', *New York Times*, 11 February 2020, at http://nyti.ms/2YBkyDL.
88 Ibid.

3

The Treaty on the Non-proliferation of Nuclear Weapons

THE RATIONALE FOR THE NPT

Since the beginning of the nuclear age, it was widely understood that the acquisition of nuclear weapons by States that did not already possess them was likely to endanger international peace and security.[1] In late 1945, the Soviet Union, the United Kingdom, and the United States agreed to establish the United Nations Atomic Energy Commission (UNAEC), in order to establish international control over the spread and development of nuclear weapons and technology. UNAEC was set up on 24 January 1946, with six permanent members (Canada, China, France, the Soviet Union, the United Kingdom, and the United States) and six rotating members.[2]

On 15 June 1946, the United States presented the 'Baruch Plan' before the newly constituted Commission for international control of atomic weapons.[3] The plan, formulated by Bernard Baruch, a long-time advisor to US presidents, called for all other nations – including, and indeed especially the Soviet Union – to forgo all development of nuclear weapons as a precondition for an eventual nuclear disarmament by the United States.[4] An Atomic Development Authority would oversee the development and use of atomic energy, manage any nuclear installation with the ability to produce nuclear weapons, and inspect any nuclear facility conducting research for peaceful purposes. The Authority would answer only to the UN Security Council, but permanent members of the Council would be stripped of their veto power concerning UN sanctions against nations that engaged in prohibited activities. But only once the plan was fully implemented would the United States begin destroying its nuclear arsenal.[5]

Within UNAEC, a vote was held on the Baruch Plan on 30 December 1946, although it was already clear that it would fail to pass. Ten of the UNAEC's twelve members voted in

[1] J. Goldblat, *Arms Control: The New Guide to Negotiations and Agreements*, Sage, Thousand Oaks, CA, 2002, p. 101. Jozef Goldblat represented Poland during the negotiation of the Treaty on the Non-proliferation of Nuclear Weapons. Though see also on this issue W. Epstein, *The Last Chance: Nuclear Proliferation and Arms Control*, The Free Press, New York, 1976, pp. 99–100.

[2] US Department of State, Office of the Historian, 'The Acheson-Lilienthal & Baruch Plans, 1946', Milestones in the History of U.S. Foreign Relations, at http://bit.ly/2SH7dro.

[3] 'The United States Presents the Baruch Plan', *History*, last updated 17 July 2019, at http://bit.ly/2SFjwnv.

[4] 'Introduction', S. I. Schwartz (ed.), *Atomic Audit: The Costs and Consequences of U.S. Nuclear Weapons since 1940*, The Brookings Institution, Washington, DC, 1998, p. 11.

[5] US Department of State, Office of the Historian, 'The Acheson-Lilienthal & Baruch Plans, 1946'.

favour, but Poland and the Soviet Union abstained, and as unanimity was required, the plan was not adopted. The United States rejected a Soviet counter-proposal for a ban on all nuclear weapons.[6]

In 1958, Ireland submitted a draft resolution to the UN General Assembly calling for efforts to prevent the spread of nuclear weapons. Talk at that time had moved on to the 'Nth-country' problem, meaning that country after country would seek to secure nuclear weapons, at best with only certain treaty-imposed limits on the number of weapons they could acquire.[7] This problem was termed 'proliferation' in 1965,[8] an expression first coined in the context of the negotiation of the Treaty on the Non-proliferation of Nuclear Weapons.[9]

For the last six decades, the NPT, as it is commonly known, has been the legal cornerstone of the global nuclear non-proliferation regime. Its second preambular paragraph expressed the belief of the States that negotiated the Treaty that nuclear proliferation 'would seriously enhance the danger of nuclear war'. In the aftermath of the Cuban missile crisis, fears had grown that many nations would act to procure nuclear weapons for their own defence. US President John F. Kennedy, for instance, believed there would be ten nuclear-armed powers by 1970, and possibly another five or even ten more by 1975.[10]

Meeting with Kennedy in Washington, DC, in December 1962, British Prime Minister Harold Macmillan informally suggested to him the elaboration of a 'non-dissemination agreement'.[11] From the seed planted by their conversation would ultimately come a global treaty that today has 190 States Parties.[12] Among arms control and disarmament treaties, only the 1992 Chemical Weapons Convention has attracted more.[13] But, despite the very broad adherence it enjoys, the NPT is under severe pressure.

From the outset, the treaty regime comprised three main pillars. The prohibition on horizontal proliferation, which lies at the heart of the NPT, was underpinned by the right of non-nuclear-weapon States to enjoy the peaceful use of nuclear energy and the duty upon nuclear-weapon States to tackle 'vertical' proliferation – where nuclear-armed States acquire ever greater numbers of nuclear weapons – and to move towards nuclear disarmament. Today, even more than in the 1960s, this latter duty remains by far the greatest challenge. As the UN Secretary-General, Ban Ki-moon, told the Ninth Review

[6] 'The United States Presents the Baruch Plan', *History*; W. Epstein, *The Last Chance: Nuclear Proliferation and Arms Control*, The Free Press, New York, 1976, pp. 10–11.

[7] Epstein, *The Last Chance: Nuclear Proliferation and Arms Control*, p. 61.

[8] B. Goldschmidt, 'The Negotiation of the Non-proliferation Treaty (NPT)', *IAEA Bulletin*, Vol. 22, Nos. 3/4 (August 1980), 73–80.

[9] Treaty on the Non-proliferation of Nuclear Weapons; opened for signature at London, Moscow, and Washington, DC, 1 July 1968; entered into force 5 March 1970 (hereinafter, NPT).

[10] R. Braithwaite, *Armageddon and Paranoia: The Nuclear Confrontation*, Profile Books, London, 2019, pp. 288–89; see 'Nuclear Proliferation Is Not Fast, but It Is Frightening', *The Economist*, 31 January 2021, at http://econ.st/3tw2aKH (subscription required).

[11] Braithwaite, *Armageddon and Paranoia: The Nuclear Confrontation*, p. 289.

[12] This is so, despite the fact that 'the precise language of the treaty leaves something to be desired from a drafting viewpoint'. Epstein, *The Last Chance: Nuclear Proliferation and Arms Control*, p. 87.

[13] Totalling 193, as of 1 January 2021. See the UN Treaty Collection webpage for the Chemical Weapons Convention, at http://bit.ly/2AdRTfs. Only the Democratic People's Republic of Korea, Egypt, Israel (a signatory), and South Sudan are States not party.

Conference of the Treaty in 2015: 'At its heart, the NPT was a 'grand bargain' underpinned by the symbiotic relationship between nuclear disarmament and non-proliferation: one could not be advanced without the other.'[14]

THE NEGOTIATION OF THE TREATY

Beyond the broader concern about the spread of nuclear weapons, a more immediate impetus for the negotiation of the NPT was the People's Republic of China's first test detonation of a nuclear explosive device in 1964.[15] China had just become the world's fifth nuclear-armed State. In June 1965, the UN Commission on Disarmament agreed to formally request the eighteen-State Disarmament Committee[16] to consider the question of a treaty on nuclear non-proliferation.[17] The shape of the future treaty was by no means either clear or certain as discussions began. Competing interests and visions, with the division of nation-states into two camps – the nuclear 'haves' and the nuclear 'have nots'[18] – would require three years of difficult, often fractious negotiations to produce a treaty text that could be adopted.[19]

The differing positions of the two nuclear superpowers, which effectively led the negotiations, were reflected in their competing drafts of the treaty. The draft submitted by the United States to the Disarmament Committee in late 1965 prohibited the transfer of nuclear weapons only to the 'national control' of a non-nuclear-weapon State,[20] leaving the door open for it to supply nuclear weapons to a group of countries and to station its nuclear weapons on the territory of its North Atlantic Treaty Organization (NATO) allies. The Soviet Union observed that one of the aims of the United States was also to find a way to provide West Germany with nuclear weapons,[21] 'the reddest of red lines' for the USSR.[22] Accordingly, the Soviet draft submitted to the UN General Assembly in 1965 sought to prohibit all non-nuclear-weapon States from ever possessing or even gaining control over the use of nuclear weapons.

The compromise solution, reached after a year of behind-the-scenes negotiations between the two superpowers, required the United States to abandon its project for

[14] UN, 'Recalling Nuclear-Non-proliferation Treaty's "Grand Bargain", Secretary-General Urges Leaders at Review Conference to "Abandon Short-Sighted Posturing"', news item, 27 April 2015, at http://bit.ly/2X56nVk.

[15] D. Bourantonis, 'The Negotiation of the Non-proliferation Treaty, 1965–1968: A Note', *International History Review*, Vol. 19, No. 2 (May 1997), 347–57, at p. 348.

[16] This body, which was formally outside the United Nations system, comprised five States from the Western bloc (Canada, France, Italy, the United Kingdom, and the United States); five States from the Soviet bloc (Bulgaria, Czechoslovakia, Poland, Romania, and the Soviet Union); and eight 'non-aligned' States (Brazil, Burma, Ethiopia, India, Mexico, Nigeria, Sweden, and the United Arab Emirates).

[17] Goldschmidt, 'The Negotiation of the Non-proliferation Treaty (NPT)', p. 73.

[18] E. Louka, *Nuclear Weapons, Justice and the Law*, Edward Elgar, Cheltenham, 2011, p. 98.

[19] For detail on the negotiations, see M. I. Shaker, *The Nuclear Non-proliferation Treaty: Origins and Implementation 1959–1979*, 3 vols., Oceana Publications, London/Rome/New York, March 1980.

[20] Art. I(1), US Draft, in Disarmament Commission Official Records, Supp. Jan.–Dec. 1965, doc. 227.

[21] Goldschmidt, 'The Negotiation of the Non-proliferation Treaty (NPT)', p. 75.

[22] G. Nystuen and T. Graff Hugo, 'The Nuclear Non-proliferation Treaty', chap. 15 in G. Nystuen, S. Casey-Maslen, and A. G. Bersagel (eds.), *Nuclear Weapons under International Law*, Cambridge University Press, Cambridge, 2014, p. 379.

a multilateral force (MLF)[23] in exchange for being allowed to retain nuclear weapons on the territory of its NATO European allies. To sweeten the pot, the Soviets also consented to the existence of NATO's nuclear planning committee.[24]

Despite their backroom deal, another fifteen months would be needed to settle on a final treaty text that was acceptable to each and every one of the seventeen participating States on the Disarmament Committee.[25] This was in large measure due to objections from among those States that did not possess nuclear weapons, particularly within the Non-aligned Movement (NAM), a grouping that had first formed in 1961.[26] The NAM sought greater influence over the content of a non-proliferation treaty, coalescing in November 1965 around a UN General Assembly resolution calling for a 'proper balance of mutual obligations and responsibilities'.[27] NAM members demanded that negotiations take place 'between nuclear and non-nuclear and between aligned and non-aligned countries', annoyed that their views on the need for nuclear disarmament and peaceful nuclear cooperation were largely being ignored.[28] That said, the non-aligned States were 'not a solid bloc with a single point of view', but rather reflected a spectrum of opinion.[29] This served to undermine the strength of the group's bargaining position.[30]

Finally, after both the Soviet Union and the United States had engaged in repeated brow-beating of the other delegations, the Conference of the Disarmament Committee in Geneva transmitted a report to the UN General Assembly in the Spring of 1968 with a single draft treaty text in attachment. In turn, the Assembly convened a special session with a view to concluding the text of the NPT. Only limited changes were incorporated at this late stage, largely at the instigation of Mexico, which concerned the sharing of knowledge and technology for peaceful purposes, combined with a marginal strengthening of the language in Article VI on nuclear disarmament.[31]

23 See, e.g., W. L. Kohl, 'Nuclear Sharing in Nato and the Multilateral Force', *Political Science Quarterly*, Vol. 80, No.1 (March 1965), 88–109.

24 Epstein, *The Last Chance: Nuclear Proliferation and Arms Control*, p. 73; Goldschmidt, 'The Negotiation of the Non-proliferation Treaty (NPT)', p. 75. The Nuclear Planning Group comprised seven ministers of defence, with the United States, the United Kingdom, West Germany, and Italy as permanent members, along with three other Committee members on a rotating basis. M. Willrich, 'The Treaty on the Non-proliferation of Nuclear Weapons', *Yale Law Journal*, Vol. 77, No. 8 (July 1968), 1447–519, at p. 1470.

25 France was 'empty chairing' the discussions, having criticised the 1963 Partial Test Ban Treaty for being discriminatory and declaring its intention that the future NPT would not concern disarmament. Goldschmidt, 'The Negotiation of the Non-proliferation Treaty (NPT)', p. 74.

26 The NAM was formed largely on the initiative of Yugoslav President Josip Broz Tito, as a grouping of States that did not seek to formally align themselves with either the United States or the Soviet Union, but wished rather to remain independent or neutral. The First NAM Summit Conference was held in Belgrade in September 1961. For details on the NAM's positions on the NPT and nuclear disarmament, see, e.g., Nuclear Threat Initiative (NTI), 'Non-aligned Movement (NAM)', last updated 31 May 2018, at http://bit.ly/3cQCZsY.

27 UN General Assembly Resolution 2028 (XX), adopted on 19 November 1965 by 93 votes to none with 5 abstentions, operative para. 2(b).

28 Bourantonis, 'The Negotiation of the Non-proliferation Treaty, 1965–1968: A Note', pp. 350, 353.

29 Epstein, *The Last Chance: Nuclear Proliferation and Arms Control*, p. 122.

30 Bourantonis, 'The Negotiation of the Non-proliferation Treaty, 1965–1968: A Note', p. 351.

31 Epstein, *The Last Chance: Nuclear Proliferation and Arms Control*, pp. 82–83.

On 12 June 1968, the UN General Assembly 'commended' the Treaty in its Resolution 2373 (XXII). A copy of the treaty was annexed to the resolution, which constituted formal adoption of the NPT by the Assembly. But Resolution 2373 was not adopted by consensus: Albania, Cuba, Tanzania, and Zambia all voted against it, while a further twenty-one States abstained.[32] The Treaty on the Non-proliferation of Nuclear Weapons was off to a rocky start.

In return for renouncing the manufacture or acquisition of nuclear weapons, the 'non-nuclear-weapon States' had sought both positive and negative assurances: positive assurances by the nuclear-weapon States that they would defend those without nuclear weapons in the event that any was the object of a nuclear attack; and negative assurances, whereby the nuclear-weapon States would never use or threaten the use of nuclear weapons against the non-nuclear-weapon States.[33] Out of concern about China, against which it had fought – and lost – a war just a few years earlier, India was especially vociferous about the need for adequate assurances, though Brazil, Romania, and West Germany were also vocal.[34] Soviet Premier Alexei Kosygin had offered to include a formal prohibition in the treaty on the use of nuclear weapons against any State that did not have nuclear weapons on its territory.[35] Ultimately, however, no assurances, either positive or negative, would be incorporated in the NPT.

The week following the Treaty's adoption, however, the Soviet Union, the United Kingdom, and the United States pledged in the UN Security Council to assist any non-nuclear-weapon State Party to the NPT in the event that it should be attacked with nuclear weapons, or where one would be threatened with such an attack. On 19 June 1968, the Security Council adopted Resolution 255, in which it referred to the commitments and recognised that 'aggression with nuclear weapons or the threat of such aggression against a non-nuclear-weapon State would create a situation in which the Security Council, and above all its nuclear-weapon State permanent members, would have to act immediately in accordance with their obligations under the United Nations Charter'.[36] Permanent member France, while undertaking to comply with the Treaty's obligations, did not adhere to the NPT for more than twenty years, finally acceding only in 1992.

But from the outset, many non-nuclear-armed States were deeply unhappy with the Treaty. Just two months after its adoption, they convened a conference in Geneva to discuss the nuclear issue. (The nuclear-weapon States had succeeded in their efforts to delay the conference until after the UN General Assembly had approved the Treaty text.) Four of the five nuclear-weapon States attended as observers, but without making any

32 UN General Assembly Resolution 2373 (XXII), adopted on 12 June 1968 by 95 votes to 4 with 21 abstentions, operative para. 1. The States abstaining were Algeria, Argentina, Brazil, Burma, Burundi, Central African Republic, Congo (Brazzaville), France, Gabon, Guinea, India, Malawi, Mali, Mauritania, Niger, Portugal, Rwanda, Saudi Arabia, Sierra Leone, Spain, and Uganda. Four UN member States did not vote: Cambodia, the Dominican Republic, the Gambia, and Haiti.

33 Bourantonis, 'The Negotiation of the Non-proliferation Treaty, 1965–1968: A Note', p. 356.

34 Nystuen and Graff Hugo, 'The Nuclear Non-proliferation Treaty', pp. 377, 384.

35 Epstein, *The Last Chance: Nuclear Proliferation and Arms Control*, pp. 138.

36 UN Security Council Resolution 255, adopted on 19 June 1968 by 10 votes to none, with 5 abstentions (Algeria, Brazil, France, India, and Pakistan), operative paras. 1 and 2.

statement. The conference took place 'in an atmosphere of bitterness, disappointment and resentment, reflecting the need of the countries in question to vent their feelings, if not to rebel, against the Great Powers, which had been exerting constant pressure on them all through the latter stages of the negotiations'.[37] The brainchild of Pakistan, the 'Forgotten Conference' as William Epstein terms it, was one more instance of the non-nuclear-weapon States being 'outmanoeuvred by the nuclear powers'.[38]

Entry into Force and Universalisation of the NPT

On 1 July 1968, the NPT was opened for signature in London, Moscow, and Washington, the three depositary States being thus the Soviet Union,[39] the United Kingdom, and the United States. The Treaty attracted fifty-eight signatory States that day, a few shy of half of all States generally recognised at the time. The NPT entered into force quickly, becoming binding international law on 5 March 1970 after forty signatories had ratified it in addition to the adherence of the three depositories.[40] Bourantonis claimed that once the NPT came into force, 'the development of nuclear weapons changed from a symbol of national pride into a violation of international law'.[41] More prosaically, Goldschmidt observed that, through their adherence to the NPT, a number of 'advanced countries', a quarter of a century after the bombing of Hiroshima, had unilaterally renounced a measure of national sovereignty for the sake of international stability while 'facilitating the world development of atomic energy'.[42]

Today, just seven States are formally outside the purview of the NPT: the Cook Islands, the Democratic People's Republic of Korea (albeit in controversial circumstances), India, Israel, Niue, Pakistan, and South Sudan.[43] Of these, the Cook Islands and Niue, which are considered 'other States' by the UN Secretary-General in his depository capacity for many other international treaties, are adjudged to be still bound by virtue of New Zealand's early adherence.[44]

37 Goldschmidt, 'The Negotiation of the Non-proliferation Treaty (NPT)', p. 76.

38 Epstein, *The Last Chance: Nuclear Proliferation and Arms Control*, pp. 126, 134.

39 Since 26 December 1991, the Russian Federation has served as the third depository to the NPT, as successor State to the Soviet Union.

40 Art. IX(3), NPT. The decision not to require all five nuclear-weapon States effectively designated under the Treaty to adhere to it in order to trigger entry into force reflected concern that Communist China might sign the Treaty and then refuse to ratify it, preventing the NPT from coming into force. Epstein, *The Last Chance: Nuclear Proliferation and Arms Control*, p. 96. Moreover, France had already made known its reluctance to ratify the NPT in the near future.

41 Bourantonis, 'The Negotiation of the Non-proliferation Treaty, 1965–1968: A Note', p. 347.

42 Goldschmidt, 'The Negotiation of the Non-proliferation Treaty (NPT)', p. 80.

43 In addition, when the State of Palestine, a UN observer State, adhered to the NPT in 2015, the United States issued the following statement: 'The Government of the United States of America does not believe the "State of Palestine" qualifies as a sovereign State and does not recognize it as such. Accession to the Treaty is limited to sovereign States. Therefore, the Government of the United States of America believes that the "State of Palestine" is not qualified to accede to the Treaty and affirms that it will not consider itself to be in a treaty relationship with the "State of Palestine" under the Treaty.' Note of the Government of the United States of America dated 21 April 2015, reported on the UK Depositary Status List of the Treaty on the Non-proliferation of Nuclear Weapons, Foreign and Commonwealth Office (FCO), London, 2016.

44 J. Prawitz, 'Negotiating Nuclear-Weapon-Free Zones', wchap. 4 in R. Avenhaus, V. Kremenyuk, and G. Sjöstedt (eds.), *Containing the Atom*, Lexington Books, New York, 2002, p. 129.

North Korea was previously a State Party, having acceded in 1985, but, as discussed in Chapter 1, it declared publicly in January 2003 that it was withdrawing immediately, to date the only State Party to have announced its withdrawal. Article X of the NPT, however, requires three months' notice not only to the other States Parties but also to the UN Security Council.[45] As the UN Office for Disarmament Affairs has observed, States Parties to the Treaty 'continue to express divergent views regarding the status' of the Democratic People's Republic of Korea under the NPT.[46]

THE (NON-)DEFINITION OF NUCLEAR WEAPONS IN THE NPT

It is surprising to say the least that in a treaty seeking to preclude the spread of the deadliest weapons ever produced by mankind, those weapons are not formally and explicitly defined in the text. In 1966, the United States seemed convinced of the need for a definition but later changed its mind.[47] No definition was included in the agreed draft text of 24 August 1967.[48]

Earlier global treaties on nuclear weapons – the 1959 Antarctic Treaty, the 1963 Partial Test-Ban Treaty, and the 1966 Outer Space Treaty – had not defined nuclear weapons, even though each had specific provisions addressing them. In contrast, Article 5 of the 1966 Treaty of Tlatelolco, adopted six months earlier,[49] defines a nuclear weapon as 'any device which is capable of releasing nuclear energy in an uncontrolled manner and which has a group of characteristics that are appropriate for warlike purposes. An instrument that may be used for the transport or propulsion of the device is not included in this definition if it is separable from the device and not an individual part thereof.'[50]

In 2015, the five permanent members of the UN Security Council – the nuclear-weapon States designated under the NPT – issued their *Glossary of Nuclear Weapons Terms*. Therein, a nuclear weapon is defined as a 'weapon assembly that is capable of producing an explosion and massive damage and destruction by the sudden release of energy instantaneously released from self-sustaining nuclear fission and/or fusion'.[51] This accurately describes a nuclear weapon for the purposes of the NPT. Excluded from the

45 See on this issue F. L. Kirgis, 'North Korea's Withdrawal from the Nuclear Nonproliferation Treaty', *ASIL Insights*, Vol. 8, No. 2 (24 January 2003), at http://bit.ly/2D6Iru8.

46 Office for Disarmament Affairs (UNODA), 'Democratic People's Republic of Korea: Accession to Treaty on the Non-proliferation of Nuclear Weapons (NPT)', undated but accessed 1 June 2020 at http://bit.ly/2S1NaSg.

47 Willrich, 'The Treaty on the Non-proliferation of Nuclear Weapons', p. 1464. US amendments to Article IV of the earlier US draft Treaty submitted on 21 March 1966 included a space for the definition of 'nuclear weapons', among other defined terms. The 1954 Atomic Energy Act in the United States had defined an 'atomic weapon' as 'any device utilizing atomic energy, exclusive of the means for transporting or propelling the device (where such means is a separable and divisible part of the device), the principal purpose of which is for use as, or for development of, a weapon, a weapon prototype, or a weapon test device'. 1954 Atomic Energy Act (as amended), §11(d), 42 US Code §2014(d) (1964).

48 US Arms Control and Disarmament Agency, *Documents on Disarmament*, 1967, p. 167.

49 Treaty for the Prohibition of Nuclear Weapons in Latin America and the Caribbean; opened for signature at Tlatelolco, Mexico, 14 February 1967; entered into force 22 April 1969.

50 The definition might usefully have incorporated the word 'explosive' before device for the purpose of clarity.

51 P5 Working Group on the Glossary of Key Nuclear Terms, *P5 Glossary of Key* Nuclear Terms, 1st ed., China Atomic Energy Press, Beijing, 2015, at https://bit.ly/36I8o1R, p. 6, para. 1.3.5.

definition are independent delivery systems for nuclear weapons, such as combat aircraft and naval vessels, particularly submarines. This is so, even if the submarine itself is nuclear-powered.[52]

THE OBLIGATIONS OF THE NUCLEAR-WEAPON STATES PARTIES

While constituting the 'cornerstone' of the nuclear non-proliferation regime,[53] the NPT is also a controversial instrument because it is deliberately discriminatory in its treatment of its parties. States are classified as either 'nuclear-weapon states' (the first five States to possess and test detonate nuclear weapons) or 'non-nuclear-weapon States' (all other States).

Article IX(3) defines, for the purposes of the Treaty, a nuclear-weapon State as 'one which has manufactured and exploded a nuclear weapon or other nuclear explosive device prior to 1 January, 1967'. This means that China, France, the Soviet Union, the United Kingdom, and the United States are the nuclear-weapon States under the NPT. All five are party, with the Russian Federation the accepted sole successor State to the Soviet Union, which ceased to exist as a legal entity in December 1991. Belarus, Kazakhstan, and Ukraine, each of which inherited Soviet nuclear weapons, voluntarily renounced them and subsequently adhered to the NPT as non-nuclear-weapon States. Ukraine, which had become the country with the third-largest nuclear arsenal in the world, had 1,900 Soviet strategic nuclear warheads and between 2,650 and 4,200 Soviet tactical nuclear weapons deployed on its territory at the time of its independence in 1991.[54] Kazakhstan (then possessing the fourth-largest arsenal) handed over 1,400 strategic nuclear warheads and 104 SS-18 ICBMs to the Russian Federation.[55]

The Prohibition on the Transfer of Nuclear Weapons

Under Article I of the NPT, each nuclear-weapon State Party undertakes not to transfer to any recipient whatsoever nuclear weapons or other nuclear explosive devices, whether directly or indirectly; not to assist, encourage, or induce any non-nuclear-weapon State to manufacture or otherwise acquire such weapons or devices; and not to transfer control over such weapons or devices to any non-nuclear-weapon State. In a number of cases,

52 On 14 March 1968, the US Department of State issued a press release in which it stated: 'For [the] purposes of the treaty a nuclear-powered submarine is not, in itself "a weapon". The treaty does not deal with such military applications of nuclear energy as nuclear propulsion of warships. Therefore, nothing in the treaty would prohibit the provision of nuclear fuel for this purpose.' Statement by US Department of State Spokesman Robert McCloskey, 14 March 1968 (unpublished). Cited by Willrich, 'The Treaty on the Non-proliferation of Nuclear Weapons', p. 1464.

53 Treaty on the Prohibition of Nuclear Weapons; adopted at New York, 7 July 2017; entered into force 22 January 2021, eighteenth preambular para. NATO also describes it as 'a cornerstone of international efforts to prevent the spread of nuclear weapons and weapons technology, and to achieve the goal of nuclear disarmament'. NATO, 'NATO and the Non-proliferation Treaty', Fact Sheet, March 2017, at https://bit.ly/3jlLL70, p. 1.

54 NTI, 'Nuclear Disarmament Ukraine', 27 January 2021, at http://bit.ly/3aXNJbo.

55 Federation of American Scientists, 'Kazakhstan Special Weapons', 6 October 2009, at https://bit.ly/3bJ8LJQ.

compliance with these obligations during the Treaty's lifetime has been questionable. It is important to recall that the obligations of States Parties comprise not only those of its armed forces and State bodies but also, depending on the circumstances, private companies and even individuals operating within its jurisdiction.

The obligation not to transfer any nuclear explosive devices to any recipient whatsoever is carefully crafted. While the *indirect* transfer of nuclear weapons *in toto* is precluded, seemingly permitted is even direct transfer of some of the key components of the weapons, especially the missiles, as long as the items supplied do not comprise an entire weapon or device.[56] Thus, for example, as discussed in Chapter 1, the United States sold the Polaris missile system to the United Kingdom in the 1960s and then sold the replacement Trident II missile system to it in the 1980s. The warheads for the UK Polaris missiles, designated ET.317, were, however, developed domestically by the British. Moreover, they differed substantively from the US W47 and later the W58 warhead used in the US Polaris missile,[57] enabling both States Parties to lay claim to compliance with the NPT prohibition on transfer.[58] The absence of an explicit definition in the NPT of a nuclear weapon is said to have further facilitated this legislative legerdemain.[59] Had the United States transferred also the warheads for the Polaris missile, this would have violated the letter as well as the spirit of the wording in Article I of the Treaty.[60]

More difficult to justify legally are the UK warheads used in its Trident missiles, which are believed to be based closely on the US W76 warhead engineering design. Writing in 2006, Hans Kristensen asked rhetorically, 'How British are the warheads on the British SSBN fleet?'[61] Recalling that the UK Ministry of Defence had claimed in a fact sheet that

56 J. Woodliffe, 'Nuclear Weapons and Non-proliferation: The Legal Aspects', chap. 5 in I. Pogany (ed.), *Nuclear Weapons and International Law*, Avebury, Aldershot, 1987, p. 89.

57 In fact, the British had concerns about the safety and reliability of both US warheads. Indeed, in the early 1960s, a number of W47 warhead primaries had to be replaced after corrosion of the fissile materials was observed during routine stockpile maintenance. Later, the entire stockpile of W47 warheads had to be rebuilt with new primaries when problems developed in a mechanical safing system. J. R. Harvey and S. Michalowski, 'Nuclear Weapons Safety: The Case of Trident', *Science & Global Security*, Vol. 4, No. 3 (1994), 261–337, at https://bit.ly/2MtnKiw, p. 292; and G. H. Miller, P. S. Brown, and C. T. Alonso, *Report to Congress on Stockpile Reliability, Weapon Remanufacture and the Role of Nuclear Testing*, Report No. UCRL-53822, Lawrence Livermore National Laboratory, Livermore, CA, October 1987, at http://bit.ly/3aA4RSW, p. 20. With respect to the W58 warhead, For instance, the 'Kinglet' boosted fission primary used in the United States' W58 warhead was initially rejected by the British for use in its own warheads, out of concern for reliability, although the United Kingdom did later adapt a version of Kinglet for reasons of effectiveness against Soviet missile defences. For details of broader challenges in ensuring safety and reliability of warheads, especially as they age, see J. Medalia, 'The Reliable Replacement Warhead Program: Background and Current Developments', US Congressional Research Service, Washington, DC, 27 July 2009, at https://bit.ly/3rpAFRm.

58 E. B. Firmage, 'The Treaty on the Non-proliferation of Nuclear Weapons', *American Journal of International Law*, Vol. 63, No. 4 (October 1969), 711–46, at p. 724.

59 Nystuen and Graff Hugo, 'The Nuclear Non-proliferation Treaty', p. 387; J. Woodliffe, 'Nuclear Weapons and Non-proliferation: The Legal Aspects', p. 89.

60 Willrich, 'The Treaty on the Non-proliferation of Nuclear Weapons', p. 1474. This is of course a theoretical example as the Polaris missiles were provided to the United Kingdom prior to the conclusion and entry into force of the NPT.

61 H. Kristensen, 'Britain's Next Nuclear Era', Federation of American Scientists, 7 December 2006, at http://bit.ly/2YN2qHi.

the warheads on the D5 missiles were 'designed and manufactured in the U.K.', Kristensen cited a declassified US Department of Energy document that demonstrated that the UK warhead was similar enough to the W76 warhead to make up an integral part of the W76 engineering, design, and evaluation schedule.[62]

Concerns about US compliance with its NPT obligations persist. As Chapter 1 described, the United Kingdom's new generation of nuclear warheads for Trident II will again be based on US technology, this time in the form of the W93 warhead.[63] The Ministry of Defence told *The Guardian* newspaper in February 2020: 'As previously stated in the 2015 defence review, we can confirm that we are working towards replacing the warhead. We have a strong defence relationship with the US and will continue to remain compatible with the US Trident missile. An announcement about the UK's replacement warhead programme will be made in due course.'[64] In August 2020, the newspaper reported that the UK Secretary of State for Defence, Ben Wallace, had written a letter urging Congress to support initial spending on the W93 warhead.[65] If authorised, the W93 will be the first 'completely new' US warhead 'in decades'.[66] The letter stated: 'Congressional funding in [2021] for the W93 program will ensure that we continue to deepen the unique nuclear relationship between our two countries, enabling the United Kingdom to provide safe and assured continuous-at-sea deterrence for decades to come.'[67]

Thus, should the United Kingdom implement its plans to not only increase its arsenal (see below) but develop a new warhead for its weapons, it must take great care to ensure that the provision in Article I of the NPT is not violated. In his statement to the House of Commons on 22 March 2021, Secretary of State for Defence Ben Wallace confirmed that each nuclear-weapon State to the NPT must develop its own nuclear weapons. He stated, 'For clarity, the United Kingdom does not buy warheads from other countries. Under the nuclear proliferation treaty, warheads have to be developed within that very country itself.'[68] This obligation must also be implemented in good faith, by both the United Kingdom and the United States.

The Integrated Review of Security, Defence, Development and Foreign Policy of March 2021 stated that the United Kingdom

62 Ibid. See also on this issue M. Clarke, 'Does My Bomb Look Big in This?', *International Affairs*, Vol. 80, No. 1 (2004), p. 37.

63 J. Doward, 'Pentagon Reveals Deal with Britain to Replace Trident', *The Guardian*, 22 February 2020, at http://bit.ly/3dio3Vs.

64 Ibid.

65 J. Borger, 'UK Lobbies US to Support Controversial New Nuclear Warheads', *The Guardian*, 1 August 2020, at http://bit.ly/3hRtqga.

66 Center for Arms Control and Non-proliferation, Fact Sheet: The W93 Warhead, 28 January 2021, at https://bit.ly/30SwkEz. There were said to be no plans to test detonate the new warhead, which the US government aims to field by 2040, though not everyone was convinced that this position would remain unchanged down the line. A. Mehta, 'Inside America's Newly Revealed Nuclear Ballistic Missile Warhead of the Future', *Defense News*, 24 February 2020, at http://bit.ly/2YJMy8m.

67 J. Borger, 'UK Lobbies US to Support Controversial New Nuclear Warheads', *The Guardian*, 1 August 2020, at https://bit.ly/3hRtqga.

68 'Integrated Review: Defence Command Paper', *Hansard*, Vol. 691, 22 March 2021, at https://bit.ly/3riQmt6, col. 648.

> will replace our existing nuclear warhead. We will work with the Atomic Weapons Establishment to build the highly skilled teams, facilities and capabilities needed to deliver this, while also sustaining the current warhead until it is withdrawn from service. We will continue to work closely with the United States to ensure our warhead remains compatible with the Trident Strategic Weapon System, our cooperation underpinned by both the MDA and the 1963 Polaris Sales Agreement.[69]

Writing on the RUSI website, two defence experts stated: 'In the case of the W93, Secretary of State for Defence Ben Wallace's lobbying of US Congressional committee members over approvals for the first stages of the W93 warhead gives a clear indication of the degree of UK dependence on that programme.'[70]

The Prohibition on the Transfer of Control over Nuclear Weapons

The prohibition on the transfer of control over nuclear weapons to a non-nuclear-weapon State under Article I of the NPT would also seemingly be violated if the United States ever decided that the bombs it holds in six air bases in Belgium, Germany, Italy, and the Netherlands needed to be used in anger.[71] Together, these bases play host to around 100 American B-61 nuclear gravity bombs on their metropolitan territories, with explosive yields which are thought to range from 0.3 kt to 170 kt. The weapons are all, at present, under the exclusive control of the United States, but arrangements are in place for the bombs to be used by the host State in an emergency.[72] Accordingly, each of those four host States retains nuclear-capable aircraft and pilots trained in their use. The aircraft are sometimes referred to as 'dual-key', as any use of nuclear weapons would have to be approved both by the US government and the government of the respective host State.

Such action would appear to contravene the language of the NPT on a plain reading. Willrich makes the case that a joint decision to use nuclear weapons is only 'control in a negative sense'. He argues that only if a non-nuclear-weapon State could make a 'unilateral and effective decision to use nuclear weapons' – a 'finger on the trigger' – would it clearly have control 'in the sense of the Treaty'.[73] Woodliffe agrees.[74] Firmage asserts that the Soviet Union had even acquiesced to potential use by NATO allies during the latter stages of the negotiation of the Treaty. The Soviet acceptance of NATO nuclear

69 HM Government, *Global Britain in a Competitive Age: The Integrated Review of Security, Defence, Development and Foreign Policy*, London, March 2021, p. 78.

70 Tom Plant and Matthew Harries, 'Going Ballistic: The UK's Proposed Nuclear Build-up', Commentary, RUSI, 16 March 2021, at https://bit.ly/3lMSmZs.

71 The bombs are believed to be located at the following five bases: Kleine Brogel Air Base in Belgium, Büchel Air Base in Germany, Aviano Air Base and Ghedi Air Base in Italy, and Volkel Air Base in the Netherlands. G. Oestern (ed.), *Nuclear Weapons Ban Monitor 2020*, Norwegian People's Aid, Oslo, January 2021, p. 55; see further T. S. Sechser, 'Sharing the Bomb: How Foreign Nuclear Deployments Shape Nonproliferation and Deterrence', *Nonproliferation Review*, Vol. 23, Nos. 3–4 (2016), 443–58.

72 That is not the case with the B61 bombs at a US airbase in Turkey.

73 Willrich, 'The Treaty on the Non-proliferation of Nuclear Weapons', p. 1470.

74 Woodliffe, 'Nuclear Weapons and Non-proliferation: The Legal Aspects', p. 90.

planning and 'participation', he intimates, is also an acknowledgment that non-nuclear-weapon States belonging to NATO could use nuclear weapons.[75]

But speaking before the Senate in 1968, Dean Rusk articulated the 'exception' in markedly different terms. The NPT, the US Secretary of State declared, 'does not deal with arrangements for deployment of nuclear weapons within allied territory as these do not involve any transfer of nuclear weapons or control over them unless and until a decision were made to go to war, at which time the treaty would no longer be controlling'.[76] The assertion is thus that the NPT does not apply during a situation of international armed conflict. There is, however, nothing in the Treaty text to indicate that this is the case.

The Prohibition on Assisting the Acquisition of Nuclear Weapons

The third primary obligation upon the five nuclear-weapon States under the NPT is not to assist any other State to manufacture or otherwise acquire nuclear weapons or other nuclear explosive devices. In the last five years, concern has been growing that the United States might breach this duty with respect to Saudi Arabia. In 2015, Saudi Arabia acquired a nuclear research reactor from Argentina, a 'stepping stone toward achieving the full nuclear fuel cycle capability'.[77] Crown Prince Mohammed bin Salman told a CBS reporter in 2018 that the kingdom would develop nuclear weapons if Iran were to do so.[78] In March 2019, Reuters news agency reported that US Secretary of Energy Rick Perry had approved, in secret, six authorisations for US companies to sell nuclear power technology and assistance to Saudi Arabia.[79]

On a separate issue, writing in 1975, William Epstein suggested that since the prohibition is on assisting non-nuclear-weapon States, it might be lawful to assist a private organisation or corporation to manufacture or otherwise acquire nuclear weapons or other nuclear explosive devices.[80] This is unpersuasive. Although the drafting of the Treaty is rather lax in this area, a private organisation or corporation located in any non-nuclear-weapon State is encompassed by the prohibition on assisting the acquisition of nuclear weapons, under both the NPT and customary international law.

75 Firmage, 'The Treaty on the Non-proliferation of Nuclear Weapons', p. 723.

76 Hearings on the Treaty on the Non-proliferation of Nuclear Weapons before the Senate Committee on Foreign Relations, 90th Congress, 2nd Session (1968), p. 5.

77 E. Gheorghe, 'Iran's Nuclear Program Seems to Be Accelerating. Will Saudi Arabia Take a Similar Path?', *The Washington Post*, 12 July 2019, at http://wapo.st/2B1UARJ.

78 T. Gardner, 'U.S. Shared Nuclear Power Info with Saudi Arabia after Khashoggi Killed', Reuters, 4 June 2019, at http://reut.rs/318CUym.

79 T. Gardner, 'U.S. Approved Secret Nuclear Power Work for Saudi Arabia', Reuters, 27 March 2019, at http://reut.rs/2BtHxZe. Under Section 123 of the 1954 Atomic Energy Act, any nation receiving help from the US agrees to abide by certain rules regarding non-proliferation technologies, the peaceful nature of a nuclear programme and IAEA inspections. Saudi Arabia has resisted these inspections. A. Harwood, 'Trump Is Helping Saudi Arabia Go Nuclear. Does the Middle East Need an Arms Race?', opinion, *Newsweek*, 12 April 2019, at http://bit.ly/2Br1RdE.

80 Epstein, *The Last Chance: Nuclear Proliferation and Arms Control*, p. 89.

Peaceful Nuclear Explosions

While the NPT does not generally address the use of nuclear weapons,[81] its Article V does implicitly permit so-called 'peaceful' nuclear explosions. As the previous chapter described, the two nuclear superpowers were engaging in a series of underground military tests while also channelling considerable sums of money into the peaceful applications of nuclear explosions in the 1960s to the 1980s, vaunting the tremendous potential advantages they believed would result.[82] The need to renounce the right to conduct peaceful nuclear explosions was 'deeply felt by a large number of non-nuclear powers', though this was 'vigorously' opposed by Brazil and India.[83] Although the Soviet Union and the United States would not agree to outlaw peaceful nuclear explosions, they were persuaded to agree to the incorporation of a clause in the Treaty promising the non-nuclear-weapon States, a share of the benefits accrued from the 'peaceful applications of nuclear explosions', at minimal cost and on 'a non-discriminatory basis'.

Article 18(1) of the 1967 Treaty of Tlatelolco had even stipulated that 'the Contracting Parties may carry out explosions of nuclear devices for peaceful purposes, including explosions which involve devices similar to those used in nuclear weapons'. In the autumn of 1968, the UN General Assembly recommended that the International Atomic Energy Agency (IAEA) conduct a study on how a service for conducting peaceful explosions could be established under international control. In fact, the United States discontinued all civil tests in the mid-1970s, and the provision in Article V of the Treaty has effectively remained a dead letter. On 31 October 2010, the General Secretariat of the Treaty of Tlatelolco's verification body, OPANAL, recommended that Article 18 be revised. In support of this recommendation, the General Secretariat memorandum observed that nuclear explosions had proven 'unnecessary for the development of nuclear technology' and noted that the Treaty's member States were all opposed to nuclear testing of any kind.[84]

In May 1974, India, a State not party to the NPT, conducted an underground nuclear explosion in an operation known officially as Pokhran I. The detonation was ostensibly for peaceful purposes and was announced as such by the government, but in reality, India was preparing the ground for the possibility of becoming a nuclear-armed power. Indeed, Raj Ramanna, the head of India's nuclear programme, would later admit that the Pokhran test 'was a bomb'.[85] India would not, however, proceed to acquire a nuclear arsenal for a further two decades.

Formally, Article V remains part of the text of the NPT, having never been either deleted or amended. At the NPT's Sixth Review Conference in 2000, however, the States Parties agreed that the provision was to be interpreted in the light of the Comprehensive

81 The first preambular paragraph notes 'the devastation that would be visited upon all mankind by a nuclear war'.

82 Goldschmidt, 'The Negotiation of the Non-proliferation Treaty (NPT)', p. 76. There was a suggestion that the term had been invented as a result of fears that a comprehensive ban might be instituted on all nuclear testing. Epstein, *The Last Chance: Nuclear Proliferation and Arms Control*, p. 172.

83 Ibid.; see Epstein, *The Last Chance: Nuclear Proliferation and Arms Control*, p. 73.

84 NTI, 'Treaty for the Prohibition of Nuclear Weapons in Latin America and the Caribbean (LANWFZ) (Tlatelolco Treaty)', last updated 29 April 2019, at http://bit.ly/2EItJc6.

85 Atomic Heritage Foundation, 'Indian Nuclear Program', 23 August 2018, at http://bit.ly/3dFIZWw.

Nuclear-Test-Ban Treaty (CTBT),[86] though only when the CTBT enters into force. Should this occur, this would preclude any test detonation of a nuclear explosive device, even for peaceful purposes, unless a prohibition on such test detonations has already crystallised in customary law.[87]

THE OBLIGATIONS OF THE NON-NUCLEAR-WEAPON STATES PARTIES

The Prohibition on Acquisition

The primary obligation on the 185 non-nuclear-weapon States Parties to the Nuclear Non-proliferation Treaty is never to acquire, in any manner and by any means, a nuclear weapon or other nuclear explosive device. Thus, under Article II of the Treaty, non-nuclear-weapon States Parties undertake not to receive the transfer from any transferor whatsoever of nuclear weapons or other nuclear explosive devices or of control over such weapons or devices directly, or indirectly; not to manufacture or otherwise acquire such weapons or devices; and not to seek or receive any assistance in their manufacture.

A Prohibition on Development?

In some respects, the undertaking 'not to manufacture or otherwise acquire' is narrower in scope than one might expect. In particular, Article II does not contain an explicit prohibition on developing a nuclear explosive device. Given this fact, a number of leading commentators have argued that preliminary activities of research and development but which fall short of the completion of a nuclear explosive device are lawful.[88] Specifically, Dan Joyner observes:

> Some current and former government officials and other observers, particularly in the United States, hold that the prohibition on manufacturing a nuclear explosive device entails a scope which reaches far back along the knowledge acquisition and development line of a nuclear weapons program to the concept, capacity building, design, research and experimentation stages. Under this interpretation, the information presented in this new IAEA report might be considered evidence of a breach. However, this interpretation is incorrect by reference to the plain meaning of the terms of Article II, as confirmed by the negotiating history of the NPT.[89]

Jozef Goldblat interpreted the provision in broadly similar terms, asserting that 'the construction of an experimental prototype nuclear explosive device would be covered by the term "manufacture"'.[90] But he broadened the understanding of this term to also encompass 'the production of components which would only have relevance to

[86] Comprehensive Nuclear-Test-Ban Treaty; adopted at New York, 10 September 1996; not yet in force.

[87] See on this issue Chapter 4.

[88] Epstein, *The Last Chance: Nuclear Proliferation and Arms Control*, p. 90; D. Joyner, 'Iran's Nuclear Program and the Legal Mandate of the IAEA', blog entry, *Jurist*, 9 November 2011, at http://bit.ly/3er3UNz.

[89] Ibid. See also Woodliffe, 'Nuclear Weapons and Non-proliferation: The Legal Aspects', p. 91.

[90] Goldblat, *Arms Control: The New Guide to Negotiations and Agreements*, p. 102.

a nuclear explosive device'.[91] If correct, this would not extend to the development and production of missiles, as they can be used to deliver a conventional explosive charge, as well as nuclear warheads.

More broad still in his interpretation of the prohibition on 'manufacture' is Andreas Persbo, who asserts that 'a more functionally consistent interpretation of the treaty is simply that any fuel cycle activity intended to support the acquisition of a nuclear device would be a matter of non-compliance with the NPT.'[92] His lines of argument include a claimed duty to interpret a term consistently throughout a treaty and that a narrower interpretation would allow a nuclear-weapon State to assist the development of a nuclear weapon right up until its physical construction.[93] These do not persuade.

First, the obligation in Article I upon the nuclear-weapon States is formulated differently, representing an undertaking 'not *in any way* to assist, encourage, or induce any non-nuclear-weapon State to manufacture or otherwise acquire nuclear weapons or other nuclear explosive devices' (emphasis added). This is far broader in scope than the simple prohibition upon each non-nuclear-weapon State of manufacture of such a weapon or device. Second, the omission of the word 'develop' in Articles I and II of the NPT was deliberate. The term does appear seven times (as a verb or its noun, 'development') elsewhere in the Treaty. The concern existed that peaceful uses of nuclear energy might somehow be captured by a prohibition of development in Article II. This explains the formulation under Article IV(1), whereby it is stipulated that 'nothing in this Treaty shall be interpreted as affecting the inalienable right of all the Parties to the Treaty to develop research, production and use of nuclear energy for peaceful purposes without discrimination and in conformity with Articles I and II of this Treaty'.

A Limited Prohibition on Assisting Another Non-nuclear-Weapon State to Acquire Nuclear Explosive Devices

Perhaps more surprising is the absence of a general prohibition upon each non-nuclear-weapon State Party of assisting another non-nuclear-weapon State to acquire nuclear explosive devices. What is only outlawed is the provision of nuclear material other than for peaceful purposes, as well as 'equipment or material especially designed or prepared for the processing, use or production of special fissionable material'.[94] This 'potentially … serious lacuna'[95] was pointed out during the drafting of the Treaty by the United Arab Republic (nowadays Egypt), but the nuclear-weapon States, particularly the Soviet Union and the United States, did not wish to amend the text.[96]

The gap is serious because assistance to acquire nuclear weapons can be provided in other forms than the supply of nuclear material and related equipment. It can be technical

91 Ibid.
92 A. Persbo, 'A Reflection on the Current State of Nuclear Non-proliferation and Safeguards', *Non-proliferation Papers*, No. 8 (February 2012), European Union (EU) Non-proliferation Consortium, at http://bit.ly/31asnTo, p. 5.
93 Ibid., p. 4.
94 Art. III(2), NPT.
95 Woodliffe, 'Nuclear Weapons and Non-proliferation: The Legal Aspects', p. 91.
96 Epstein, *The Last Chance: Nuclear Proliferation and Arms Control*, p. 73.

(to guide another State in how to manufacture nuclear weapons, including through secondment of a State's nuclear physicians); financial (in the form of a loan or other financing by a bank within the assisting State's jurisdiction to support a nuclear weapons programme); material (such as through the supply of missiles for the delivery of nuclear warheads); or technological (through the provision of missile technology, such as advanced guidance systems, or assistance in the development of solid-fuel rockets).

The Sixth Review Conference of the NPT, recalling the obligations of all the States Parties under Articles I, II, and III, called upon all States Parties 'not to cooperate or give assistance in the nuclear or nuclear-related field to States not party to the Treaty in a manner which assists them in manufacturing nuclear weapons or other nuclear explosive devices'.[97] The chosen language illustrates the voluntary nature of the entreated restraint.

A non-nuclear-weapon State Party is also not precluded under the NPT from supplying nuclear material to any of the five nuclear-weapon States.[98] That said, in the Outcome Document of the Sixth Review Conference of the NPT, the Conference recognised that 'nuclear material supplied to the nuclear-weapon States for peaceful purposes should not be diverted for the production of nuclear weapons or other nuclear explosive devices, and should be, as appropriate, subject to IAEA safeguards agreements'.[99] But that carefully worded phrase does not equate to a call never to supply nuclear material to the nuclear-weapon States for non-peaceful purposes.

Domestic Implementation and Reporting

Aside from the provisions on safeguards with the IAEA, discussed below, the NPT contains no national implementation clause, requiring its States Parties to take the necessary measures to give effect to the Treaty obligations at the domestic level, including through the criminalisation of certain prohibited acts. There is also no general reporting obligation in the Treaty. Both are staples of arms control and disarmament treaties.

Verification: The IAEA Safeguards Agreements

Verification of the NPT is limited to safeguards agreements to be concluded with the IAEA.[100] Each non-nuclear-weapon State Party undertakes to accept safeguards in an agreement with the IAEA 'for the exclusive purpose of verification of the fulfilment' of its NPT obligations

97 2000 Review Conference of the Parties to the Treaty on the Non-proliferation of Nuclear Weapons, Final Document, Vol. I, Part I: Review of the operation of the Treaty, taking into account the decisions and the resolution adopted by the 1995 Review and Extension Conference, at https://bit.ly/39P5RTU, 'Article III and fourth and fifth preambular paragraphs, especially in their relationship to article IV and the sixth and seventh preambular paragraphs', para. 34.

98 Ibid., p. 90; Woodliffe, 'Nuclear Weapons and Non-proliferation: The Legal Aspects', p. 91.

99 2000 Review Conference of the Parties to the Treaty on the Non-proliferation of Nuclear Weapons, Final Document, Vol. I, Part I, 'Article III and fourth and fifth preambular paragraphs, especially in their relationship to article IV and the sixth and seventh preambular paragraphs', para. 25.

100 Although the IAEA is best known for its verification of compliance with the NPT, it was established in 1957 with a view to promoting peaceful use of nuclear energy following Eisenhower's famous 'Atoms for Peace' speech in December 1953 to the UN General Assembly. This followed a softening of Soviet stance since the

'with a view to preventing diversion of nuclear energy from peaceful uses to nuclear weapons or other nuclear explosive devices'.[101] It is further stipulated that the requisite safeguards 'shall be applied on all source or special fissionable material in all peaceful nuclear activities within the territory of such State, under its jurisdiction, or carried out under its control anywhere'.[102] Each State Party to the Treaty also undertakes not to provide either a source of special fissionable material or any 'specially designed or prepared' equipment or material for processing, use, or production of special fissionable material to any non-nuclear-weapon State for peaceful purposes, unless the material is subject to the safeguards required by Article III.[103]

The Comprehensive Safeguards Agreement

The IAEA, based in Vienna, produced a new model agreement specifically to support the implementation of Article III of the NPT in 1971.[104] The provision on safeguards, which inevitably involved inspections by an international body, was one of the hardest pills for the non-nuclear-weapon States to swallow during the negotiation of the Treaty. The five nuclear-weapon States were formally exempt from such a requirement, which 'accentuated the discriminatory nature of the restrictions'.[105] Objections to any form of international verification of an arms control treaty are often reflective of the fear that inspections will be unlawfully exploited for the purpose of spying, and the case of safeguards under the NPT was no exception. Japan and the Federal Republic of Germany (erstwhile West Germany) each claimed that the risk of industrial espionage was significant.[106]

With a view to rebutting the allegation, in 1967 US President Lyndon Johnson and British Prime Minister Harold Wilson solemnly undertook, in formal statements, to open voluntarily their peaceful facilities to inspection by the IAEA, 'thereby running the same risks of industrial espionage as the other powers subject to safeguards'. The Soviet Union, however, would not do so 'under any circumstances'. In any event, given that the nuclear-weapon States could decide which installations would be exempt from safeguards on grounds of national security, 'this voluntary submission to inspection may be compared to the attitude of a traveller who has a right to show the customs officials which of his suitcases should be examined'.[107]

death of Stalin and the end of the Korean War. Epstein, *The Last Chance: Nuclear Proliferation and Arms Control*, p. 14.

101 Art. III(1), NPT.

102 The term 'source material' includes uranium containing the mixture of isotopes occurring in nature, uranium depleted in the isotope 235, and thorium. The term 'special fissionable material' means ^{239}Pu, ^{233}U, and 'uranium enriched in the isotopes 235 or 233'. See Art. XX, Statute of the IAEA, and NSG Part 1 Guidelines – INFCIRC/254/Rev.13/Part 1, 'Material and Equipment', at http://bit.ly/2EzebK6, paras. 1.1 and 1.2.

103 Art. III(2), NPT.

104 IAEA doc. INFCIRC/153. Text available at IAEA, 'The Structure and Content of Agreements between the Agency and States Required in Connection with the Treaty on the Non-proliferation of Nuclear Weapons', at http://bit.ly/3iyTmON. See also Woodliffe, 'Nuclear Weapons and Non-proliferation: The Legal Aspects', p. 94.

105 Goldschmidt, 'The Negotiation of the Non-proliferation Treaty (NPT)', p. 78.

106 Ibid., p. 79.

107 Ibid.

The limitations of a Comprehensive Safeguards Agreement are clear. As Hans Blix wrote in 1985, 'Safeguards cannot prevent a violation of obligations – the diversion of fissile material – any more than bank of company audits can prevent a misappropriation of funds. All they can do is expose infringements or arouse suspicions, in effect sound the alarm.'[108] A Comprehensive Safeguards Agreement permits the IAEA to verify declared quantities of nuclear material but is relatively easy to bypass, given sufficient funding and political will, as Chapter 7 describes. Iran, Iraq, and Libya all managed to do so, despite their adherence to the NPT (in 1970, 1969, and 1975, respectively).

The IAEA Additional Protocol

An Additional Protocol to a Comprehensive Safeguards Agreement, which is not required by the NPT,[109] but whose conclusion has been encouraged by successive review conferences of the Treaty, offers far stronger reassurance that no clandestine nuclear weapons programme is in operation. Under the Protocol, the IAEA is granted significantly expanded rights of access to both information and sites within the territory of a party. As of the end of 2020, 136 States had concluded and brought in force an Additional Protocol with the IAEA.[110] In addition, Iran had been – but had recently stopped, as of this writing – provisionally applying the Protocol, in compliance with a commitment to do so under the Joint Comprehensive Plan of Action (JCPOA).[111] Agreements between the IAEA and a further fourteen States for an Additional Protocol had been approved but were not yet in force.[112] For details of verification measures performed under a Comprehensive Safeguards Agreement and an Additional Protocol, respectively, see Chapter 7.

Small Quantities Protocol

For States with little or no nuclear material and no nuclear material in a 'facility', a Small Quantities Protocol with the IAEA can reduce the administrative burden of nuclear safeguards.[113] The original Small Quantities Protocol suspended the application of many provisions of the Comprehensive Safeguards Agreement. This can be problematic in the case of certain States, when they later secure a domestic nuclear energy and research infrastructure. In exceptional cases, a proliferation concern may arise.

[108] H. Blix, 'Safeguards and Non-proliferation: The IAEA and Efforts to Counteract the Spread of Nuclear Weapons', *IAEA Bulletin*, Summer 1985, p. 5.

[109] S. Hill, 'NATO and the Treaty on the Prohibition of Nuclear Weapons', Research Paper, Chatham House, London, January 2021, p. 16.

[110] IAEA, 'Additional Protocol', 1 February 2021, at http://bit.ly/2Ieeg5W.

[111] IAEA, 'IAEA Verification in Iran', at https://bit.ly/39OgDtM.

[112] IAEA, 'Additional Protocol', 1 February 2021, at http://bit.ly/2Ieeg5W.

[113] To qualify for a Small Quantities Protocol, nuclear material in the State may not exceed 1 kg in total of special fissionable material (plutonium, uranium enriched to 20 per cent and above, and uranium enriched to less than 20 per cent after its weight is multiplied by five times the square of its enrichment); 10 metric tons in total of natural uranium and depleted uranium with an enrichment above 0.5 per cent; 20 metric tons of depleted uranium with an enrichment of 0.5 per cent or below; and 20 metric tons of thorium. See IAEA doc. INFCIRC/153 (corrected), para. 37.

This is currently the case with Saudi Arabia, which in January 2021 was described by Mark Fitzpatrick, who had earlier overseen non-proliferation policy at the US Department of State, as 'the proliferation concern number one around the world'.[114] For although Saudi Arabia is party to a Comprehensive Safeguards Agreement with the IAEA, its old Small Quantities Protocol to that Agreement suspends most inspection and reporting requirements.[115] Calls have been made by non-governmental experts (as well as by the IAEA in direct communication with the Kingdom) for Saudi Arabia to rescind its Small Quantities Protocol and bring into force an Additional Protocol with the IAEA, allowing the Agency to search for undeclared materials and activities.[116]

The Small Quantities Protocol that binds with Saudi Arabia is of a standard that has been deemed 'simply not adequate' by the IAEA Director-General, Rafael Grossi.[117] For instance, the old version does not even allow the IAEA to perform verification activities in order to confirm that the State meets the eligibility criteria for the Protocol, and the contracting State is not required to provide the IAEA with an initial report on all nuclear material which is subject to safeguards.[118] As of writing, it remained to be seen whether President Joe Biden's tougher stance on the Saudi regime than this predecessor in the White House[119] would enable progress to be made on this issue and preclude the possibility of a break-out by a non-nuclear-weapon State Party to the NPT.

THE PEACEFUL USE OF NUCLEAR ENERGY

The right to engage in the peaceful use of nuclear energy was a critical element in securing agreement from non-nuclear-armed States for the conclusion of the NPT. The preamble to the Treaty affirms the principle that the benefits of peaceful applications of nuclear technology should be available to all its States Parties and that, in furtherance of this principle, all 'are entitled to participate in the fullest possible exchange of scientific information for, and to contribute alone or in co-operation with other States to, the further development of the applications of atomic energy for peaceful purposes'.[120]

Under Article IV, States Parties undertake to facilitate the transfer of knowledge, materials, and equipment, and to promote international cooperation, especially with respect to the Global South ('the developing areas of the world'). The provision further specifies that 'nothing in this Treaty shall be interpreted as affecting the inalienable right of all parties to

114 'Nuclear Proliferation Is Not Fast, But It Is Frightening', *The Economist*, 31 January 2021.

115 Agreement between the Kingdom of Saudi Arabia and the International Atomic Energy Agency for the Application of Safeguards in Connection with the Treaty on the Non-proliferation of Nuclear Weapons, IAEA doc. INFCIRC/746, 16 February 2009, at https://bit.ly/39Utue4.

116 Oestern (ed.), *Nuclear Weapons Ban Monitor 2020*, p. 32; and E. O. Lisman, 'Reinforcing Saudi Arabia's Non-proliferation Obligations', blog entry, Center for Arms Control and Non-proliferation, 11 December 2020, at http://bit.ly/3ayJVM9.

117 'Saudi Arabia, IAEA Discuss Safeguards', *Arms Control Today*, October 2020, at http://bit.ly/3cMeh07.

118 IAEA, *Safeguards Implementation Guide for States with Small Quantities Protocols*, Vienna, 2016, at https://bit.ly/3pTo3i1, p. 4.

119 See, e.g., 'Joe Biden Puts Saudi Arabia on Notice', *The Economist*, 5 February 2021, at http://econ.st/2LoHfrM.

120 NPT, seventh and eight preambular paras.

the Treaty to engage in research, production and use of nuclear energy for peaceful purposes without discrimination and in conformity with Articles I and II of this Treaty'. One commentator has suggested that the NPT 'can be summed up in one simple phrase: a nuclear explosion is prohibited, but everything not prohibited is allowed, including all the stages of the fuel cycle, even if they make it possible to produce nuclear explosives'.[121]

Nuclear energy is the fourth largest source of energy, with around 10 per cent of the world's electricity generated by a global total of 440 nuclear reactors. A total of 32 States plus Taiwan had operational nuclear reactors on their territory as of January 2021.[122] The United States has more nuclear power plants (96) than any other nation, while France's 56 nuclear reactors produce 70 per cent of its electricity needs (though it is eager to cut this figure in half).[123] Ukraine, whose reactor at Chernobyl exploded in 1986, causing the worst nuclear disaster in history, plans to add 11 more reactors to its existing 15 plants, in order to double its production of nuclear energy. But in the aftermath of the Fukushima-Daiichi Nuclear Disaster in 2011, Germany, Belgium, and Switzerland decided to stop nuclear production completely: by 2022, 2025, and 2035, respectively.[124]

THE DUTY TO PURSUE NUCLEAR DISARMAMENT

By far the most contested of all the provisions in the NPT – with respect to both its interpretation and its application – is Article VI. This provides in full: 'Each of the Parties to the Treaty undertakes to pursue negotiations in good faith on effective measures relating to cessation of the nuclear arms race at an early date and to nuclear disarmament, and on a Treaty on general and complete disarmament under strict and effective international control.' Thus, under the provision, States Parties agree to negotiate, not within the NPT framework but in a separate, unspecified forum (or forums), both an end to the arms race and comprehensive nuclear disarmament.[125] The formal undertaking is to 'pursue

121 Goldschmidt, 'The Negotiation of the Non-proliferation Treaty (NPT)', p. 78.

122 Argentina, Armenia, Belarus, Belgium, Brazil, Bulgaria, Canada, China, Czechia, Finland, France, Germany, Hungary, India, Iran, Japan, the Republic of Korea, Mexico, the Netherlands, Pakistan, Romania, Russia, Slovakia, Slovenia, South Africa, Spain, Sweden, Switzerland, Ukraine, the United Arab Emirates, the United Kingdom, and the United States, and Taiwan. World Nuclear Association, 'World Nuclear Power Reactors & Uranium Requirements', January 2021, at http://bit.ly/2MYwa1a. In addition, in 2019 Algerian President Abdelaziz Bouteflika gave the green light to the exploitation of nuclear energy for peaceful purposes. A new law on nuclear activities, which will allow Algeria to use nuclear energy for scientific research, especially medicine, is part of a broader nuclear strategy aiming at the diversification of energy sources in the country. A. Lefevre, 'Algeria Is Promoting the Nuclear Energy', *NBN*, 4 February 2019, at http://bit.ly/2B4b37X; see also Algeria Press Service, 'Algeria Seeks to Generate Electricity from Nuclear Energy', 15 July 2019, at http://bit.ly/2BwltNw. Algeria adhered to the NPT in 1995. Iraq had three nuclear reactors at Tuwaitha, its main nuclear research site, south of Baghdad. One was destroyed by an Israeli air raid, in 1981, and the two others were blown up by US aircraft during the 1991 Gulf War. In 2017, Iraq asked for international assistance to build a nuclear reactor for peaceful purposes. M. Nichols and M. Chmaytelli, 'Iraq Asks U.N. for Help to Build New Nuclear Power Reactor', Reuters, New York, 23 September 2017, at http://reut.rs/2Z3B5QH.

123 World Nuclear Association, 'World Nuclear Power Reactors & Uranium Requirements', January 2021; World Nuclear Association, 'Nuclear Share Figures, 2009–2019', September 2020, at http://bit.ly/3aAXfQb.

124 Ibid.

125 According to Epstein, by 'cessation' is meant not only qualitative accumulations but also qualitative developments and improvements. Epstein, *The Last Chance: Nuclear Proliferation and Arms Control*, p. 183.

negotiations in good faith', but not specifically to conclude those negotiations successfully. By accepting the language of Article VI, therefore, non-nuclear-weapon States had been constrained 'to be content with pious assurances, rather than specific nuclear disarmament commitments, on the part of the military nuclear powers'.[126]

The five nuclear-weapon States recognised by the NPT have argued for some time that implementation of Article VI, and especially moves towards comprehensive nuclear disarmament, depend on the regional and global political and security environment.[127] This perception has been accentuated in recent years by the United States' dedicated initiative, 'Creating an Environment for Nuclear Disarmament' (CEND), launched in 2019 in the lead-up to the NPT's Tenth Review Conference.[128] An advocate for the initiative claimed in February 2020 that what makes CEND 'unique' is its participation and format. The CEND initiative was launched at the 2019 NPT Preparatory Committee, with an invitation from the United States to other States to engage in a new dialogue to address the 'deteriorating security conditions [that] have made near-term prospects for progress on disarmament bleak'.[129]

In November 2019, at a second meeting of thirty-one participating States, which included both nuclear-weapon and non-nuclear-weapon States Parties to the NPT, as well as an unknown number of States not party, the Initiative's path was mapped out in greater detail.[130] Three subgroups were created to tackle, respectively: the reduction of the perceived incentives for States to acquire or increase nuclear stockpiles, the functioning and effectiveness of existing nuclear disarmament mechanisms and institutions, and potential interim measures to reduce risks related to nuclear weapons. The first of the subgroups, chaired by the Netherlands and Morocco, would consider a range of issues, including improved dialogue among States on threat perceptions, improved approaches to addressing non-compliance with international obligations, and possible avenues for future dialogue on nuclear deterrence and the humanitarian consequences of using nuclear weapons.

The second of the subgroups, chaired by South Korea and the United States, was planning to identify best practices of nuclear non-proliferation and disarmament mechanisms and institutions. It would further seek to develop proposals to maintain and improve the functioning of those bodies. The third subgroup, led by Germany and Finland, aimed to explore nuclear risk-reduction measures and to analyse their practicality.[131]

All three subgroups were supposed to report within two years, though whether the initiative would survive the global coronavirus pandemic and the change in US

[126] Goldschmidt, 'The Negotiation of the Non-proliferation Treaty (NPT)', p. 78.

[127] Partially on this basis, in 2014, Dan Joyner argued that the United States has been breaching its duty under Article VI to negotiate in good faith an agreement for nuclear disarmament. D. Joyner, 'The Legal Meaning and Implications of Article VI of the Non-proliferation Treaty', chap. 16 in Nystuen, Casey-Maslen, and Bersagel (eds.), *Nuclear Weapons under International Law*, p. 414.

[128] H. Williams, 'CEND and a Changing Global Nuclear Order', commentary, European Leadership Network, 18 February 2020, at http://bit.ly/3eB1dJq.

[129] Ibid.

[130] S. Bugos, 'CEND Establishes Two-Year Work Program', Arms Control Today, January/February 2020, at http://bit.ly/3drGs1m.

[131] Ibid.

administration in January 2021 remained to be seen. In any event, even among supporters of the CEND initiative, there was little optimism that any concrete disarmament outcome would result.

In contrast, in the view of the overwhelming majority of the members of the NPT, Article VI is a binding obligation upon all States Parties – but especially the nuclear-weapon States – to take concrete steps to both negotiate and conclude an agreement on comprehensive nuclear disarmament. For sure, the nuclear disarmament measures many repeatedly sought during the Treaty negotiations 'in order to strike a fair balance in the concessions made' did not materialise.[132] Indeed, Goldschmidt argued that the nuclear-weapon States had 'managed to divest them entirely of their binding nature'.[133] But this goes too far. Article VI certainly does contain legally binding disarmament obligations, as the International Court of Justice has made clear, even though officials in the nuclear-weapon States 'have intentionally attempted to obfuscate' them.[134]

In 1996, in its Advisory Opinion on the threat or use of nuclear weapons, the International Court of Justice determined, by unanimous agreement among its judges, that 'there exists an obligation to pursue in good faith and bring to a conclusion negotiations leading to nuclear disarmament in all its aspects under strict and effective international control'.[135] At first sight, the reference to a duty to successfully conclude an agreement for nuclear disarmament goes beyond the strictures of Article VI. Upon closer examination, however, given that the obligation is (with added emphasis) 'to pursue negotiations *in good faith* on *effective* measures relating to cessation of the nuclear arms race at an early date and to nuclear disarmament', there is rather less progressive development of international law than appears to be the case. Good faith implies a persistent readiness to try to achieve an agreement,[136] while the reference to effective measures means that they must result in both an end to the arms race and in disarmament. The difference between the tenets of Article VI and the dispositif in the 1996 Advisory Opinion is indeed 'important', but it is also 'small'.[137]

The Non-aligned Movement has gone further than the International Court of Justice, with those of its members who are States Parties to the NPT (i.e., all except India, North Korea, and Pakistan) arguing that the modernisation of nuclear arsenals is in and of itself a violation of Article VI. Speaking on behalf of the NAM Group in 2013, Indonesia declared that 'in order to comply with their obligations under Article VI of the Treaty', the nuclear-weapon States 'must immediately cease their plans to further invest in modernizing, upgrading, refurbishing, or extending the lives of their nuclear weapons

132 Goldschmidt, 'The Negotiation of the Non-proliferation Treaty (NPT)', p. 77.

133 Ibid.

134 Joyner, 'The Legal Meaning and Implications of Article VI of the Non-proliferation Treaty', p. 397.

135 ICJ, *Legality of the Threat or Use of Nuclear Weapons*, Advisory Opinion, 8 July 1996, para. 105(2), dispositif F.

136 In its 1982 decision in the *Kuwait* v. *Aminoil* arbitration, the Tribunal held that the substance of an 'obligation to negotiate' implied 'sustained upkeep of the negotiations over a period appropriate to the circumstances'. *Arbitration Tribunal: Award in the Matter of an Arbitration between Kuwait and the American Independent Oil Company* (AMINOIL), 24 March 1982; see Joyner, 'The Legal Meaning and Implications of Article VI of the Non-proliferation Treaty', pp. 409–10.

137 Joyner, 'The Legal Meaning and Implications of Article VI of the Non-proliferation Treaty', p. 405.

and related facilities'.[138] The statement further noted the NAM's view 'that the indefinite extension of the Treaty does not imply the indefinite possession' by the nuclear-weapon States of their nuclear arsenals. 'Any assumption of indefinite possession of nuclear weapons is incompatible with the integrity and sustainability of the nuclear non-proliferation regime, both vertical and horizontal, and with the broader objective of maintaining international peace and security.'[139]

The extension of the NPT by the Fifth Review Conference in 1995, discussed below, was only consented to by the non-nuclear-weapon States Parties on the basis of strong language in favour of nuclear disarmament in a separate decision. Thus, it was declared that achievement of the following measures 'is important in the full realization and effective implementation of article VI':

(a) The completion by the Conference on Disarmament of the negotiations on a universal and internationally and effectively verifiable Comprehensive Nuclear-Test-Ban Treaty no later than 1996. Pending the entry into force of a Comprehensive Test-Ban Treaty, the nuclear-weapon States should exercise utmost restraint;
(b) The immediate commencement and early conclusion of negotiations on a non-discriminatory and universally applicable convention banning the production of fissile material for nuclear weapons or other nuclear explosive devices, in accordance with the statement of the Special Coordinator of the Conference on Disarmament and the mandate contained therein;
(c) The determined pursuit by the nuclear-weapon States of systematic and progressive efforts to reduce nuclear weapons globally, with the ultimate goals of eliminating those weapons, and by all States of general and complete disarmament under strict and effective international control.[140]

Modernisation is sometimes considered as falling within the duty to pursue nuclear disarmament rather than pertaining to the arms race.[141] The extent of modernisation programmes, however, and the likelihood of a new nuclear arms race (this time potentially involving also China, in addition to Russia and the United States) make the NAM's interpretation of Article VI considerably more persuasive. In June 2020, Joyner recalled that in 2002 when the Strategic Offensive Reductions Treaty (SORT) was signed with the Russian Federation,

> the mood certainly in the U.S. was that the arms race was over. Now it was just a question of continuing to reduce numbers of deployed nuclear weapons. The war on terror was starting and attention had turned away from Big Power rivalry between the US and Russia.

138 'Cluster 1 Specific Issues: Nuclear Disarmament and Security Assurance', statement by Edi Yusup, Ambassador and Deputy Permanent Representative of the Republic of Indonesia in Geneva, on behalf of the Group of Member States of the Non-aligned Movement Parties to the NPT, Geneva, 25 April 2013, at http://bit.ly/2BvRDbV.

139 Ibid.

140 The CTBT was indeed adopted in 1996, but only after it was submitted to the UN General Assembly for adoption by vote, and it has not entered into force. There has been no concrete progress on the elaboration of a fissile material cut-off treaty.

141 Joyner, 'The Legal Meaning and Implications of Article VI of the Non-proliferation Treaty', p. 411.

> I would say that all changed with the invasion of Ukraine in 2014. After that we have returned to a footing of Big Power rivalry with Russia, and modernization of nuclear stockpiles, along with the death of arms control agreements . . . mean[ing] that we are now in a new arms race.[142]

In a formal Decision of the 1995 Review and Extension Conference, the nuclear-weapon States reaffirmed 'their commitment, as stated in article VI, to pursue in good faith negotiations on effective measures relating to nuclear disarmament'.[143] It was further stated in the Decision that the achievement of a number of measures was 'important in the full realization and effective implementation of article VI'. These measures included '[t]he determined pursuit by the nuclear-weapon States of systematic and progressive efforts to reduce nuclear weapons globally, with the ultimate goals of eliminating those weapons'.[144] The 2000 Review Conference of the NPT formally agreed on the 'practical steps for the systematic and progressive efforts' to implement Article VI, in particular that the 'principle of irreversibility' would 'apply to nuclear disarmament, nuclear and other related arms control and reduction measures'.[145] This may be considered an authoritative interpretation by the States Parties to the NPT of Article VI.[146]

Since the end of the Cold War, the number of nuclear weapons possessed by France, the Russian Federation, the United Kingdom, and the United States have decreased. China's nuclear arsenal is not known with certainty and previous projections have overestimated the number of nuclear warheads it possesses. A United States Defense Intelligence Agency study from 1984 estimated that China had between 150 and 360 nuclear warheads and projected it could increase to more than 800 by 1994. That projection did not come true. Another Defense Intelligence Agency study from 1999 projected that China might have more than 460 nuclear weapons by 2020. That projection also did not come true. The Federation of American Scientists has calculated that from around 180 warheads in the late 1990s, China now has around 300 warheads (operational and in stockpiles).[147]

Successive British governments have stated that, as a 'responsible' nuclear-weapon State and a party to the NPT, since the end of the Cold War they have been reducing the number of nuclear warheads they possess and deploy. This was the case for thirty years until March 2021. The plan set forth in the 2015 Strategic Defence Review was to reduce the number of warheads to 'no more than 180' by the mid-2020s and to reduce operationally available warheads to 120. The United Kingdom stated that it had, since 2010, reduced

[142] Email to the author, 23 June 2020.

[143] Paragraph 3 of Decision 2: 'Principles and Objectives for Nuclear Non-proliferation and Disarmament', Doc. NPT/CONF.1995/32 (Part I), Annex.

[144] Paragraph 4(c) of Decision 2: 'Principles and Objectives for Nuclear Non-proliferation and Disarmament'.

[145] 2000 Review Conference of the Parties to the Treaty on the Non-proliferation of Nuclear Weapons, Final Document, Vol. I, Review of the operation of the Treaty, taking into account the decisions and the resolution adopted by the 1995 Review and Extension Conference, Doc. NPT/CONF.2000/28, 2000, Part I, paragraph 15(5).

[146] See Art. 31(3)(a), Vienna Convention on the Law of Treaties; adopted at Vienna, 23 May 1969; entered into force 27 January 1980.

[147] Hans M. Kristensen and Matt Korda, 'Nuclear Notebook: Chinese Nuclear Forces, 2020', *Bulletin of the Atomic Scientists*, 7 December 2020, at https://bit.ly/3tRUim1.

warheads on each submarine from 48 to 40 and the number of operational missiles on each submarine to not more than 8. The United Kingdom remained, it stated, committed to achieving the long-term reduction in the overall nuclear weapon stockpile. This was evidence, the Ministry of Defence stated, of the United Kingdom's 'leading role in multilateral nuclear disarmament'. This information has now been removed from the Government website on the United Kingdom's nuclear deterrent.

The UK government announced on 16 March 2021 that it could seek to significantly increase its nuclear arsenal.[148] The new cap on the number of warheads in the United Kingdom's nuclear arsenal of 260 is an increase of more than 40 per cent and represents its largest and swiftest increase since the 1960s. The increase was justified on the basis of 'the evolving security environment, including the developing range of technological and doctrinal threats'.[149] This is a vague statement of justification and does not necessarily describe the motivating factors behind the decision.[150]

Speaking on the record in the House of Commons on 22 March 2021, the Secretary of State for Defence, Ben Wallace, defended the increase. He stated that 'on the nuclear deterrent, we do not believe that the changes to the number of warheads in any way breach the nuclear non-proliferation treaty, and that advice is backed up by the Attorney General.'[151] In response to a question from a Member of Parliament, he declined to publish the advice, stating that 'Governments do not publish the Attorney General's advice. We do not believe in any way that we are breaking the nuclear proliferation treaty, and what we really need to do is make sure that we maintain a credible deterrent.'[152]

In a statement to the Conference on Disarmament on 26 March 2021, James Cleverly, Minister of State at the Foreign, Commonwealth and Development Office, declared: 'The UK's unequivocal undertaking, with the other nuclear weapons states, to eliminate our nuclear arsenals persists; as do our obligations under Article 6 of the Non Proliferation Treaty. As such, the UK has taken, and will continue to take, a consistent and leading approach to nuclear disarmament.'[153]

The spokesperson of the Secretary-General of the United Nations (UN) stated on 17 March 2021 that 'we do express our concern at the UK's decision to increase its nuclear weapons arsenal, which is contrary to its obligations under Article VI of the NPT. It could have a damaging impact on global stability and efforts to pursue a world free of nuclear weapons.'[154] The following day, the spokesperson stated that 'while the United Kingdom continues to support the goal of a world free of nuclear weapons and many efforts to

148 HM Government, *Global Britain in a Competitive Age: The Integrated Review of Security, Defence, Development and Foreign Policy*, London, March 2021, at https://bit.ly/3vWpSkw, p. 76.

149 Ibid.

150 M. Harries, 'Why Is the United Kingdom Raising Its Nuclear Stockpile Limits?', *Bulletin of the Atomic Scientists*, 2 April 2021, at https://bit.ly/3fRGioF.

151 'Integrated Review: Defence Command Paper', *Hansard*, Vol. 691, 22 March 2021, at https://bit.ly/3riQmt6, col. 644.

152 Ibid., col. 651.

153 'Conference on Disarmament: Minister Cleverly's Address on the UK Integrated Review', Geneva, 26 March 2021, at https://bit.ly/2PKaV4j.

154 United Nations, 'Daily Press Briefing by the Office of the Spokesperson for the Secretary-General', New York, 17 March 2021, at https://bit.ly/3d9kLoq.

achieve it, we feel this announcement is not consistent with the disarmament commitments all nuclear-weapon States have undertaken'.[155] In response to a question from a journalist, he stated that 'it will be up to the parties to the treaty to express a more legal opinion'.[156]

The Elders are a group of 'independent leaders using their collective experience and influence for peace, justice and human rights worldwide'.[157] The group was founded by Nelson Mandela in 2007. Mary Robinson, the Chair of the Elders, was formerly the UN High Commissioner for Human Rights. She stated:

> The announcement today by the UK Government of its intention to increase by over 40% the cap on its nuclear warhead numbers is surprising and deeply alarming. This would be incompatible with the UK's international obligations to pursue disarmament under the Non-Proliferation Treaty (NPT), and risks contributing to a dangerous new nuclear arms race. It also risks undermining the NPT Review Conference due to take place in August this year.[158]

On 18 March 2021, the German Minister of Foreign Affairs Heiko Maas criticised the United Kingdom's plans to increase its nuclear arsenal in an interview with German news agency *Deutsche Welle*. He stated that 'we don't want nuclear weapons arsenals to grow. If you don't want that to happen, you can't expand them.'[159] Mark Fitzpatrick, from the International Institute of Strategic Studies and a former acting Deputy Assistant Secretary for Non-proliferation in the United States, stated in an interview with the BBC that the United Kingdom announcement was 'not an NPT violation, at least not in the letter of international law, although one could argue that it violates the spirit of the NPT'.[160] Paul O'Neill, Senior Research Fellow in Military Sciences at the Royal United Services Institute (RUSI), stated that 'increasing the nuclear arsenal in a breach of the spirit (at least) of the Non-Proliferation Treaty'.[161]

Under international law, a treaty must be interpreted and applied in good faith. Known by its Latin moniker, *pacta sunt servanda*, the rule exists as a matter of customary international law[162] and treaty law. Under Article 26 of the 1969 Vienna Convention on

155 United Nations, 'Daily Press Briefing by the Office of the Spokesperson for the Secretary-General', New York, 18 March 2021, at https://bit.ly/3tSkSf4.

156 Ibid.

157 The Elders are Ban Ki-moon (Deputy Chair), Lakhdar Brahimi, Gro Harlem Brundtland, Zeid Raad Al Hussein, Hina Jilani, Ellen Johnson Sirleaf, Ricardo Lagos, Graça Machel (Deputy Chair), Juan Manuel Santos, Mary Robinson (Chair) and Ernesto Zedillo. Martti Ahtisaari, Ela Bhatt, Fernando Henrique Cardoso, Jimmy Carter and Desmond Tutu are Elders Emeritus.

158 The Elders, 'UK Nuclear Announcement "Shocking and Alarming" Warn the Elders', London, 16 March 2021.

159 'Exclusive: Germany's Heiko Maas Criticizes UK Plans to Expand Nuclear Arsenal', *Deutsche Welle*, 18 March 2021, at https://bit.ly/3d2yZrj.

160 BBC News (Reality Check team), 'Integrated Review: Fact-Checking Claims about the Army, Aid and Nuclear Weapons', 16 March 2021, at https://bbc.in/31eIUnZ.

161 P. O'Neill, 'The UK's Integrated Review: Seeing through a Glass Darkly', Commentary, RUSI website, 18 March 2021, at https://bit.ly/3m4fvXf.

162 J. Salmon, 'Article 26 (1969)' in O. Corten and P. Klein (eds.), *The Vienna Conventions on the Law of Treaties: A Commentary*, Oxford University Press, Oxford, 2011.

the Law of Treaties, 'Every treaty in force is binding upon the parties to it and must be performed by them in good faith.'[163] Article 27 of the Convention stipulates that: 'A party may not invoke the provisions of its internal law as justification for its failure to perform a treaty.' This is also a rule of customary international law.[164] The United Kingdom is a State Party to the Vienna Convention on the Law of Treaties.

Unless and until the legal advice of the Attorney-General for England and Wales is published, it is not possible to parse or analyse the text. But in September 2020, it was reported that the Attorney-General had seemingly argued, in relation to another treaty binding on the United Kingdom, that domestic law could override international legal obligations:

> All law officers agree that it is an established principle of international law that a state, acting through its executive government, is obliged to discharge its treaty obligations in good faith. ... However in the difficult circumstances in which we find ourselves, the attorney general and solicitor general consider it is important to remember that an established principle of international law is subordinate to the much more fundamental principle of parliamentary sovereignty.[165]

A good faith interpretation of Article VI is that no nuclear-weapon State may seek to provoke or act to cause a new nuclear arms race. Following the UK announcement, Russia stated that it would take the change in United Kingdom nuclear policy into account when working on its own military planning. Kremlin spokesman Dmitry Peskov stated: 'We are very sorry that Britain has chosen the path of increasing the number of nuclear warheads. This decision will harm international stability and strategic security.'[166] German Foreign Minister Heiko Maas stated: 'The past has shown that if one side has more nuclear weapons, the other side will try to catch up. And that is the disastrous arms race we have been in for decades.' He further stressed the importance of international treaties in that regard, stating that people must be able to count on them limiting arsenals and prohibiting their expansion.[167]

A good faith interpretation of Article VI is that each nuclear-weapon State must engage in negotiations on nuclear disarmament in good faith. In 1996, the International Court of Justice determined, by unanimous agreement among its judges, that 'there exists an obligation to pursue in good faith and bring to a conclusion negotiations leading to nuclear disarmament in all its aspects under strict and effective international control'.[168]

163 Art. 26, Vienna Convention on the Law of Treaties.

164 A. Schaus, 'Article 27 (1969)' in Corten and Klein (eds.), *The Vienna Conventions on the Law of Treaties: A Commentary*.

165 Reported in P. Lewis and O. Bowcott, 'Government's Top Legal Advisers Divided over Move to Override Brexit Deal', *The Guardian*, 10 September 2020, at https://bit.ly/3ckHy1z. The text published by the Government differed slightly but materially: 'However, in the difficult and highly exceptional circumstances in which we find ourselves, it is important to remember the fundamental principle of Parliamentary sovereignty.' 'HMG Legal Position: UKIM Bill and Northern Ireland Protocol', at https://bit.ly/3vY8Tyl.

166 Reported in A. Forrest, 'Russia Condemns UK Plan to Increase Nuclear Weapons as Threat to "International Stability"', *The Independent*, 17 March 2021, at https://bit.ly/3lNrJ6J.

167 'Germany's Heiko Maas Criticizes UK Plans to Expand Nuclear Arsenal', Deutsche Welle, 18 March 2021.

168 International Court of Justice, *Legality of the Threat or Use of Nuclear Weapons*, Advisory Opinion, 8 July 1996, para. 105(2), dispositif F.

The increase in any nuclear-weapon State's nuclear arsenal runs counter to this obligation. In announcing the increase in the United Kingdom nuclear arsenal, the British Prime Minister, Boris Johnson, stated that 'we're committed to nuclear arms reduction, and indeed we believe that China should be brought into strategic nuclear arms reduction'.[169]

Both China and the United Kingdom will be in violation of the NPT by the fact and manner of increases in the number of nuclear weapons they hold. Expanding the size of nuclear arsenals contravenes the obligations in Article VI, at the least when this is not accompanied by initiation or engagement in good faith negotiations on nuclear disarmament. In June 2020, a joint paper by the European Leadership Network and the Centre for Science and Security Studies at King's College London noted the 'lack of significant steps towards nuclear disarmament over the past five years'.[170] Provoking a renewed nuclear arms race would be a serious violation of the NPT.

NPT REVIEW CONFERENCES

Article VIII(3) of the NPT provided that five years after its entry into force, 'a conference of Parties to the Treaty shall be held in Geneva, Switzerland, in order to review the operation of this Treaty with a view to assuring that the purposes of the Preamble and the provisions of the Treaty are being realised'. The First Review Conference was therefore obligatory. The paragraph continued by offering the opportunity, at 'intervals of five years thereafter' and if a simple majority of the States Parties agree – by the agency of a proposal to this effect submitted to the three depositary States – to convene 'further conferences with the same objective of reviewing the operation of the Treaty'. In fact, entering into force in 1970, conferences to review the NPT have been convened every five years since the First Conference in 1975. This was so, until the 2020 conference was postponed for public health reasons, owing to the global COVID-19 pandemic.

There was significant concern from the early days of the Treaty that it would not be successful in stemming horizontal proliferation. But the lack of progress in stemming vertical proliferation, addressed in Article VI, was also a huge concern. Thus the Final Declaration of the First Review Conference noted that the nuclear arms race was continuing 'unabated', with claims made back in 1975 in the aftermath of the Conference that 'the treaty seems weaker and in greater peril today than at any time since its approval'.[171]

The Fifth Review Conference in 1995 had an especially important task – 'the ultimate test', in one commentator's words[172] – which was to determine whether the Treaty would come to an end at a certain point in time or endure. Article X(2) of the NPT had stipulated that twenty-five years after its entry into force, 'a conference shall be convened to decide whether the Treaty shall continue in force indefinitely, or shall be extended for an

[169] W. James, 'China Should Be Brought into Strategic Nuclear Arms Reductions – UK PM Johnson', Reuters, 16 March 2021, at https://bit.ly/3tQndqI.

[170] Shatabhisha Shetty and Heather Williams, *The P5 Process: Opportunities for Success in the NPT Review Conference*, European Leadership Network and the Centre for Science and Security Studies at King's College London, London, June 2020, at https://bit.ly/3i2ZjCD, p. 11.

[171] Epstein, *The Last Chance: Nuclear Proliferation and Arms Control*, p. 124.

[172] Woodliffe, 'Nuclear Weapons and Non-proliferation: The Legal Aspects', p. 101.

additional fixed period or periods'. In accordance with the provision, the decision would be taken by a simple majority of the States Parties. The 1995 Review and Extension Conference of the Parties to the NPT was held on 17 April–12 May 1995 in New York. The decision was taken that, 'as a majority exists among States party to the Treaty for its indefinite extension, . . . the Treaty shall continue in force indefinitely'.[173]

The States Parties also decided at the Fifth Review Conference, in accordance with the power granted in Article VIII(3) of the NPT, 'that Review Conferences should continue to be held every five years and that, accordingly, the next Review Conference should be held in the year 2000'.[174] That review conference, the Treaty's sixth, managed to reach agreement on a final document. In it, the Conference 'deplore[d] the nuclear test explosions carried out by India and then by Pakistan in 1998' and declared that 'such actions do not in any way confer a nuclear-weapon-State status or any special status whatsoever'.[175] The Sixth Review Conference noted with concern that the IAEA 'continues to be unable to verify the correctness and completeness of the initial declaration of nuclear material made by the Democratic People's Republic of Korea, and is therefore unable to conclude that there has been no diversion of nuclear material in that country'.[176] The Conference further recalled the 'unequivocal undertaking by the nuclear-weapon States' at the Fourth Review Conference 'to accomplish the total elimination of their nuclear arsenals leading to nuclear disarmament, to which all States parties are committed under article VI'.[177]

The latest review conference of the Treaty – its tenth – had been due to take place in New York in April to May 2020. As of this writing, the conference was expected to take place at some undefined point in early 2022, still in New York, at least as things stood. Whether the outcome of the Conference would be positive – depending on how one defines success in the febrile atmosphere permeating global arms control – remained unclear as of this writing. In 2005, during the Bush presidency in the United States, States Parties had been unable to agree on the text of an outcome document. The failure of the Ninth Review Conference in 2015 to produce a consensus outcome document was attributed rather to discussions around the establishment of a zone free of weapons of mass destruction in the Middle East, an issue linked to a resolution adopted at the 1995 NPT Review and Extension Conference.[178]

[173] Decision 3: 'Extension of the Treaty on the Non-proliferation of Nuclear Weapons', Doc. NPT/CONF.1995/32 (Part I), Annex. Arguably, the fact that the Fifth Review Conference was being held in the aftermath of the end of the Cold War, with huge concomitant reductions in the nuclear arsenals held by both the Russian Federation and the United States since 1987, was fortuitous timing from the perspective of the nuclear-weapon States. In the absence of such reductions, it is questionable whether objections to the permanent extension of the Treaty might have been louder and broader.

[174] Decision 1: 'Strengthening the Review Process for the Treaty', Doc. NPT/CONF.1995/32 (Part I), Annex.

[175] 2000 Review Conference of the Parties to the Treaty on the Non-proliferation of Nuclear Weapons, Final Document, Vol. I, Part I, 'Articles I and II and first to third preambular paragraphs', para. 9.

[176] Ibid., 'Article III and fourth and fifth preambular paragraphs, especially in their relationship to article IV and the sixth and seventh preambular paragraphs', para. 14.

[177] Ibid., 'Article VI and eighth to twelfth preambular paragraphs', para. 15.

[178] According to the head of the United Kingdom's delegation, 'this issue and this issue alone was the stumbling block'. W. Wan, 'Why the 2015 NPT Review Conference Fell Apart', article, United Nations University, 28 May 2015, at http://bit.ly/2Lt8LVe.

It was widely believed that the Tenth Review Conference might also not be able to agree upon a final declaration. In a joint paper published at the end of June 2020, King's College London's Centre for Science and Security Studies and the European Leadership Network acknowledged that a 'lack of significant steps towards nuclear disarmament over the past five years' risked 'derailing' the Review Conference.[179] The report called on the five permanent members of the UN Security Council to 'clearly demonstrate their support for Article VI and that their disarmament obligations are being taken seriously despite setbacks'. The P5 should, the report affirmed, 'restate' their commitment to Article VI and explicitly inform the non-nuclear-weapon States 'how they will move forward with Article VI commitments as opposed to discussing this in the abstract'.

CONCLUDING REMARKS

How one views the NPT depends, in part, on whether it is an end in itself or rather, in Woodliffe's words, a 'means to an end, namely, general and complete disarmament'.[180] It has been argued that the primary ambition for the NPT among the nuclear-weapon States was to 'freeze' the status quo with regard to possession of nuclear weapons.[181] Seen in those terms, the conclusion and implementation of the Treaty represented 'a major success' for both the Soviet Union and the United States. During the negotiations, Epstein recalls, one US diplomat conceded privately that the NPT was one of the 'greatest con games of modern times'.[182] The two global superpowers had 'succeeded, if not in imposing this "nuclear Yalta", then at least in getting it accepted, by conjuring up the spectre of the threat to world peace if countries not possessing nuclear weapons were to acquire them.'[183] While this approach would work for most States, it would not work for all.

India, smarting from military humiliation in 1962 at the hands of its Chinese neighbour, was confronted with the reality of China becoming a nuclear-armed power just two years later. It would ultimately decide not to join the NPT in the absence of a firm commitment by the nuclear powers to disarm, and chose instead to acquire a nuclear capability. Pakistan saw nuclear weapons as an essential deterrent to conventional military action by India and believed that it would counterbalance the significant imbalance in conventional forces between the two nations. Israel determined that its survival should be guaranteed by becoming a nuclear-armed power; for analogous though sharply distinct reasons, North Korea would arrive at the same decision four decades later. None is a State Party to the NPT – North Korea having effectively withdrawn in 2003 – and none is likely to adhere any time soon.

Undeniably, the NPT 'has played, and continues to play, a crucial role in limiting nuclear arsenals in the world, and to limiting the number of States that have access to these

[179] Centre for Science and Security Studies of King's College London and the European Leadership Network, *The P5 Process: Opportunities for Success in the NPT Review Conference*, London, June 2020, p. 11.

[180] Woodliffe, 'Nuclear Weapons and Non-proliferation: The Legal Aspects', p. 87.

[181] Nystuen and Graff Hugo, 'The Nuclear Non-proliferation Treaty', p. 393.

[182] Epstein, *The Last Chance: Nuclear Proliferation and Arms Control*, p. 118.

[183] Goldschmidt, 'The Negotiation of the Non-proliferation Treaty (NPT)', p. 80.

weapons'.[184] In those terms, it has been a considerable success. But whether it will continue to play this role depends to a large extent on whether serious efforts are made by the nuclear-armed States to end the new nuclear arms race and make serious efforts towards comprehensive nuclear disarmament.

In March 2020, to celebrate the fiftieth anniversary of the Treaty's entry into force, the five nuclear-weapon States Parties declared that the NPT 'has provided the essential foundation for international efforts to stem the looming threat – then and now – that nuclear weapons would proliferate across the globe. In so doing, it has served the interests of all its Parties.'[185] Whether this persists for the next fifty years remains to be seen. 'As a norm', wrote two experts in 2014, the Treaty 'remains unimpressive'.[186] While enduring reports of its demise have, so far, been exaggerated, the future success of the NPT is inextricably linked to a renewed and genuine commitment towards nuclear disarmament.

184 Nystuen and Graff Hugo, 'The Nuclear Non-proliferation Treaty', pp. 392–93.

185 'Fiftieth Anniversary of the Treaty on the Non-proliferation of Nuclear Weapons', Joint Statement by the Foreign Ministers of China, France, Russia, the United Kingdom and the United States, 10 March 2020, at http://bit.ly/3dyEnkl.

186 Nystuen and Graff Hugo, 'The Nuclear Non-proliferation Treaty', p. 396.

4

The Testing of Nuclear Weapons

Since July 1945, more than 2,000 nuclear explosive devices have been detonated in tests in more than 60 different locations.[1] Nuclear weapons or other nuclear explosive devices have been detonated on or above the ground (termed atmospheric tests), underground, underwater, and in outer space.[2] They have been exploded on the top of towers, on board ships or barges, when suspended from balloons, at depths of 600 metres underwater, and at depths of more than 2,400 metres underground. In addition to the dropping of bombs from aircraft, nuclear weapons have been fired by rockets into space and exploded at altitudes of more than 400 kilometres above the earth's surface.[3]

The precise number of nuclear detonations is not known as a number of tests were conducted in secret or involved the detonation of multiple devices but were not reported as such. But through to the conclusion of the Comprehensive Nuclear-Test-Ban Treaty (CTBT)[4] in 1996, the United States conducted some 1,000 tests (ending in 1992); the Soviet Union carried out more than 700 tests between 1949 and 1990; France carried out more than 200 tests between 1960 and 1996; the United Kingdom carried out 45 tests between 1952 and 1991; and China carried out 45 tests between 1964 and 1996.[5] India detonated a nuclear explosive device in 1974, while Israel is believed to have conducted at least one nuclear test detonation (in 1979), possibly in concert with South Africa.[6]

1 This figure excludes the approximately 160 detonations conducted for 'peaceful purposes', as described in Chapter 2, but does include test detonations conducted by the Soviet Union as part of its research into the design of devices for its Nuclear Explosions for the National Economy programme.

2 A test is deemed atmospheric until the point of detonation reaches the Kármán line, which is generally considered to represent the boundary between Earth's atmosphere and outer space. Usually set at 100 kilometres in altitude, more recently it has been proposed to define the boundary at 80 kilometres above sea level. J. C. McDowell, 'The Edge of Space: Revisiting the Karman Line', *Acta Astronautica*, Vol. 151 (October 2018), 668–77, at http://bit.ly/2MzqYxl.

3 Preparatory Commission for the Comprehensive Nuclear-Test-Ban Treaty Organization (CTBTO), 'Types of Nuclear Weapons Tests', accessed 1 June 2020 at http://bit.ly/3cFhQl2.

4 Comprehensive Nuclear-Test-Ban Treaty; adopted at New York, 10 September 1996; not yet in force.

5 Preparatory Commission for the CTBTO, 'History of Nuclear Testing: World Overview', accessed 1 June 2020 at http://bit.ly/2z9YBm5.

6 J. Borger, 'The Truth about Israel's Secret Nuclear Arsenal', *The Guardian*, 15 January 2014, at http://bit.ly/30aMxwb.

The total yield of nuclear tests conducted in the 50 years following the first in 1945 has been estimated at some 510 MT,[7] equivalent in TNT yield to 34,000 Hiroshima-size bombs. Atmospheric tests have accounted for more than 80 per cent of all explosive yield.[8]

Since the CTBT was adopted by the UN General Assembly in 1996, banning all nuclear explosive tests, seventeen further tests have been conducted in three States. India conducted a series of five tests over two days in May 1998[9] and Pakistan conducted a total of six tests over a two-day period later the same month.[10] The Democratic People's Republic of Korea (North Korea) conducted one nuclear test in 2006, 2009, and 2013; two in 2016 (in January and September); and one (a thermonuclear device) in early September 2017.[11] Following this last nuclear explosive test, Lassina Zerbo, Executive Secretary of the Preparatory Commission for the Comprehensive Nuclear-Test-Ban Treaty Organization (CTBTO), declared in Vienna, 'I sincerely hope that this will serve as the final wake-up call to the international community to outlaw all nuclear testing by bringing the CTBT into force.'[12]

NUCLEAR TESTING BY THE NPT NUCLEAR-WEAPON STATES

This section summarises nuclear testing by the five nuclear-weapon States designated by the Treaty on the Non-proliferation of Nuclear Weapons[13] (NPT): the five permanent members of the UN Security Council.

Nuclear Testing by the United States

The Trinity test of 16 July 1945, as described in Chapter 1, was the world's first detonation of a nuclear explosive device. Following the Trinity test, the United States conducted

7 C. E. Paine, T. B. Cochran, and R. S. Norris, 'The Arsenals of the Nuclear Weapon Powers: An Overview', Natural Resources Defense Council, Washington, DC, 4 January 19, at https://bit.ly/3acHJL8, Table 6: Nuclear Milestones.

8 See ibid.

9 Shakti I was a two-stage thermonuclear device with fusion boosted primary, intended for a missile warhead; the test design yield was a reported 45 kt. Shakti II was a pure fission tactical bomb/missile warhead, with a 12 kt design yield. The other three detonations were of experimental devices and so are not counted by certain authorities. Shakti III was a fission device, reportedly made with reactor-grade plutonium. It may have been a fusion boosted design without the fusion fuel. The design yield was 0.3 kt. Shakti IV was a 0.5 kt experimental device while Shakti V was a 0.2 kt experimental device. 'India's Nuclear Weapons Program. Operation Shakti: 1998', *Nuclear Weapon Archive*, last updated 30 March 2001, at http://bit.ly/2Ct3XKJ.

10 On 28 May 1998, five nuclear explosive devices were detonated simultaneously underground at the test site in the Chagai district of Baluchistan province in western Pakistan. The explosive yields are not known with any degree of reliability. C. Sublette, 'Pakistan's Nuclear Weapons Program. 1998: The Year of Testing', *Nuclear Weapon Archive*, last updated 10 September 2001, at http://bit.ly/30YYgyf.

11 Preparatory Commission for the CTBTO, 'History of Nuclear Testing: World Overview'. See also Preparatory Commission for the CTBTO, 'DPRK Nuclear Tests', accessed 1 June 2020 at http://bit.ly/3bxvveu.

12 Preparatory Commission for the CTBTO, 'CTBTO Executive Secretary Lassina Zerbo on the Unusual Seismic Event Detected in the Democratic People's Republic of Korea', accessed 1 June 2020 at http://bit.ly/3h2b1xr.

13 Treaty on the Non-proliferation of Nuclear Weapons; opened for signature at London, Moscow, and Washington, DC, 1 July 1968; entered into force 5 March 1970 (hereinafter, NPT).

nuclear tests between 1945 and 1992: at the Nevada Test Site; in Colorado, Mississippi, and New Mexico; in Amchitka Island of the Alaska peninsula; and at sites in the Pacific Ocean.[14] In the state of Nevada, tests were conducted in the atmosphere until 1962 and were even something of a tourist attraction.[15] On 19 May 1953, the United States conducted the 'Harry' nuclear test at the Nevada Test Site, one of a series of eleven tests dubbed Operation Upshot-Knothole. The 32 kt detonation generated more radioactive fallout than any other continental US test, leading the test to be later nicknamed 'Dirty Harry', in an ironic reference to the 1971 film starring Clint Eastwood.[16]

Between 1946 and 1958, the United States carried out 67 nuclear weapons tests at Bikini and Enewetak atolls in the Marshall Islands, a set of 29 atolls halfway between Australia and Hawaii. The atolls were some of the main sites included in the so-called Pacific Proving Grounds. The populations of Bikini and Enewetak had been relocated to other atolls before the testing with a view to ensuring their safety. But following the detonation of the 15 MT Castle Bravo test on 1 March 1954, the most powerful nuclear device ever detonated by the United States, fallout was unexpectedly deposited on the surrounding atolls of Rongelap and Utrik. Other atolls to the east and south-east of Bikini atoll were all affected. The fallout contaminated an area of more than 11,000 square kilometres, spreading radioactive material as far as Australia, India, Japan, the United States, and even parts of Europe.

A few hours after the explosion, fallout from the explosion began sprinkling over a Japanese fishing boat, *Lucky Dragon Number* 5. The fallout consisted of coral rock, soil, and other debris sucked up in the fireball and rendered intensely radioactive by the nuclear reaction. The boat was some 145 kilometres downwind of the explosion point at the time. Many of the Lucky Dragon's crew became ill, and one crew member died. Several of the 64 inhabitants of Rongelap experienced immediate radiation sickness, including vomiting, skin damage, and hair loss. By the time they were evacuated from the area, 2 days after the detonation of the Castle Bravo device, some of the islanders had received 175 rads from gamma radiation and 160 rads from iodine-131.[17]

On 9 July 1962, the United States conducted the 'Starfish Prime' nuclear test, one of a series of five aimed at testing the effects of nuclear weapons in outer space. The explosion, which occurred 400 kilometres above the Johnston atoll in the Northern Pacific ocean, had an explosive yield of 1.45 MT. The test experimented with radiation belts in the Earth's magnetosphere, known as Van Allen belts. The crucial role of these belts in shielding life from solar winds was not fully understood until later.[18] The test-detonation temporarily altered the shape and intensity of the lower Van Allen belt while

14 Preparatory Commission for the CTBTO, 'The United States' Nuclear Testing Programme'.

15 R. Braithwaite, *Armageddon and Paranoia: The Nuclear Confrontation*, Profile Books, London, 2019, p. 274.

16 Preparatory Commission for the CTBTO, '19 May 1953 – Dirty Harry', accessed 1 June 2020 at http://bit.ly/2MBa9Sz.

17 Preparatory Commission for the CTBTO, 'The United States' Nuclear Testing Programme'. A dose of 100 to 200 rads delivered to the entire body in less than a day may cause acute radiation syndrome. It is usually not fatal.

18 Preparatory Commission for the CTBTO, '9 July 1962: "Starfish Prime", Outer Space', accessed 1 June 2020 at http://bit.ly/2zdZOZK.

the electro-magnetic pulse (EMP) produced by the explosion caused significant damage to both civilian and military electrical systems throughout the Hawaiian Islands, more than 800 miles away from Ground Zero. The effects were such that physicist Lowell Wood declared that if the test had taken place at the Nevada Test Site, the consequences 'would still be indelibly imprinted in the minds of citizenry of the western US, as well as in history books'.[19]

Tests were not only of the devices themselves. In Operation Desert Rock, the aim of the series of tests that were conducted at the Nevada Proving Grounds between 1951 and 1957, was to assess the operational ability of US soldiers to fight on irradiated battlegrounds. A declassified US Army report on the tests stated that 'Exercise Desert Rock I marked the first time that . . . troops have had the opportunity to receive realistic training in the tactical aspects of atomic warfare. . . . By the end of the project, the American troops had participated in eight separate Desert Rock events . . . which all involved nuclear detonations.'[20]

In 1990, President George H. W. Bush signed into law the Radiation Exposure Compensation Act. Under the legislation, anyone who worked on atmospheric nuclear tests, including the Desert Rock exercises, could receive a one-time payment of $75,000.[21]

The United States announced a national moratorium on nuclear testing in 1992 under the presidency of Bill Clinton. In May 2020, the Trump administration is believed to have contemplated the resumption of explosive nuclear testing.[22] A month later, it was reported that the Senate Armed Services Committee had set aside $10 million for fiscal year 2021, with a view to speeding up preparations for a new nuclear test, should one be ordered.[23]

Nuclear Testing by the Soviet Union

In 1949, Kazakhstan was the site of the first nuclear weapon test detonation by the Soviet Union. Tests were later conducted in the mountainous Russian archipelago of Novaya Zemlya in the Arctic, in the Urals, and at the Semipalatinsk Test Site in Kazakhstan. Between 1949 and 1989, more than 450 atomic and thermonuclear devices were exploded at the Semipalatinsk Test Site. Five surface tests were unsuccessful, resulting in the dispersion of plutonium into the environment, while the first test on 29 August 1949 is said to have 'unexpectedly' contaminated villages north-east of the Site.[24]

More than 300 test explosions were conducted underground after 1961. Semipalatinsk's Degelen mountain test facility was the largest underground nuclear test site in the world, consisting of 181 separate tunnels. Between October 1961 and October 1989, 224 tests were

[19] Statement by Dr Lowell Wood, Subcommittee on Government Programs and Oversight of the Committee on Small Business, House of Representatives, Washington, DC, 1 June 1999, at http://bit.ly/2Ad6Dem.

[20] Cited in J. Trevithick, 'During the 1950s, the Pentagon Played War Games with Troops and Nukes', *Medium*, 20 April 2015, at http://bit.ly/2ZRzHCT.

[21] Ibid.

[22] J. Hudson and P. Sonne, 'Trump Administration Discussed Conducting First U.S. Nuclear Test in Decades', *Washington Post*, 23 May 2020, at http://wapo.st/2yv76ba.

[23] Arms Control Association, 'Reaction to White House Nuclear Testing Proposal Strongly Negative', *Issue Briefs*, Vol. 12, No. 4 (16 June 2020), at http://bit.ly/3hMiYHp.

[24] Preparatory Commission for the CTBTO, 'The Soviet Union's Nuclear Testing Programme', accessed 1 June 2020 at http://bit.ly/2XEMwif.

conducted therein.[25] The last test, which took place on 12 February 1989, is said to have resulted in leakage of large amounts of xenon and krypton. Effective dose estimates due to external and internal exposure attributable to the 1949 and 1953 tests in villages near the test zones range from 70 mSv to 4,470 mSv.[26]

On 14 September 1954, near the village of Totskoye in the Ural mountains 600 miles south-east of Moscow, the Soviet armed forces air-detonated a 20 kt bomb as part of a military exercise. The detonation was deliberately close to where 45,000 Red Army troops and thousands of civilians were gathered. The purpose of the exercise, which was filmed, was to assess the extent to which troops could fight in an area immediately after it had been hit by an atomic bomb. The film documents the explosion and its aftermath, showing soldiers with little or no protective gear running through 'an inferno of dust, heat and radiation'.[27] In *The Red Bomb*, a television documentary from 1994, Ivan Skvortsov and Vasily Kovalyov, two Soviet Army veterans who took part in the Totskoye exercise, described their experiences. Dr Nikolay Sidorov reported that the number of people suffering from tumorous illnesses in the province increased by 500 per cent between 1950 and 1994.[28]

Consisting of two islands approximately 450 kilometres from the Arctic Circle, Novaya Zemlya was inhabited by nomadic peoples and large numbers of reindeer before nuclear testing started. Around 500 people were relocated due to the testing programme. Between 1954 and 1990, 130 nuclear tests were conducted at Novaya Zemlya: in the atmosphere, underground, and in the surrounding oceans. Although the site accounts for only one quarter of all Soviet testing, the aggregate yield of tests at Novaya Zemlya is estimated at 273 MT, representing 94 per cent of the total yield for all Soviet tests. The 'Tsar Bomba' device alone, which was dropped by a Tupolev Tu-95 heavy bomber in October 1961 on Mityushikha Bay on the island of Severny in the Arctic Circle, accounted for a yield of 57 MT. The top of the mushroom cloud was more than 65 kilometres above ground.[29] Testing on Novaya Zemlya represents the greatest single source of artificial radioactive contamination throughout the Arctic.[30]

25 Ibid.

26 B. I. Gusev, Z. N. Abylkassimova, and K. N. Apsalikov, 'The Semipalatinsk Nuclear Test Site: A First Assessment of the Radiological Situation and the Test-Related Radiation Doses in the Surrounding Territories', *Radiation Environmental Biophysics*, Vol. 36, No. 3 (September 1997), 201–4.

27 M. Simons, 'Soviet Atom Test Used Thousands as Guinea Pigs, Archives Show', *New York Times*, 7 November 1993, at http://bit.ly/3gZDQut. Pravda reported on the exercise at the time: 'The purpose of the test was to examine the effects of nuclear explosion. Valuable results have been obtained that will help Soviet scientists and engineers to successfully solve the task of protecting the country from nuclear attack.' *Pravda*, 17 September 1954.

28 E. Carter, 'The Soviets Trained to Fight under Nuclear Detonations. Soldiers Suffered as a Result', *War Is Boring*, 7 February 2015, at http://bit.ly/3h5WYHs.

29 National World War Two Museum New Orleans, 'Tsar Bomba: The Largest Atomic Test in World History', 29 August 2020, at http://bit.ly/3qigFzQ. In August 2020, Rosatom State Atomic Energy Corporation (Russia's national atomic agency) released forty minutes of previously classified footage, showing the bomb's journey from manufacture to detonation. See the YouTube video at https://bit.ly/3agmh87; and B. Specktor, 'Russia Declassifies Footage of "Tsar Bomba" – The Most Powerful Nuclear Bomb in History', Live Science, 31 August 2020, at http://bit.ly/3dfliXT.

30 Preparatory Commission for the CTBTO, 'The Soviet Union's Nuclear Testing Programme'.

Nuclear Testing by the United Kingdom

The United Kingdom conducted twelve atmospheric tests between 1952 and 1957 on Australian territories at Emu Field, Maralinga, and Monte Bello Island. In 1957–58, nine atmospheric test detonations occurred over Christmas Island (Kiritimati) and Malden Island in the central Pacific Ocean. The remaining twenty-four UK nuclear tests were conducted jointly with the United States at its Nevada Test Site.[31] In addition to the test detonations, a long series of 'minor trials' were performed at Maralinga (as many as six hundred), which were designed to test the safety and security of British nuclear weapons in case of an accident. Considerable contamination resulted, with plumes of radioactive material in the form of fine particles spread over a wide area of the test range and, in some cases, beyond it. Maralinga was contaminated with approximately 8 tons of uranium, 24 kg of plutonium, and 100 kg of beryllium.[32]

'Operation Grapple' consisted of nine detonations over Christmas Island and Malden Island in the South Pacific (both now part of the State of Kiribati) in 1957 and 1958.[33] The Grapple X test on 8 November 1957 saw a thermonuclear detonation equating to 1.8 MT.[34] On 28 April 1958, in the Grapple Y test, a Royal Air Force plane dropped the United Kingdom's largest ever hydrogen bomb, a 3 MT detonation.

The British government has refused to pay any compensation to the soldiers from Fiji, Kiribati, New Zealand, and the United Kingdom present at the test detonations, arguing that the tests caused no ill effects and maintaining that there is no conclusive link between the tests and the high rates of cancer suffered among veterans.[35] No nuclear weapon was ever test-detonated on British metropolitan territory.

Nuclear Testing by France

France detonated its first nuclear explosive device in Algeria on 13 February 1960 at a site in the Sahara 50 kilometres south of Reggane. Named '*Gerboise bleue*' ('blue jerboa') in a reference that combined the hue of the tricolour French flag with a small rodent living in the Sahara, the device detonated with an explosive yield of 70 kt.[36] Over the next five years, France conducted seventeen nuclear weapons tests at two locations in Algeria. Four were atmospheric tests while the remainder of the devices were detonated underground.[37]

France's other 193 test detonations occurred at Moruroa and Fangataufa atolls in French Polynesia. In 2013, declassified French Ministry of Defence documents revealed that nuclear

31 Preparatory Commission for the CTBTO, 'The United Kingdom's Nuclear Testing Programme', accessed 1 June 2020 at http://bit.ly/3czjYuQ.

32 Report by the Maralinga Rehabilitation Technical Advisory Committee (MARTAC) on the Rehabilitation of Former Nuclear Test Sites at Emu and Maralinga (Australia), 2003.

33 See, e.g., R. Gibson, 'Operation Grapple: The Groundbreaking British Nuclear Test Series', *ArcGIS Story Maps*, 1 November 2019, at http://bit.ly/2MDoFck.

34 Preparatory Commission for the CTBTO, 'The United Kingdom's Nuclear Testing Programme'.

35 J. Tahana, 'For Veterans of British Nuclear Tests, a 60-Year Fight for Recognition Goes On', *RNZ Radio*, 29 April 2018, at http://bit.ly/3cHnogq.

36 J. Magdaleno, 'Algerians Suffering from French Atomic Legacy, 55 Years after Nuke Tests', *Aljazeera*, 1 March 2015, at http://bit.ly/2UW3KFs.

37 Preparatory Commission for the CTBTO, 'France's Nuclear Testing Programme', accessed 1 June 2020 at http://bit.ly/2UjsQhK.

tests in the South Pacific in the 1960s and 1970s had been far more toxic than previously acknowledged, affecting a vast swath of Polynesia with nuclear fallout. As Chapter 8 recalls, France's public pledges in the early 1970s that it would cease atmospheric testing in the Pacific were deemed by the International Court of Justice to be binding upon them under international law. France ratified the CTBT in 1998 and closed its nuclear test site in the Pacific.[38]

No nuclear weapon was ever test-detonated on French metropolitan territory.

Nuclear Testing by China

As described in Chapter 1, Operation 59-6 was carried out on 16 October 1964 at the Lop Nur test site in the Gobi desert in Xinjiang province. The device's detonation, which produced an explosive yield of 22 kt,[39] was the first of 45 Chinese nuclear tests, all of which were conducted at Lop Nur. Twenty-three of the tests were atmospheric with the remainder conducted underground, generating explosive yields ranging from 1 kt to 4 MT.[40] The largest atmospheric test of 4 MT is said to have been conducted on 17 November 1976; China's largest underground test, on 21 May 1992, was of 660 kt.[41]

The total amount of plutonium-239 released to the atmosphere as a result of the 23 atmospheric nuclear tests is estimated at 3,300 curies, representing approximately 48 kg of ^{239}Pu in weight.[42] One-millionth of a gram of plutonium, one of the world's most poisonous substances, can cause cancer if inhaled. A modelling study by a Japanese doctor published in 2009 claimed that as many as 190,000 people might already have died as a result of China's testing.[43]

THE INTERNATIONAL LEGAL REGIMES FOR NUCLEAR TESTING

The regulation of nuclear testing under international law is spread across a range of treaties: the 1959 Antarctic Treaty,[44] the 1963 Partial Test-Ban Treaty,[45] the 1966 Outer Space Treaty, the 1974 Threshold Test-Ban Treaty,[46] the CTBT, adopted in 1996, and most recently, the 2017 Treaty on the Prohibition of Nuclear Weapons. In addition, several

38 A. Chrisafis, 'French Nuclear Tests "Showered Vast Area of Polynesia with Radioactivity"', *The Guardian*, 3 July 2013, at http://bit.ly/2Ul5mJ9.

39 Preparatory Commission for the CTBTO, '16 October 1964 – First Chinese Nuclear Test', accessed 1 June 2020 at http://bit.ly/2MssQYv.

40 Preparatory Commission for the CTBTO, 'China's Nuclear Testing Programme', accessed 1 June 2020 at http://bit.ly/2AOZIYJ.

41 Ibid.

42 IPPNW, *Radioactive Heaven and Earth: The Health and Environmental Effects of Nuclear Weapons Testing in, on, and above the Earth*, Apex Press, New York, 1991.

43 S. Das, 'China's Nuclear Tests Allegedly Caused 190k Deaths', *Digital Journal*, 20 April 2009, at http://bit.ly/3h1oa6Y.

44 The Antarctic Treaty; adopted at Washington, DC, 1 December 1959; entered into force 23 June 1962.

45 Treaty Banning Nuclear Weapon Tests in the Atmosphere, in Outer Space and Under Water; opened for signature at London, Moscow, and Washington, DC, 8 August 1963; entered into force 10 October 1963.

46 Treaty between the United States of America and the Union of Soviet Socialist Republics on the Limitation of Underground Nuclear Weapon Tests (and Protocol Thereto); signed at Moscow, 3 July 1974; entered into force 11 December 1990.

States (most notably India and Pakistan) have made political commitments not to test-detonate nuclear weapons or have announced a national moratorium on explosive nuclear testing (the case of the United States).

The 1959 Antarctic Treaty

The Antarctic is the southernmost continent, stretching across 14.2 million square kilometres, more than a third greater in extent than continental Europe. Originally named *Terra Australis* ('land of the south'), its existence was deduced by Aristotle;[47] in the sixteenth century, the continent appeared on maps even before it had been physically discovered.[48] The 1959 Antarctic Treaty was the first formal Cold War–era arms control agreement. The International Geophysical Year of 1957–58 (IGY) was a joint scientific effort by 12 States – Argentina, Australia, Belgium, Chile, France, Japan, New Zealand, Norway, South Africa, the Soviet Union, the United Kingdom, and the United States – to conduct studies of the Earth and its cosmic environment. As interest grew in keeping the continent from becoming militarised, diplomatic discussion began about the possibility of formalising a demilitarisation agreement.[49]

On 3 May 1958, the United States proposed to the other eleven nations participating in the IGY that a diplomatic conference be held to formalise agreements that had been reached informally: that the legal status quo of Antarctica remain unchanged, that scientific cooperation continue, and that the continent be used for peaceful purposes only.[50] What the other States did not know was that the United States was using the IGY as cover for the launch and test detonation of three nuclear weapons from the South Atlantic ocean in order to assess whether detonating nuclear weapons in outer space would create an artificial radiation belt in the Earth's magnetic field that would effectively destroy incoming Soviet warheads in flight.[51]

The three secret tests, the first nuclear detonations in outer space, were conducted between 27 August and 9 September 1958 over the South Atlantic Ocean as part of an operation code-named Argus.[52] Three W25 warheads, each of which yielded an explosive equivalent of between 1 kt and 2 kt, were delivered into outer space in a specially modified Lockheed X-17 three-stage ballistic missile and detonated at altitudes of between 200 and 483 kilometres.[53] The

47 'Terra Australis', Princeton University Library, 2010, at http://bit.ly/3p8v1kT; Oxford Reference, 'Terra Australis Incognita', at https://bit.ly/372qb2e.

48 For example, zum Barth, C. J., *Astronomia: Teutsch Astronomei*, Frankfurt, 1545. The use of the term *Antarctica* on maps in 1887 is generally accredited to the Scottish cartographer, John George Bartholomew.

49 US Department of State, Bureau of Arms Control, Verification, and Compliance, 'Antarctic Treaty', 2017, at http://bit.ly/3paFlcj.

50 Ibid.

51 M. Wolverton, 'How the World Learned about the Pentagon's Sky-High Nuclear Testing', *The Atlantic*, 24 November 2018, at http://bit.ly/3d2Madd; and M. Wolverton, *Burning the Sky: Operation Argus and the Untold Story of the Cold War Nuclear Tests in Outer Space*, Abrams Press, United States, 2018.

52 'Operation Argus, 1958, United States Atmospheric Weapons Tests, Nuclear Test Personnel Review', Technical Report No. DNA 6039F, Defense Nuclear Agency, Washington, DC, 30 April 1982, at https://bit.ly/3a7rU8s.

53 Ibid., p. 36.

conduct of the secret tests was revealed by two journalists at the *New York Times* in an exclusive front-page scoop in March 1959.[54] This public exposure would not derail the negotiation of the Antarctic Treaty.

The Washington Conference on Antarctica was convened from 15 October to 1 December 1959, culminating in the conclusion of a treaty that was signed by all 12 participating nations. The 1959 Antarctic Treaty provides that Antarctica – defined in its Article VI as the area south of 60 degrees south latitude – 'shall be used for peaceful purposes only'.[55] To this end, it prohibits 'any measures of a military nature',[56] while Article V(1) of the Treaty stipulates that 'any nuclear explosions in Antarctica . . . shall be prohibited'.[57] The Treaty provides for the designation of observers to conduct inspections throughout Antarctica,[58] each of whom is granted complete freedom of access, at any time, to all areas of the continent.[59]

The 1959 Antarctic Treaty entered into force on 23 June 1961, following the deposit of the twelfth ratification, and remains in force today.[60] As of 1 January 2021, fifty-four States were party to it, the latest being Slovenia which adhered in April 2019.[61] That year, the sixtieth anniversary of the Treaty's adoption, a declaration was issued at the formal Treaty Meeting in Czechia. In the Prague Declaration, the 'Consultative' States Parties[62] recognised that 'it is in the interest of all humankind that Antarctica continue to be used exclusively for peaceful purposes'. They reaffirmed the 'comprehensive protection of the Antarctic environment and dependent and associated ecosystems, and the designation of Antarctica as a natural reserve, devoted to peace and science'.[63]

To this day, however, the impact of global nuclear testing continues to be registered in Antarctica. Marine nuclear bomb tests in the late 1950s produced anthropogenic chlorine-36, which was injected into the stratosphere and spread around the globe. Scientific

54 H. W. Baldwin, '3 Atomic Devices Detonated 300 Miles Up', *New York Times*, 19 March 1959, p. 1; W. Sullivan, 'Radiation and Geomagnetic Phenomena Probed and Revealed by Test Outlined', *New York Times*, 19 March 1959, p. 1. An unclassified report by the Defense Nuclear Agency on the operation, and its possible effects on the personnel engaged in it (a 'Nuclear Test Personnel Review'), was published in 1982. The report stated that 'the detonations occurred at such distances above the Earth that there was no possibility of exposure of task force personnel to ionizing radiation'. 'Operation Argus, 1958, United States Atmospheric Weapons Tests, Nuclear Test Personnel Review', p. 1.

55 Art. I, 1959 Antarctic Treaty.

56 Art. I(1), 1959 Antarctic Treaty.

57 Technically, therefore, the US launching of nuclear missiles a year earlier was not in contradiction with Article V, as the detonations took place in outer space. Such test detonations would later be prohibited in 1963 by the Partial Test-Ban Treaty (as discussed below). In addition, the warheads were neither launched south of the 60 degree south latitude nor did they detonate over Antarctica.

58 Art. VII, 1959 Antarctic Treaty.

59 See, e.g., Bureau of Arms Control, Verification, and Compliance, 'Antarctic Treaty'; and Secretariat of the Antarctic Treaty (ATS), 'Peaceful Use and Inspections', 2021, at http://bit.ly/2LEhbsL.

60 Art. XIII(5), 1959 Antarctic Treaty.

61 See the latest ATS list of States Parties, at http://bit.ly/2xjIVLO.

62 Of the fifty-four States Parties, twenty-nine are Consultative Parties, which entitles them to participate in decision-making at the annual Antarctic Treaty Consultative Meetings (ATCMs). No ATCM was held in 2020 owing to the COVID-19 global epidemic, but the forthcoming meeting, the Treaty's forty-third, was due to be held in Paris in June 2021.

63 'Prague Declaration on the Occasion of the Sixtieth Anniversary of the Antarctic Treaty', adopted at Prague, 8 July 2019, at https://bit.ly/372Wlea.

research published in September 2019 showed that deposits in Vostok, the site of a Russian research facility in inland Princess Elizabeth Land in Antarctica, remain contaminated with ^{36}CI, a radioactive isotope with a half-life of more than 300,000 years.[64]

The 1963 Partial Test-Ban Treaty

A proposal for a legally binding treaty outlawing all explosive nuclear testing was made by Indian Prime Minister, Jawaharlal Nehru, in 1954. But his call for a 'standstill agreement' was not yet acceptable to either nuclear superpower. In 1957, President Eisenhower announced that the United States would be willing, as part of a first-step disarmament agreement, to suspend testing of nuclear weapons for up to two years. But he made the offer conditional on Soviet acceptance of a permanent end to the production of fissionable material for weapons purposes and physical inspections of Soviet sites to verify compliance.[65] Neither stipulation would meet with a positive response from Moscow.

In March 1958, however, Soviet Premier Nikita Khrushchev wrote to Eisenhower to announce that the Soviet Union was halting all nuclear testing and he called on the United States to reciprocate.[66] Later that year, the Soviet Union, the United Kingdom, and the United States opened discussions at a 'Conference on the Discontinuance of Nuclear Weapon Tests' in Geneva, but the prospects for an agreement foundered on the thorny issue of verification. The diplomatic reverse occurred despite support for the initiative by US Secretary of State, Allen Dulles, who viewed with concern the changing role of nuclear weapons in military strategy,[67] as well as the developing 'nth country problem' of nuclear weapon proliferation.[68]

The more immediate genesis of the Treaty Banning Nuclear Weapon Tests in the Atmosphere, in Outer Space and Under Water – better known as the Partial Test-Ban Treaty[69] – was to be found in the Cuban Missile Crisis in 1962. In December of that year, while British Prime Minister Harold Macmillan was meeting with President Kennedy and urging an abandonment of the spiralling arms race between the two superpowers, a message arrived for the American President from Khrushchev exhorting 'an end once and for all to nuclear tests'.[70] With a view to breaking the impasse on verification, the Soviet Premier offered to grant up to three on-site inspections a year in the Soviet Union. Although the negotiations fell short of a comprehensive test ban, Khrushchev, Kennedy,

64 S. Pivot, M. Baroni, E. Bard, and X. Giraud, 'A Comparison of 36Cl Nuclear Bomb Inputs Deposited in Snow from Vostok and Talos Dome, Antarctica, Using the 36Cl/Cl– Ratio', *Journal of Geophysical Research*, Vol. 124, No. 20 (27 October 2019), at https://bit.ly/3p9zoxM.

65 Federation of American Scientists, 'Comprehensive Test Ban Treaty Chronology', undated but accessed 1 February 2021 at http://bit.ly/3tQuxmS.

66 W. Epstein, *The Last Chance: Nuclear Proliferation and Arms Control*, The Free Press, New York, 1976, p. 49.

67 Among other issues, 'limited' nuclear war was being actively wargamed. See, e.g., M. H. Halperin, 'Nuclear Weapons and Limited War', *Journal of Conflict Resolution*, Vol. 5, No. 2 (June 1961), 146–66.

68 H. K. Jacobson and E. Stein, *Diplomats, Scientists, and Politicians: The United States and the Nuclear Test Ban Negotiations*, University of Michigan Press, Ann Arbor, 1966, p. 88.

69 At the time, it was also referred to as the Moscow Treaty because of the location for its negotiation (not to be confused with the later Strategic Offensive Reductions Treaty (SORT) of 2002).

70 Braithwaite, *Armageddon and Paranoia: The Nuclear Confrontation*, p. 288.

and Macmillan all deserve credit for doggedly pursuing agreement on what would become the centrepiece of international limitations on nuclear test detonations for the coming three decades.

Six months later, in his oft-quoted Commencement Address at the American University in Washington, DC, President Kennedy announced a unilateral moratorium on US atmospheric testing, calling on other nations to follow the American lead. He noted the 'ironic but accurate fact' that the two greatest military powers were also the two 'in the most danger of devastation'. 'All we have built, all we have worked for', he said, 'would be destroyed in the first 24 hours'.[71] In Moscow, Khrushchev told a visiting Harold Wilson, the leader of the British Labour Party (and future prime minister), that it was 'the greatest speech by any American President since Roosevelt'.[72]

Kennedy himself favoured a total prohibition of all nuclear testing. Pressure was also growing from the public for concrete action as the human and environmental effects of atmospheric tests were starting to become known.[73] But amid scepticism across the US Senate and among the Joint Chiefs of Staff as to its desirability, and with many in the West beset by doubts about Soviet bona fides, prospects for an end to all nuclear testing, already faint, were dimming further.[74]

Those doubts only grew when, on 2 July 1963, speaking in East Berlin, Khrushchev publicly scotched the possibility of on-site inspections, declaring that it was 'time for the imperialist gentlemen to know that the Soviet Government will never abandon the security interests of its country and all the Socialist countries and will not open its doors to NATO intelligence agents'. This was, he declared, 'no subject for bargaining'.[75] Instead, he argued that underground nuclear tests could be monitored by national detection systems combined with automatic seismic stations, and that on-site inspections were thus unnecessary. The Soviet Union would, he announced, be willing to conclude a treaty banning nuclear tests in the atmosphere, in outer space, and underwater.[76] The die was effectively cast for the scope and content of the future treaty.

The formal negotiation of the treaty was conducted in the Kremlin by three of the four nuclear powers of the time, taking just ten days beginning on 15 July 1963. France had conducted its first explosive test three years before in Algeria, becoming the world's fourth nuclear power, but had not been invited to take part in the talks. No agreement to outlaw all underground testing could be reached, although an underground detonation would still be deemed unlawful under the Treaty if it were to cause radioactive debris to be present outside the territory of the State responsible for the test. In other respects, the provisions were those that had been sketched out by Khrushchev in his East Berlin address

71 'Commencement Address at American University, Washington, D.C., June 10, 1963', John F. Kennedy Presidential Library and Museum, at http://bit.ly/3gzTE6V.

72 Jacobson and Stein, *Diplomats, Scientists, and Politicians: The United States and the Nuclear Test Ban Negotiations*, p. 453.

73 Epstein, *The Last Chance: Nuclear Proliferation and Arms Control*, p. 54.

74 Jacobson and Stein, *Diplomats, Scientists, and Politicians: The United States and the Nuclear Test Ban Negotiations*, pp. 449–50.

75 Ibid., p. 453.

76 Ibid.

earlier in July. On 26 July 1963, the day after the treaty's conclusion, President Kennedy went on television to tell Americans that 'a shaft of light' had 'cut into the darkness'.[77]

The Partial Test-Ban Treaty was opened for signature at London, Moscow, and Washington on 8 August 1963, entering into force on 10 October 1963. The three negotiating States – the Russian Federation (as successor State to the Soviet Union), the United Kingdom, and the United States – are its three depositaries.[78] On 29 July 1963, France announced it would not adhere to the Treaty; China followed suit with a similar statement two days later. Neither has ever joined. As of 1 January 2021, however, 125 States were party to the Treaty while a further 9 States were signatories.[79] The Partial Test-Ban Treaty, which is of 'unlimited duration', remains in force today.[80]

The Partial Test-Ban Treaty requires its States Parties to prohibit, prevent, and abstain from the carrying out of nuclear weapons tests or any other nuclear explosions in the atmosphere, in outer space, and underwater.[81] At the instigation of the Soviets, no exception was provided for the possibility of explosions in these environments for 'peaceful purposes'. The Treaty further obligates States Parties to refrain from causing, encouraging, or in any way participating in any nuclear weapon test explosion or other nuclear explosion anywhere in any of the proscribed environments.[82]

The Treaty, a simple text comprising only five articles, was the first arms control treaty to contain a withdrawal clause. Inserted at the demand of the US delegation – the Soviets just assumed that a right of withdrawal existed by virtue of sovereignty – each State Party is granted the right to withdraw at the expiry of three months' notice if it determines that 'extraordinary events' related to the subject of the Treaty have 'jeopardized' its 'supreme interests'.[83] No State Party has, though, ever sought to withdraw. In any event, as discussed below, a detonation in the atmosphere, in outer space, or underwater today would contravene a rule of customary international law.

Prime Minister Macmillan greatly regretted that the Treaty did not comprehensively outlaw nuclear testing.[84] The preamble does note the desire of its States Parties to seek to achieve 'the discontinuance of all test explosions of nuclear weapons for all time' while Article I(1) refers to the partial prohibition as being 'without prejudice to the conclusion of a Treaty resulting in the permanent banning of all nuclear test explosions, including all such explosions underground'. But nuclear-armed States would continue to conduct nuclear explosive tests in that environment for the following three decades: more than 1,500 devices would be detonated up until the 1990s, equivalent to about one nuclear test a week over the course of thirty years.[85] Underground test detonations would only be

77 President John F. Kennedy, Address to the Nation on the Nuclear Test Ban Treaty, 26 July 1963, at http://bit.ly/3tRobRe.
78 Art. III(2), 1963 Partial Test Ban Treaty.
79 See, e.g., the list maintained by the UN Office for Disarmament Affairs (UNODA), at http://bit.ly/3aUnctV.
80 Art. IV, 1963 Partial Test Ban Treaty.
81 Art. I(1), 1963 Partial Test Ban Treaty.
82 Art. I(2), 1963 Partial Test Ban Treaty.
83 Art. IV, 1963 Partial Test Ban Treaty.
84 Braithwaite, *Armageddon and Paranoia: The Nuclear Confrontation*, p. 291.
85 P. G. Richards and J. Zavales, 'Seismological Methods for Monitoring a CTBT: The Technical Issues Arising in Early Negotiations', at http://bit.ly/3a9XVgi.

comprehensively prohibited in the CTBT, adopted in 1996 – a treaty that has still not entered into force.

The Partial Test-Ban Treaty does not provide for any mechanism of international verification, the result of implacable Soviet opposition, but States Parties are not prohibited from engaging in verification on the basis of their own 'national technical means'.[86] In this regard, Project Vela (Spanish for 'watchman' or 'wakefulness') was created by the United States with the express purpose of verifying compliance with the provisions of the Treaty.

Developed by scientists at the Los Alamos laboratory, the Vela satellites were launched into outer space and orbited about 95,000 kilometres from Earth. The sensors deployed on the first pair of satellites, which were launched a week after the Treaty's entry into force, monitored for optical and electromagnetic signatures of nuclear explosions in the earth's atmosphere as well as in outer space.[87] Each satellite had a sensing range of 200 million miles, and the on-board equipment was capable of detecting x-rays, gamma rays, and neutrons.[88] Ultimately, twelve satellites (six pairs, 1A and 1B through to 6A and 6B) would be launched as part of the project. The last functioning Vela satellite was turned off in 1985.

A corresponding project (Vela Uniform) sought to develop seismic methods for detecting underground nuclear tests. The project, which was conducted jointly by the US Atomic Energy Commission and the Department of Defense, involved seven test detonations in the United States between October 1963 and July 1971. Seismic traces from multiple locations were analysed for each of the explosions to develop methods for differentiating underground nuclear tests from other seismic events, such as earthquakes, and to determine the location of any test site.[89] The project also included experiments using conventional high explosives.[90] Seismology as a scientific discipline was said to be 'transformed' by the need to detect even low-yield underground or underwater nuclear detonations.[91]

The 1966 Outer Space Treaty

The Treaty on Principles Governing the Activities of States in the Exploration and Use of Outer Space, including the Moon and Other Celestial Bodies (Outer Space Treaty), was concluded under the auspices of the UN General Assembly and 'commended' by Resolution 2222 (XXI) in December 1966.[92] The Treaty is largely based on the 'Declaration of Legal Principles Governing the Activities of States in the Exploration

86 Epstein, *The Last Chance: Nuclear Proliferation and Arms Control*, p. 52.
87 DARPA, 'VELA: Nuclear Explosion Detection', undated but accessed 1 June 2020, at http://bit.ly/3dnz7AK.
88 V. Grant, 'Cold War Watchmen', Los Alamos National Laboratory, 13 July 2020, at http://bit.ly/376s2Dl.
89 'Decoupling' is a considerable challenge for seismic detection. This evasion method involves detonating a nuclear device in a large underground cavity so as to muffle the seismic signal.
90 US Department of Energy, 'Plowshare and Vela Uniform', Fact Sheet, 2020, at https://bit.ly/3aVyq1r.
91 K.-H. Barth, 'The Politics of Seismology: Nuclear Testing, Arms Control, and the Transformation of a Discipline', *Social Studies of Science*, Vol. 33, No. 5 (October 2003), 743–81.
92 UN General Assembly Resolution 2222 (XXI), adopted without a vote on 19 December 1966.

and Use of Outer Space', which had been adopted by the General Assembly three years earlier.[93]

Article IV(2) of the Outer Space Treaty stipulates that the Moon and other celestial bodies shall be used by all States Parties exclusively for peaceful purposes. The testing of any type of weapons on celestial bodies, including the Moon, is expressly prohibited. The use in outer space of nuclear weapons – as opposed to their testing (already outlawed under the Partial Test-Ban Treaty) – is not, though, rendered illegal under the Outer Space Treaty; nor is the launching of weapons from Earth into space.

The 1966 Treaty was opened for signature by the three depository States (the Soviet Union, the United Kingdom, and the United States) in January 1967, entering into force in October of the same year. As of 1 January 2020, 110 States were party to the Outer Space Treaty and a further 23 were signatories.

The 1974 Threshold Test-Ban Treaty

The Treaty on the Limitation of Underground Nuclear Weapon Tests, better known as the Threshold Test-Ban Treaty, was concluded by the United States and the Soviet Union in July 1974. The Treaty, which restricted the underground testing of nuclear weapons from 31 March 1976 to explosive yields of no greater than 150 kt, was signed by the two States on 3 July 1974.[94] But for many years, neither the United States nor the Soviet Union ratified the Treaty, with verification once again proving to be the sticking point. In 1976, however, each State announced its intention to observe the stipulated Treaty limit of 150 kt, pending ratification.[95]

The two nations began negotiations in November 1987 with a view to reaching an agreement on additional verification measures. Agreement on verification was set out in a new protocol, concluded in June 1990. The verification protocol provides for the use of the hydrodynamic yield measurement method,[96] as well as seismic monitoring with respect to all tests with a planned yield exceeding 50 kt. With respect to all tests having a planned yield exceeding 35 kt, the option of on-site inspections was foreseen.[97] The Threshold Test-Ban Treaty finally entered into force on 11 December 1990, more than sixteen years after its original adoption.

93 UN General Assembly Resolution 1962 (XVIII), adopted without a vote on 13 December 1963.

94 See generally R. W. Helm and D. R. Westervelt, 'The New Test Ban Treaties: What Do They Mean? Where Do They Lead?', *International Security*, Vol. 1, No. 3 (Winter 1977), 162–78.

95 US Department of State, 'Treaty between the United States of America and the Union of Soviet Socialist Republics on the Limitation of Underground Nuclear Weapon Tests (and Protocol Thereto) (TTBT)', at http://bit.ly/2O05W8Q.

96 The 'hydro-dynamic yield measurement method' is formally defined as 'the method whereby the yield of a test is derived from on-site, direct measurement of the properties of the shock wave as a function of time during the hydrodynamic phase of the ground motion produced by the test'. Protocol to the Treaty between the United States of America and the Union of Soviet Socialist Republics on the Limitation of Underground Nuclear Weapon Tests, §1, para. 10.

97 Ibid., §3, para. 1(a).

The 1996 Comprehensive Nuclear-Test-Ban Treaty

Back in 1968, the preamble to the NPT had recalled the determination of the States Parties to the Partial Test-Ban Treaty 'to seek to achieve the discontinuance of all test explosions of nuclear weapons for all time and to continue negotiations to this end'. It would take until 1996 for a treaty to be concluded that would outlaw all such test detonations. Yet, despite widespread adherence, the CTBT[98] is not yet in force, and prospects for its entry into force in the short to medium term continue to be slim. This is primarily due to the demanding conditions set for entry into force which include the nomination of a list of forty-four States in an annex to the Treaty every one of which must adhere in order to trigger entry into force.

The Negotiation of the Treaty

In 1992, following the end of the Cold War and the successful negotiation of the Chemical Weapons Convention, there was a sense of optimism in the international community that real progress towards nuclear disarmament was possible. With the non-aligned nations at the forefront, the non-nuclear-weapon States designated under the NPT increased pressure on the nuclear-weapon States to fulfil their disarmament obligations under Article VI.[99]

The task of negotiating an end to all explosive nuclear testing was entrusted to the Conference on Disarmament, which had successfully adopted the Chemical Weapons Convention. But this time, and for the first time in its history, the Conference on Disarmament would fail to agree upon the text of a Treaty that it had been mandated – and had undertaken – to negotiate.[100] Ultimately, the conclusion of the CTBT in the Conference on Disarmament would be blocked by India alone. The formal 'rules of procedure' that govern the organisation the Conference require that its substantive decisions be adopted by consensus.

On 22 August 1996, Belgium submitted as a national paper to the Conference on Disarmament the text of the CTBT that had otherwise been settled, permitting the Conference to forward the Treaty to the General Assembly. On 9 September, Australia, along with 127 co-sponsors, introduced a resolution into the General Assembly that contained the Treaty text. The very next day, the Assembly formally adopted the CTBT by 158 votes to 3 (Bhutan, India, and Libya), with 5 abstentions (Cuba, Lebanon, Mauritius, Syria, and Tanzania). On 24 September 1996, US President William J. Clinton became the first leader to sign the CTBT at the United Nations in New York, famously referring to the treaty as 'the longest-sought, hardest-fought prize in arms control history'.[101]

As of 5 February 2021, 170 States had ratified the Treaty[102] – the latest to adhere being Comoros – and a further 15 States had signed but not ratified.[103] Despite this impressive

[98] Comprehensive Nuclear-Test-Ban Treaty; adopted at New York, 10 September 1996; not yet in force.
[99] Preparatory Commission for the CTBTO, '1993–95: Prelude and Formal Negotiations', at http://bit.ly/38utOxH.
[100] Preparatory Commission for the CTBTO, '1996: CTBT: A Long-Sought Success', at http://bit.ly/38wxoHJ.
[101] Preparatory Commission for the CTBTO, 'FAQs', at http://bit.ly/2Z3fSrp.
[102] Under Article XIII of the Treaty, accession to the CTBT is only possible after its entry into force.
[103] UN Treaty Collection, Status of the Comprehensive Nuclear-Test-Ban Treaty, at http://bit.ly/2ZILMss.

level of universalisation, however, to enter into force as an instrument of binding international law, as of this writing the CTBT still requires the full adherence of China (a signatory), the Democratic People's Republic of Korea, Egypt (a signatory), India,[104] Iran (a signatory), Israel (a signatory), Pakistan, and the United States (a signatory).[105]

The Content of the Treaty

Under the CTBT, its States Parties undertake not to carry out 'any nuclear weapon test explosion or any other nuclear explosion', and to prohibit and prevent any such nuclear explosion at any place under their jurisdiction or control.[106] The CTBT further prohibits 'causing, encouraging, or in any way participating in the carrying out of any nuclear weapon test explosion or any other nuclear explosion'.[107] These substantive rules are detailed in a single article, entitled 'Basic Obligations'. As is the case with the NPT and the Partial Test-Ban Treaty, the term 'nuclear weapon' is not defined in the Comprehensive Nuclear-Test-Ban Treaty.

Each State Party is required to take 'any necessary measures to implement its obligations' under the Treaty. This includes 'in particular' any necessary measures to 'prohibit natural and legal persons anywhere on its territory or in any other place under its jurisdiction as recognized by international law' from undertaking any activity that is prohibited to a State Party under the Treaty.[108] The CTBT further obligates the prohibition's extension to preclude natural and legal persons from undertaking any such activity 'anywhere under its control' and 'natural persons possessing its nationality from undertaking any such activity anywhere'.[109]

Two annexes to the Treaty, respectively, detail the location of various Treaty monitoring assets associated with the International Monitoring System (Annex 1), and list the States that must ratify the Treaty for it to enter into force (Annex 2). Since the conclusion of the Treaty, three of the Annex 2 States that have not adhered have conducted nuclear test explosions: India and Pakistan in May 1998, and the Democratic People's Republic of Korea on six separate occasions, most recently (as of this writing) in early September 2017. No reservation may be made by a contracting State to either the articles of the Treaty or the two Annexes to it.[110]

The Treaty also includes an extensive Protocol, which is separated into three parts. Part I details the International Monitoring System (IMS). Part II governs on-site inspections. Part III pertains to confidence-building measures.[111] Article X of the CTBT makes it

104 For a discussion of the (non-)likelihood of Indian adherence to the CTBT, see B. Gopalaswamy, 'India and the Comprehensive Nuclear-Test-Ban Treaty: To Sign or Not to Sign?', Stockholm International Peace Research Institute (SIPRI), Policy Brief, January 2010, at https://bit.ly/3d85wxU.

105 On 13 October 1999, the US Senate voted against ratification of the CTBT.

106 Art. I(1), CTBT.

107 Art. I(2), CTBT.

108 Art. III(1)(a), CTBT.

109 Art. III(1)(b) and (c), CTBT.

110 Art. XV, CTBT.

111 See, e.g., Nuclear Threat Initiative (NTI), 'Comprehensive Nuclear-Test-Ban Treaty (CTBT)', last updated 23 April 2020, at http://bit.ly/3b34gcw.

explicit that the annexes to the Treaty, the Protocol, and indeed also the annexes to the Protocol 'form an integral part' of the CTBT. These are discussed further in Chapter 7.

The Treaty establishes a Comprehensive Nuclear Test-Ban Treaty Organization (CTBTO), to be headquartered in Vienna.[112] A Preparatory Commission for the CTBTO exists, based on a resolution adopted by the 'States Signatories' to the CTBT, which is installed in Vienna pending the Treaty's entry into force.[113] In late January 2021, speaking at a virtual event organised by the Vienna Center for Disarmament and Non-proliferation (VCDNP), Lassina Zerbo, the Executive Secretary of the CTBTO Preparatory Commission, warned against forgetting or underestimating the great danger of a resumption of nuclear testing, and reiterated the importance of a legally binding ban on such tests. 'We have to finish the unfinished business for the CTBT entry into force', she said.[114]

The 2017 Treaty on the Prohibition of Nuclear Weapons

The initial drafts of the Treaty on the Prohibition of Nuclear Weapons at the 2017 UN diplomatic conference that negotiated the treaty text reproduced the language of the CTBT verbatim. Thus the second formal draft text of 27 June 2017 maintained the formulation whereby States Parties would undertake never under any circumstances to 'carry out any nuclear weapon test explosion or any other nuclear explosion'.[115]

There was a general desire to ensure the complete consistency of the Treaty on the Prohibition of Nuclear Weapons with the CTBT, as evidenced by the wording in its preamble: '*Recognizing* the vital importance of the Comprehensive Nuclear-Test-Ban Treaty and its verification regime as a core element of the nuclear disarmament and non-proliferation regime.' But there was also a dogged determination among many of the negotiating States to outlaw other forms of testing than explosive testing in which the nuclear material goes critical. Ecuador in particular wished to see subcritical testing explicitly prohibited.[116] In this form of testing, a quantity of high explosive is detonated beside weapons-grade fissile material to assess how the material reacts, but no critical mass is formed. This means that no self-sustaining nuclear fission chain reaction occurs as it would in the detonation of a nuclear explosive device.[117]

112 Art. II(1) and (3), CTBT.

113 Resolution establishing the Preparatory Commission for the Comprehensive Nuclear Test-Ban Treaty Organization, adopted on 19 November 1996 by a Meeting of States Signatories, at https://bit.ly/3tPq50B.

114 CTBTO Preparatory Commission, '"Strengthening the CTBT": High-Level Speakers Reaffirm Treaty's Key Role', 1 February 2021, at http://bit.ly/3qhKvo1.

115 Art. 1(1)(e), Draft Treaty on the Prohibition of Nuclear Weapons of 27 June 2017.

116 Comments in plenary by Ecuador on 16 June 2017. Peru supported Ecuador's call in comments in the plenary on 17 June 2017.

117 See, e.g., F. von Hippel, 'Subcritical Experiments', *Bulletin of the Atomic Scientists*, 14 December 2012, at http://bit.ly/3jGyia7; Los Alamos National Laboratory, 'Do Subcritical Experiments Help?', December 2016, at https://bit.ly/3tRZrvm; and D. C. Conrad, 'Underground Explosions Are Music to their Ears', *Science and Technology Review*, Lawrence Livermore National Laboratory, July/August 2000, 4–11, at https://bit.ly/3jJlrUn. As one US expert, David Conrad, has observed, such subcritical tests 'have become largely accepted internationally for ensuring the safety and reliability of a nation's nuclear force without resorting to nuclear testing'. The experiments are, he observes, 'permitted

Following informal consultations with participating States, a revised draft Treaty text was issued on 3 July 2017.[118] A compromise on testing was found by including an undertaking never under any circumstances to 'test' nuclear weapons or other nuclear explosive devices in the first subparagraph of Article 1(1). The relevant text, which remained unchanged through to the Treaty's adoption, read as follows: '(a) Develop, test, produce, manufacture, otherwise acquire, possess or stockpile nuclear weapons or other nuclear explosive devices.'

Subcritical testing is effectively illegal for States Parties to the TPNW, but this is so under the prohibition on developing nuclear weapons or other nuclear explosive devices in the Treaty and not the prohibition on testing. A critical mass is an inherent feature of the detonation of any prohibited nuclear explosive device. Nonetheless, in the declaration it submitted upon ratification of the TPNW, Cuba claimed that 'the prohibition on the testing of nuclear weapons contained in Article 1(a) encompasses all forms of testing, including those performed using non-explosive methods such as subcritical testing and computer simulation'.[119]

EXPLOSIVE NUCLEAR TESTING UNDER CUSTOMARY INTERNATIONAL LAW

The explosive testing of nuclear weapons is not only restricted under treaty law; a number of these rules have also crystallised as international custom. Writing in 1987, Nicholas Grief suggested that the fact that it was considered necessary to conclude the Partial Test-Ban Treaty is evidence that customary law did not, in 1963, prohibit atmospheric nuclear tests.[120] This assertion is undoubtedly correct. Moreover, the claim made by Anthony D'Amato only a few years after the treaty's adoption that the rule effectively became an instant custom in 1963 is not persuasive.[121] Among other contrary practices, long-standing opposition to the core rules laid down in the Partial Test-Ban Treaty until the early 1990s by China and France – both specially affected States – acted to preclude the formation of general international law prohibiting at least the test detonation of nuclear devices in the atmosphere.

Today, however, all test detonations of nuclear explosive devices in the atmosphere, underwater, and in outer space, including very-low-yield 'hydro-nuclear' tests,[122] are prohibited by customary international law.[123] No State may claim persistent objector status

within the Comprehensive Test Ban Treaty signed by President Clinton in 1998'. Conrad, 'Underground Explosions Are Music to Their Ears', at p. 4.

118 Draft treaty on the prohibition of nuclear weapons, UN doc. A/CONF.229/2017/L.3, 3 July 2017.

119 Text available on the UN Treaty Section website, at http://bit.ly/2Zognf7.

120 N. Grief, 'Nuclear Tests and International Law', chapter 9 in I. Pogany (ed.), *Nuclear Weapons and International Law*, Avebury, Aldershot, 1987, 217–44, at p. 227.

121 A. D'Amato, 'Legal Aspects of the French Nuclear Tests', *American Journal of International Law*, Vol. 61, No. 1 (January1967), 66–77.

122 There is, however, no customary international rule precluding subcritical nuclear testing. It is prohibited to States Parties to the TPNW but not to other States. For details of low-yield tests, see, e.g., M. B. Schneider, 'Yes, the Russians Are Testing Nuclear Weapons and It Is Very Important', *Real Clear Defense*, 8 August 2019, at http://bit.ly/2ZHwp3m.

123 D. MacKay, 'The Testing of Nuclear Weapons under International Law', chapter 12 in G. Nystuen, S. Casey-Maslen, and A. G. Bersagel (eds.), *Nuclear Weapons under International Law*, Cambridge University Press, Cambridge, 2014, 292–318, at pp. 306, 307, 316, 317.

to these exclusionary rules. Despite fears expressed in certain quarters, even pariah State North Korea has not conducted atmospheric nuclear tests: all of its six test detonations have occurred underground.[124]

In addition, all underground explosive test detonations are prohibited to any signatory or ratifying State to the Comprehensive Nuclear-Test-Ban Treaty, as being acts that would serve to defeat the object and purpose of the CTBT. This was explicitly recognised by the five NPT nuclear-weapon States in a joint statement on 15 September 2016: 'a nuclear-weapon test explosion or any other nuclear explosion would defeat the object and purpose of the CTBT'.[125] Thus, should the United States or any other signatory or contracting NPT nuclear-weapon State wish to resume explosive testing, it would need to declare that it does not intend to become a party to the CTBT. This is in full accord with the rule codified in the 1969 Vienna Convention on the Law of Treaties.[126] Any nuclear test detonation of any magnitude by China, France, Russia, or the United Kingdom would thus similarly violate its respective obligations under international law.

Is there also a general international law prohibition of all explosive nuclear testing? While discerning the requisite *opinio juris* is always challenging, the evidence supports the contention that the rule has become *lex lata*. The adoption of and widespread adherence to the CTBT is itself evidence of significant State practice towards a customary prohibition. India's opposition to the adoption of the Treaty is contrary evidence, but India may come to be considered as, at the most, a persistent objector, and its objections do not serve to frustrate the crystallisation of a customary norm. In 1998, in its Resolution 1172, the UN Security Council 'demand[ed]' that India and Pakistan refrain from further nuclear tests. Also 'in this context' it 'call[ed] upon all States not to carry out any nuclear weapon test explosion or any other nuclear explosion in accordance with the provisions of the Comprehensive Nuclear Test Ban Treaty'.[127]

State practice since 1998 has been highly consistent. The United States has made unsubstantiated claims, including in 2020, that China and Russia have engaged in low-yield test detonations. This indirectly reinforces the existence of the norm. But only the Democratic People's Republic of Korea has certainly test-detonated a nuclear explosive device since 1998: first in 2006 and then a further five times through to September 2017. This makes North Korea the only nation to have conducted explosive tests of nuclear weapons in the twenty-first century.[128] Furthermore, North Korea has been sharply

[124] H. Shin and L. Sieg, 'A North Korea Nuclear Test over the Pacific? Logical, Terrifying', Reuters, 22 September 2017, at http://reut.rs/2ZcVO4U.

[125] Statement issued jointly by the Governments of China, France, the Russian Federation, the United Kingdom, and the United States, Media Note, Office of the Spokesperson, US Department of State, Washington, DC, 15 September 2016, at http://bit.ly/2Z56ymV.

[126] Art. 18, Vienna Convention on the Law of Treaties; adopted at Vienna, 23 May 1969; entered into force 27 January 1980. The United States is a signatory not a State Party but considers, through its practice in relation to other treaties, such as the 1998 Rome Statute of the International Criminal Court, this rule to be customary.

[127] UN Security Council Resolution 1172, adopted unanimously on 6 June 1998, operative para. 3. In adopting the resolution, the Council was not ostensibly acting under Chapter VII of the UN Charter.

[128] T. Rauf, '"Unfinished Business" on the Anniversary of the Comprehensive Nuclear-Test-Ban Treaty', Commentary, SIPRI, Stockholm, 26 September 2016, at http://bit.ly/3gweO5b.

condemned by the UN Security Council as a result, with reproval beginning after its first test detonation.[129] The very widespread adherence to the CTBT – 170 ratifying States and 15 signatories – supported by the conclusion of the 2017 Treaty on the Prohibition of Nuclear Weapons, with its broad prohibition of testing, is further evidence of State practice and *opinio juris* in support of a customary prohibition.

In signing the CTBT in September 1996, China declared that it has 'all along stood for the complete prohibition and thorough destruction of nuclear weapons and the realization of a nuclear-weapon-free world. It is in favour of a comprehensive ban on nuclear weapon test explosions in the process towards this objective.'[130] Iran, which has signed but not ratified the CTBT, complained that the Treaty did not go far enough: 'We had not perceived a CTBT only as non-proliferation instrument. The Treaty must have terminated fully and comprehensive further development of nuclear weapons. However, the Treaty bans explosions, thus limiting such development only in certain aspects, while leaving other avenues wide open.'[131]

Twenty years later, in 2016, UN Security Council Resolution 2310 again called upon all States to refrain from carrying out nuclear-weapon test explosions and urged all States that have either not signed or not ratified the treaty, particularly the eight CTBT Annex 2 States, to do so without delay.[132]

Writing in 2014, Don MacKay argued that the 'options' for States to test underground 'are clearly closing'.[133] The option of a nuclear explosive test detonation has now closed. Even though the CTBT is not in force, the norm that it codifies is today a rule of general international law.

[129] In its Resolution 1718 (2006), the UN Security Council, acting under Chapter VII of the UN Charter, condemned the nuclear test by DPR Korea on 9 October 2006 'in flagrant disregard of its relevant resolutions', on the basis that such a test would 'represent a clear threat to international peace and security', and demanded that North Korea 'not conduct any further nuclear test'. UN Security Council Resolution 1718, adopted unanimously on 14 October 2006, operative paras. 1 and 2.

[130] Text available on the UN Treaty Collection website at http://bit.ly/3gy4olk.

[131] Ibid.

[132] UN Security Council Resolution 2310, adopted on 23 September 2016 by 14 votes to nil but with one abstention (Egypt), operative paras. 1 and 4.

[133] MacKay, 'The Testing of Nuclear Weapons under International Law', p. 318.

5

Agreements between Russia and the United States

The sole remaining bilateral nuclear arms control treaty between the Russian Federation and the United States of America, aside from the functionally obsolete 1974 Threshold Test Ban Treaty[1] and 1976 Peaceful Nuclear Explosions Treaty,[2] is the 2010 New Strategic Arms Reduction Treaty.[3] Extended in extremis in early February 2021 for a further five years, once New START expires on 5 February 2026, unless a new agreement is negotiated and enters into force by then, no international legal restraint will apply to the arsenals of the two nuclear superpowers for the first time since 1972.

This chapter begins by describing the negotiation and content of New START and the details of its extension. It then looks at the other main nuclear arms control treaties concluded between the Soviet Union/Russian Federation and the United States over the past fifty years, beginning with the multipartite 1987 Intermediate-Range Nuclear Forces Treaty[4] (INF Treaty), which had eliminated short- and intermediate-range missiles as a category, but which effectively became defunct in August 2019 following the withdrawal of first the United States and later Russia.

The chapter then traces the elaboration and content of the first nuclear arms control treaties, beginning with the 1972 Anti-ballistic Missile (ABM) Treaty[5] and the Interim

[1] Treaty between the United States of America and the Union of Soviet Socialist Republics on the Limitation of Underground Nuclear Weapon Tests (and Protocol Thereto); signed at Moscow, 3 July 1974; entered into force 11 December 1990.

[2] Treaty between the United States of America and The Union of Soviet Socialist Republics on Underground Nuclear Explosions For Peaceful Purposes (and Protocol Thereto); signed at Washington and Moscow, 28 May 1976; entered into force 11 December 1990.

[3] The Treaty between the United States of America and the Russian Federation on Measures for the Further Reduction and Limitation of Strategic Offensive Arms; signed at Prague, 8 April 2010; entered into force 5 February 2011.

[4] Treaty between the United States of America and the Union of Soviet Socialist Republics on the Elimination of Their Intermediate-Range and Shorter-Range Missiles; adopted at Washington, DC, 8 December 1987; entered into force 1 June 1988; expired 2 August 2019.

[5] Treaty between the United States of America and the Union of Soviet Socialist Republics on the Limitation of Anti-Ballistic Missile Systems (ABM Treaty); adopted at Moscow, 26 May 1972; entered into force 3 October 1972; expired 13 June 2002.

Strategic Arms Limitation Treaty (SALT I).[6] These were concluded by President Richard Nixon and General Secretary Leonid Brezhnev in the Strategic Arms Limitation Talks between the Americans and the Soviets that opened in the late 1960s. US withdrawal from the ABM Treaty in 2002 and its persistent pursuit of more elaborate missile defence systems triggered a new nuclear arms race, whose effects reverberate today, and would act to preclude the entry into force and conclusion of two important arms control treaties.

Consideration thus turns to the negotiation of the three START treaties, beginning with the 1991 START I[7] between the United States and the Soviet Union (later Russia and other successor States to the USSR) that New START effectively replaced, as well as the ill-fated START II and START III. The importance of the 2002 Strategic Offensive Reductions Treaty (SORT)[8] between Russia and the United States is often underestimated. The chapter concludes with an assessment of what, if anything, might ensue in treaty terms in 2026 upon the final expiry of New START.

THE 2010 NEW STRATEGIC ARMS REDUCTION TREATY (NEW START)

US President Barack Obama had set the scene for what he would term 'the most comprehensive arms control agreement in nearly two decades' in a noted speech in Prague on 5 April 2009. Focusing on the issue he termed 'fundamental' to the security of nations and world peace – the future of nuclear weapons in the twenty-first century – he stated 'clearly and with conviction' the commitment of the United States 'to seek the peace and security of a world without nuclear weapons'.[9] The speech and the vision he outlined would win him the Nobel Peace Prize for 2009,[10] but the award was one that the Secretary of the Norwegian Nobel Committee, Geir Lundestad, would later regret.[11]

The Negotiation of New START

The New Strategic Arms Reduction Treaty (New START) was envisaged as a seamless replacement for START I, the Treaty signed with the Soviet Union at the end of July 1991,

[6] Interim Agreement between the United States of America and the Union of Soviet Socialist Republics on Certain Measures with Respect to the Limitation of Strategic Offensive Arms (SALT I); adopted at Moscow, 26 May 1972; entered into force 3 October 1972; expired 3 October 1977.

[7] Treaty between the United States of America and the Union of Socialist Soviet Republics on Further Reduction and Limitation of Strategic Offensive Arms (START I); adopted at Moscow, 31 July 1991; entered into force 5 December 1994; expired 5 December 2009.

[8] Treaty between the United States of America and the Russian Federation on Strategic Offensive Reductions; signed at Moscow, 24 May 2002; entered into force 1 June 2003; expired, 5 February 2011.

[9] Office of the Press Secretary, The White House, 'Remarks By President Barack Obama in Prague As Delivered', 5 April 2009, at http://bit.ly/2MUj6u8.

[10] 'The Nobel Peace Prize for 2009', press release, Oslo, 9 October 2009, at http://bit.ly/3p11pkY. In announcing the award, the Norwegian Nobel Committee 'attached special importance to Obama's vision of and work for a world without nuclear weapons'.

[11] BBC, 'Nobel Secretary Regrets Obama Peace Prize', 17 September 2015, at http://bbc.in/3pcWof3.

a few months before the Union's demise.[12] In accord with its terms and without extension, START I would expire on 5 December 2009, fifteen years after the treaty's delayed entry into force. Negotiations for its more progressive surrogate began in April 2009 following a face-to-face meeting in London between the US President and his Russian counterpart, Dmitry Medvedev. The US delegation for the talks was led by Rose Gottemoeller, appointed for the task as Assistant Secretary for Arms Control, Verification and Compliance at the Department of State. Her book, *Negotiating the New START Treaty*, published in 2021, is a fascinating personal account of the trials and tribulations the negotiators would endure. Russia's delegation was headed by Anatoly Antonov, Director of Security and Disarmament at the Russian Ministry of Foreign Affairs, and now Russia's Ambassador to the United States.

The negotiation of New START, which would take ten months to conclude (four longer than planned), began well but became problematic, not only due to the perennially thorny issue of verification but also owing to the duty to exchange data on missile test launches ('telemetry'), another concern for the Russians. Especially at the eleventh hour, Russia's longstanding apprehension at US plans for missile defence reared its head once again.[13] A senior Obama administration official involved in the process admitted to a journalist at the *New York Times* in 2010, 'We thought it would be relatively easy.'[14]

Russia did want to retain some of START I's extensive monitoring and verification provisions, but it wanted to make them less costly and cumbersome.[15] According to some reports, Russia was also hoping the new treaty would ease some of the restrictions that START I had imposed on mobile ICBMs.[16] More problematic from the US perspective was Russia's desire to link limits on strategic offensive nuclear forces to potential limits on ballistic missile defences.[17] In June 2009, President Medvedev reportedly declared that proposed cuts in offensive weapons would only be possible if the United States relieved Russian concerns about missile defence. 'In any case', the Russian president said, 'the link between strategic offensive and defensive weapons must be clearly fixed in the treaty'.[18]

But on 8 April 2010, after compromises and climbdowns on both sides, and amid sometimes fractious telephone calls between the leaders of the two nations, New

12 That is not to say that the new treaty was simply an extension of START I. As Amy Woolf observes, START I's negotiation during the latter years of the Cold War occurred when the two nations were bitter adversaries, each wary of the other's capabilities and intentions. New START was a product of 'a different era and a different relationship between the United States and Russia'. A. F. Woolf, *'The New START Treaty: Central Limits and Key Provisions'*, *Congressional Research Service*, Washington, DC, updated 3 February 2021, at https://bit.ly/2ZfR2Ug, p. 4. That remains the case today, despite the tense and difficult relations in play between the two nations.

13 Ms Gottemoeller's personal account of the troubled elaboration of the Treaty, *Negotiating the New START Treaty*, was published by Cambria Press in the Spring of 2021.

14 P. Baker, 'Twists and Turns on Way to Arms Pact With Russia', *New York Times*, 26 March 2010, at http://nyti.ms/3jMKtSx.

15 A. F. Woolf, 'Strategic Arms Control after START: Issues and Options', Congressional Research Service, Washington, DC, updated 6 May 2010, at https://bit.ly/2Zc2zE2, p. 15.

16 A. Diakov and E. Miasnikov, 'ReSTART: The Need for a New U.S.-Russian Strategic Arms Agreement', *Arms Control Today*, September 2006.

17 Woolf, 'Strategic Arms Control After START: Issues and Options', p. 16.

18 A. Max, 'Russia Wants U.S. Assurances on Missile Defense', *Associated Press*, 19 June 2009.

START was signed in Prague by President Medvedev and President Obama. Following legislative approval in both nations, the Treaty entered into force on 5 February 2011 upon the exchange of instruments of ratification between Russian Minister for Foreign Affairs Sergei Lavrov and US Secretary of State Hillary Clinton. In addition to replacing START I, as of the date of its entry into force, New START also superseded the 2002 SORT ('Moscow Treaty') between the two States, which thus formally terminated on 5 February 2011.[19]

The duration of New START was explicitly limited to ten years from entry into force, but the Treaty incorporated the option, by mutual agreement, of a single extension for a further period of up to five years thereafter.[20] The challenge for the future US president of needing to secure Senate approval to prolong the Treaty was thereby avoided. Although the Trump administration engaged in direct talks with Russia about the possible extension of New START, in April 2019, President Trump had directed his staff to develop proposals for expanded arms control efforts that would include China as a party. He told them to persuade China to join an arms-control agreement, for the first time, that would limit or verify Chinese nuclear capabilities.[21] Realistically, this aim was never going to be achieved, in no small measure given the huge imbalance in nuclear forces between the United States and China.[22] This suggested to certain commentators that the administration, which was already in the process of withdrawing from the INF Treaty, was ready and willing to let New START lapse.[23] Retrospectively, this seemed to be also the interpretation of US behaviour by the Russian Ministry of Foreign Affairs.[24] When Donald Trump lost the presidential election to Joe Biden in November 2020, the Russians decided to sit tight and wait.

On 21 January 2021, the day after Joseph Robinette Biden took the oath of office as the forty-sixth president of the United States, the incoming US administration indicated that it would seek a full five-year extension of the Treaty. The same day, a press release by the Russian Ministry of Foreign Affairs declared:

> We believe that the treaty can only be extended as it was signed and without any preconditions. The best option would be to extend New START for five years as it is stipulated in the text of the treaty. This would give Russia and the United States enough time to get down to a joint search for answers to the international security and strategic

[19] Art. XIV(2), New START.

[20] Art. XIV(4), New START.

[21] P. Sonne and J. Hudson, 'Trump Orders Staff to Prepare Arms-Control Push with Russia and China', *Washington Post*, 25 April 2019, at http://wapo.st/3daAAwY.

[22] Moreover, as Frank Rose observes: 'Like Russia, China is especially concerned about the development of U.S. missile defenses and the potential impact of those systems on its strategic nuclear deterrent. U.S. deployment of missile defenses is most likely the key driver behind China's decision to deploy multiple independent re-entry vehicles (MIRVs) on some of its ICBMs.' F. Rose, '*Bringing China into the Fold on Arms Control and Strategic Stability Issues*', The Brookings Institution, Washington, DC, 25 September 2019, at http://brook.gs/3jIboiA.

[23] See, e.g., K. Reif and S. Bugos, 'U.S., Russia Hit Impasse on New START', *Arms Control Today*, October 2020, at http://bit.ly/3ph8thN.

[24] On the day of Joe Biden's inauguration as US President, the Ministry of Foreign Affairs issued a 'Press Release on the Future of New START', in which it declared that 'judging by the counterproductive and openly aggressive negotiating policy of the Trump administration on extending the New START treaty, Washington was preparing an unenviable fate for that last remaining international legal mechanism of mutual restrictions on the nuclear missile arsenals of the world's two largest nuclear powers.' See http://bit.ly/3pfDra5.

stability questions that are currently emerging. At the same time, this would preserve the current level of transparency and predictability in the sphere of strategic offensive weapons, which will be in the interests of both parties and the rest of the world.[25]

On 3 February 2021, two days before its expiry, the final exchange of diplomatic notes between Russia and the United States took place, confirming the extension of New START, unamended, until 5 February 2026. The new US Secretary of State, Anthony Blinken, publicly welcomed the extension and the continued security that it would ensure.[26] Publishing a series of 'myth-busters' on its website on the day of the exchange of instruments extending the Treaty, the US Department of State declared:

> Without New START, the Russian Federation could significantly increase the number of warheads deployed on its ballistic missiles and our window of transparency into Russian intercontinental-range nuclear forces would shrink. Over time we would have less confidence in our assessments of Russian intercontinental-range nuclear forces and would have less information upon which to base decisions about U.S. nuclear forces.[27]

The State Department did acknowledge, however, that the 'substantial projected growth' in China's nuclear arsenal 'remains a key concern for the United States and its allies and partners'. China's 'continued resistance to engaging in a meaningful dialogue on nuclear weapons and risk reduction is destabilizing', calling into question 'its intentions'. To prevent an 'unconstrained nuclear arms competition and enhance stability', the Department of State concluded, the world will need nuclear arms control that includes China. The United States 'has not lost sight of this objective', it said.[28]

The Content of New START

The centrepiece of New START is a series of aggregate limits for deployed strategic nuclear weapons stipulated by the Treaty. Their progressive implementation over seven years following its entry into force in February 2011 meant that the final deadline for their achievement was set at 5 February 2018. The aggregate limits are as follows:

- A maximum of 1,550 nuclear warheads on deployed intercontinental ballistic missiles (ICBMs), deployed submarine-launched ballistic missiles (SLBMs), and deployed heavy bombers equipped for nuclear armaments (although each heavy bomber counts as only one warhead toward this limit, irrespective of how many bombs it actually carries)[29]

[25] Russian Ministry of Foreign Affairs, 'Press Release on the Future of New START', Moscow, 20 January 2021.
[26] 'On the Extension of the New START Treaty with the Russian Federation', press statement by Antony J. Blinken, Secretary of State, 3 February 2021, at http://bit.ly/3cEegLV.
[27] US Department of State, 'Myth: Allowing the New START Treaty to Expire Does Not Harm U.S. Security', New START Treaty Mythbusters Fact Sheet, 3 February 2021, at https://bit.ly/3tUkmxI.
[28] Ibid., 'Myth: Extending the New START Treaty Allows the People's Republic of China (PRC) to Continue an Unconstrained Nuclear Build-Up'.
[29] Art. III(1)(c), New START.

- Up to 700, in total, deployed ICBMs, deployed SLBMs, and deployed heavy bombers equipped for nuclear armaments
- A total of no more than 800 deployed and non-deployed ICBM launchers, SLBM launchers, and heavy bombers equipped for nuclear armaments.[30]

Both States reported meeting their obligations under New START by the February 2018 deadline,[31] which equated to a cut – of about one-third – in the strategic nuclear weapons the United States and Russia were allowed to deploy as of that date compared to the status of deployment at the Treaty's conclusion.[32]

The Treaty does not restrict the stockpiling of nuclear warheads. Between September 2009 and the beginning of 2018, though, the US nuclear arsenal reduced from 5,113 nuclear warheads to an estimated total stockpile of 4,000.[33] Some 1,800 warheads were deployed, of which roughly 1,650 strategic warheads were deployed on ballistic missiles and at bomber bases in the United States. Another 150 tactical bombs continue to be deployed in Europe. The remaining warheads – approximately 2,200, or 55 per cent of the total – are in storage 'as a so-called hedge against technical or geopolitical surprises'. Several hundred warheads are scheduled to be retired 'before 2030'.[34]

Russia is in 'the second half of a decades-long modernization of its strategic and non-strategic nuclear forces to replace Soviet-era weapons with newer systems'.[35] Its total arsenal has reduced significantly since late 2009, when it had approximately 4,600 operational warheads (some 2,600 strategic warheads and 2,000 non-strategic warheads) with a further 7,300 warheads in reserve or awaiting dismantlement, for a total of approximately 12,000 nuclear warheads.[36]

Russia's nuclear arsenal, as of early 2018, was estimated at approximately 4,350 nuclear warheads assigned for use by long-range strategic launchers and shorter-range tactical nuclear forces. Of these, roughly 1,600 strategic warheads were deployed on ballistic missiles and at heavy bomber bases, while another 920 strategic warheads were in storage along with about 1,830 non-strategic warheads. In addition to the military stockpile for operational forces, up to 2,500 retired but still largely intact warheads were awaiting dismantlement, for a total inventory of more than 6,850 nuclear warheads.[37] To meet the New START aggregate limits, experts suggested

30 Art. II(1), New START; see also US Department of State, 'New START', at https://bit.ly/3jSsUAQ.

31 H. Nauert, '*New START Treaty Central Limits Take Effect*', press statement, US Department of State, Washington, DC, 5 February 2018, at http://bit.ly/3pjPsLP; and 'Russia Confirms Commitment to New START Treaty – Foreign Ministry', *TASS*, 5 February 2018, at http://bit.ly/3rN9iRi.

32 J. Lee, 'President Obama Announces the New START Treaty', The White House, 26 March 2010, at http://bit.ly/2NrPfco.

33 H. M. Kristensen and R. S. Norris, 'United States Nuclear Forces, 2018', *Nuclear Notebook, Bulletin of the Atomic Scientists*, 4 March 2018, at http://bit.ly/3jPk32M.

34 Ibid.

35 H. M. Kristensen and R. S. Norris, 'Russian Nuclear Forces, 2018', *Nuclear Notebook, Bulletin of the Atomic Scientists*, 4 May 2018, at http://bit.ly/3jRabW6.

36 H. M. Kristensen and R. S. Norris, 'Russian Nuclear Forces, 2010', *Bulletin of the Atomic Scientists*, Vol. 66, No.1 (2010), 74–81, at p. 74.

37 Kristensen and Norris, 'Russian Nuclear Forces, 2018', *Nuclear Notebook*.

that the number of warheads on each SS-18 and SS-27 Mod 2 ICBM, as well as on each SS-N-32 SLBM, had been reduced.[38]

Extending New START, the Department of State further declared: 'The Russian Federation has the capacity to deploy many more than 1,550 warheads on its modernized ICBMs and SLBMs, as well as heavy bombers, but is constrained from doing so by New START.'[39] The Treaty specifically allows for 'modernization and replacement of strategic offensive arms' to be carried out, subject of course to compliance with the provisions of the Treaty and, in particular, full respect for the aggregate limits.[40]

New START did not and does not require destruction of specific nuclear weapons or weapons delivery systems per se, at least not in the same manner as the earlier INF Treaty (see the discussion below), but it did make explicit at the outset that 'each Party shall reduce and limit its strategic offensive arms in accordance with the provisions of this Treaty'.[41] The particular means by which those reductions could occur, however, was left to the discretion of the two parties. They could be destroyed, they could be converted, or they could be stockpiled.

Various options for destruction exist. To eliminate bombers, for instance, a wing or tail section could be cut from the fuselage at locations that were obviously not assembly joints, or the fuselage could be cut into two parts at a location obviously not an assembly joint. There was no requirement to remove the wings from the fuselage as was the case under START I. To convert a heavy bomber to one that was no longer equipped to carry nuclear armaments, either the weapons bays and external attachments for pylons could be modified so that they could not carry nuclear armaments, or all internal and external launcher assemblies could be modified so that they could carry nuclear armaments, or another procedure to carry out the conversion could be developed.[42]

Neither State has accused the other of a serious violation of the Treaty provisions (in marked contradistinction to the situation with respect to the INF Treaty), although the United States acknowledges that Russia has criticised US procedures used to convert its B-52H heavy bombers and Trident-II SLBM launchers. In response, the United States declares that it 'stands by its conversion procedures, which render the converted SLBM launchers and heavy bombers incapable of employing nuclear weapons[,] thereby removing them from accountability under the treaty'.[43]

The aggregate limits set out above remain those applicable throughout the extended five-year lifetime of New START through to 5 February 2026. At the same time, as Article II(2) clarifies, each Party to the Treaty continues to have the right 'to determine for itself the composition and structure of its strategic offensive arms', giving both powers a continued degree of flexibility. Following the extension decision in early February 2021, the US Department of State observed that New START limits all Russian deployed intercontinental-range nuclear weapons,

38 H. M. Kristensen and R. S. Norris, 'Russian Nuclear Forces, 2018', *Bulletin of the Atomic Scientists*, Vol. 74, No.3 (2018), 185–95, at p. 185.

39 US Department of State, 'New START Treaty', accessed 13 February 2021, at https://bit.ly/3jSsUAQ.

40 Art. V(1), New START.

41 Art. I(1), New START.

42 Woolf, 'The New START Treaty: Central Limits and Key Provisions', p. 11.

43 US Department of State, 'New START Treaty', accessed 13 February 2021.

including every Russian nuclear warhead loaded onto an ICBM 'that can reach the United States in approximately 30 minutes'. The Treaty applies to some of the new weapons developed by the Russian Federation, including the deployed Avangard and the under-development Sarmat, 'the two most operationally available of the Russian Federation's new long-range nuclear weapons that can reach the United States'.[44]

In addition to the main New START treaty text, a Protocol signed in 2010 on the same day as the treaty contains a set of legally binding terms and definitions,[45] provisions on data exchange, and measures for verification. The definitions section of the New START Protocol (part one of ten) defines such straightforward terms as 'aircraft' ('any manned machine that can derive support in the atmosphere from interaction with the air other than the interaction of the air with the Earth's surface')[46] and 'airplane' ('a power-driven, heavier-than-air aircraft that derives its lift in flight chiefly from aerodynamic reactions on surfaces that remain fixed under given conditions of flight').[47]

More significantly, it defines 'deployed launcher of ICBMs' as 'an ICBM launcher that contains an ICBM and is not an ICBM test launcher, an ICBM training launcher, or an ICBM launcher located at a space launch facility'.[48] Nuclear armaments are defined, for heavy bombers, as long-range nuclear air-launched cruise missiles, nuclear air-to-surface missiles, or nuclear bombs.[49] The terms 'nuclear bomb' and 'nuclear weapon' are not defined in either New START or its Protocol.

Monitoring and verification measures are detailed in the Annex on Inspection Activities, the Annex on Notifications, and the Annex on Telemetric Information. Stung by criticism from President Trump's Special Presidential Envoy for Arms Control, Marshall Billingslea, that the Obama administration had negotiated 'a very weak verification regime' with 'significant loopholes in the way verification is physically conducted', Rose Gottemoeller bit back. In a detailed rebuttal published on the website of the *Bulletin of the Atomic Scientists*, she wrote:

> In the end, the United States got what it wanted in the New START verification regime: streamlined inspection procedures at a sufficient level of detail to be effectively implemented. We made good use of what had been in previous treaties, but we were not trapped into perpetuating problems, such as over-counting of warheads, that were not in the interest of the United States. Most important, we ended up with detailed procedures that make the inspections reliable in confirming information that the Russians provide us. The same, of course, goes for them, since everything is done on a reciprocal basis.'[50]

The verification of New START is discussed in detail in Chapter 7.

44 Ibid.

45 That the definitions in the Protocol are binding interpretations of the Treaty text is made explicit. Art. I(2), New START.

46 Protocol to the Treaty between the United States of America and the Russian Federation on Measures for the Further Reduction and Limitation of Strategic Offensive Arms, Part One, Definition 2, at https://bit.ly/3pq4nnX.

47 Ibid., Part One, Definition 5.

48 Ibid., Part One, Definition 14.

49 Ibid., Part One, Definition 53.

50 R. Gottemoeller, 'The New START Verification Regime: How Good Is It?', *Bulletin of the Atomic Scientists*, 21 May 2020, at http://bit.ly/3qho2o9.

THE 1987 INTERMEDIATE-RANGE NUCLEAR FORCES (INF) TREATY

New START concerned the strategic arsenals of the two nuclear superpowers. But in Cold War Europe, another central concern had been the short- and intermediate-range forces of the Soviet Union aimed at North Atlantic Treaty Organization (NATO) allies across the region. As an analyst at the RAND Corporation recalled, Soviet deployment of SS-20 intermediate-range ballistic missiles (IRBMs) in Europe risked 'nuclear decoupling', allowing the Soviet Union to conduct nuclear strikes on Western European capitals without attacking the United States.[51] 'The shorter the range, the deader the German', went a popular, if cynical, refrain of the time.

With tensions between the two superpowers rising rapidly in the early 1980s, at the prodding of West German Chancellor Helmut Schmitt, US President Ronald Reagan proposed the 'zero-zero' option to the Soviets, then under the leadership of the ailing Brezhnev. The proposal concerned a commitment from the United States not to deploy its Pershing II or cruise missiles in Western Europe if the Soviet Union would withdraw its RSD-10 Pioneer (designated SS-20 by NATO) IRBMs. Unsurprisingly, the Soviets rejected the proposal out of hand, with Yuli Kvitsinsky, who would go on to serve as the Soviet's initial negotiator for the INF Treaty, describing it as a 'formula for unilateral disarmament by our side, and, frankly, an insult to our intelligence'.[52]

The head of the Central Intelligence Agency (CIA), William Casey, and the Secretary of State for Defense, Casper Weinberger, both opposed the elaboration of the INF Treaty. Former US President Nixon even predicted that a crisis would erupt within NATO if it were concluded.[53] Their fears were ill-founded. In fact, at least until the strictest verification measures came to an end, the Treaty was a great success.[54] Concluded in 1987, the INF Treaty eliminated a dangerous class of weapons from Europe. The armaments were especially dangerous because their presence encouraged a 'launch on warning' procedure for strategic weapons, so short was the time between launch and impact of these shorter-range weapons. It was a concrete outcome from the Summit between President Reagan and General Secretary Gorbachev in Reykjavik a year earlier. Those face-to-face talks had come close to reaching an agreement to eliminate all nuclear weapons but had fallen short. The failure was down to the US Strategic Defense Initiative.

The 1987 Treaty on the Elimination of Intermediate-Range and Shorter-Range Missiles required the United States and the Soviet Union to eliminate all nuclear and conventional ground-launched ballistic and cruise missiles with ranges of between 500 and 5,500

[51] S. Charap, 'The Demise of the INF: Implications for Russia-China Relations', RAND Corporation, document submitted on 9 April 2019, to the US-China Economic and Security Review Commission as a statement for the record for the hearing on 21 March 2019, at https://bit.ly/3rY1H2a, p. 2.

[52] S. Breyman, *Why Movements Matter: The West German Peace Movement and U.S. Arms Control*, SUNY Press, New York, 12 July 2001, p. 78.

[53] T. Downing, *1983: The World at the Brink*, Little, Brown, London, 2018, p. 320.

[54] J. V. Anderson and A. J. Nelson, 'The INF Treaty: A Spectacular, Inflexible, Time-Bound Success', *Strategic Studies Quarterly*, Summer 2019, 90–122.

kilometres. The INF Treaty was the first agreement between the two nuclear superpowers that eliminated an entire category of nuclear weapons. It required physical destruction of the weapons, to be verified by extensive on-site inspections. While the authority to conduct inspections ended on 31 May 2001, the use of surveillance satellites ('national technical means') was permitted to continue.

The INF Treaty was signed in Washington, DC, on 8 December 1987, entering into force on 1 June 1988. The two States Parties, the United States and the Soviet Union, destroyed a total of 2,692 short-, medium-, and intermediate-range missiles, with each meeting the Treaty-imposed deadline for completion of all disarmament of 1 June 1991. Most of the missiles were eliminated by detonation while they were unarmed, with their stages burnt, or else the missiles were cut in half and their wings and tail sections were severed.

On 10 February 2007, however, President Vladimir Putin declared that the Treaty 'no longer' served Russia's interests, presaging future troubles. In July 2014, the United States alleged that Russia, as the primary successor State Party to the obligations of the Soviet Union,[55] was in violation of the Treaty rules 'not to possess, produce, or flight-test' a ground-launched cruise missile with a range of between 500 and 5,500 kilometres or to possess or produce launchers of such missiles.[56] The cruise missile in question was believed at the time to be the Russian R-500, derived from the land-based Iskander-K.[57] In response to a letter from President Obama on the issue, the Russian Ministry of Foreign Affairs issued a statement in which it declared, 'There is absolutely no evidence provided to support [the allegations].'[58]

In February 2017, Senator Tom Cotton of Arkansas along with Senators Ron Johnson of Wisconsin and Marco Rubio of Florida introduced a bill that would declare Russia in material breach of the INF Treaty, a precursor to possible withdrawal.[59] The bill would also authorise transferring intermediate-range systems to allied countries, establish a new programme for ground-launched missiles within the banned ranges, and provide US$500 million to fund countervailing-strike options. In June 2017, with rumours continuing to circulate that the Trump administration was considering US withdrawal from the Treaty, the content of a US Department of Defense report to Congress from the year before cautioning against such a course of action was publicly cited in the press. The Pentagon said that Russia's compliance 'remains the preferable outcome, which argues against unilateral U.S. withdrawal from or abrogation of the INF Treaty at this time'.[60]

55 The treaty's membership expanded in 1991 to include Belarus, Kazakhstan, and Ukraine as successor States to the former Soviet Union, as they had inspectable facilities on their territories at the time of the Soviet Union's dissolution. Turkmenistan and Uzbekistan also possessed INF Treaty-range facilities (SS-23 operating bases) but forwent Treaty meetings with the consent of the other States Parties. D. Kimball and K. Reif, 'The Intermediate-Range Nuclear Forces (INF) Treaty at a Glance', Fact Sheet, Last reviewed August 2019, Arms Control Association, Washington, DC, at http://bit.ly/2T6lziN.

56 Anderson and Nelson, 'The INF Treaty: A Spectacular, Inflexible, Time-Bound Success'.

57 J. Marcus, 'US Briefs NATO on Russian "Nuclear Treaty Breach"', *BBC*, 30 January 2014, at http://bit.ly/2yn5UmU.

58 Cited in 'Russia: US Claims on Nuclear Missiles Treaty Unfounded, We Have Questions Too', *RT*, 30 July 2014, at http://bit.ly/2OAvcIg.

59 Sen. Tom Cotton (Senatorial website), 'Cotton, Johnson, Rubio, Poe, and Rogers Introduce Intermediate-Range Forces Treaty Preservation Act', press release, 16 February 2017, at http://bit.ly/2PIrl8H.

60 G. Hellman and B. Bender, 'The Other Treaty on the Chopping Block', *Politico*, 24 June 2017, at http://bit.ly/2PEEKyt.

Speaking publicly in July 2017, Senator Cotton said, 'Vladimir Putin is violating the letter, so if the U.S. violates the spirit, I'm not terribly concerned.'[61]

In late November 2017, a senior US national security official stated that the Novator 9M729, a land-based cruise missile, was in fact the weapon that the United States believed was in violation of the INF Treaty.[62] The following month, NATO issued a public statement affirming that the Treaty had 'contributed to strategic stability and reduced the risk of miscalculation leading to conflict'.[63] As such, the organisation noted, 'full compliance with the INF Treaty is essential', affirming at the same time that it remained 'fully committed to the preservation of this landmark arms control treaty'. It did, though, observe that 'a situation whereby the United States and other parties were abiding by the treaty and Russia were not – would be a grave and urgent concern'.[64]

For its part, Russia alleged that the United States had violated the Treaty by deploying a component of a missile defence system – the Mark 41 Vertical Launch System (VLS) – that is capable of launching offensive missiles. It also claimed that the United States had used prohibited missiles in defence tests and that some US armed drones were effectively unlawful cruise missiles.[65] A further complicating factor was the perceived threat from China whose growing nuclear and conventional missile arsenal was mostly composed of weapons in the INF Treaty-prohibited range.[66]

On 8 December 2017, the thirtieth anniversary of the treaty's conclusion and signature, the United States announced a new strategy to respond to alleged Russian violations. This response encompassed 'economic and military measures intended to induce the Russian Federation to return to compliance'.[67] Military options could, the Trump administration declared, include research and development of conventional ground-launched intermediate-range missile systems, which it said would not violate the treaty.[68]

The United States formally withdrew from the INF Treaty on 2 August 2019, following a treaty-mandated six-month period of suspension. Russia announced it was doing likewise, putting an effective end to the INF Treaty.[69] None of the nuclear-weapon States is

61 N. Ault, 'Sen. Cotton: Army Modernization Crucial for Challenging Russia', *Washington Times*, 17 July 2017, at http://bit.ly/2R1MZET.

62 D. Majumdar, 'Novator 9M729: The Russian Missile that Broke INF Treaty's Back?', *The National Interest*, 7 December 2017, at http://bit.ly/2P7C3bI.

63 Statement by the North Atlantic Council on the Intermediate-Range Nuclear Forces (INF) Treaty, press release (2017) 180, 15 December 2017, at http://bit.ly/2OzJFnY.

64 Ibid.

65 Kimball and Reif, 'The Intermediate-Range Nuclear Forces (INF) Treaty at a Glance'.

66 Ibid.

67 'Trump Administration INF Treaty Integrated Strategy', press Statement by Heather Nauert, Spokesperson for the US Department of State, Washington, DC, 8 December 2017, at http://bit.ly/2NqzBhn.

68 Ibid.; and see A. Panda, 'The Uncertain Future of the INF Treaty', Backgrounder, Council on Foreign Relations, last updated 21 February 2018, at http://bit.ly/2OvuwUy.

69 The other States Parties to the INF Treaty (Belarus, Kazakhstan, Turkmenistan, Ukraine, and Uzbekistan) did not formally withdraw. In August 2019, however, Ukraine's Minister for Foreign Affairs declared in a statement that it had the right to develop intermediate-range missiles to protect itself from Russian aggression following Russian and US withdrawal from the INF Treaty. C. Maza, 'Ukraine Has Right to Develop Missiles Now That Russia-U.S. Nuclear Treaty Is Canceled, Foreign Ministry Announced', *Newsweek*, 3 August 2019, at http://bit.ly/3qroowT.

today prohibited by treaty from developing or deploying short-range or intermediate-range nuclear or conventional missiles anywhere in the world. In withdrawing from and ending the INF Treaty, there was a strong suspicion that, in addition to reflecting longstanding concern about Russian compliance, some in the United States were keen to have the option of placing intermediate-range missiles in Asia, with a view to confronting a security threat from China that was widely perceived to be increasing.[70] This issue was also firmly in the minds of the Russian authorities, as it had been from the start of negotiations in the second half of the 1980s.[71]

THE STRATEGIC ARMS LIMITATION TALKS (SALT)

In January 1964, at the Disarmament Committee in Geneva, the United States proposed to explore with the Soviet Union 'a verified freeze of the number and characteristics of their strategic nuclear offensive and defensive vehicles'. On 1 July 1968, at the signing of the Nuclear Non-proliferation Treaty, President Lyndon Johnson announced that an agreement had been reached with the Soviets to begin discussions on limiting and reducing both strategic nuclear weapons delivery systems and defence against ballistic missiles.[72] The Strategic Arms Limitation Talks (SALT) had been due to start later that year but were delayed following the Soviet invasion of Czechoslovakia.[73]

The first series of Strategic Arms Limitation Talks began in November 1969 under the Johnson administration, first in Helsinki and later in Vienna, and continued through to May 1972 under President Nixon. The first round of SALT talks ended with the successful conclusion of two treaties, one addressing defensive systems against ballistic missiles and the other imposing a very limited capping of the two nations' strategic nuclear arsenals. Subsequent SALT talks would take place in Geneva.

In the late 1960s, the Soviet Union had a limited anti-ballistic missile (ABM) system around Moscow; the United States had shifted from an earlier plan for a 'thin' anti-ballistic missile defence of certain American cities and instead began to deploy ABM systems at two ICBM missile sites to protect its retaliatory forces, with the full programme envisaging 12 ABM complexes.[74] ABM systems called into question the effectiveness of the mutual assured destruction strategy that had emerged in the 1960s and which was deemed to preserve strategic stability: 'Without effective national defenses, each superpower remained vulnerable, even at reduced or low offensive force holdings, to the other's

[70] See further on this issue D. M. Allison and S. Herzog, '"What about China?" and the Threat to US–Russian Nuclear Arms Control', *Bulletin of the Atomic Scientists*, Vol. 76, No.4 (2020), 200–5.

[71] As Charap recalls, already during the drafting of the Treaty, the possibility of addressing the European and Asian theatres separately came up at several points, and when the negotiations began, 'it was not at all clear that the eventual agreement would extend east of the Urals'. Charap, 'The Demise of the INF: Implications for Russia-China Relations', p. 3, and cf. also p. 4.

[72] Federation of American Scientists, 'Strategic Arms Limitation Talks (SALT I)', at http://bit.ly/3tTLFsd.

[73] W. Epstein, *The Last Chance: Nuclear Proliferation and Arms Control*, The Free Press, New York, 1976, p. 27. For detail on the SALT talks, see generally M. J. Ambrose, *The Control Agenda: A History of the Strategic Arms Limitation Talks*, Cornell University Press, Ithaca NY, 2018.

[74] Federation of American Scientists, 'Strategic Arms Limitation Talks (SALT I)'.

nuclear weapons, thereby deterring either side from launching an attack first because it faced a potential retaliatory strike that would assure its own destruction.'[75]

Difficulties in reaching an agreement to restrict strategic nuclear weapons led the Soviets to argue that the issue be postponed for future consideration while negotiating efforts concentrate on defensive systems. On 20 May 1971, it was announced that an understanding had been reached to concentrate on a permanent treaty to limit ABM systems, while agreeing on certain limitations on offensive weapons, but it was further stated that negotiations would continue thereafter with a view to concluding a more comprehensive and long-term agreement on strategic arsenals. At a Summit in Moscow on 26 May 1972, after two-and-a-half years of negotiations, the first round of SALT was brought to a conclusion, when Nixon and Brezhnev signed both the ABM Treaty and the Interim Agreement on strategic offensive arms.[76]

There was no intrusive verification system to verify compliance with either Treaty. 'Intensive research' had been dedicated to finding ways to verify the agreements without the need to access the other's territory. Both the ABM Treaty and the Interim Agreement stipulate that compliance is to be assured by 'national technical means of verification' and prohibit action to interfere with these means or to deliberately conceal illegal conduct.[77]

The 1972 Anti-Ballistic Missile Treaty

The link between offensive and defensive systems is explicitly highlighted in the preamble to the ABM Treaty, recording the view of both parties that effective limits on anti-missile systems would be a 'substantial factor in curbing the race in strategic offensive arms'.[78] The preamble further noted that the parties were 'mindful' of their obligations under Article VI of the NPT,[79] with the Nuclear Non-proliferation Treaty having entered into force two years earlier.

The Treaty defined an ABM system as 'a system to counter strategic ballistic missiles or their elements in flight trajectory', consisting of interceptor missiles, launchers, and radars.[80] Substantively, the Treaty limited strategic missile defences for both the Soviet Union and the United States to the deployment of two fixed, ground-based defence sites comprising no more than one hundred missile interceptors each. One site could protect the national capital while the second could be used to guard an ICBM site.[81] The Treaty otherwise prohibited the deployment of ABM systems for national defence,[82] as well as the development, testing, or deployment of ABM systems or components which are sea-based, air-based, space-based, or mobile land-based.[83]

75 D. Kimball, '*The Anti-Ballistic Missile (ABM) Treaty at a Glance*', Fact Sheet, last reviewed December 2020, Arms Control Association, Washington, DC, at http://bit.ly/3soWoRr.
76 Federation of American Scientists, 'Strategic Arms Limitation Talks (SALT I)'.
77 Ibid.
78 ABM Treaty, second preambular para.
79 ABM Treaty, fourth preambular para.
80 Art. II, ABM Treaty.
81 Art. III, ABM Treaty.
82 Art. I(2), ABM Treaty.
83 Art. V(1), ABM Treaty.

In a Protocol to the Treaty, signed on 3 July 1974, the two parties reduced the number of permitted defences to a single site of no more than one hundred missile interceptors.[84] In implementing this revised treaty, the Soviet Union opted to keep its existing missile defence system around Moscow, while the United States eventually fielded its one hundred permitted interceptors to protect an ICBM base near Grand Forks, North Dakota. The Arms Control Association notes that Moscow's ABM defence system still exists, but questions its effectiveness.[85] The United States shut down its permitted ABM defence system only a few months after activating it in October 1975 'because the financial costs of operating it were considered too high for the little protection it offered'.[86]

The ABM Treaty, whose duration was unlimited (in distinction to the SALT I treaty), survived the end of the Cold War. But on 13 December 2001, following the 9/11 attacks, President George W. Bush announced that the United States would withdraw from the ABM Treaty, claiming that it prevented US development of defences against possible terrorist or 'rogue State' ballistic missile attacks. The ABM Treaty permitted each State Party to withdraw if 'extraordinary events' had jeopardised its supreme interests. The US withdrawal took effect on 13 June 2002, rendering the treaty defunct.

The ABM Treaty had not delimited the distinction between strategic and non-strategic ('theatre') missile defence systems. The United States and Russia, as well as the other designated successor States to the Soviet Union as party to the 1972 Treaty (Belarus, Kazakhstan, and Ukraine), had negotiated and signed a binding interpretation of this issue in September 1997.[87] The First Agreed Statement considered anti-missile systems as those 'not to have been given capabilities to counter strategic ballistic missiles or their elements in flight trajectory and not to have been tested in an ABM mode'. This was so, if, 'in the course of testing them separately or in a system',

- the velocity of the interceptor missile did not exceed 3 kilometres per second over any part of its flight trajectory;
- the velocity of the ballistic target-missile did not exceed 5 kilometres per second over any part of its flight trajectory; and
- the range of the ballistic target-missile did not exceed 3,500 kilometres.[88]

While Russia ratified the 1997 Memorandum of Understanding in May 2000, it was never sent to the US Senate for consent, and thus the agreement did not enter into force.

The US withdrawal from the ABM Treaty was not without significant consequence. Already in April 2001, two experts had published an Opinion Editorial on the Brookings Institution website cautioning against such action and warning that, far from being a Cold

[84] Art. I(1), Protocol to the ABM Treaty, signed at Moscow, 26 May 1972.

[85] Kimball, 'The Anti-Ballistic Missile (ABM) Treaty at a Glance'.

[86] Ibid.

[87] Memorandum of Understanding Relating to the Treaty between the United States of America and the Union of Soviet Socialist Republics on the Limitation of Anti-Ballistic Missile Systems of May 26, 1972; adopted at New York, 26 September 1997; never entered into force.

[88] First Agreed Statement Relating to the Treaty between the United States of America and the Union of Soviet Socialist Republics on the Limitation of Anti-Ballistic Missile Systems of May 26, 1972, 26 September 1997, para. 1(1).

War 'relic', a unilateral withdrawal from the Treaty would be 'a foreign policy disaster'.[89] They concluded: 'It is not too late for President Bush to reverse course. Rather than abandon the ABM Treaty, he should make clear that the United States will live within its strictures provided that Moscow commits to a serious effort to negotiate the necessary modifications, or even a mutually acceptable replacement, that enable limited defense deployments to go forward.'[90] Their warnings went unheeded.

The head of the Russian armed forces at the time, General Anatoly Kvashnin, predicted the withdrawal would 'alter the nature of the international strategic balance in freeing the hands of a series of countries to restart an arms build-up'.[91] Vladimir Volkov, deputy head of the Defence Committee in Russia's parliament (State Duma), warned that the US decision to develop a missile defence shield outlawed under the ABM could force China to beef up its strategic arsenal, thus prompting India and Pakistan to follow suit. 'All in all, the US move will spark a new nuclear arms race and lead to a reduction in the level of security', Volkov said.

The most immediate consequences of the US withdrawal were to prevent the entry into force of START II (the 'deMIRVing' agreement; see below), as Russia denounced the Treaty after its domestic ratification. The negotiation of START III, which until then had been progressing well, was also torpedoed. While the main thrust of START III would effectively be replaced by New START, the chance to end the incorporation of multiple re-entry vehicles in each missile was a significant opportunity missed. It has never presented itself since. Seventeen years after the end of the ABM Treaty, President Vladimir Putin reiterated publicly that the arms race between Russia and the United States had followed the US withdrawal.[92] At the time, while declaring that this unilateral action would not threaten Russia's security, President Putin nonetheless cautioned that 'we must not allow a legal vacuum in the sphere of strategic stability. We must not undermine the regime of non-proliferation of weapons of mass destruction.'[93]

The 1972 Strategic Arms Limitation Treaty (SALT I)

SALT I was an interim treaty of a set five-year lifetime that, in practice, allowed both the Soviet Union and the United States to increase some of their nuclear forces. Specifically, the United States was allowed to add three nuclear-armed submarines and to carry up to 710 missiles, while the Soviet Union could build up to 62 submarines carrying 950 nuclear missiles. No limitation was placed on incorporating MIRVs to either land-based or sea-based missiles.[94]

89 I. H. Daalder and J. M. Lindsay, 'Unilateral Withdrawal from the ABM Treaty Is a Bad Idea', Op-Ed, The Brookings Institution, 30 April 2001, at http://brook.gs/2B6OWuZ.

90 Ibid.

91 S. Shane, 'Russia Warns of New Arms Race If US Tears Up ABM Treaty', Agence France-Presse, 13 December 2001, at http://bit.ly/3rMXzlM.

92 'Putin Says Arms Race between US, Russia Followed Washington's Withdrawal from ABM Treaty', TASS, 2 March 2018, at http://bit.ly/3qnePoE.

93 'Russian President Vladimir Putin's Response to the U.S. Decision to Withdraw from the ABM Treaty', Atomic Archive, 13 December 2001, at http://bit.ly/3b5K1vo.

94 Epstein, *The Last Chance: Nuclear Proliferation and Arms Control*, pp. 28–29.

The SALT treaties did stabilise mutual deterrence between the two superpowers, helping to usher in the spirit of détente, but they did not bring an end to or even impose any real limitation on the arms race, much less move positively towards nuclear disarmament.[95]

Under SALT I, both sides pledged not to construct new ICBM silos nor to increase the size of existing ICBM silos 'significantly', while the numbers of permissible SLBM launch tubes and SLBM-carrying submarines were capped. The agreement limited the United States to 1,054 ICBM silos and 656 SLBM launch tubes. The Soviet Union was limited to 1,607 ICBM silos and 740 SLBM launch tubes. But the agreement did not restrict the number of strategic bombers either side could have, nor did it even cap the total number of warheads allowable, leaving both sides free to enlarge their strategic forces by increasing their bomber-based forces and by exploiting the newly developed MIRV technology on both ICBMs and SLBMs.

The Federation of American Scientists described the Interim Agreement as essentially a 'holding action', complementing the ABM Treaty by limiting competition in certain strategic armaments and providing time for further negotiation.[96] While formally SALT I expired on 3 October 1977, on 23 September 1977, the United States unilaterally announced that it would continue to honour the Agreement while SALT II was still being negotiated, provided the Soviet Union would do the same. On 25 September 1977, the USSR made a similar declaration.[97]

The 1979 Strategic Arms Limitation Treaty (SALT II)

The 1979 Strategic Arms Limitation Treaty (SALT II)[98] was explicitly intended to build on SALT I and to enter into force upon its expiry, as the joint 1974 Vladivostok agreement had foretold.[99] It would set specific aggregate limits on strategic nuclear weapon delivery systems and the number of MIRVs that could be incorporated in each ballistic missile.[100] But SALT II, which was signed by both the Soviet Union and the United States in June 1979, would never enter into force.

A highly complex agreement, SALT II would prove to be one of the most controversial US-Soviet pacts of the Cold War.[101] The treaty was denounced by hawks in the US Congress as a 'sell-out' to the Soviets – one that would leave America defenceless against a whole range of new weapons not governed by the agreement. One of the examples often cited was the Soviet 'Backfire' bomber (its NATO designation), which US negotiators believed could reach the United States, but which the Soviets refused to include in the

95 Ibid., pp. 33–34.

96 Federation of American Scientists, 'Strategic Arms Limitation Talks (SALT I)'.

97 Nuclear Threat Initiative (NTI), 'Strategic Arms Limitation Talks (SALT I)', last updated 26 October 2011, at http://bit.ly/37kcsUS.

98 Treaty between the United States of America and the Union of Soviet Socialist Republics on the Limitation of Strategic Offensive Arms; adopted and signed at Vienna, 18 June 1979; never entered into force.

99 'The new agreement will cover the period from October 1977 through December 31, 1985.' 'Joint US-Soviet statement of 24 November 1974 (Vladivostok Agreement)', *Atomic Archive*, at http://bit.ly/2AdCMCN.

100 P. H. Nitze, 'The Vladivostok Accord and SALT II', *Review of Politics*, Vol. 37, No.2 (April 1975), 147–60.

101 See, e.g., NTI, 'Strategic Arms Limitation Talks (SALT II)', last updated 26 October 2011, at http://bit.ly/2VuYbi9.

SALT negotiations.[102] Supporters of arms control, on the other hand, criticised SALT II for doing little to actually restrict the development of nuclear weapons and the arms race.[103]

The Treaty prohibited the construction of new fixed ICBM launchers and the development, testing, or deployment of ICBMs with a launch-weight or a throw-weight greater than that of the heaviest of the heavy ICBMs deployed by either State as of the date of signature of the Treaty (18 June 1979). SALT II further prohibited the flight-testing or deployment of new types of ICBMs (those not flight-tested as of 1 May 1979, except for a single new type of light ICBM), and set the maximum number of re-entry vehicles at 10 for an ICBM and at 14 for an SLBM.

An equal aggregate limit of 2,400 was set for strategic nuclear weapon delivery systems (ICBMs, SLBMs, and heavy bombers). Within the aggregate limit, the Treaty also fixed the following sub-limits:

- no more than 1,320 ICBM and SLBM launchers to be equipped with MIRVs, when counted together with air-to-surface ballistic missiles equipped with MIRVs and heavy bombers equipped for cruise missiles capable of a range in excess of 600 kilometres;
- no more than 1,200 total ICBM and SLBM launchers equipped with MIRVs when counted together with air-to-surface ballistic missiles equipped with MIRVs; and
- no more than 820 ICBM launchers to be equipped with MIRVs.[104]

The Treaty obligated the two States to dismantle or destroy all strategic offensive arms in excess of the Treaty's aggregate numbers by 31 December 1981 and strategic offensive arms prohibited by the Treaty no later than six months after its entry into force.[105]

Debate over SALT II in the US Congress persisted without resolution for months. In December 1979, however, the Soviet invasion of Afghanistan put paid to any chance of SALT II being approved by the Senate, and President Jimmy Carter withdrew the request for consent for its ratification in January 1980. During the 1980s, both nations made

102 US Department of State, Office of the Historian, 'Strategic Arms Limitations Talks/Treaty (SALT) I and II', at http://bit.ly/3dqnGsj. As the Federation of American Scientists recalled, arms control opponents contended that the United States had left a loophole the Soviets would eventually exploit. The United States stated that as it can be refuelled in flight, allowing it to reach the United States, the Backfire was an intercontinental bomber and should be subject to the same restrictions as other strategic bombers. The Soviets consistently maintained that the Backfire was not a strategic bomber because of its non-intercontinental range. J. Pike, C. Vick, M. Jacubowski, and P. Garrett, 'Tu-22M Backfire (Tupolev)', updated 8 August 2000, Federation of American Scientists, at http://bit.ly/3beqXuz. On 16 June 1979, President Brezhnev handed President Carter a written statement with the following text: 'The Soviet side informs the US side that the Soviet "Tu-22M" airplane, called "Backfire" in the USA, is a medium-range bomber, and that it does not intend to give this airplane the capability of operating at intercontinental distances. In this connection, the Soviet side states that it will not increase the radius of action of this airplane in such a way as to enable it to strike targets on the territory of the USA. Nor does it intend to give it such a capability in any other manner, including by in-flight refueling. At the same time, the Soviet side states that it will not increase the production rate of this airplane as compared to the present rate.' 'Soviet Backfire Statement', Federation of American Scientists, at http://bit.ly/37jKJDQ.

103 '1979, June 18: Jimmy Carter and Leonid Brezhnev Sign the SALT-II Nuclear Treaty', *History*, last updated 27 July 2019, at http://bit.ly/2Zo1dFY.

104 Art. V, SALT II.

105 Arts. X and XI, SALT II.

a political commitment to respect the agreement until such time as new arms negotiations could take place. In 1991, with the Cold War over, SALT II was effectively superseded by the first Strategic Arms Reduction Treaty (START I).

THE STRATEGIC ARMS REDUCTION TREATIES (START)

Carter's successor as US president, Ronald Reagan, had been a vehement critic of SALT II during the 1980 presidential campaign. Nonetheless, President Reagan agreed to abide by the terms of SALT II until its treaty-designated expiration on 31 December 1985.[106] In resuming strategic arms negotiations with the Soviet Union in 1982, however, the Reagan administration proposed radical reductions, rather than merely limitations, in each superpower's existing stocks of missiles and warheads. Reagan thus renamed the talks 'START' (an acronym for Strategic Arms Reduction Talks).[107]

In 1983, the Soviet Union quit the talks in protest at the deployment of US intermediate-range missiles in Western Europe. Two years later, however, talks resumed, culminating in July 1991 with the signature of START I by US President George H. W. Bush and Soviet leader Mikhail Gorbachev. While the Treaty's entry into force was complicated by the collapse of the Soviet Union, as a result of START I, by the late 1990s, Russian and US arsenals were down to around 10,000 warheads each,[108] a reduction of two-thirds from the heights of the Cold War in the mid-1980s.[109]

The fate of START II and START III was far less auspicious. START II was signed by both nations' heads of State in January 1993, but on 14 June 2002, despite its domestic ratification by both nations, Russia denounced the Treaty in response to US withdrawal from the ABM Treaty. That same withdrawal also scuppered the negotiations underway for START III, which never resulted in a signed treaty. Negotiations had begun in 1997 between President Bill Clinton and President Boris Yeltsin, with Russian officials suggesting they might accept an upper limit of 1,500 strategic nuclear warheads within the context of the agreement.[110]

START I

START I was swiftly ratified in the US Senate, but in late December 1991, the Soviet Union disintegrated, leaving four independent States with strategic nuclear weapons: Belarus, Kazakhstan, the Russian Federation, and Ukraine. The US Congress passed the Soviet Threat Reduction Act in November 1991, providing US funding and expertise to the

[106] US Department of State, Office of the Historian, 'Strategic Arms Limitations Talks/Treaty (SALT) I and II'.
[107] L. D. Freedman, 'Strategic Arms Reduction Talks', *Britannica*, 20 July 1988, at http://bit.ly/3prcOPE.
[108] 'Introduction', in Schwartz (ed.), *Atomic Audit: The Costs and Consequences of U.S. Nuclear Weapons Since 1940*, p. 2.
[109] H. M. Kristensen and M. Korda, 'Nuclear Notebook', Federation of American Scientists, accessed 1 February 2021, at http://bit.ly/2miTj16.
[110] Arms Control Association, 'The START III Framework at a Glance', updated April 2019, at http://bit.ly/3deEQvc.

former Soviet Union States to secure and dismantle nuclear weapons and their delivery systems (as well as other weapons of mass destruction).[111]

Signed in May 1992, the Lisbon Protocol allowed all four former Soviet States to become party to START I, giving Belarus, Kazakhstan, and Ukraine the option to either destroy their strategic nuclear warheads or to transfer them to Russia. All five parties to START I exchanged the instruments of ratification in Budapest on 5 December 1994 with the Treaty entering into force the same day, for an initial duration of fifteen years.[112]

START I set limits to be reached in a first phase within three years and then a second phase within five years of the Treaty's entry into force. By the end of the second phase, in 1999, both the United States and Russia were permitted a total of 7,950 warheads on a maximum of 1,900 delivery vehicles (missiles and bombers). Of these 7,950 permitted warheads, no more than 6,750 could be mounted on deployed ICBMs and SLBMs. The treaty included intrusive verification measures, including on-site inspection, the stationing of US monitors at the Russian mobile ICBM factory at Votkinsk, and access to missile telemetry (see further Chapter 7). By early 1997, Belarus and Kazakhstan had no remaining nuclear warheads, and Ukraine destroyed its last ICBMs in 1999. The United States and Russia reached the required levels for the second phase during 1997.

START I was the first treaty between the two superpowers to provide for deep reductions of US and Soviet/Russian strategic nuclear weapons. In the view of the Nuclear Threat Initiative, it played 'an indispensable role in ensuring the predictability and stability of the strategic balance' serving as a 'framework' for even deeper cuts in strategic arsenals. 'Even though many elements of START I – first and foremost the limits on the number of warheads and delivery vehicles – quickly became outdated, its verification and transparency provisions maintained their value until the treaty's last days.'[113]

START II

START II, the 'deMIRVing' agreement, prohibited all use of multiple independently targetable re-entry vehicles on ICBMs. It stipulated that the maximum number of warheads attributed to deployed ICBMs of types to which more than one warhead is attributed was 'zero'.[114] In an instance of the contorted drafting to which the negotiators were constrained to resort, Article II(1) provides as follows:

> No later than January 1, 2003, each Party undertakes to have eliminated or to have converted to launchers of ICBMs to which one warhead is attributed all its deployed and non-deployed launchers of ICBMs to which more than one warhead is attributed under Article III of this Treaty (including test launchers and training launchers), with the exception of those launchers of ICBMs other than heavy ICBMs at space launch facilities allowed under the START Treaty, and not to have thereafter launchers of ICBMs to

111 Cooperative Threat Reduction Program, Fact Sheet, at https://bit.ly/2XJVIkn.

112 Art. XVII(2), START I.

113 NTI, 'Treaty between the United States of America and the Union of Soviet Socialist Republics on Strategic Offensive Reductions (START I)', last updated 26 October 2011, at http://bit.ly/350KRpu.

114 Art. I(4)(b), START II.

> which more than one warhead is attributed. ICBM launchers that have been converted to launch an ICBM of a different type shall not be capable of launching an ICBM of the former type. Each Party shall carry out such elimination or conversion using the procedures provided for in the START Treaty, except as otherwise provided for in paragraph 3 of this Article.

Behind the complexity of the drafting, the Treaty was a major step forward in arms control. It stipulated that from 1 January 2003, each Party was prohibited from producing, acquiring, flight-testing (except for flight tests from space launch facilities conducted in accordance with the provisions of the START Treaty), and deploying ICBMs to which more than one warhead was attributed.[115] In addition, each Party undertook 'not to transfer heavy ICBMs to any recipient whatsoever, including any other Party to the START [I] Treaty'.[116] Taken together with the duties of conversion or elimination of MIRVed weapons, this was – or would have been – a disarmament treaty in the true sense of the word.

For START II would never enter into force. It was signed by US President George H. W. Bush and Russian President Boris Yeltsin on 3 January 1993, but on 14 June 2002, despite ratification by both States, Russia denounced the Treaty. Russia's ratification legislation had required the US Senate to ratify the START II Extension Protocol and the 1997 ABM Demarcation Agreements for START II to enter into force.[117] The end of the ABM Treaty spelled the end of START II.

START III

During their March 1997 Summit in Helsinki, President Clinton and President Yeltsin agreed upon a framework for START III negotiations. At their Moscow Summit in September 1998, Clinton and Yeltsin reiterated their commitment to begin formal negotiations on START III as soon as Russia ratified START II.[118] The basic elements of START III were to be that by the end of 2007, coterminous with START II, the United States and Russia would each deploy an aggregate of no more than 2,500 strategic nuclear warheads on ICBMs, SLBMs, and heavy bombers.[119] Russian officials had indicated a willingness to consider negotiated levels as low as 1,500 strategic warheads within the context of a START III agreement (very close to what would later be agreed upon in the New START Treaty).

The United States and Russia also intended to negotiate measures relating to the transparency of strategic warhead inventories and the destruction of strategic warheads, as well as other jointly agreed technical and organisational measures to promote the irreversibility of deep reductions. In addition, the two parties would endeavour to resolve issues related to the goal of making the START I and II treaties unlimited in duration.

115 Art. II(9), START II.
116 Art. II(8), START II.
117 NTI, 'Treaty between the United States of America and the Union of Soviet Socialist Republics on Strategic Offensive Reductions (START II)', last updated 26 October 2011, at http://bit.ly/2R6JU6T.
118 D. Kimball, 'The START III Framework at a Glance', updated April 2019, Arms Control Association, at https://bit.ly/3deEQvc.
119 Ibid.

But the abortive START III negotiations never resulted in a signed treaty. As was the case with START II, the decision by the Bush administration to withdraw from the ABM Treaty effectively put an end to hopes for START III. Arguably, however, in this case, the consequences for arms control were less damaging, given the subsequent achievement of New START.

THE SORT TREATY

Also called the Moscow Treaty, the 2002 Strategic Offensive Reductions Treaty entered into force on 1 June 2003 following domestic ratification by the Senate and the State Duma, respectively, and the subsequent exchange of diplomatic instruments. SORT would have expired at the end of 2012 if it not been superseded earlier by New START. The Treaty, which is sometimes derided as more of a policy statement than a legally binding instrument, limited the United States and Russia to no more than 2,200 strategic nuclear warheads each.[120] This was the size of arsenal that the Bush administration's 2001 Nuclear Posture Review had concluded was necessary for the United States, regardless of the levels of nuclear arms other nations possessed. Indeed, President Bush had originally proposed that he and President Putin merely make statements of national policy setting out their intended strategic force levels, but he later agreed to negotiate a treaty at Putin's insistence.[121]

SORT was, in the view of one commentator, 'not much of a treaty'. While START I and New START 'each made a good-sized book, SORT barely filled two pages. Curiously, it did not define a "strategic nuclear warhead" ... or any other term for that matter. Lacking any monitoring provisions, SORT was unverifiable.'[122] But Steven Pifer was too dismissive of the Strategic Offensive Reductions Treaty, which was indeed a legally binding treaty and whose main provisions were implemented in practice. President George W. Bush directed the US military to cut its stockpile of both deployed and reserve nuclear weapons in half by 2012. That goal was said to have been achieved in 2007, a reduction in the US nuclear arsenal to just over half of the 2001 total of warheads.[123]

[120] Art. I, SORT: 'Each Party shall reduce and limit strategic nuclear warheads ... so that by December 31, 2012, the aggregate number of such warheads does not exceed 1700–2200 for each Party.'

[121] S. Pifer, 'SORT vs. New START: Why the Administration Is Leery of a Treaty', The Brookings Institution, Washington, DC, 15 March 2013, at http://brook.gs/3pq20Qm.

[122] Ibid.

[123] J. Trebes and T. Lavietes, 'Monitoring a Nuclear Weapon from the Inside', *Science & Technology Review*, July/August 2008, Lawrence Livermore National Laboratory, 12–19, at https://bit.ly/3b6Xrqu, at p. 15. Less complementary, initially, was the *Bulletin of the Atomic Scientists*, which reported in 2007 that 'slow reductions' were continuing under the 2002 Moscow Treaty. 'U.S. Nuclear Forces', *Bulletin of the Atomic Scientists*, Vol. 63, No. 1 (2007), 79–82, at p. 79. But a year later, the Bulletin was estimating that the US stockpile contained 5,400 nuclear warheads (approximately 4,075 operational warheads, of which 3,575 were strategic and 500 were non-strategic warheads), along with about 1,260 additional warheads held in the responsive force or inactive stockpile. The Department of Defense had removed an additional 5,150 warheads from the stockpile for future dismantlement . R. S. Norris and H. M. Kristensen, 'U.S. Nuclear Forces', *Bulletin of the Atomic Scientists*, 1 March 2008, at http://bit.ly/3qqxSXL.

CONCLUDING REMARKS

Have two become three? The Cold War was characterised by the overriding rivalry between the United States and the Soviet Union, two nuclear superpowers whose global hegemony was fought out on a regional and national basis around the world. But the growing influence of China, the economic powerhouse that is today flexing its military muscles across Asia, further complicates the nuclear arms control and disarmament landscape. Despite China's numerical inferiority in strategic nuclear armaments, the arms race is perhaps no longer a two-horse race in strategic military terms.

Frank Rose, Senior Fellow for Security and Strategy in Foreign Policy at the Brookings Institution, has suggested that containing China's perceived expansionism should begin with a US build-up of conventional forces in the Western Pacific. Now unconstrained by the INF Treaty from deploying, anywhere in the world, ground-launched conventional and nuclear cruise and ballistic missiles with a range of between 500 and 5,500 kilometres, he argued that the United States could also begin laying the groundwork to bring China into a future nuclear arms control regime over the longer term. In a blog entry on the Brookings Institution website, he offered a few 'practical ideas' for engaging China.[124] For example, the United States could

- convene bilateral strategic stability talks with China;
- develop a bilateral pre-launch missile notification regime;
- invite China to observe a New START inspection;
- establish a link between the US Nuclear Risk Reduction Center[125] and a similar Chinese entity;
- negotiate bilateral space norms for outer space, an area where the Obama administration made some progress with China; and
- hold trilateral strategic stability talks with Russia and China, or broader talks with the five permanent members of the UN Security Council.[126]

Where does this leave the future of arms control between Russia and the United States? The preamble to New START notes the commitment of the two parties to the 'fulfilment of their obligations under Article VI of the Treaty on the Non-Proliferation of Nuclear Weapons of July 1, 1968, and to the achievement of the historic goal of freeing humanity from the nuclear threat'.[127] Despite the conclusion of New START, however, the Obama administration embarked on a massive nuclear modernisation programme of nuclear ballistic missiles and of new submarines and bombers to deliver nuclear weapons.[128]

[124] Rose, 'Bringing China into the Fold on Arms Control and Strategic Stability Issues', The Brookings Institution, Washington, DC, 25 September 2019.

[125] Officially renamed the National and Nuclear Risk Reduction Center (NNRRC) pursuant to National Security Presidential Memorandum 34. US Department of State, 'Renaming of the National and Nuclear Risk Reduction Center', 8 February 2021, at http://bit.ly/3k3JE8k.

[126] Rose, 'Bringing China into the Fold on Arms Control and Strategic Stability Issues'.

[127] New START, fifth preambular para.

[128] Elisabeth Eaves characterises the modernisation programme as a straightforward quid pro quo for Senate approval of New START. E. Eaves, 'Why Is America Getting a New $100 billion Nuclear Weapon?', *Bulletin*

But what above all is preventing moves towards nuclear disarmament is the unrelenting US investment in its missile defence systems. Reacting to new plans announced by the Pentagon in January 2019, Russia said the new US missile defence strategy would trigger an arms race in space and further undermine global stability. The strategy advocates the development of new space-based sensors and systems to more quickly detect and shoot down incoming missiles. It made clear that the new defence technologies are needed to counter advanced weapons being developed by Russia and China along with threats from North Korea and Iran.[129] The Russian Ministry of Foreign Affairs portrayed the strategy as proof of 'Washington's desire to ensure uncontested military domination in the world'. Describing the plans as an attempt to reproduce President Reagan's 'Star Wars' missile defence plans on a new technological level, Russia urged the Trump administration to 'come to its senses' and engage in arms control talks with Russia.[130]

In 2009, President Obama had pledged that the United States would seek a world without nuclear weapons. His then vice-president, now the US president, has a huge challenge if he is to pursue the goal of a nuclear-free world. With the duration of New START extended until 2026, the Tenth Review Conference of the NPT, due to finally occur in January 2022, will be the next major test of his administration's ability to steer the world in this fundamental issue: the future of nuclear weapons in the twenty-first century.

of the Atomic Scientists, 8 February 2021, at http://bit.ly/3bfyUPX. The $100 billion weapon she refers to is the ground-based strategic deterrent to be developed for the Pentagon by Northrop Grumman to replace the Minuteman III missile fleet.

129 V. Isachenkov, 'Russia Warns US Missile Defense Plans Will Fuel Arms Race', Associated Press, 18 January 2019, at http://bit.ly/3k1nnI7.

130 Ibid.

6

Treaties Prohibiting Nuclear Weapons

While nine States in Asia, Europe, and North America retain and modernise their nuclear arsenals, projecting to retain nuclear weapons for the rest of the century, most of the world and beyond is subject to a regional nuclear-weapon-free zone. The 1968 Treaty on the Non-proliferation of Nuclear Weapons (NPT) had explicitly reaffirmed the right of any group of States to conclude regional treaties to assure 'the total absence of nuclear weapons in their respective territories'.[1]

This chapter considers, in chronological order, the comprehensive regional zones established by treaties for Antarctica, Latin America and the Caribbean, Outer Space, the sea bed and the ocean floor, the South Pacific, Africa, South-East Asia, and Central Asia, as well as noting the national nuclear-free status of Mongolia. As of 1 January 2021, a total of 103 States were prohibited by international treaty, on a regional basis, from acquiring or using nuclear weapons in Africa, the Americas, Asia, and the Pacific (in addition to their obligations under the NPT). The chapter also explains the failure, thus far, to conclude a nuclear-weapon-free zone for the Middle East.

In 1975, United Nations (UN) General Assembly Resolution 3472 (XXX) B defined a Nuclear-Weapon-Free Zone as being 'as a general rule':

> any zone recognized as such by the General Assembly of the United Nations, which any group of States, in the free exercises of their sovereignty, has established by virtue of a treaty or convention whereby:

(a) The statute of total absence of nuclear weapons to which the zone shall be subject, including the procedure for the delimitation of the zone, is defined;
(b) An international system of verification and control is established to guarantee compliance with the obligations deriving from that statute.[2]

In 2017, a treaty with global reach outlawing all development, possession, transfer, and use of nuclear weapons – the Treaty on the Prohibition of Nuclear Weapons (TPNW) – was

[1] Art. VII, Treaty on the Non-proliferation of Nuclear Weapons; opened for signature at London, Moscow, and Washington, DC, 1 July 1968; entered into force 5 March 1970.

[2] UN General Assembly Resolution 3472 (XXX) B, adopted on 11 December 1975 by 82 votes to 10, with 36 abstentions, operative para. 1.

concluded within the United Nations. Entering into force in January 2021 for its first fifty States Parties, it is the first comprehensive treaty prohibition of nuclear weapons at global level. Among its fifty-four States Parties (as of the end of June 2021), eight were not already bound by a regional prohibition on the use of nuclear weapons.[3] The likely impact of the TPNW on the behaviour of the nuclear-armed States is sharply disputed.

THE REGIONAL NUCLEAR PROHIBITION TREATIES

The 1959 Antarctic Treaty

Adopted and signed in Washington, DC, in December 1959, the Antarctic Treaty entered into force in June 1962. As of 1 January 2021, 54 States were party to the Treaty.[4] As Chapter 4 described, the 1959 Antarctic Treaty was the first legally binding Cold War–era agreement governing nuclear weapons. Described by the US Department of State as a 'non-armament' treaty, it 'demilitarized the Antarctic Continent and provided for its cooperative exploration and future use'.[5]

Each State Party is prohibited generally from conducting 'any measures of a military nature' and the 'testing of any type of weapons'.[6] Specifically prohibited are '[a]ny nuclear explosions in Antarctica' or the disposal of radioactive waste material anywhere on the world's southernmost continent.[7] Despite the lack of any international verification measures, there have been no reports of violations of the Antarctic Treaty provisions pertaining to nuclear weapons.

The 1966 Outer Space Treaty

The Treaty on Principles Governing the Activities of States in the Exploration and Use of Outer Space (commonly known as the Outer Space Treaty) was concluded under the auspices of the UN General Assembly and 'commended' by Resolution 2222 (XXI) in December 1966.[8] The Treaty was opened for signature by the three depository States – the Soviet Union, the United Kingdom, and the United States – the following month, entering into force in October 1967.[9] As of 1 January 2021, 111 States were party to the Outer Space Treaty, including space powers China, India, Japan, Russia, and the United States. As of this writing, the latest adherence to the Treaty had occurred in September 2020 from Bosnia and Herzegovina. Twenty-three States are signatories.

3 Austria, Bangladesh, Holy See, Ireland, Malta, Palau, Palestine, and San Marino were not so bound.

4 See the latest list of States Parties to the Treaty, at http://bit.ly/2xjIVLO.

5 US Department of State, 'Antarctic Treaty', Bureau of Arms Control, Verification, and Compliance, at https://bit.ly/3paFlcj.

6 Art. I(1), 1959 Antarctic Treaty.

7 Art. V(1), 1959 Antarctic Treaty.

8 Treaty on Principles Governing the Activities of States in the Exploration and Use of Outer Space, including the Moon and Other Celestial Bodies; concluded under UN General Assembly Resolution 2222 (XXI), adopted without a vote on 19 December 1966.

9 The UK government version of the text is available at https://bit.ly/2OIiiJ7.

The Outer Space Treaty prohibits the stationing of nuclear weapons in space or on celestial bodies, including the Moon. Under Article IV(1), States Parties undertake not to place in orbit around the Earth any objects carrying nuclear weapons or any other weapons of mass destruction, not to install such weapons on celestial bodies, and not to station such weapons in outer space in 'any other manner'. Article IV(2) stipulates that the Moon and other celestial bodies shall be used by all States Parties exclusively for peaceful purposes. The testing of any type of weapons on celestial bodies, including the Moon, is expressly prohibited. The testing of nuclear weapons in outer space had earlier been outlawed under the 1963 Partial Test-Ban Treaty (see Chapter 4), and this prohibition is reflective of customary law.

Neither the launching of weapons from Earth into space nor their use in outer space (for instance, to destroy an enemy satellite during an international armed conflict) is a violation of the Outer Space Treaty.[10] Indeed, according to the US Department of Defense, 'lawful military activities in self-defense (e.g., missile early warning, use of weapon systems) would be consistent with the use of space for peaceful purposes, but aggressive activities that violate the Charter of the United Nations would not be permissible.'[11] The US Department of Defense further notes that the Outer Space Treaty 'does not ban the use of nuclear or other weapons of mass destruction that go into a fractional orbit or engage in suborbital flight'. For example, intercontinental ballistic missiles (ICBMs) will travel a portion of their trajectory in outer space, but because this entry into outer space would be only temporary, ICBMs with nuclear warheads would not violate the prohibitions in the Outer Space Treaty.[12]

Nuclear weapons are not explicitly defined in the Treaty, but they are understood in the same terms as they were under the Partial Test-Ban Treaty and later the NPT, a definition that is reflective of customary law. While the definition ordinarily excludes methods of transportation, such as an aircraft, the carrying of nuclear weapons on an orbital spacecraft would be captured by the prohibition in the Outer Space Treaty on stationing such weapons in outer space in any manner.

While there have been, to date, no alleged violations of the Treaty's provisions pertaining to nuclear weapons, the risk of an arms race in space is growing. Beginning in the early 1980s, the Conference on Disarmament considered proposals under an agenda item 'prevention of an arms race in outer space'. This comprised drafts of treaties aimed at preventing the placement of all weapons in outer space and prohibiting the use of anti-satellite weapons. In 2008, China and Russia introduced the draft text of such a treaty to the Conference on Disarmament, offering a revised draft in 2014.[13] The United States and

10 That said, New START prohibits Russia and the United States from interfering with the other's National Technical Means for verifying compliance, 'which is understood to include satellite reconnaissance systems as well as other intelligence collection methods'. J. Lauder, F. G. Klotz, and W. Courtney, 'How to Avoid a Space Arms Race', The RAND Blog, 26 October 2020, at http://bit.ly/3avlMac.

11 US Department of Defense, *Law of War Manual*, June 2015 (Updated December 2016), at https://bit.ly/3dnoHAI, §14.10.4.

12 Ibid., §14.10.3.1.

13 UN Office for Disarmament Affairs (UNODA), 'Outer Space', at https://bit.ly/3prGmMX.

a number of other nations continue to oppose such legislative development, ostensibly 'because it is not possible to verify such a treaty'.[14]

In 2017, the General Assembly decided to establish a Group of Governmental Experts to consider and make recommendations on substantial elements of an international legally binding instrument on the prevention of an arms race in outer space.[15] In 2020, the Assembly adopted Resolution 75/35 in which it reaffirmed 'the importance and urgency of preventing an arms race in outer space and the readiness of all States to contribute to that common objective', in 'conformity with' the provisions of the Outer Space Treaty.[16] The resolution was adopted by a recorded vote of 185 votes to 2, with Israel and the United States voting against it.

The 1967 Tlatelolco Treaty

The Treaty for the Prohibition of Nuclear Weapons in Latin America and the Caribbean (better known as the Treaty of Tlatelolco, in recognition of the district of Mexico City where it was negotiated) was concluded and opened for signature on 14 February 1967, entering into force on 22 April 1968. As of 1 January 2021, thirty-three States from Latin America and the Caribbean were party to the Treaty.

Costa Rica had first proposed the negotiation of a Latin American nuclear arms control regime at an Organization of American States (OAS) Council meeting in 1958. Three years later, Brazil advocated the creation of a nuclear-weapon-free zone within the Americas. The more formal starting point of the effort, though, was the Joint Declaration issued on 29 April 1963 by five Latin American presidents, led by the President of Mexico Adolfo López Mateos, who invited the presidents of Bolivia, Brazil, Chile, and Ecuador to jointly announce with him that their respective Governments were prepared to sign a multilateral Latin American agreement undertaking not to manufacture, receive, store, or test nuclear weapons 'or nuclear launching devices'.[17]

In October 1963, a draft resolution on the initiative was submitted to the First Committee of the UN General Assembly with the co-sponsorship of 11 Latin American States.[18] In its Resolution 1911 (XVIII) on the 'Denuclearization of Latin America', adopted

14 Cited in L. Schlein, 'Nuclear Arms Race, Weaponization of Outer Space High on US Disarmament Agenda', *Voice of America*, 1 October 2020, at http://bit.ly/3duu8Rk. In August 2020, the US Space Force, formally created in 2019, issued its first statement on doctrine in which it determined that the primary purpose of the military in space is 'to secure U.S. interests through deterrence and, when necessary, the application of force'. A. M. Wright, 'Space Force Releases 1st Doctrine, Defines "Spacepower" as Distinct Form of Military Power', US Space Force, 10 August 2020, at http://bit.ly/3dn7omg.

15 UN General Assembly Resolution 72/250, adopted on 24 December 2017 by 108 votes to 5 (France, Israel, Ukraine, United Kingdom, and the United States), with 47 abstentions.

16 UN General Assembly Resolution 75/35, adopted on 7 December 2020 by 185 votes to 2 and no abstentions, operative para. 1.

17 A. García Robles, 'The Prohibition of Nuclear Weapons in Latin America, Summary of the Main Working Phases', Agency for the Prohibition of Nuclear Weapons in Latin America (OPANAL), undated but accessed 1 February 2021, at http://bit.ly/3qv2eIR.

18 Bolivia, Brazil, Costa Rica, Chile, Ecuador, El Salvador, Haiti, Honduras, Mexico, Panama, and Uruguay.

after a vote, the General Assembly noted 'with satisfaction' the proposal and requested the Secretary-General to provide technical support.[19]

The Treaty for the Prohibition of Nuclear Weapons in Latin America[20] was formally negotiated in a body termed the Preliminary Commission for the Denuclearization of Latin America (COPREDAL), established for the purpose by committed States in the region. The process, which convened between March 1965 and February 1967, was supported by three working groups. Working Group 'A' was responsible for identifying the geographic boundaries of the area to which it felt the future treaty should apply, as well as to seek to bring on board other countries falling within that geographical area. Group B was tasked with studying the methods by which the treaty's implementation could be verified. Group C was mandated with obtaining a commitment from the nuclear Powers – then five – to respect the treaty.[21]

The Preliminary Draft of the Treaty for the Denuclearization of Latin America was prepared by 14 March 1966. A key omission in the text was the phrase 'launching devices', drawing a distinction between the means for the transportation and launching of nuclear weapons and the weapons themselves. This is said to have been necessary for 'otherwise the absurd situation would arise where most commercial aircraft would be prohibited, since they are capable of being used as vehicles for the launching of certain nuclear weapons'.[22] As Chapter 3 described, this exclusion of combat aircraft, heavy bombers, and nuclear-armed submarines is fully consistent with the definition of nuclear weapons that has evolved under customary law, although the particular explanation proffered for the formulation in the context of the Treaty of Tlatelolco does not fully persuade.

The entry-into-force provisions of the Treaty were hard fought over. They are also unusual. The Treaty required an exacting and cumulative set of conditions to trigger its entry into force, which included adherence by all States in the region, adherence to the First Additional Protocol to the Treaty by 'all extra-continental or continental States having de jure or de facto international responsibility for territories situated in the zone of application of the Treaty', adherence to the Second Additional Protocol to the Treaty by all nuclear weapons possessors, and conclusion by the Contracting States of safeguards agreements with the International Atomic Energy Agency (IAEA).[23]

Given that these cumulative conditions could have caused the Treaty never to enter into force, a further provision allowed each Contracting State to make a declaration upon or following ratification by which it waived these conditions and formally brought the Treaty into force for it.[24] The Treaty of Tlatelolco duly became formally binding on 22 April 1968,

19 UN General Assembly Resolution 1911 (XVIII), adopted on 27 November 1963 by 91 votes to 0, with 15 abstentions (primarily Soviet bloc countries), operative paras. 1 and 4.

20 By its Resolution 267 (E-V) of 3 July 1990, the General Conference of OPANAL formally amended the title of the Treaty to include the words 'and the Caribbean'. As of 1 January 2021, twenty-four States Parties to the Treaty had ratified this amendment to the Treaty.

21 García Robles, 'The Prohibition of Nuclear Weapons in Latin America, Summary of the Main Working Phases'.

22 Ibid.

23 Art. 28(1), Treaty of Tlatelolco.

24 Art. 28(2), Treaty of Tlatelolco.

following its signature and ratification by Brazil and El Salvador, the first two States to make such a declaration. In 2002, Cuba became the last of the thirty-three States Parties to adhere; its ratification was accompanied by a diatribe against the United States for its 'policy of hostility' towards Cuba and 'illegal occupation of part of the national territory'.[25] Forty years previously, the world had nearly come to grief as a result of the covert introduction of Soviet nuclear missiles onto the island of Cuba.

The Treaty of Tlatelolco prohibits all use, testing, production, or acquisition by any means of any nuclear weapons by its States Parties, as well as the storage, installation, deployment of any nuclear weapons.[26] Nuclear weapons are defined in the Treaty as 'any device which is capable of releasing nuclear energy in an uncontrolled manner and which has a group of characteristics that are appropriate for use for warlike purposes'.[27] The definition clarifies that an 'instrument that may be used for the transport or propulsion of the device is not included in this definition if it is separable from the device and not an indivisible part thereof'.[28]

The Treaty does not prohibit the development of nuclear weapons; nor does it outlaw the production or even the detonation of other 'nuclear devices' for peaceful purposes – quite the contrary. Thus, Article 18 of the Treaty ('Explosions for peaceful purposes') stipulates in its first paragraph that the Contracting Parties 'may carry out explosions of nuclear devices for peaceful purposes – including explosions which involve devices similar to those used in nuclear weapons – or collaborate with third parties for the same purpose, provided that they do so in accordance with the provisions of this article and the other articles of the Treaty'. Today, of course, this apparent permission is more than just an anachronism, given the unequivocal obligations of non-nuclear-weapon States Parties under Article II of the 1968 Nuclear Non-proliferation Treaty (NPT).[29] It would also contravene customary law. The offending provision has, however, not been formally deleted from the Treaty of Tlatelolco.

Additional Protocol I to the Treaty applies its provisions to territories for which France, the Netherlands, the United Kingdom, and the United States are 'internationally responsible' within the limits of the geographic zone established by the Treaty. These four States are all party to the Protocol. Additional Protocol II obligates the five nuclear-weapon States

[25] Cuba's ratification on 23 October 2002 was accompanied by a reservation that achieving a solution to the United States hostility to Cuba and the use of the Guantánamo Bay military base for US nuclear weapons was a precondition to Cuba's continued membership of the Treaty: 'The Government of the Republic of Cuba declares that the obstacles which, up to the present time, have prevented the Republic of Cuba from fully acceding to the Treaty for the Prohibition of Nuclear Weapons in Latin America and the Caribbean still exist and continue to have serious implications for Cuba's security. The only nuclear Power in this part of the world, the United States of America, is maintaining a policy of hostility against Cuba; tightening its economic, commercial and financial embargo; strengthening its campaign against our country; and continuing, by force and against the wishes of our people, its illegal occupation of part of the national territory, and even allowing its ships to pass through that area when they are carrying nuclear weapons. In the future, the solution of this problem must be considered a precondition for our country's continued adherence to this Treaty.'

[26] Art. 1(1), Treaty of Tlatelolco.

[27] Art. 5, Treaty of Tlatelolco.

[28] Ibid.

[29] See further on this issue Chapter 4.

recognised by the NPT, all of which are party to the Protocol, to respect the status of denuclearisation of the relevant geographic zone, committing them not to use or threaten to use nuclear weapons against any party to the Treaty.[30]

The Agency for the Prohibition of Nuclear Weapons in Latin America (OPANAL) is responsible for overseeing the implementation of the Treaty. At the inauguration of the First Session of the General Conference of OPANAL in Mexico in September 1969, the UN Secretary-General, U Thant, declared as follows:

> The Treaty of Tlatelolco is unique in several respects. It is true that the Antarctic Treaty and the Outer Space Treaty have prevented an arms race from taking place in those regions, and that concerted international efforts are now being undertaken to keep the arms race from spreading to the sea-bed and the ocean floor. All these regions have an element in common in that they are not inhabited. The Treaty of Tlatelolco is unique in that it applies to an important inhabited area of the earth. It is also unique in that the Agency which is being established at this session will have the advantage of a permanent and effective system of control with a number of novel features. In addition to applying the safeguards of the International Atomic Energy Agency, the regime under the Treaty also makes provision for special reports and enquiries and, in cases of suspicion, for special inspections. There is embodied in your Treaty a number of aspects if the system known as 'verification-by-challenge', which is one of the more hopeful new concepts introduced into the complicated question of verification and control.[31]

There have been no reports of violations by any of the parties to either the Treaty or the two annexed Protocols.

The 1970 Sea-Bed Treaty

The Treaty on the Prohibition of the Emplacement of Nuclear Weapons and Other Weapons of Mass Destruction on the Sea-Bed and the Ocean Floor and in the Subsoil Thereof (Sea-Bed Treaty) prohibits the placement of nuclear weapons on the sea-bed restricting exploration of the sea-bed and the ocean floor to peaceful purposes. Adopted in December 1970, the Sea-Bed Treaty was opened for signature in London, Moscow, and Washington, DC, on 11 February 1971, entering into force on 18 May 1972, following adherence by the Soviet Union, the United Kingdom, and the United States, and nineteen other States.[32] As of 1 January 2021, ninety-four States were party to the Sea-Bed Treaty.

Following a proposal to the UN Secretary-General from Malta in August 1967, the UN General Assembly had established an ad hoc committee to study ways of reserving the seabed for peaceful purposes, with the objective of ensuring that 'the exploration and use of the seabed and the ocean floor should be conducted in accordance with the principles and purposes of the Charter of the United Nations, in the interests of maintaining

30 Art. 3, Additional Protocol II to the Treaty of Tlatelolco.

31 Declaration of U Thant, UN Secretary-General, to the General Conference of OPANAL, Mexico, 2 September 1969, text in: Report of the Conference on the Committee on Disarmament, CCD doc. CCD/268, 25 September 1969, at https://bit.ly/37ps1dR, Annex III.

32 Art. X(3), Sea-Bed Treaty.

international peace and security and for the benefit of all mankind'.[33] After more than two years of negotiations, the text of the Treaty was formally 'commended' by the UN General Assembly on 7 December 1970.[34]

Article I sets out the main obligation of the Treaty, prohibiting States Parties from emplacing on the sea-bed and the ocean floor beyond a twelve-mile coastal zone nuclear weapons or other weapons of mass destruction (neither of which is formally defined).[35] Procedures for verification are set out in Article III of the Treaty. Parties are empowered to undertake verification either using their own means, with the assistance of other parties, or through appropriate international procedures within the framework of the United Nations and in accordance with the UN Charter. These provisions 'permit parties to assure themselves the Treaty obligations are being fulfilled without interfering with legitimate seabed activities'.[36]

The 1985 Treaty of Rarotonga

The South Pacific Nuclear Free Zone Treaty was concluded and signed at Rarotonga in the Cook Islands on 6 August 1985, the fortieth anniversary of the dropping of the atomic bomb on Hiroshima. The Treaty of Rarotonga, as it is commonly referred to, entered into force on 11 December 1986. As of 1 January 2021, thirteen States from among the eighteen members of the Pacific Islands Forum were party to it.[37]

In 1975, the South Pacific Forum, a regional organisation that promotes cooperation among Pacific nations,[38] had responded positively to a proposal by New Zealand for the establishment of a nuclear-weapon-free zone in the Pacific region. The proposal was endorsed by the UN General Assembly the same year,[39] although the text of the South Pacific Nuclear Free Zone Treaty would take another ten years to conclude.

The Treaty of Rarotonga prohibits the manufacture, acquisition, possession, and control of all nuclear explosive devices by its States Parties, as well as the dumping of radioactive waste at sea within a defined zone.[40] Under Annex I, the 'Treaty Zone' covers

33 UN General Assembly Resolution 2340 (XXII), adopted on 18 December 1967 by 99 votes to 0 (without abstention).

34 UN General Assembly Resolution 2660 (XXV), adopted on 7 December 1970 by 104 votes to 2 (El Salvador and Peru), with two abstentions (Ecuador and France), operative para. 1.

35 The sea-bed in the Treaty is thus defined as anywhere on the floor of the seas beyond twelve-mile limits from State territory. Art. II, Sea-Bed Treaty.

36 US Department of State, 'Treaty on the Prohibition of the Emplacement of Nuclear Weapons and Other Weapons of Mass Destruction on the Seabed and the Ocean Floor and in the Subsoil Thereof', at http://bit.ly/3pDwY93.

37 Australia, the Cook Islands, Fiji, Kiribati, Nauru, New Zealand, Niue, Papua New Guinea, Samoa, Solomon Islands, Tonga, Tuvalu, and Vanuatu. Pacific Islands Forum members that are not party to the Treaty are the following: the Marshall Islands, Micronesia, and Palau – all UN member States – as well as French Polynesia and New Caledonia, neither of which is recognised as a State by the UN Secretary-General as they fall under France's dominion.

38 The South Pacific Forum was renamed the Pacific Islands Forum in 2000.

39 UN General Assembly Resolution 3477 (XXX), adopted on 11 December 1975 by 110 votes to 0, with 20 abstentions.

40 Art. 3(1), Treaty of Rarotonga.

an extensive part of the South Pacific. The Treaty further requires States Parties to prevent the testing or stationing of any nuclear explosive devices within their territories.[41]

According to Article 1(c) of the Treaty, a nuclear explosive device is defined as 'any nuclear weapon or other explosive device capable of releasing nuclear energy, irrespective of the purpose for which it could be used'. The term, it is further stipulated, 'includes such a weapon or device in unassembled and partly assembled forms, but does not include the means of transport or delivery of such a weapon or device if separable from and not an indivisible part of it'. There is no dedicated body established to oversee the implementation of the Treaty. Under Article 8(1), the States Parties agree to establish a 'control system' for the purpose of verifying compliance with their obligations under the Treaty. It is stipulated that the control system comprises reports and the exchange of information, consultations, the application to peaceful nuclear activities of IAEA safeguards, and a complaints procedure (set out in Annex 4 to the Treaty).[42]

There are three protocols to the Treaty of Rarotonga, which are open to adherence by certain nuclear-weapon States. Protocol I, which was open to adherence by France, the United Kingdom, and the United States, obliges each party to apply the prohibitions of the Treaty to territories within the South Pacific Nuclear Free Zone for which it is internationally responsible. France and the United Kingdom are States Parties while the United States is a signatory.

Protocol II, which is open to adherence by all five NPT-designated nuclear-weapon States, obligates its States Parties not to use or threaten to use nuclear explosive devices against any party to the Treaty or against each other's territories located within the zone. China, France, Russia, and the United Kingdom are States Parties to the Protocol while again the United States is a signatory.

Protocol III obliges the five nuclear-weapon States not to test any nuclear explosive devices within the zone established by the Treaty. Once again, China, France, Russia, and the United Kingdom are all States Parties while the United States is a signatory. In a statement of reservation and interpretation, however, France affirmed that it did not consider its inherent right to self-defence as set out in the UN Charter to be limited by the Protocols.[43] The United States has stated that its practices and procedures in the South Pacific are 'not inconsistent' with the Treaty and its protocols but has affirmed that the zone arrangement does not 'impose restrictions on the exercise of rights recognized under international law, particularly the high seas freedoms of navigation and overflight, the right of innocent passage of territorial and archipelagic seas, the right of transit passage of international straits, and the right of archipelagic sea lanes passage of archipelagic

[41] Arts. 5 and 6(1), Treaty of Rarotonga.

[42] Art. 8(2), Treaty of Rarotonga.

[43] The Secretary General of the Pacific Islands Forum Secretariat as depositary of the Treaty received France's ratification on 20 September 1996 with the following statement: 'no provision of the Protocols or the articles of the Treaty to which the Protocols refer shall impair the full exercise of the inherent right of self-defence provided for in Article 51 of the United Nations Charter'.

waters'.[44] This would allow the United States to move vessels with nuclear weapons through the zone.[45]

The 1995 Bangkok Treaty

The Treaty on the Southeast Asia Nuclear-Weapon-Free Zone (also called the SEANWFZ Treaty or the Bangkok Treaty) was concluded on 15 December 1995 and entered into force on 28 March 1997. As of 1 January 2021, all ten members of the Association of Southeast Asian Nations (ASEAN) were party to the Treaty.[46]

The idea for the Southeast Asia Nuclear-Weapon-Free Zone was first mooted in 1971, when the original five members of ASEAN – Indonesia, Malaysia, Philippines, Singapore, and Thailand – signed a Declaration on a Zone of Peace, Freedom, and Neutrality in Kuala Lumpur. But negotiations on a nuclear-weapon-free zone did not start until the mid-1980s and were slow to progress, concluding with the opening for signature of the Treaty only in late 1995.

States Parties to the Bangkok Treaty are obligated not to develop, manufacture or otherwise acquire, possess, or 'exercise control over' nuclear weapons; to station nuclear weapons; or to test or use nuclear weapons anywhere inside or outside the designated Treaty zone.[47] The Treaty defines nuclear weapons as 'any explosive device capable of releasing nuclear energy in an uncontrolled manner but does not include the means of transport or delivery of such device if separable from and not an indivisible part thereof'.[48]

States Parties are further prohibited from assisting or encouraging the manufacture or acquisition by any State of any nuclear explosive device – not defined in the Treaty – and undertake not to provide source or special fissionable material or equipment to any nuclear-weapon State as well as any non-nuclear-weapon State, unless that material or equipment is subject to a relevant safeguards agreement with the IAEA.[49] States Parties are also required to prevent the stationing of any nuclear explosive device in their respective territories and to prevent the testing of any nuclear explosive device.[50] In distinction to other nuclear-weapon-free zones, the Treaty's zone of application also includes the continental shelves and exclusive economic zones (EEZ) of the States Parties.[51]

44 US Department of State, 'South Pacific Nuclear Free Zone Treaty and Protocols', Bureau of International Security and Nonproliferation, at http://bit.ly/370Uf8q.

45 Ibid.; and see also NTI, 'South Pacific Nuclear-Free Zone (SPNFZ) Treaty of Rarotonga', last updated 30 November 2020, at http://bit.ly/3azZKDD.

46 Brunei Darussalam, Cambodia, Indonesia, the Lao People's Democratic Republic, Malaysia, Myanmar, Philippines, Singapore, Thailand, and Vietnam. As of this writing, two further States – Papua New Guinea and Timor-Leste – were seeking to join ASEAN. On 26 September 2018, Timor-Leste signed the Treaty on the Prohibition of Nuclear Weapons.

47 Art. 3(1), Treaty of Bangkok.

48 Art. 1(c), Treaty of Bangkok.

49 Art. 4(3), Treaty of Bangkok.

50 Art. 3(2), Treaty of Bangkok.

51 Art. 2(1), Treaty of Bangkok. The Treaty defines the 'Southeast Asia Nuclear-Weapon-Free Zone' as 'the area comprising the territories of all States in Southeast Asia, namely, Brunei Darussalam, Cambodia, Indonesia, Laos, Malaysia, Myanmar, Philippines, Singapore, Thailand and Vietnam, and their respective continental shelves and Exclusive Economic Zones (EEZ)'. Art. 1(a), Treaty of Bangkok.

A Commission for the Southeast Asia Nuclear-Weapon-Free Zone was created to 'oversee the implementation of' the Treaty and to 'ensure compliance with its provisions'.[52] An Annex to the Bangkok Treaty sets out the procedure for a fact-finding mission to a State Party, which may be authorised by the Executive Committee (a subsidiary organ of the Commission) upon request of a State Party.[53] The aim of a fact-finding mission is to 'clarify and resolve a situation which may be considered ambiguous or which may give rise to doubts about compliance' with the provisions of the Treaty.[54]

A Protocol to the Bangkok Treaty, open to adherence by the five NPT-designated nuclear-weapon States, would oblige them not to use or threaten to use nuclear weapons against any State Party to the treaty and not to use or threaten to use nuclear weapons within the region.[55] None of the nuclear-weapon States has yet adhered to or even signed the Protocol, on the basis that they consider the zone of application to be too broad or its precise scope unclear. The Nuclear Threat Initiative notes the United States' concern regarding the negative security assurances required of the parties to the Protocol; the ambiguity it perceives in the treaty language regarding the permissibility of port calls by ships carrying nuclear weapons; and the procedural rights of the parties to the Protocol to be represented before the executive bodies set up by the Treaty to ensure its implementation.[56]

The 1996 Pelindaba Treaty

The text of the African Nuclear-Weapon-Free Zone Treaty (Pelindaba Treaty) was concluded at experts' meetings in South Africa and approved by the African Heads of State on 23 June 1995. The Pelindaba Treaty was opened for signature in Cairo on 11 April 1996, entering into force on 15 July 2009 on the date of deposit of the twenty-eighth instrument of ratification (Burundi). As of 1 January 2021, forty-two States were party to the Treaty,[57] including the Sahrawi Arab Democratic Republic (Western Sahara), which is a member of the African Union but is not recognised as a State by the UN Secretary-General.[58]

In 1961, the UN General Assembly adopted Resolution 1652 (XVI), which called upon UN Member States to respect the continent of Africa as a denuclearised zone.[59] In 1964,

52 Art. 8(1) and (3), Treaty of Bangkok.

53 Arts. 9(1) and 13, Treaty of Bangkok.

54 Art. 13, Treaty of Bangkok.

55 Art. 2, Protocol to The Treaty on the Southeast Asia Nuclear-Weapon-Free Zone.

56 NTI, 'Southeast Asian Nuclear-Weapon-Free-Zone (SEANWFZ) Treaty (Bangkok Treaty)', last updated 30 October 2020, at http://bit.ly/3pBpMKB.

57 Algeria, Angola, Benin, Botswana, Burkina Faso, Burundi, Cameroon, Cabo Verde, Chad, Comoros, Congo, Côte d'Ivoire, Equatorial Guinea, Eswatini, Ethiopia, Gabon, Gambia, Ghana, Guinea, Guinea-Bissau. Kenya, Lesotho, Libya, Madagascar, Malawi, Mali, Mauritania, Mauritius, Mozambique, Namibia, Niger, Nigeria, Rwanda, Saharawi Arab Democratic Republic, Senegal, Seychelles, South Africa, Tanzania, Togo, Tunisia, Zambia, and Zimbabwe.

58 A further twelve States are signatories. Of the fifty-five member States of the African Union, as of this writing only South Sudan had neither adhered to nor signed the Treaty.

59 UN General Assembly Resolution 1652 (XVI) adopted on 24 November 1961 by 55 votes to 0, with 44 abstentions.

the Organization of African Unity (OAU) issued the Declaration on the Denuclearization of Africa, which was subsequently endorsed by the General Assembly.[60] The OAU and the UN established a Joint Group of Experts to draft a treaty creating a nuclear-weapon-free zone in Africa, which first met in Addis Ababa in April 1991. The Treaty text would take another four years to conclude.

States Parties to the Treaty are obligated not to conduct research on, develop, manufacture, stockpile, or otherwise acquire, possess, or have control over any nuclear explosive device by any means anywhere.[61] They are prohibited from taking 'any action' to assist or encourage such research, development, manufacture, stockpiling or other acquisition, or possession of any nuclear explosive device.[62]

The parties also undertake to prohibit, in their respective territories, the stationing of any nuclear explosive device.[63] They are explicitly permitted to decide whether to allow visits by foreign ships and aircraft to their ports and airfields, transit of their airspace by foreign aircraft, and navigation by foreign ships in their territorial seas or archipelago waters.[64] The Treaty further prohibits States Parties from testing or allowing testing in their territory, or assisting or encouraging the testing of any nuclear explosive device.[65]

The Pelindaba Treaty defines *nuclear explosive device* (not *nuclear weapon*) as 'any nuclear weapon or other explosive device capable of releasing nuclear energy, irrespective of the purpose for which it could be used'.[66] The term, the definition confirms, 'includes such a weapon or device in unassembled and partly assembled forms, but does not include the means of transport or delivery of such a weapon or device if separable from and not an indivisible part of it'.[67]

The States Parties undertake to declare any capability for the manufacture of nuclear explosive devices; dismantle and destroy any nuclear explosive device that they have manufactured prior to the coming into force of this Treaty; destroy facilities for the manufacture of nuclear explosive devices or, where possible, convert them to peaceful uses; and permit the IAEA to verify the processes of dismantling and destruction of the nuclear explosive devices, as well as the destruction or conversion of the facilities for their production.[68] The parties further undertake not to take, or assist, or encourage any action aimed at an armed attack by conventional or other means against nuclear installations in the Treaty's zone of application.[69]

To ensure compliance with their 'undertakings' under the Pelindaba Treaty, the Parties established the African Commission on Nuclear Energy (AFCONE).[70] At the first Treaty conference in November 2010, South Africa was selected to host the Commission headquarters. AFCONE promotes the peaceful application of nuclear science and technology

60 UN General Assembly Resolution 45/56A, adopted on 4 December 1990 by 145 votes to 0, with 4 abstentions.
61 Art. 3(a), Pelindaba Treaty.
62 Art. 3(c), Pelindaba Treaty.
63 Art. 4(1), Pelindaba Treaty.
64 Art. 4(2), Pelindaba Treaty.
65 Art. 5, Pelindaba Treaty.
66 Art. 1(c), Pelindaba Treaty.
67 Ibid.
68 Art. 6, Pelindaba Treaty.
69 Art. 11, Pelindaba Treaty.
70 Art. 12(1), Pelindaba Treaty.

in Africa and is also 'actively engaged in global and regional efforts towards disarmament and non-proliferation'.[71]

Protocol I to the Pelindaba Treaty obligates the NPT nuclear-weapon States not to use or threaten to use a nuclear explosive device against any State Party to the Treaty and any territory within the regional zone. China, France, Russia, and the United Kingdom are States Parties to the Protocol, while the United States is a signatory. Neither the United Kingdom nor the United States recognises Diego Garcia as being subject to the Treaty.[72]

Protocol II calls on the nuclear-weapon States not to test or assist or encourage the testing of any nuclear explosive device anywhere within the regional zone. Again, China, France, Russia, and the United Kingdom are States Parties, while the United States is a signatory. Protocol III to the Pelindaba Treaty calls on each State Party, with respect to the territories for which it is internationally responsible within the region, to apply the provisions of the Treaty to it. It is only open to adherence by France and Spain. France is a State Party to Protocol III, while Spain is a State not party.

The 2006 Treaty of Semipalatinsk

The Treaty on a Nuclear-Weapon-Free Zone in Central Asia, usually referred to as the Treaty of Semipalatinsk (which is where the Soviet Union tested its first nuclear explosive device), was formally adopted on 8 September 2006, entering into force on 21 March 2009. All five Central Asian republics – Kazakhstan, Kyrgyzstan, Tajikistan, Turkmenistan, and Uzbekistan – are States Parties. Kyrgyzstan is the designated depositary for the Treaty of Semipalatinsk.[73]

The idea of a nuclear-weapon-free zone for Central Asia had originated in the 1992 initiative by Mongolia declaring itself a nuclear-weapon-free zone (see below) and which had also called for a regional zone in addition to its own nuclear-weapon-free status. On 27 February 1997, the presidents of the five Central Asian States issued the Almaty Declaration endorsing the creation of a regional nuclear-weapon-free zone. The Treaty of Semipalatinsk was formally concluded and opened for signature on 8 September 2006.

Under the Treaty, the States Parties undertake not to research, develop, manufacture, stockpile, acquire, possess, or have any control over any nuclear weapon or other nuclear explosive device.[74] Each State Party is also obligated, 'in accordance with' the Comprehensive Nuclear-Test-Ban Treaty, not to carry out nuclear weapon tests or any other nuclear explosion as well as to prevent any such nuclear explosion at any place under its control.[75] They are further required to maintain effective physical protection of nuclear material, facilities, and equipment.[76]

The Treaty defines 'nuclear weapon or other nuclear explosive device' as 'any weapon or other explosive device capable of releasing nuclear energy, irrespective of the military or

[71] The African Commission on Nuclear Energy, 'About AFCONE', at http://bit.ly/3dlQjt7.

[72] See, e.g., P. H. Sand, 'Diego Garcia: British–American Legal Black Hole in the Indian Ocean?', *Journal of Environmental Law*, Vol. 21, No. 1 (1 January 2009), 113–37.

[73] Art. 18(a), Treaty of Semipalatinsk.

[74] Art. 3(1)(a), Treaty of Semipalatinsk.

[75] Art. 5(a) and (b), Treaty of Semipalatinsk.

[76] Art. 9, Treaty of Semipalatinsk.

civilian purpose for which the weapon or device could be used'. Similar to the other regional nuclear-weapon-free zone treaties, it is further clarified that the term includes such a weapon or device 'in unassembled or partly assembled forms, but does not include the means of transport or delivery of such a weapon or device if separable from and not an indivisible part of it'.[77]

The Treaty does not affect the rights and obligations of its States Parties under other international treaties concluded prior to the entry into force of the Treaty of Semipalatinsk.[78] This is contentious because of the 1992 Collective Security Treaty to which Kazakhstan, Kyrgyzstan, and Tajikistan have adhered. France, the United Kingdom, and the United States have expressed concern that the 1992 agreement could allow Russia to deploy nuclear weapons in Central Asian nations that are party to the Collective Security Treaty.[79] Thus the prohibition on allowing in the territory of a State Party the installation of any nuclear weapon or other nuclear explosive device could potentially be overridden.[80] Kazakhstan, however, is a State Party to the Treaty on the Prohibition of Nuclear Weapons (TPNW), which prohibits without exception '[a]llow[ing] any stationing, installation or deployment of any nuclear weapons or other nuclear explosive devices in its territory or at any place under its jurisdiction or control'.[81] On the other hand, Kyrgyzstan and Tajikistan are both States not party to the TPNW.

Under the Protocol to the Treaty of Semipalatinsk, each State Party to that Protocol undertakes not to use or threaten to use a nuclear weapon or other nuclear explosive device against any State Party to the Treaty and not to contribute to any act that constitutes a violation of the Treaty. China, France, Russia, and the United Kingdom are States Parties to the Protocol, while the United States is a signatory.

The Nuclear-Weapon-Free 'Status' of Mongolia

In September 1992, in an address to the UN General Assembly, the President of Mongolia declared his country's territory a nuclear-weapon-free zone.[82] During the Cold War, the Soviet Union is believed to have stationed nuclear weapons in Mongolia.[83]

Mongolia adopted a law on its nuclear-weapon-free 'status' in early 2000.[84] Article 4 of the Law prohibits any natural or legal person or any foreign State from involvement in the development, manufacture, acquisition, possession, or control over nuclear weapons, their stationing or transportation, or their testing or use anywhere on Mongolian territory.

77 Art. 1(b), Treaty of Semipalatinsk.

78 Art. 12, Treaty of Semipalatinsk. The Parties shall, though, 'take all necessary measures for effective implementation of the purposes and objectives of this Treaty in accordance with the main principles contained therein'.

79 See, e.g., C. Ibragimova, 'Free Zone: Greater Security for the Region?', Russian International Affairs Council, 24 July 2015, at http://bit.ly/37owSfy.

80 Art. 3(1)(d)(ii), Treaty of Semipalatinsk.

81 Art. 1(1)(g), Treaty on the Prohibition of Nuclear Weapons. See further below.

82 N. Tuya, 'Mongolia's Nuclear-Weapon-Free Status: Recognition vs. Institutionalization', The Brookings Institution, 31 August 2012, at http://brook.gs/3qEkvUg.

83 J. Enkhsaikhan, 'Mongolia's Nuclear-Weapon-Free Status: Concept and Practice', *Asian Survey*, Vol. 40, No.2 (2000), p. 344.

84 Law of Mongolia on its nuclear-weapon-free status, adopted on 3 February 2000.

In the Final Document of the 2000 Review Conference of the Parties to the NPT, held at the UN in New York from 24 April to 19 May 2000, the Conference welcomed the declaration by Mongolia of its nuclear-weapon-free status. On 5 October 2000, the five nuclear-weapon States jointly issued a statement detailing the provision of security assurances in connection with Mongolia's non-nuclear status. The following month, the UN General Assembly recognised this status in its Resolution 55/33S.[85]

Mongolia's hope for a trilateral treaty with Russia and China, however, endorsing its non-nuclear-weapon status has not been fulfilled.[86] Perhaps its concern not to irritate its two superpower neighbours helps explain why, as of this writing, Mongolia had not signed the Treaty on the Prohibition of Nuclear Weapons.

The Conferences of Nuclear-Weapon-Free Zones and Mongolia

To date, three Conferences of Nuclear-Weapon-Free Zones and Mongolia have been held. The first Conference was proposed by OPANAL and was held in Mexico in 2005 under the coordination of Mexico. The second and third Conferences, in 2010 and 2015, were held in New York one day before the NPT Review Conference, and were coordinated, respectively, by Chile and Indonesia. In response to the global COVID-19 pandemic, the UN Office for Disarmament Affairs (UNODA) postponed the Fourth Conference of Nuclear-Weapon-Free Zones and Mongolia, due to be held in 2020, until 2021.

The Proposal for a Nuclear-Weapon-Free Zone in the Middle East

The aim of a nuclear-weapon-free (or more broadly a weapons of mass destruction (WMD)-free) zone in the Middle East is long-standing, and the failure to create such a zone continues to be a source of irritation to many governments in the region.[87] The failure of the Ninth Review Conference of the NPT in 2015 to generate a consensus outcome document was specifically attributed to discussions around the establishment of a WMD-free zone in the Middle East.[88]A resolution adopted at the Sixth NPT Review (and Extension) Conference in 1995 had called on States to take 'practical steps' to make progress in the establishment of a WMD-free zone in the region. Agreement on this resolution was seen as 'key' to securing the indefinite extension of the NPT.[89]

85 UN General Assembly Resolution 55/33S ('Mongolia's international security and nuclear-weapon-free status'), adopted on 20 November 2000 without a vote.

86 For a discussion of the thought processes of the Mongolian government and the chronology of events, see Tuya, 'Mongolia's Nuclear-Weapon-Free Status: Recognition vs. Institutionalization', esp. pp. 10–12.

87 See generally M. Roscini, 'International Law, Nuclear Weapon-Free Zones and the Proposed Zone Free of Weapons of Mass Destruction in the Middle East', chapter 13 in G. Nystuen, S. Casey-Maslen, and A. G. Bersagel (eds.), *Nuclear Weapons under International Law*, Cambridge University Press, Cambridge, 2014, 321–46.

88 According to the head of the United Kingdom's delegation, 'this issue and this issue alone was the stumbling block'. W. Wan, 'Why the 2015 NPT Review Conference Fell Apart', Article, United Nations University, 28 May 2015, at http://bit.ly/2Lt8LVe.

89 K. Davenport, 'WMD-Free Middle East Proposal at a Glance', Fact Sheet, Arms Control Association, last reviewed December 2018, at http://bit.ly/2Nj2Jav.

But proposals for a nuclear-weapon-free zone in the Middle East were put forward as far back as 1962, while in 1974 Egypt and Iran had formally submitted a draft resolution to the UN General Assembly calling for the establishment of such a zone.[90] Since then, despite 'extensive international support' for the notion and a 'catalogue of resolutions' endorsed by all regional States, 'practical progress has been stymied by sharp disagreements between countries in the region over the terms and the sequence of steps leading to the establishment of the zone'.[91] Israel has closely linked discussions on the establishment of such a zone with the existence of durable peace and compliance with international obligations by States in the region. Arab States have said that no such linkage should exist and that the establishment of the zone would contribute to peaceful relations.[92]

It remains to be seen if Israel's recent peace agreements with Bahrain and the United Arab Emirates (in September 2020), and its warming of relations with Saudi Arabia, might ease the path towards at least renewed discussion of a nuclear-weapon-free zone in the Middle East, even if the institution of such a zone seems as far away as ever. Adopted on 7 December 2020 by 174 votes to 2 (Israel and the United States) with 1 abstention (Cameroon), UN General Assembly Resolution 75/33 on the establishment of a nuclear-weapon-free zone in the region of the Middle East urged all parties directly concerned to consider taking the practical and urgent steps required for the implementation of the proposal to establish such a zone and invited the 'countries concerned' to adhere to the NPT.[93] The resolution further requested the UN Secretary-General to 'continue to pursue consultations with the States of the region and other concerned States' with a view to moving 'towards' the establishment of a nuclear-weapon-free zone in the region of the Middle East.[94]

THE TREATY ON THE PROHIBITION OF NUCLEAR WEAPONS

The Treaty on the Prohibition of Nuclear Weapons (TPNW) was adopted at United Nations Headquarters in New York on 7 July 2017 at a diplomatic conference convened under the auspices of the UN General Assembly and entered into force on 22 January 2021 following adherence by fifty States. As of the end of June 2021, fifty-four States had either signed and ratified or acceded to the Treaty[95] and a further thirty-four States were signatories.[96]

90 Roscini, 'International Law, Nuclear Weapon-Free Zones and the Proposed Zone Free of Weapons of Mass Destruction in the Middle East', p. 322.

91 Davenport, 'WMD-Free Middle East Proposal at a Glance'.

92 Ibid.

93 UN General Assembly Resolution 75/33, adopted on 7 December 2020 by 174 votes to 2, with 1 abstention, operative para. 1.

94 UN General Assembly Resolution 75/33, operative para. 10.

95 Antigua and Barbuda, Austria, Bangladesh, Belize, Benin, Bolivia, Botswana, Cambodia, Comoros, Cook Islands, Costa Rica, Cuba, Dominica, El Salvador, Ecuador, Fiji, Gambia, Guyana, Holy See, Honduras, Ireland, Jamaica, Kazakhstan, Kiribati, Lao PDR, Lesotho, Malaysia, Maldives, Malta, Mexico, Namibia, Nauru, New Zealand, Nicaragua, Nigeria, Niue, Palau, Palestine, Panama, Paraguay, Philippines, Saint Kitts and Nevis, Saint Lucia, Saint Vincent and the Grenadines, Samoa, San Marino, South Africa, Thailand, Trinidad and Tobago, Tuvalu, Uruguay, Venezuela, Vanuatu, Vietnam.

96 Algeria, Angola, Brazil, Brunei Darussalam, Cabo Verde, Central African Republic, Chile, Colombia, Congo, Côte d'Ivoire, Democratic Republic of Congo, Dominican Republic, Ghana, Grenada, Guatemala, Guinea-Bissau, Indonesia, Libya, Liechtenstein, Madagascar, Malawi, Mozambique, Myanmar,

The Negotiation of the TPNW

The mandate for the negotiation of the Treaty was given by the UN General Assembly on 23 December 2016. Resolution 71/258 ('Taking forward multilateral nuclear disarmament negotiations'), adopted by 113 votes[97] to 35[98] with 13 abstentions,[99] decided to convene in 2017 a UN conference 'to negotiate a legally binding instrument to prohibit nuclear weapons, leading towards their total elimination'.[100] The resolution followed the convening of an Open-Ended Working Group on taking forward multilateral nuclear disarmament negotiations, itself mandated by the General Assembly. The Open-Ended Working Group had met for three sessions in 2016.[101] Among the Working Group's recommendations had been to hold a conference in 2017, open to all States, with the participation and contribution of international organisations and civil society, to negotiate a legally binding instrument to prohibit nuclear weapons, leading towards their total elimination.[102]

At a preparatory organisational meeting on 16 February 2017, Ambassador Elayne Whyte Gómez of Costa Rica was elected President of the United Nations diplomatic conference for the negotiation of the Treaty by acclamation.[103] Two sessions of the diplomatic conference were held. The first, a week-long session adopted in late March 2017, focused on adopting the rules of procedure and hearing statements of a general nature as to the desired content of the future treaty. The second session, of three weeks duration, was the

Nepal, Niger, Peru, Sao Tome and Principe, Seychelles, Sudan, Tanzania, Timor-Leste, Togo, Zambia, and Zimbabwe. The Seychelles ratified the TPNW on 9 July 2021.

97 Afghanistan, Albania, Algeria, Angola, Antigua and Barbuda, Argentina, Austria, Azerbaijan, the Bahamas, Bahrain, Bangladesh, Barbados, Bhutan, Bolivia, Botswana, Brazil, Brunei Darussalam, Burkina Faso, Cabo Verde, Cambodia, Chad, Chile, Colombia, Comoros, Congo, Costa Rica, Côte d'Ivoire, Cuba, Cyprus, Djibouti, Dominican Republic, Ecuador, Egypt, El Salvador, Equatorial Guinea, Eritrea, Estonia, Ethiopia, Fiji, Gabon, Ghana, Guatemala, Guyana, Honduras, Indonesia, Iran, Iraq, Ireland, Italy, Jamaica, Jordan, Kazakhstan, Kenya, Kiribati, Kuwait, Lao PDR, Lebanon, Lesotho, Libya, Liechtenstein, Madagascar, Malaysia, the Maldives, Malta, the Marshall Islands, Mauritania, Mauritius, Mexico, Mongolia, Mozambique, Myanmar, Namibia, Nepal, New Zealand, Niger, Nigeria, Oman, Palau, Panama, Papua New Guinea, Paraguay, Peru, Philippines, Qatar, Saint Kitts and Nevis, Saint Lucia, Saint Vincent and the Grenadines, San Marino, Saudi Arabia, Senegal, Sierra Leone, Singapore, South Africa, Sri Lanka, Suriname, Sweden, Tajikistan, Tanzania, Thailand, the former Yugoslav Republic of Macedonia, Timor-Leste, Togo, Tonga, Trinidad and Tobago, Tunisia, Uganda, United Arab Emirates, Uruguay, Vanuatu, Venezuela, Vietnam, Yemen, and Zimbabwe.

98 Andorra, Australia, Belgium, Bosnia and Herzegovina, Bulgaria, Canada, Croatia, the Czech Republic, Denmark, France, Germany, Greece, Hungary, Iceland, Israel, Japan, Latvia, Lithuania, Luxembourg, Micronesia, Monaco, Montenegro, Norway, Poland, Portugal, the Republic of Korea, Romania, Russia, Serbia, Slovakia, Slovenia, Spain, Turkey, the United Kingdom, and the United States.

99 Armenia, Belarus, China, Finland, India, Mali, Morocco, The Netherlands, Nicaragua, Pakistan, Sudan, Switzerland, and Uzbekistan.

100 UN General Assembly Resolution 71/258, adopted on 23 December 2016 by 113 votes to 35 with 13 abstentions, operative para. 8.

101 UN General Assembly Resolution 70/33; and see 'Taking forward multilateral nuclear disarmament negotiations. Note by the Secretary-General', UN doc. A/71/371, 1 September 2016.

102 'Taking forward multilateral nuclear disarmament negotiations. Note by the Secretary-General', para. 67, p. 18.

103 UN, 'United Nations Conference to Negotiate Ban on Nuclear Weapons Holds First Organizational Meeting, Adopts Agenda for 2017 Substantive Session', UN doc. DC/3685, 16 February 2017, at http://bit.ly/2EwlK41.

occasion for the substantive negotiations. These worked on the basis of a draft 'Convention' prepared by Ambassador Whyte Gómez, which was published on 22 May 2017.[104]

The draft text was in some respects a curious creation, formulated as a disarmament treaty with undertakings to 'never under any circumstances' engage in certain conduct but without incorporating explicit disarmament provisions. Instead, a draft article stipulated that 'proposals for further effective measures relating to nuclear disarmament, including provisions for the verified and irreversible elimination of any remaining nuclear weapon programmes under strict and effective international control, which may take the form of additional protocols to this Convention, may be considered at the Meetings of States Parties or Review Conferences.'[105] A prohibition on the use of nuclear weapons was supplemented by the language of the CTBT prohibiting the carrying out of 'any nuclear weapon test explosion or any other nuclear explosion'.[106]

In comments on the draft in plenary, many States called for the threat of use of nuclear weapons to be added as an explicit prohibition in the treaty. Despite the desire on the part of a number of negotiating States to address extended nuclear deterrence, the articulation of such a prohibition would need to be restricted to States Parties, given that the customary international law of treaties precludes the binding of third States without their consent.[107] Several negotiating States, beginning with South Africa, called for the title of the draft 'Convention' to be changed to 'Treaty', in order to reflect the language of the 1968 Treaty on the Non-proliferation of Nuclear Weapons and the 1996 Comprehensive Nuclear-Test-Ban Treaty.[108]

The Conference President published her second draft of what was now titled the Draft Treaty on the Prohibition of Nuclear Weapons on 27 June 2017.[109] Again, however, the draft did not refer to a prohibition of the threat of use. None of the nine nuclear-weapons-possessor States attended either session of the UN Diplomatic Conference and only one State benefitting from extended nuclear deterrence – the Netherlands – was a participant. That said, former nuclear-armed States Kazakhstan and South Africa each made important contributions to the drafting. For example, the text on reporting obligations and the disarmament provisions (discussed below) owed much to a composite proposal by South Africa. The relatively high threshold of fifty States to trigger entry into force, intended to reflect broad support for the norms codified in the Treaty, was inserted following a proposal by Kazakhstan.

A third draft of the treaty was published on 3 July 2017.[110] This time a broad prohibition was included whereby States Parties undertook never to 'use or threaten to use nuclear weapons or

104 Draft Convention on the Prohibition of Nuclear Weapons, UN doc. A/CONF.229/2017/CRP.1, 22 May 2017.

105 Art. 5, Draft Convention on the Prohibition of Nuclear Weapons, 22 May 2017.

106 Art. 1(1)(e), Draft Convention on the Prohibition of Nuclear Weapons, 22 May 2017.

107 This rule is codified in the Article 34 of the Vienna Convention on the Law of Treaties; adopted at Vienna, 23 May 1969; entered into force 27 January 1980.

108 In fact, given that the Treaty as adopted incorporates disarmament provisions, this marked a break from broader international precedent given that the other five global disarmament treaties – outlawing anti-personnel mines, biological weapons, chemical weapons, and cluster munitions – are all entitled 'Convention'.

109 'Draft Treaty on the Prohibition of Nuclear Weapons', UN doc. A/CONF.229/2017/CRP.1/Rev.1, 27 June 2017.

110 Draft Treaty on the Prohibition of Nuclear Weapons, UN doc. A/CONF.229/2017/L.3, 3 July 2017.

other nuclear explosive devices'.[111] But drafting errors and the omission of a negotiated provision addressing the responsibility of States Parties that had used or tested nuclear weapons led to a revised text being issued on 5 July 2017.[112] The final draft of the treaty, which included an amended provision on this issue, was issued on 6 July 2017 to comply with the '24-hour rule', allowing States one day to consult with capitals before the treaty's adoption.

On 7 July 2017, the Conference President put the Draft Treaty on the Prohibition of Nuclear Weapons before the Conference for adoption. The Netherlands, the only nuclear 'umbrella' State with nuclear weapons stationed on its territory to participate in the Conference, took the floor to ask for a vote, stating its objection to the treaty text. The Treaty on the Prohibition of Nuclear Weapons was then adopted by the Conference on 7 July 2017 by 122 votes to 1 (the Netherlands) with 1 abstention (Singapore). It was opened for signature on 20 September 2017 and remains open for signature since its entry into force.[113]

The Prohibitions in the TPNW

The language of the TPNW in its Article 1 is one of disarmament. The wording whereby each State Party 'undertakes never any circumstances' to engage in certain conduct, first incorporated in the 1971 Biological Weapons Convention[114] and then consolidated as a standardised formulation in the 1992 Chemical Weapons Convention,[115] is deliberately broad in scope and unequivocal in nature. Such an undertaking embraces conduct in peacetime as well as during situations of armed conflict, and does not allow certain actions to be taken even in self-defence when the State Party is the subject of an armed attack.[116] As is the case in the Partial Test-Ban Treaty, the NPT, and the CTBT, nuclear weapons are not defined in the TPNW, despite a number of calls during the negotiations for a definition to be included.[117] That said, no other global disarmament treaty that comprehensively prohibits a weapon omits to define what is being outlawed.[118]

The prohibitions in Article 1 of the TPNW are detailed and extremely broad in compass:

111 Art. 1(1)(e), Draft Treaty on the Prohibition of Nuclear Weapons, 3 July 2017.

112 Draft Treaty on the Prohibition of Nuclear Weapons, UN doc. A/CONF.229/2017/L.X, undated but 5 July 2017.

113 Art. 13, TPNW.

114 'Each State Party to this Convention undertakes never in any circumstance to develop, produce, stockpile or otherwise acquire or retain . . . .' Art. I, Convention on the Prohibition of the Development, Production and Stockpiling of Bacteriological (Biological) and Toxin Weapons and on Their Destruction; adopted at New York, 16 December 1971; entered into force 26 March 1975.

115 Art. I(1), Convention on the Prohibition of the Development, Production, Stockpiling and Use of Chemical Weapons and on Their Destruction; adopted at Geneva, 3 September 1992; entered into force 29 April 1997.

116 While the Chemical Weapons Convention frames the core undertakings as 'General Obligations', given that its Article I contains also positive obligations upon States Parties (to destroy chemical weapons), the TPNW, which does not have such obligations in its Article 1, entitles the article 'Prohibitions'.

117 During the negotiations, Sweden, for example, had proposed using language from that incorporated by the five permanent members of the UN Security Council in their 2015 *P5 Glossary of Key Nuclear Terms*: 'Weapon assembly that is capable of producing an explosion and massive damage and destruction by the sudden release of energy instantaneously released from self-sustaining nuclear fission and/or fusion.'

118 See Art. I(1) and (2), Biological Weapons Convention; Art. II(1), (2), and (3), Chemical Weapons Convention; Art. 2(1) and (2), 1997 Anti-Personnel Mine Ban Convention; and Arts. 1(2) and (2) and 2(2), 2008 Convention on Cluster Munitions.

- Develop, test, produce, manufacture, or otherwise acquire, possess, or stockpile nuclear weapons or other nuclear explosive devices[119]
- Transfer to any recipient whatsoever or control over such weapons or explosive devices directly or indirectly[120]
- Receive the transfer of or control over such weapons or other devices, directly or indirectly[121]
- Use or threaten to use such weapons or devices[122]
- Allow any stationing, installation, or deployment of any nuclear weapons or other nuclear explosive devices in its territory or at any other place under its jurisdiction or control[123]
- Seek or receive any assistance, in any way, from anyone to engage in any of the above activities[124]
- Assist, encourage, or induce, in any way, anyone to engage in any of the above prohibited activities.[125]

The prohibition on testing nuclear explosive devices pertains to completed devices. Other forms of development, including computer modelling and subcritical detonations, as well as the partial assembly of such devices, are encompassed by the prohibition on development. A preambular paragraph emphasises, though, that nothing in the TPNW 'shall be interpreted as affecting the inalienable right of its States Parties to develop research, production and use of nuclear energy for peaceful purposes without discrimination'. The reference to the right being 'inalienable', as codified in Article IV(1) of the NPT, recalls its customary law nature.

The language on seeking or receiving any assistance to engage in any of the prohibited activities was adopted from Article II of the NPT, which had prohibited such action, for non-nuclear-weapon States only, in relation to the manufacture of nuclear weapons or other nuclear explosive devices. The conduct was thus significantly broadened in the TPNW to encompass any of the proscribed activities in Article 1(1). The prohibition on threatening to use any nuclear explosive devices reflected language from the regional nuclear-weapon-free zone treaties.

The prohibition on allowing the stationing, installation, or deployment of any nuclear weapons or other nuclear explosive devices in its territory or at any place under its jurisdiction or control was adapted from language incorporated in the Treaty of Rarotonga, the Bangkok Treaty, and the Pelindaba Treaty.[126] As noted above, the corresponding prohibition in the Treaty of Semipalatinsk was subjugated to the obligations of its

119 Art. 1(1)(a), TPNW.
120 Art. 1(1)(b), TPNW.
121 Art. 1(1)(c), TPNW.
122 Art. 1(1)(d), TPNW.
123 Art. 1(1)(f), TPNW.
124 Art. 1(1)(g), TPNW.
125 Art. 1(1)(e), TPNW.
126 The corresponding language in the Treaty of Tlatelolco was less clear in this regard. According to Article 1(1)(b) of the Treaty, the installation or deployment of any nuclear weapons, 'directly or indirectly', was prohibited when it occurred 'by the Parties themselves, by anyone on their behalf or in any other way'.

States Parties under other international treaties concluded prior to the entry into force of that 2006 Treaty.[127] This is contentious because of the prior existence of the 1992 Collective Security Treaty with the Russian Federation, which is interpreted by some such as to potentially permit the placement by Russia of nuclear weapons on the territory of the other States Parties to that agreement.

In some respects, the prohibition in Article 1(1)(g) of the TPNW on allowing the stationing, installation, or deployment of any nuclear weapons or other nuclear explosive devices on the territory of a State Party or at any other place under its jurisdiction or control forbids conduct which would already be captured by the prohibition on assisting other activities rendered illegal in Article 1(1). But its express prohibition does serve to clarify the legal situation. The stationing of nuclear weapons on the territory of another State without that State's valid consent would contravene the prohibition in general international law on inter-State use of force. As an act breaching the territorial integrity or political independence of another State, it would likely amount also to an act of aggression. The prohibition of aggression is a peremptory (*jus cogens*) norm of international law.[128]

The most contentious provision in Article 1 of the TPNW is the prohibition on assisting or encouraging prohibited activities. During the negotiations at the Second Session of the Diplomatic Conference, the Netherlands had called for the notions of assist, encourage, and induce to be each defined.[129] Singapore subsequently stated that the provision as a whole was 'not clear'.[130] A prohibition on complicit action by States Parties has, however, been a standard clause in global disarmament treaties since the Biological Weapons Convention in 1972. The undertaking by each State Party never under any circumstances to assist, encourage, or induce, in any way, anyone to engage in prohibited activities was included in every draft of the TPNW, with the text remaining materially alike through to its adoption.

One specific bone of contention is the issue of transit of nuclear weapons across the territory of States Parties. Several States had called for transit or 'allowing' the transit of nuclear weapons to be rendered illegal. This was difficult for both practical and legal reasons. Legally, the right of innocent passage through the territorial waters of States pertains to maritime vessels, including nuclear-armed submarines, as long as they do not engage in any hostile act.[131] Practically, enforcing a prohibition on allowing transit of all nuclear-armed aircraft or missiles through a State's airspace would be impossible. The failure to prohibit the transit of nuclear weapons by a State not party to the TPNW is thus

[127] Art. 12, Treaty of Semipalatinsk.

[128] See, e.g., International Law Commission, *Report of the International Law Commission*, Seventy-first session, UN doc. A/74/10, 2019, Chap. V, Annex, para. (a).

[129] Remarks of the Netherlands in plenary, Second Session of the UN Diplomatic Conference, 16 June 2017.

[130] Remarks of Singapore in plenary, Second Session of the UN Diplomatic Conference, 16 June 2017. This is despite the corresponding provision in Article 3(4) of the Bangkok Treaty, to which Singapore is a party, whereby each State Party undertakes not to 'take any action to assist or encourage the commission of any act in violation of the provisions of paragraphs 1, 2 and 3 of this Article'.

[131] The UN Convention on the Law of the Sea makes it clear that passage is not innocent where it is effected with a view to committing aggression against the coastal State. Art. 19(2), Convention on the Law of the Sea; adopted at Montego Bay, 10 December 1982; entered into force 16 November 1994. This is reflective of customary law.

not a violation of the Treaty.[132] This is so, as long as the territorial State Party does not either act to assist or encourage the possession by the nuclear-armed State of its nuclear weapons during transit or allow passing transit to amount to the stationing, installation, or deployment of any nuclear weapons or other nuclear explosive devices in or on its territory.

Another issue of concern during the negotiations was the treatment of military preparations for use of nuclear weapons, such as through participation in military exercises that trained for the possible use of nuclear weapons. A number of States, beginning with Indonesia, as well as the International Committee of the Red Cross (ICRC) had called unsuccessfully for such acts to be explicitly prohibited,[133] as they are in the Chemical Weapons Convention with respect to chemical weapons.[134] Certain military preparations may amount to prohibited assistance with or encouraging the possession of nuclear weapons, and potentially even of threatening to use, but in general the TPNW does not restrict its States Parties from participating in training exercises.

More broadly, the participation in a 'nuclear' military alliance, most notably the North Atlantic Treaty Organization (NATO), is not per se rendered unlawful by the prohibition on assisting or encouraging prohibited activities. An endorsement of NATO's Strategic Concept, however, which stipulates that NATO members will ensure that NATO will 'maintain an appropriate mix of nuclear and conventional forces',[135] would contravene the prohibition on encouraging possession of nuclear weapons.

In contrast, the financing of nuclear weapons programmes in another State, for example by support from sovereign funds or by private banks headquartered or located on the territory of a State Party, would always constitute prohibited assistance.[136] Thus, for instance, if 'funding in the form of an earmarked loan or a credit line is provided to a company for the development or maintenance of nuclear weapons, this is unlawful assistance with the development or possession of nuclear weapons'.[137]

Positive Obligations of States Parties

In addition to complying with the prohibitions set forth in Article 1 of the TPNW, States Parties also have a number of 'positive' obligations under the Treaty. Every State Party must make an initial declaration of its nuclear status and adopt the necessary measures at

[132] Nonetheless, in its declaration upon ratification of the TPNW, Cuba affirmed that 'the transit of nuclear weapons and other nuclear explosive devices through territory under the jurisdiction of the States Parties to this Treaty is also a prohibited activity according to the provisions of Article 1(e).' Text available on the UN Treaty Section website, at http://bit.ly/2AlahjS.

[133] The ICRC recommended that a new paragraph be inserted to prohibit engagement in any military preparations to use nuclear weapons. See ICRC, 'Comments of the International Committee of the Red Cross on key provisions of the Draft Convention on the Prohibition of Nuclear Weapons', UN doc. A/CONF.229/2017/CRP.2, 14 June 2017, p. 4.

[134] Article I(1)(c) of the Chemical Weapons Convention prohibits a State Party from engaging in 'any military preparations to use chemical weapons'.

[135] *Strategic Concept for the Defence and Security of the Members of the North Atlantic Treaty Organization*, adopted by Heads of State and Government at the NATO Summit in Lisbon, 19–20 November 2010, p. 5.

[136] This was stated by Austria in a plenary session of the Second Diplomatic Conference on 16 June 2017.

[137] G. Oestern (ed.), *Nuclear Weapons Ban Monitor 2020*, Norwegian People's Aid, Oslo, January 2021, p. 53.

the domestic level to implement the Treaty as well as a complementary duty to promote signature and adherence to the TPNW by other States. Obligations of international cooperation and assistance on each State Party 'in a position to do so' support efforts by affected States Parties to assist the victims of past nuclear weapons use and testing and to carry out environmental remediation of irradiated land. Specific obligations pertain to certain former and all existing nuclear-armed States Parties to the TPNW.

The Declaration of Nuclear Status

The most straightforward of the positive obligations is the duty on each State Party to submit a declaration to the UN Secretary-General within thirty days of becoming party to the Treaty detailing its nuclear status. Article 2 requires that this declaration clarify whether the State Party has 'ever' owned, possessed, or controlled nuclear weapons or other nuclear explosive devices. If it has, it must further declare whether it has already eliminated its nuclear-weapon programme, including by destroying or irreversibly converting all nuclear-weapons-related facilities, or whether it still owns, possesses, or controls any such devices. Finally, the declaration must state whether nuclear weapons or nuclear explosive devices belonging to a foreign State are located in its territory or in any other place under its jurisdiction or control.

For the first fifty States Parties to the Treaty, the deadline for this obligation expired on 21 February 2021. As of that date, 42 States Parties had made the requisite declaration, although all fifty had complied with their obligation to do so as of end-June 2021.[138] Of the States Parties at that date, only Kazakhstan and South Africa were former nuclear-armed States. Kazakhstan recalled the 'devastating consequences' of the 456 nuclear tests conducted on its soil over four decades and the 'bold and historic' decision in 1991 of the First President of Kazakhstan, Nursultan Nazarbayev, to close the Semipalatinsk nuclear test site and 'renounce the fourth largest nuclear arsenal in the world'.[139] It declared that, in accordance with the 1992 Protocol (Lisbon Protocol) to the Strategic Arms Reduction Treaty (START I), on 14 February 1994 Kazakhstan acceded to the NPT as a non-nuclear weapons State Party, and that 'in that connection it voluntarily renounced its inherited part of the Soviet Union's nuclear arsenal and dismantled all related military and technical infrastructure'; in addition, 'all nuclear weapons and nuclear explosive devices on its

[138] Antigua and Barbuda, Austria, Bangladesh, Bolivia, Botswana, Cook Islands, Costa Rica, Ecuador, El Salvador, Fiji, Guyana, Holy See, Ireland, Jamaica, Kazakhstan, Kiribati, Lao People's Democratic Republic, Lesotho, Malaysia, Malta, Mexico, Namibia, Nauru, New Zealand, Nicaragua, Nigeria, Niue, Palau, Palestine, Panama, Paraguay, Saint Kitts and Nevis, Saint Lucia, Saint Vincent and the Grenadines, South Africa, Thailand, Trinidad and Tobago, Tuvalu, Uruguay, Vanuatu, Venezuela, and Vietnam. Belize and the Maldives submitted their respective Article 2 declarations on 22 February 2021. Samoa did so on 23 February 2021. Cuba followed on 26 February 2021. San Marino did so on 9 March 2021, followed by The Gambia and Honduras on 15 March 2021. The last of the first fifty States Parties to submit its Article 2 declaration was Dominica, on 26 April 2021. Cambodia, which became a State Party on 21 February 2021 with a consequent deadline on 23 March, submitted its requisite declaration on 12 May 2021. Comoros, whose deadline was on 20 April 2021, had not submitted its declaration as of 20 June 2021. Benin submitted its Article 2 declaration on 9 April 2021, while the Philippines did so on 17 June 2021, in each case a few weeks past their respective deadline.

[139] TPNW Article 2 Declaration of Kazakhstan, Deputy Prime Minister and Minister of Foreign Affairs of Kazakhstan, 18 February 2021, at https://bit.ly/2MtrpN1, first and third preambular paras.

territory were transported to the Russian Federation while all nuclear-weapons-related facilities were irretrievably eliminated'.[140]

South Africa declared that it had developed nuclear explosive devices in the 1970s and 1980s but had abandoned its nuclear weapons programme in 1989.[141] It further noted that in 1994 the International Atomic Energy Agency (IAEA) had confirmed that one partially completed nuclear weapon and six completed weapons had been dismantled by South Africa. Since abandoning its nuclear weapons programme and adhering to the NPT, 'no other nuclear explosive devices have ever been manufactured, stationed or tested in the South African territory.'[142]

Cuba, which had Soviet nuclear missiles stationed on its territory in 1962, and had stated upon ratification of the TPNW that the declarations that States Parties are required to make under Article 2 'must include information on any activity they carry out that is prohibited under Article 1' submitted its own declaration on 26 February 2021. Cuba stated that it could not guarantee that the United States had not placed nuclear weapons on the territory it occupied 'illegally' in the province of Guantánamo but over which the Cuban State 'does not exercise any jurisdiction'.

Once the Article 2 declaration has been submitted, any State Party that does not have outstanding obligations arising under Article 4 with respect to disarmament has fulfilled its reporting duties under the TPNW. It is regrettable that no duty is imposed to report on the national implementing measures demanded by Article 5 (see below). On this issue, the *Nuclear Weapons Ban Monitor 2020* published by the non-governmental organisation Norwegian People's Aid 'would encourage voluntary reporting under the TPNW on legislative and other measures taken to implement the Treaty ... and on other issues such as cooperation and assistance, victim assistance, and environmental remediation'.[143] This call could be made by the First Meeting of States Parties, due to be held in Vienna on 22–24 March 2022.[144]

National Implementation Measures

Article 5(1) of the TPNW obligates each State Party to adopt 'the necessary measures to implement its obligations' under the Treaty. This could include, for example, instructions to a State Party's nuclear energy industry (should it have one) not to engage in any prohibited research; to its armed forces not to assist the armed forces of any nuclear-armed State to undertake prohibited activities; and to its Ministry of Foreign Affairs not to encourage the development or possession of nuclear explosive devices by any other State.

In addition, each State Party is required to assure the imposition of penal sanctions for any activity prohibited to a State Party. This is so, at the least when illegal acts are perpetrated by

140 Ibid., p. 2.
141 TPNW Article 2 Declaration of South Africa, Department of International Relations and Cooperation, Pretoria, 18 February 2021, at https://bit.ly/3aEen8W, p. 1.
142 Ibid.
143 Oestern (ed.), *Nuclear Weapons Ban Monitor 2020*, p. 59.
144 Art. 8(2), TPNW.

persons or on territory under its jurisdiction or control.[145] While acts pertaining to nuclear material and especially nuclear weapons would ordinarily be criminal through more general provisions in the penal codes of the overwhelming majority of States, there is merit in adopting specific legislation. In Ireland, the only State to do so as of this writing, dedicated legislation was adopted in 2019 to comply with the general principle of legality.

Ireland's Prohibition of Nuclear Weapons Act,[146] which was signed into law by the Irish President in December 2019, details criminal offences in its Section 2, reflecting the prohibitions in Article 1 of the TPNW.[147] The Act defines a nuclear explosive device rather narrowly as 'any weapon or other explosive device capable of releasing nuclear energy that is designed for a hostile purpose or for use in armed conflict, and includes such a weapon or device in unassembled or partly assembled forms but does not include the means of transport or delivery of such a weapon or device if separable from, and not an indivisible part of, such a weapon or device'.[148] Of 'course', as Grethe Oestern observes, 'a nuclear explosive device designed for "peaceful purposes" would also be unlawful'.[149]

The Duty to Promote the Universalisation of the TPNW

Under Article 12 of the TPNW, each State Party is required to 'encourage States not party to this Treaty to sign, ratify, accept, approve or accede to the Treaty, with the goal of universal adherence of all States to the Treaty'. The fora within which this encouragement should occur is not specified but would presumably include the UN General Assembly, review conferences of the NPT, and bilateral meetings with States not party. It is of course an obligation of reasonable effort, not one of successful outcome.

The *Nuclear Weapons Ban Monitor 2020* offers particular examples of support for universalisation in the course of 2020 by a number of contracting States (now States Parties), including Antigua and Barbuda,[150] Bangladesh,[151] Benin,[152] Costa Rica,[153] Cuba,[154] and New Zealand.[155] Fiji delivered a statement at the 2020 UN General Assembly's High-Level Plenary Meeting to Commemorate and Promote the International Day for the Total Elimination of Nuclear Weapons on behalf of the Pacific Small Island Developing States, encouraging UN member States to adhere to

[145] Art. 5(2), TPNW. The provision does not specify that legal persons (e.g., companies) or natural persons should be the focus of the penal law, the undertaking never under any circumstances to engaged in prohibited activities dictates that this should be the case.

[146] Prohibition of Nuclear Weapons Act 2019 (Act 40 of 2019), at http://bit.ly/39vSl4b. The law is formally entitled the 'Act to give effect to the Treaty on the Prohibition of Nuclear Weapons done at New York on 7 July 2017 and for those purposes to provide for offences relating to acts prohibited by that Treaty; and to provide for related matters'.

[147] Oestern (ed.), *Nuclear Weapons Ban Monitor 2020*, p. 70.

[148] S. 1, Prohibition of Nuclear Weapons Act 2019 (Act 40 of 2019).

[149] Oestern (ed.), *Nuclear Weapons Ban Monitor 2020*, p. 70.

[150] Ibid., p. 84.

[151] Ibid., p. 86.

[152] Ibid., p. 88.

[153] Ibid., p. 92.

[154] Ibid., p. 93.

[155] Ibid., p. 80.

the TPNW and the CTBT for it 'is morally right, and we owe it to ourselves and our future generations'.[156]

Victim Assistance

The duty to provide assistance to the victims of past nuclear weapons use and testing is required of all States Parties with respect to such individuals who are under their jurisdiction.[157] Assistance must be 'adequate' and both age- and gender-sensitive, comprising medical care, rehabilitation, and psychological support, as well as providing for the social and economic inclusion of nuclear weapon victims. The provision of assistance, which must occur 'without discrimination', must comply with 'applicable international humanitarian and human rights law'.[158]

Those caught in the explosion of a nuclear weapon and who survive may suffer horrific burns. Harder to treat, though, are the effects of radiation poisoning. A person who has survived a nuclear explosion ordinarily receives two doses of radiation, the first as a direct result of the explosion and a second from fallout, when radioactive particles float down to the ground later. According to the US Centers for Disease Control and Prevention (CDC), radiation sickness ('acute radiation syndrome') is diagnosed when a person receives more than 70 rads from a source outside their body. The dose affects the whole body, or most of it, and is able to penetrate to the internal organs. It is received in a short time, usually within minutes.[159]

There is no cure for acute radiation syndrome, although barriers can prevent exposure and certain medication may remove some of the radiation from the body.[160] The main treatment goals are to prevent further radioactive contamination, to treat life-threatening injuries (such as those resulting from burns and trauma), to reduce the symptoms of radiation sickness, and to manage the pain. Decontamination involves removing as many external radioactive particles as possible to help prevent further distribution of radioactive materials and lowering the risk of internal contamination from inhalation, ingestion, or open wounds.[161]

A protein called granulocyte colony-stimulating factor, which promotes the growth of white blood cells, may be used to counter the effect of radiation sickness on bone marrow. But severe damage to the marrow may also necessitate transfusions of red blood cells or blood platelets. Potassium iodide, a non-radioactive form of iodine, can help to fill 'vacancies' in the thyroid and prevent absorption of radioiodine. Radioiodine is eventually cleared from the body in urine. Prussian blue, a type of dye, binds to particles of caesium

156 Ibid., p. 97.

157 Art. 6(1), TPNW.

158 Ibid. IHL will of course not be applicable to test detonations of nuclear explosive devices, but only to those used in the conduct of hostilities during an armed conflict (i.e., the bombs dropped at Hiroshima and Nagasaki).

159 CDC, 'Acute Radiation Syndrome: A Fact Sheet for Clinicians', Booklet, information last reviewed on 4 April 2018, at https://bit.ly/3sgoQdl.

160 Y. Brazier, 'What's to Know about Radiation Sickness?', *Medical News Today*, 15 August 2017, at http://bit.ly/3k4TzKP.

161 Mayo Clinic, 'Radiation Sickness', 7 November 2020, at http://mayocl.in/2PNSBm7.

and thallium, which are then excreted in faeces. This treatment speeds up the elimination of the radioactive particles and reduces the amount of radiation cells may absorb. Pentetic acid (diethylenetriaminepentaacetic acid) binds to particles of plutonium, americium, and curium, which then pass out of the body in urine, reducing the amount of radiation absorbed.[162]

In addition to the serious health problems due to radiation, the victims of nuclear weapons use in Japan – known as the *hibakusha* – have also suffered societal harm as a result of discrimination at the hands of fellow Japanese. In 1945, ignorance about the effects of radioactive contamination led to the spread of rumours that radiation exposure was akin to an infectious disease. Already traumatised by their experience of the 'unforgettable fire', the *hibakusha* were often considered ineligible for work and marriage.[163]

It is important to note also the transgenerational impact caused by the detonation of nuclear explosive devices. A study after the end of the Cold War in a rural district neighbouring the Semipalatinsk Test Site found a nearly 80 per cent increase in the mutation rate in individuals directly exposed to the radioactive fallout compared to people living in a non-irradiated population elsewhere in Kazakhstan. Even the children of affected individuals showed a 50 per cent mutation rate increase over their non-irradiated counterparts although the mutation rates declined steadily after the 1950s.[164]

Genetic disorders resulting from radiation poisoning, caused by proximity to a test explosion, can thus be passed on to a survivor's children, grandchildren, and even great-grandchildren. This has been witnessed, for example, in the families of military veterans who witnessed the test detonations of British nuclear weapons at Christmas Island (now part of Kiribati). In the case of one serviceman interviewed by the BBC in 2018, the eighty-three-year-old great-grandfather recounted his belief that three generations of his family are living with the 'genetic curse' of those explosions. Sixteen of his twenty-one descendants have had birth defects or health problems of some form. His youngest daughter has thyroid problems and severe breathing difficulties, and her teeth fell out prematurely.[165]

Environmental Remediation of Irradiated Land

Treating irradiated land is both highly challenging, dangerous, and extremely expensive. The accident on 17 January 1966 at Palomares in Spain (see Chapter 2) released 'only' three kilograms of radioactive plutonium, which spread out over two square kilometres of land.[166] As the *Washington Post* reports, the US Air Force dispatched 1,600 troops to work on the clean-up. Over the course of several weeks, the troops collected wreckage, destroyed crops, and shovelled soil contaminated by the explosions. The US shipped 1,700 tonnes of irradiated soil back to South Carolina. Some of the military personnel wore thin surgical

[162] Ibid.

[163] 'Who Are the Hibakusha?', Hibakusha Stories, accessed 1 February 2021, at http://bit.ly/2Cx3rcB.

[164] G. Mone, 'Cold War Weapons Testing Increased Human DNA Mutation Rate', Scientific American, 8 February 2002, at http://bit.ly/3s4ftR8.

[165] S. Corker, 'DNA Tests for UK's Nuclear Bomb Veterans', *BBC News*, 16 February 2018, at http://bit.ly/2CwWUP2.

[166] M. Gonzalez, 'Trump Presidency Will Force Renegotiation of Palomares Nuclear Clean-Up', *El País*, 27 January 2017, at http://bit.ly/2Ak8iMH.

masks, while others had no protection at all. Over the following decades, signs of radiation exposure manifested in many of the airmen: 'everything from hair loss to blood disorders to cancers'.[167] Tests of the soil at Palomares in the 1990s revealed high levels of americium, a decay product of plutonium, with further tests showing that 50,000 cubic metres of earth were still contaminated.[168]

There is no agreed international standard for environmental remediation of former nuclear test sites. In the context of the testing on the Marshall Islands, the Marshall Islands Government proposed adopting the national guidance established by the US Environmental Protection Agency for the clean-up of radioactive contamination at affected sites in the United States.[169] This limits annual exposure at such sites after clean-up to 15 millirems of radiation above natural background levels from all sources. In the past, the US Department of Energy used a 100 millirem standard for the clean-up efforts in the Marshall Islands.[170]

Forty-three nuclear weapons test detonations occurred between 1948 and 1958 on the Marshall Islands, especially on Enewetak Atoll. About 5,600 US military personnel were sent to the Islands between 1977 and 1980 to try to make the atoll fit for human habitation again.[171] The final plan for the remediation efforts called for the removal of all radioactive and non-radioactive debris (e.g., equipment, concrete, scrap metal); removal of all soil that exceeded 14.8 Bq (400 pCi) of plutonium per gram of soil; depending on ultimate land-use, removal also of soil between 1.48 and 14.8 Bq (40 and 400 pCi) of plutonium per gram of soil; and disposal and stabilisation of all the accumulated radioactive waste into the crater on Runit Island, which was then capped with a concrete dome.[172] US soldiers were tasked with walking on the irradiated beaches in 'shorts, rubber boots and a painter's mask'.[173]

In June 2020, a report to Congress by the US Department of Energy admitted that the dome was leaking radioactive waste, but it also indicated that there was 'no evidence to suggest that the containment structure represents a significant source of radiation exposure relative to other sources of residual radioactive fallout contamination on the atoll'.[174] The report noted that while sea-level rise could increase storm surge and swells, and cause 'wave-induced over-wash of lower sections of the dome', definitive data did not permit the determination of 'how these events might impact on the environment'.[175]

167 D. Hawkins, 'These Airmen Cleaned Up an H-Bomb Disaster. Decades Later, They're Still Fighting for Benefits', *Washington Post*, 5 October 2017, at http://bit.ly/2J7Plzu.

168 S. Burgen, 'US to Clean Up Spanish Radioactive Site 49 Years after Plane Crash', *The Guardian*, 19 October 2015, at http://bit.ly/2DomXz4.

169 T. Lum et al., 'Republic of the Marshall Islands Changed Circumstances Petition to Congress', Congressional Research Service Report, updated 16 May 2005, available at http://bit.ly/2JbjOfU, p. 4.

170 Ibid., p. 5.

171 C. Shearer, 'Remembering America's Forgotten Nuclear Cleanup Mission', *Vice World News*, 28 December 2020, at https://bit.ly/3urWJxo.

172 Marshall Islands Dose Assessment and Radioecology Program, 'Enewetak', Lawrence Livermore National Laboratory, Last modified 25 August 2020, at http://bit.ly/2NKq98I.

173 Shearer 'Remembering America's Forgotten Nuclear Cleanup Mission'.

174 US Department of Energy, Report on the Status of the Runit Dome in the Marshall Islands, June 2020, at https://bit.ly/3ugLDL5, p. 8.

175 Ibid., p. 10. See also S. Rust, 'U.S. Says Leaking Nuclear Waste Dome Is Safe; Marshall Islands Leaders Don't Believe It', *Los Angeles Times*, 1 July 2020, at http://lat.ms/3dqBrtw.

Disarmament Obligations

Specific obligations pertain to certain former or all existing nuclear-armed States Parties to the TPNW. These are set out in Article 4 of the Treaty. Nuclear-armed States are given the option of either 'destroy and join' the TPNW or 'join and destroy', with obligations pertaining to them dependent on the decision they make.

For States Parties that possessed or controlled nuclear weapons after 7 July 2017 and destroyed them before joining the Treaty, there are enhanced verification obligations (discussed below).[176] Disarmament obligations pertain to States that are still nuclear armed upon becoming party to the TPNW. Thus Article 4(2) stipulates in part:

> Notwithstanding Article 1 (a), each State Party that owns, possesses or controls nuclear weapons or other nuclear explosive devices shall immediately remove them from operational status, and destroy them as soon as possible but not later than a deadline to be determined by the first meeting of States Parties, in accordance with a legally binding, time-bound plan for the verified and irreversible elimination of that State Party's nuclear-weapon programme, including the elimination or irreversible conversion of all nuclear-weapons-related facilities.

Therefore 'immediately' upon becoming a party to the TPNW, a nuclear-armed State must remove all its nuclear weapons from 'operational status'. The nuclear-armed State Party must then elaborate a plan for the destruction of the weapons and any other nuclear explosive devices and for the elimination of the nuclear weapons programme. The deadline for completion of destruction of the weapons must comply with the deadline that will be set by the First Meeting of States Parties to the Treaty. It may be that the elimination or irreversible conversion of all nuclear-weapons-related facilities may legitimately take longer than this. Paragraph 2 of Article 4 further requires that the nuclear-armed State Party must submit the plan it has elaborated, either to the other States Parties or to a 'competent international authority' they designate, within sixty days of becoming party to the TPNW.

The plan will be the subject of negotiation with this competent international authority, which will then submit it to the subsequent meeting of States Parties or review conference, whichever comes first, 'for approval in accordance with its rules of procedure'.[177] The requirement that the plan be legally binding does not clarify whether that should be in the form of a treaty or domestic legislation (or both). It is to be assumed that the plan should at the least be binding under international law, which would imply that the competent international authority is an international organisation with the power to conclude treaties with States[178] in the same way that the IAEA can do with respect to safeguards.[179]

[176] Art. 4(1), TPNW.

[177] Art. 4(2), TPNW.

[178] According to the 1986 Vienna Convention on the Law of Treaties between States and International Organizations or between International Organizations, the 'capacity of an international organization to conclude treaties is governed by the rules of that organization'. Art. 6, Vienna Convention on the Law of Treaties between States and International Organizations or between International Organizations; adopted at Vienna, 21 March 1986; not yet in force. Although the 1986 Vienna Convention is not yet in force, this rule is reflective of customary law.

[179] See further on this issue Chapter 7.

During the course of the destruction programme, there are reporting obligations for the nuclear-armed State Party (to each meeting of States Parties and review conference), as well as enhanced verification requirements. The Treaty makes it explicit that the costs related to the destruction of nuclear weapons or other nuclear explosive devices, and the elimination of nuclear-weapon programmes, including the elimination or conversion of all nuclear-weapons-related facilities, 'should be' borne by the nuclear-armed States Parties themselves.[180]

States Parties that join the TPNW with nuclear weapons belonging to a third State either on their territory or in any place under their jurisdiction or control must ensure the 'prompt' removal of the weapons, 'as soon as possible but not later than a deadline to be determined by the first meeting of States Parties'. It is assumed that this deadline will be markedly shorter than the deadline set down for the destruction of a domestic nuclear weapons programme. Until the removal of the foreign State's weapons is complete, the concerned State Party must report to each meeting of States Parties and review conference. Once the weapons and any other nuclear explosive devices have been removed, the State Party must submit a declaration of completion to the UN Secretary-General.

Unless and until a nuclear-armed State adheres to the TPNW, the obligations in Article 4 will remain purely theoretical. It would have been possible for the Treaty to eschew the membership of such a State. Indeed, the first draft of the Treaty had incorporated an article detailing measures 'for States that have eliminated their nuclear weapons',[181] while foreseeing the possibility of proposals for further effective measures relating to nuclear disarmament, including provisions for the conclusion of additional protocols to the treaty for 'the verified and irreversible elimination of any remaining nuclear weapon programmes under strict and effective international control'.

The Obligations of International Cooperation and Assistance

Article 7 addresses the duties of each State Party with respect to international cooperation and assistance. Paragraph 1 of the article obligates each State Party to cooperate with other States Parties to 'facilitate the implementation' of the Treaty. There is a further reference to the right of each State Party to seek and 'where feasible' to receive assistance from the other States Parties to support the fulfilment of its respective obligations.[182] This may be for environmental remediation or for the victims of the use or testing of nuclear weapons or other nuclear explosive devices.[183] As of this writing, there was no information on assistance that had been provided.

There is no explicit authorisation in the Treaty of the provision of assistance for the destruction of nuclear weapons in a nuclear-armed State Party, but equally no bar is imposed on it occurring. Such assistance could be in the form of technical, human, or material assistance, as well as being potentially financial in nature given the

180 Art. 9(3), TPNW.
181 Art. 4, Draft Convention on the Prohibition of Nuclear Weapons, 22 May 2017.
182 Art. 7(2), TPNW.
183 Art. 7(3) and Art. 7(4), TPNW.

recommendation that the nuclear-armed State Party should bear the costs of the destruction and the elimination of its nuclear-weapons programme.

Verification of Compliance

There are limited verification measures set out in the TPNW, which focus on safeguards agreements with the IAEA. In general, duties to maintain or bring into force such safeguards are slightly stronger than, but largely replicate, those set out in the NPT. Suggestions made by diplomats or commentators opposed to the TPNW that the safeguards requirements in that Treaty are weaker than they are in the NPT (which does not require that any State Party have an IAEA Additional Protocol) are incorrect. Specific provision is also made in the TPNW for regular meetings of the States Parties 'in order to consider and, where necessary, take decisions in respect of any matter with regard to the application or implementation' of the Treaty,[184] as well as a conference after five years following entry into force 'to review the operation of the Treaty and the progress in achieving the purposes of the Treaty'.[185]

Safeguards Agreements

The obligation under the TPNW to negotiate and bring into force nuclear safeguards is more stringent than is the case with the NPT, but is also rather more complicated. Each State Party to the TPNW must either maintain in force its existing IAEA standards agreement,[186] or if it does not yet have one in force, it must conclude and bring into force the latest version of the IAEA Comprehensive Standards Agreement (INFCIRC/153 Corrected) within eighteen months of becoming party to the Treaty.[187] Upon the entry into force of the TPNW in January 2021, this concerned only Palestine, which had signed a Comprehensive Standards Agreement in 2019 but had not yet brought it into force.

In addition, every State Party to the TPNW that had an IAEA Additional Protocol in force as of 22 January 2021 – the date of entry into force of the Treaty – must maintain it in force.[188] As of that date, the following thirty States Parties were so obligated: Antigua and Barbuda, Austria, Bangladesh, Botswana, Costa Rica, Cuba, Ecuador, Fiji, Gambia, Holy See, Honduras, Ireland, Jamaica, Kazakhstan, Lesotho, Malta, Mexico, Namibia, New Zealand, Nicaragua, Nigeria, Palau, Panama, Paraguay, Saint Kitts and Nevis, South Africa, Thailand, Uruguay, Vanuatu, and Vietnam.

Stricter safeguards standards also apply to existing or former nuclear-armed States that adhere to the TPNW. They must conclude an agreement for implementation and verification of the Treaty's disarmament obligations and also conclude and bring into force within eighteen months both a Comprehensive Standards Agreement and an Additional Protocol, which, combined, are 'sufficient to provide credible assurance of

184 Art. 8(1), TPNW.
185 Art. 8(4), TPNW.
186 Art. 3(1), TPNW.
187 Art. 3(2), TPNW.
188 Art. 3(1), TPNW.

the non-diversion of declared nuclear material from peaceful nuclear activities and of the absence of undeclared nuclear material or activities in that State Party as a whole'.[189]

The First Meeting of States Parties

Austria has already announced that it will host the First Meeting of States Parties to the TPNW, and that its 'ambition and aim is clear: to lay the foundations for a world free of nuclear weapons'.[190] This meeting, which was required to occur at the latest by 21 January 2022 in order to comply with Article 8(2) of the Treaty, was set for 22–24 March 2022 in Vienna, as of this writing.

The Impact of the TPNW

It is too soon to judge the effectiveness of the TPNW in promoting nuclear disarmament – if that is indeed the goal of its architects. The object and purpose of the Treaty are narrower: to prevent 'the catastrophic humanitarian consequences that would result from any use of nuclear weapons'.[191] That said, its States Parties recognise 'the consequent need to completely eliminate such weapons, which remains the only way to guarantee that nuclear weapons are never used again under any circumstances'.[192]

No nuclear-armed State has yet signed the TPNW and the prospects of one doing so appeared remote as of this writing. More credible is that, within the medium term, a State under a nuclear 'umbrella' might decide to adhere to the Treaty, or at least to sign it. Signature would not render illegal its protection by a nuclear-armed State, but would enable the signatory State to signal its support for the humanitarian objectives of the TPNW. While a NATO member could disassociate itself from specific documents promulgated by the Alliance, including the Strategic Concept, such a stance with respect particularly to nuclear weapons would undoubtedly prove politically difficult. As of this writing, no NATO member had signed the TPNW.

Nuclear-armed States have been unclear as to whether they consider the TPNW to be ineffective (in disarmament terms) or deeply damaging to existing disarmament initiatives (such as they are), or to have both effects simultaneously. Concern about the normative implications of the Treaty has prompted several such States to emphasise that the Treaty does not contribute to the emergence of customary international law pertaining to nuclear weapons. In 2018, for instance, the five permanent members of the UN Security Council issued a joint statement in which they asserted that they 'do not accept any claim that it contributes to the development of customary international law; nor does it set any new standards or norms'.[193] This statement is,

189 Art. 4(1) and (3), TPNW.

190 Oestern (ed.), *Nuclear Weapons Ban Monitor 2020*, p. 85.

191 TPNW, second preambular para.

192 Ibid.

193 Joint Statement by China, France, Russian Federation, United Kingdom and United States, First Committee Thematic Debate (Nuclear Weapons), Seventy-Third Session of the UN General Assembly, New York, 22 October 2018, at https://bit.ly/3ugzjdL.

however, incorrect as a matter of both fact and law. The Treaty is both State practice and evidence of *opinio juris*, and it clearly establishes new norms, such as through the comprehensive prohibition of using or threatening to use nuclear weapons. What is true to say, given the implacable opposition of the five nuclear-weapon States, is that a customary prohibition of all use will not crystallise as custom in any foreseeable future. This issue is discussed further in Chapter 8.

7

Verification

From the earliest days of the nuclear age, the issue of verification has plagued efforts to restrain the development, testing, and deployment of nuclear weapons and to ensure their destruction. It continues to do so. Agreement after agreement has foundered on the fear that verification, especially when it concerns on-site inspections of military facilities (or those of a sensitive commercial nature), is not only a licence to engage in intelligence gathering but even an invitation to conduct espionage by the front door. In contrast, the lack of such intrusive verification measures is used by some to deride a Treaty as worthless. The consequence of such mistrust has been to reduce rather than to build confidence in arms control. But when verification is effective, as it has been with respect to several nuclear treaties (especially a number of those adopted between the Soviet Union/Russian Federation and the United States) the results are both manifest and significant.

This chapter considers verification thematically, first by reference to methods to substantiate compliance with prohibitions on nuclear testing. It then discusses, in turn, the means and methods of verification devised with a view to preventing nuclear proliferation, ensuring the destruction of nuclear weapons, and confirming respect for the limitations on the deployment of nuclear weapons. Some verification regimes are global in nature while others are bilateral, reflecting the nature of the agreement. Many nuclear treaties, especially those adopted in the early decades of the Cold War, either allowed States Parties to rely on 'national technical means' of verification or simply eschewed verification altogether. Later, certain agreements provided for on-site inspections – routine, spontaneous, and/or challenge in nature – with the 'teeth' intended to deter violations as well as to detect them.

As of this writing, while the International Atomic Energy Agency (IAEA), entering its sixty-fifth year of operation, continues to work to prevent nuclear proliferation, no international disarmament body existed that could support and verify national disarmament of nuclear weapons and the ambient programme in nuclear-armed States. Indeed, as the Netherlands has observed, nuclear disarmament verification is a capability that the international community as a whole has 'just started to develop'.[1]

[1] 'Explanation of Vote of the Netherlands on Text of Nuclear Ban Treaty', 7 July 2017, available at https://bit.ly/2PokJHd.

If the IAEA is to become such a body, it will need both a new mandate and a huge injection of resources. More probable is that a new institution dedicated to the task will need to be created, should the opportunity arise whereby any or all of the nine nuclear-armed States accept to disarm in a multilateral treaty. What is certain, however, is that success in nuclear disarmament – as with nuclear non-proliferation and arms control – tends to go hand in hand with effective verification.

VERIFICATION OF TESTING

Verification of the Treaty Prohibitions of Explosive Nuclear Testing

Three main global treaties restrain nuclear explosive testing: the Partial Test-Ban Treaty,[2] the Comprehensive Nuclear-Test-Ban Treaty (CTBT),[3] and the Treaty on the Prohibition of Nuclear Weapons.[4] Of these, only one – the CTBT – has an international verification regime that is associated with and established by it. This is despite the fact that the CTBT has still to enter into force, 25 years after its adoption by the United Nations (UN) General Assembly.

As Chapter 3 described, the negotiation of the Partial Test-Ban Treaty in 1963 brought with it a specific verification challenge. In fact, to be precise, there were two main challenges, given that no international verification mechanism was acceptable to the Soviets. One task pertained to verification of the prohibition on detonating nuclear weapons in the atmosphere and outer space. The second pertained to assuring compliance with the prohibition on detonating nuclear weapons underwater as well as, albeit only in limited circumstances, on detonating nuclear weapons underground. The solutions found by the United States were implemented in two distinct projects: Project Vela and Project Vela Uniform.

The ability to detect every underground detonation has been necessary since the adoption of the CTBT in 1996 and its comprehensive prohibition of explosive nuclear testing. Although the treaty is not in force and therefore on-site inspections are not permissible, the international monitoring system (IMS) created to verify compliance with the norm against all explosive testing established by the CTBT has been progressively established over the last two decades and is effectively functioning. The IMS is described once the main elements of Project Vela have been outlined.

Project Vela

Project Vela was created by the United States with the express purpose of verifying compliance with the provisions of the Partial Test-Ban Treaty it was negotiating with the

[2] Treaty Banning Nuclear Weapon Tests in the Atmosphere, in Outer Space and Under Water; concluded at Moscow, 25 July 1963; entered into force 10 October 1963.

[3] Comprehensive Nuclear-Test-Ban Treaty; adopted at New York, 10 September 1996; not yet in force.

[4] Treaty on the Prohibition of Nuclear Weapons; adopted at New York, 17 July 2017; entered into force 22 January 2021.

Soviet Union following the Cuban Missile Crisis. Developed by scientists at the Los Alamos laboratory in Nevada, the project involved the placing of satellites in geospatial orbit. The first pair of satellites (Vela 1A and Vela 1B) were launched a week after the Treaty entered into force; ultimately, a total of 12 satellites, each weighing 150 kilograms, would be launched under the Project between October 1963 and April 1970.[5] Sensors on each satellite monitored for the optical and electromagnetic signatures of nuclear explosions in the earth's atmosphere as well as in outer space.[6] Each satellite had a sensing range of 200 million miles, and the on-board equipment was capable of detecting X-rays, gamma rays, and neutrons.[7]

The effectiveness of this 'national technical means' of verification was demonstrated in September 1979, when satellite Vela 5B (also referred to as Vela 6911) detected the double-flash typical of a nuclear weapon test off the coast of South Africa.[8] The so-called Vela incident is widely believed to have been a test detonation of an Israeli nuclear explosive device.[9] At the time, Israel and South Africa were both States Parties to the 1963 Partial Test-Ban Treaty and had therefore accepted the prohibition on all atmospheric nuclear tests.

Studies by Christopher Wright and Lars-Erik De Geer, published jointly in 2017 and 2018, analysed data on radioactivity found in the thyroids of sheep in Australia following the flash, meteorological data from the time, and radionuclide and hydro-acoustic data released by the US government. Their analysis led them to conclude that the flash was in all likelihood a small-yield nuclear explosion, possibly equating to 2 kt of TNT.[10] If true, this would constitute a serious violation of the Partial Test-Ban Treaty by Israel, possibly with the assistance of South Africa.[11] Writing in 2018 on the *Bulletin of the Atomic Scientists* website following the publication of the studies, Leonard Weiss, the chief architect of the US's Nuclear Nonproliferation Act of 1978, questioned whether the United States and the international community were 'serious about nuclear arms control'.[12]

Project Vela Uniform involved the development of seismic methods for detecting underground nuclear tests. The challenge for the project, which was conducted jointly by the US Atomic Energy Commission and the Department of Defense in the 1960s even before the adoption of the Partial Test-Ban Treaty, was to differentiate underground nuclear tests from other seismic events, such as earthquakes, and to identify the location

5 While all the Vela satellites remain in orbit today, they no longer gather data. The last functioning Vela satellite was switched off in 1985.

6 DARPA, 'VELA: Nuclear Explosion Detection', undated but accessed 1 June 2020, at http://bit.ly/3dnz7AK.

7 V. Grant, 'Cold War Watchmen', Los Alamos National Laboratory, 13 July 2020, at http://bit.ly/376s2Dl.

8 Atmospheric nuclear explosions produce a unique signature: a short and intense flash lasting around one millisecond, followed by a second prolonged, but less intense emission of light.

9 See, e.g., J. Borger, 'The Truth about Israel's Secret Nuclear Arsenal', *The Guardian*, 15 January 2014, at http://bit.ly/30aMxwb.

10 C. M. Wright and L.-E. De Geer, 'The 22 September 1979 Vela Incident: The Detected Double-Flash', *Science & Global Security*, Vol. 25, No. 3 (2017), 95–124, at https://bit.ly/2NpYw4U; and C. M. Wright and L.-E. De Geer, 'The 22 September 1979 Vela Incident: Radionuclide and Hydroacoustic Evidence for a Nuclear Explosion', *Science & Global Security*, Vol. 26, No. 1 (2018), 1–35, at https://bit.ly/3sgM3zs.

11 As such, it would amount to a violation of Article I(1) of the Treaty by Israel and of Article I(2) by South Africa.

12 L. Weiss, 'A Double-Flash from the Past and Israel's Nuclear Arsenal', *Bulletin of the Atomic Scientists*, 3 August 2018, at http://bit.ly/3kaSZuM.

of any test site.[13] The principal work areas for Vela Uniform comprised 'classical and explosion seismology' and involved the development of field equipment, prototype observatories, and data centres as well as the conduct of an extensive monitoring programme of seismic and other unique signatures from a series of US subsurface nuclear detonations.[14]

In particular, through its measurement of seven nuclear detonations in the continental United States in the 1960s, as well as smaller experiments using conventional high explosives, the Project developed technologies to verify whether and, if so, where underground and underwater nuclear detonations had occurred. Especially important was the ability, fine-tuned over time, to distinguish such detonations from, in particular, earthquakes.[15] The work conducted as part of Project Vela Uniform fed into the international monitoring system developed for the verification of underground nuclear detonations prohibited under the CTBT while also transforming seismology as a scientific discipline.[16] Indeed, as Barth reports, funding under Vela Uniform supported almost every US seismologist in the 1960s.[17]

Verification of the CTBT

In order to verify compliance with the CTBT, a verification regime 'shall be established' consisting of an International Monitoring System (IMS); consultation and clarification; on-site inspections; and confidence-building measures.[18] The IMS has been established by the Contracting States to the CTBT even though the treaty has not entered into force. Confidence-building measures include the duty on every State Party to provide notification 'of any chemical explosion using 300 tonnes or greater of TNT-equivalent blasting material detonated as a single explosion anywhere on its territory, or at any place under its jurisdiction or control'.[19]

The International Monitoring System

Described as 'one of the most ambitious global projects ever undertaken', the IMS plays a central role in monitoring compliance with the CTBT.[20] The System is, in the words of the Preparatory Commission for the Comprehensive Nuclear-Test-Ban Treaty Organization (CTBTO), 'unique'. It consists of 321 facilities worldwide that use four

13 'Decoupling' is a considerable challenge for seismic detection. This evasion method involves detonating a nuclear device in a large underground cavity so as to muffle the seismic signal.

14 C. C. Bates, 'Detection and Identification of Nuclear Explosions Underground (Project VELA UNIFORM)', Proceedings of the *Institute of Radio Engineers*, Vol. 50, No. 11 (November 1962). (Note this journal no longer exists.)

15 See, e.g., A. L. Lange, 'Seismic Aftershock Investigations – Project Vela Uniform Recording of Micro-Earthquakes Near Socorro, New Mexico, December 24–27, 1961', Technical Report No. 2, Stanford Research Institute, Washington, DC, February 1963, at https://bit.ly/3qG1GQd.

16 K.-H. Barth, 'The Politics of Seismology: Nuclear Testing, Arms Control, and the Transformation of a Discipline', *Social Studies of Science*, Vol. 33, No. 5 (October 2003), 743–81.

17 Ibid., p. 744.

18 Art. IV(1), CTBT.

19 Protocol to the CTBT, Part III, para. 1.

20 Preparatory Commission for the Comprehensive Nuclear-Test-Ban Treaty Organization (CTBTO), 'The Future Role of the International Monitoring System', at http://bit.ly/3qInNpj.

different technologies – seismic, infrasound, hydroacoustic, and radionuclide – to monitor the globe for nuclear explosions. The system is supported by a network of 16 radionuclide laboratories. Shock waves emanating from a nuclear explosion underground, in the seas, or in the air are registered, and any radioactive debris released into the atmosphere can be detected.[21]

The IMS has successfully detected all six nuclear test detonations by the Democratic People's Republic of Korea (North Korea) between 2006 and 2017. This is so even though North Korea has not signed the Treaty. (Its signature and ratification are required for the entry into force of the CTBT.) The System's 'baptism of fire' came with North Korea's first nuclear explosive test on 9 October 2006.[22] While the intention to conduct a nuclear test had been announced some days earlier, Pyongyang had not provided any details of when it would occur. The detonation was recorded by the IMS, despite its small yield and the fact that the System was only 60 per cent operational at the time. Twenty-two IMS seismic stations, including one as far away as South America, registered the shock waves 'which clearly showed explosion-like characteristics'. The signal's origin was eventually narrowed down to an area covering significantly less than 1,000 square kilometres[23] – the size of the area that may be investigated during an on-site inspection according to the CTBT.[24] Two weeks after the test, the IMS radionuclide station at Yellowknife, Canada, registered an increased level of xenon. 'The prevailing meteorological conditions showed that these findings could be attributed to the explosion, thus providing the radioactive "smoking gun" evidence that the explosion was indeed nuclear.'[25]

While the 2006 test was detected by twenty-two IMS stations, the 2009 test was detected by sixty-one of the System's stations and the 2013 test was detected by ninety-six, demonstrating the development of the facilities' capabilities over the course of a decade.[26] The last test by North Korea (as of this writing), a thermonuclear detonation in early September 2017, was sensed or analysed by more than 100 monitoring stations. The initial estimate for the magnitude of the blast of 5.8 body-wave magnitude (mb) was subsequently revised up to 6.1 and even higher,[27] and the location estimate showed that the event took place in the area of North Korea's nuclear test site.[28]

As of 1 February 2021, a total of 302 facilities worldwide had been certified for the IMS by the Preparatory Commission for the CTBTO.[29]

21 Preparatory Commission for the CTBTO, 'Maps of Monitoring Facilities', at http://bit.ly/2Mb2HRz.
22 Preparatory Commission for the CTBTO, '9 October 2006 – First DPRK Nuclear Test', at http://bit.ly/3aBXUlx.
23 Ibid.
24 Protocol to the CTBT, Part II, para. 3.
25 Preparatory Commission for the CTBTO, '9 October 2006 – First DPRK Nuclear Test'.
26 Preparatory Commission for the CTBTO, 'Update on CTBTO Findings Related to the Announced Nuclear Test by North Korea', Vienna, 15 February 2013, at http://bit.ly/2NjkJBO.
27 See, e.g., A. Arimuko, E. Sujarwanto, and A. Marsono, 'Measurements of Earthquake Moment Magnitude (Mw) to Estimate Detonation Energy of a Nuclear Bomb as Plutonium-240', *Journal of Physics Conference Series*, March 2020, at https://bit.ly/3aG8t6W.
28 Preparatory Commission for the CTBTO, 'DPRK: Sept 2017 Unusual Seismic Event', at http://bit.ly/3bxvveu.
29 Preparatory Commission for the CTBTO Homepage, at http://bit.ly/3qKHYD6.

On-Site Inspections under the CTBT

The fact that the CTBT has not entered into force has precluded the conduct of on-site inspections: the 'final verification measure' under the Treaty.[30] An on-site inspection is launched to establish whether or not a nuclear explosion has been carried out. Indeed, the Convention confirms: 'The *sole purpose* of an on-site inspection shall be to clarify whether a nuclear weapon test explosion or any other nuclear explosion has been carried out in violation of Article I and, to the extent possible, to gather any facts which might assist in identifying any possible violator.'[31]

Although not formally labelled as such in the Convention, on-site inspections under the CTBT are 'challenge inspections', as they can only be carried out upon request from a State Party.[32] The State Party subjected to such an inspection is not entitled to refuse to allow it to take place.[33] If a decision is taken to authorise an on-site inspection (by the Executive Council of the CTBTO, once established), it must be conducted 'without delay' by an inspection team designated by the Director-General of the Organization.[34]

As ever with inspections, the negotiation of the relevant provisions proved challenging, generating a need to 'strike a fine balance between the expected benefits and the political risks'.[35] No fewer than thirty-five of the sixty-eight paragraphs of the article in the Treaty dealing with verification (Article IV) are dedicated to the on-site inspections regime. A separate Protocol to the CTBT provides further detail on the conduct of an inspection. It is stipulated that '[w]ithout prejudice to the right of any State Party to request an on-site inspection, States Parties should, whenever possible, first make every effort to clarify and resolve, among themselves or with or through the Organization, any matter which may cause concern about possible non-compliance with the basic obligations of this Treaty.'[36]

Despite the difficulty in agreeing upon the possibility of inspections, the Preparatory Commission stresses that a key benefit of the regime is its deterrence value, increasing confidence in compliance with the Treaty by the States Parties. 'Provisions for on-site inspections strengthen the notion of a verifiable Treaty and thus help garner support for it.'[37]

Verification of the Prohibition of Testing under the TPNW

There is a comprehensive prohibition of nuclear testing under the Treaty on the Prohibition of Nuclear Weapons. In addition to a prohibition of explosive testing, all other forms of development of nuclear weapons, such as computer modelling and subcritical testing, are outlawed. There is no verification system established under the TPNW to verify compliance with these prohibitions.

30 Preparatory Commission for the CTBTO, 'The Final Verification Measure', at http://bit.ly/2ZCa7R2.
31 Art. IV(34), CTBT (emphasis added)
32 Art. IV(34), CTBT.
33 Preparatory Commission for the CTBTO, 'The Final Verification Measure'.
34 Art. IV(53), CTBT.
35 Ibid.
36 Art. IV(29), CTBT.
37 Preparatory Commission for the CTBTO, 'The Final Verification Measure'.

PREVENTING THE PROLIFERATION OF NUCLEAR WEAPONS

The Development of IAEA Safeguards

As Chapter 4 described, the IAEA had already developed 'safeguards' for nuclear material in the 1960s, prior to the negotiation and adoption of the Treaty on the Non-proliferation of Nuclear Weapons.[38] The NPT's conclusion in 1968, however, prompted the Agency to revise its safeguards agreement and, in 1972, issue the model for the Comprehensive Safeguards Agreement that reflects these treaty obligations on non-nuclear-weapon States Parties.[39] The Comprehensive Safeguards Agreement or 'CSA' is itself a bilateral treaty between the Agency and each contracting State.[40] A CSA in force permits the IAEA to verify that disclosed nuclear material is not being diverted from peaceful purposes in that State. The Agreement is the basis for the verification of compliance with the NPT, the regional nuclear-weapons-free-zone treaties, and latterly, also the TPNW.

The model for a Comprehensive Safeguards Agreement has been the legal basis for the IAEA's work for the last fifty years. For half of that period, until the elaboration of the more intrusive Additional Protocol, it was the sole international legal basis by which the IAEA could act to prevent and detect diversion of disclosed nuclear material in a State. Following concealment by a number of States, whose actions are described below, the Additional Protocol was developed to grant the Agency the power also to seek to detect the presence or use of undisclosed nuclear material and facilities. The failure to inform the IAEA about certain nuclear material or facilities would be prima facie evidence of the existence of a programme for the development of nuclear weapons.

As of this writing, no arms control or disarmament treaty required that all its States Parties conclude and maintain in force an Additional Protocol. As its name suggests, a Protocol can only be adopted further to a Comprehensive Safeguards Agreement.[41] For States without a nuclear energy programme and without significant uranium deposits or stockpiles, a Small Quantities Protocol (SQP) reduces the administrative burdens of the safeguards

38 Treaty on the Non-proliferation of Nuclear Weapons; opened for signature at London, Moscow, and Washington, DC, 1 July 1968; entered into force 5 March 1970.

39 The latest version, concluded in 1971 and adopted by the IAEA Board of Governors in 1972 with some textual corrections, is IAEA doc. INFCIRC/153 (Corrected). The document is entitled 'The Structure and Content of Agreements between the Agency and States required in connection with the Treaty on the Non-proliferation of Nuclear Weapons'.

40 International organisations are subjects of international law with international personality, denoting that they can contract obligations under international law as well as having obligations imposed upon them. In the preamble to the 1986 Vienna Convention on the Law of Treaties between States and International Organizations, reference is made to 'the specific features of treaties to which international organizations are parties as subjects of international law distinct from States'.

41 As discussed below, the TPNW requires all States that had in force an Additional Protocol as of 22 January 2021 and which were either already party to the Treaty on that date or which later become a State Party to it, must maintain in force that Protocol.

agreement.[42] No arms control treaty requires – or even expressly permits – the conclusion of an SQP.[43]

The IAEA Safeguards

The Comprehensive Safeguards Agreement

Verification of compliance with the NPT is limited to safeguards agreements to be concluded with the IAEA by every non-nuclear-weapon State Party over nuclear material and related equipment under its jurisdiction or control. The 'exclusive purpose' of such an agreement is the 'verification of the fulfilment' of the party's NPT obligations, 'with a view to preventing diversion of nuclear energy from peaceful uses to nuclear weapons or other nuclear explosive devices'. The requisite safeguards must be applied on 'all source or special fissionable material in all peaceful nuclear activities within the territory of such State, under its jurisdiction, or carried out under its control anywhere'.[44] The term 'source material' comprises uranium containing the mixture of isotopes occurring in nature, uranium depleted in the isotope 235, and thorium. The term 'special fissionable material' means plutonium-239 and uranium enriched in the isotopes 235 or 233.[45]

Each State Party to the Treaty undertakes not to provide either a source of special fissionable material or any 'specially designed or prepared' equipment or material for processing, use, or production of special fissionable material to any non-nuclear-weapon State for peaceful purposes, unless the material is subject to these safeguards.[46] There are no corresponding safeguards obligations imposed by the NPT on the five nuclear-weapon States Parties.

Under the TPNW, all States Parties must maintain in force the latest version of the Comprehensive Safeguards Agreement (INFCIRC/153 (Corrected)), should it have one with the IAEA, or else it must conclude and bring one into force within eighteen months of becoming a State Party.[47] Stricter safeguards are required for all nuclear-armed States Parties or for those that were nuclear-armed after 7 July 2017 and which disarm before adhering to the TPNW.[48]

42 To qualify for a Small Quantities Protocol, nuclear material in the State may not exceed 1 kg in total of special fissionable material (plutonium; uranium enriched to 20 per cent and above; and uranium enriched to less than 20 per cent after its weight is multiplied by five times the square of its enrichment); 10 metric tons in total of natural uranium and depleted uranium with an enrichment above 0.5 per cent; 20 metric tons of depleted uranium with an enrichment of 0.5 per cent or below; and 20 metric tons of thorium. See IAEA doc. INFCIRC/153 (Corrected), para. 37.

43 Surprisingly, one leading commentator appears to regret the absence of such a reference in the TPNW. S. Hill, 'NATO and the Treaty on the Prohibition of Nuclear Weapons', Research Paper, Chatham House, London, January 2021, at https://bit.ly/2MYhyyQ, p. 16.

44 Art. III(1), NPT.

45 See Art. XX, Statute of the IAEA; and NSG Part 1 Guidelines – INFCIRC/254/Rev.13/Part 1, 'Material and Equipment', at http://bit.ly/2EzebK6, paras. 1.1 and 1.2.

46 Art. III(2), NPT.

47 Art. 3(1) and (2), TPNW.

48 Art. 4(1) and (3), TPNW.

A CSA allows the IAEA to audit a State's 'nuclear material accounting system'.[49] Thus safeguards are based on 'assessments of the correctness and completeness of a State's declared nuclear material and nuclear-related activities'. Verification measures include on-site inspections and visits, as well as containment and surveillance techniques, such as tamper-proof seals and cameras that the IAEA installs at nuclear facilities.[50]

The IAEA carries out different types of on-site inspections and visits under comprehensive safeguards agreements. Ad hoc inspections verify a State's initial report of nuclear material or subsequent changes to it, and are also used to verify nuclear material that is the subject of an international transfer. Routine inspections – the type most frequently used by the Agency – can be conducted under a defined schedule or have an 'unannounced or short-notice character'. The Agency's right to carry out routine inspections under a CSA is limited to those locations within a nuclear facility, or other locations containing nuclear material, through which nuclear material is expected to flow. These are called *strategic points*. Special inspections may be carried out if the IAEA considers that information from a State is not adequate or raises issues of particular concern.[51]

Safeguards visits may be made to declared facilities at appropriate times during the lifecycle for verifying the safeguards relevant design information. They may be carried out during the construction of the facility to determine the completeness of the declared design information; during routine facility operations and following maintenance, in order to confirm that no modification was made that would allow unreported activities to take place; and during the decommissioning of a facility, to confirm that sensitive equipment is indeed rendered unusable.[52]

While highly valuable, the limitations of a Comprehensive Safeguards Agreement are well understood, in particular to the Agency itself. As Hans Blix, then Director General of the IAEA, wrote in 1985, 'Safeguards cannot prevent a violation of obligations – the diversion of fissile material – any more than bank of company audits can prevent a misappropriation of funds. All they can do is expose infringements or arouse suspicions, in effect sound the alarm.'[53] Iran, Iraq, and Libya all managed to initiate a nuclear weapons programme – although none constructed a complete nuclear explosive device – despite adhering to the NPT (in 1970, 1969, and 1975, respectively) and having in place a safeguards agreement.

IAEA Safeguards and Iran's Nuclear Weapons Programme

Iran is alleged to have had a covert nuclear weapons programme for several years in the early 2000s, terminating in 2003. Iran's first nuclear reactor, the Tehran Research Reactor,

49 See, e.g., R. Parsick and J. Sanborn, 'INFCIRC/153 as the Basis for Verification of a Special Nuclear Materials Production Cutoff Convention', Brookhaven National Laboratory, United States, August1994, at http://bit.ly/3uhpwEt.

50 IAEA, 'IAEA Safeguards Overview: Comprehensive Safeguards Agreements and Additional Protocols', 2020, at http://bit.ly/353kpLS.

51 Ibid.

52 Ibid.

53 H. Blix, 'Safeguards and Non-proliferation: The IAEA and Efforts to Counteract the Spread of Nuclear Weapons', *IAEA Bulletin*, Summer 1985, p. 5.

which was built with assistance from the United States, first went critical in November 1967. It operated for 25 years on uranium enriched to about 93 per cent, which was also supplied by the United States, but was later changed, with help from Argentina, to operate on low enriched uranium. Iran's safeguards agreement with the IAEA entered into force in 1974.[54] That year, the Shah established the Atomic Energy Organisation of Iran and announced plans to construct twenty-three nuclear power plants and develop a full nuclear fuel cycle.[55]

In August 2002, the National Council of Resistance of Iran, the political wing of the People's Mujahedin Organisation of Iran (Mujahideen-e Khalq), convened a press conference in which it declared that Iran had secretly built nuclear facilities near Natanz and Arak.[56] During the September 2002 regular session of the IAEA General Conference, the Director General met with Iran's Vice President (who was also President of the Atomic Energy Organisation of Iran), and asked him to confirm whether Iran was building a large underground nuclear-related facility at Natanz and a heavy water production plant at Arak.[57] US President George W. Bush observed to media the following year that the facilities were discovered not because of Iran's compliance with the IAEA or the NPT, 'but because a dissident group pointed it out to the world'.[58] In subsequent years, the IAEA discovered other safeguards violations. Efforts by the Agency to resolve compliance issues in Iran were said to be 'intense and difficult'.[59]

In early March 2006, at the close of the Agency's Board of Governors meeting in Vienna, IAEA Director General Mohamed ElBaradei sent his report on Iran's nuclear programme to the UN Security Council.[60] Speaking to the press, the Director General called for a 'cool-headed approach' from all parties.[61] At the end of July 2006, the Security Council adopted Resolution 1696, in which it noted 'with serious concern' that the Director General's report had listed a number 'of outstanding issues and concerns on Iran's nuclear programme, including topics which could have a military nuclear dimension'. The Council demanded that Iran 'suspend all enrichment-related and reprocessing activities, including research and development, to be verified by the IAEA', giving it a deadline of one month to comply before facing the possibility of economic and diplomatic sanctions.[62]

54 IAEA doc. INFCIRC/214, 13 December 1974, at https://bit.ly/3up7pMA.

55 K. Davenport, 'Timeline of Nuclear Diplomacy with Iran', Fact Sheet, last reviewed January 2021, Arms Control Association, at http://bit.ly/3seIJ7O.

56 Remarks by Alireza Jafarzadeh on New Information on Top Secret Projects of the Iranian Regime's Nuclear Program, Private Viewpoints, Iran Watch, 14 August 2002, at http://bit.ly/37zw5rV.

57 Implementation of the NPT safeguards agreement in the Islamic Republic of Iran, Report by the Director General, IAEA doc. GOV/2003/40, 6 June 2003, at https://bit.ly/3dCoo6U, paras. 2, 3.

58 Cited by P. Kerr, 'Exiles and Iran Intel', Blog entry, Arms Control Wonk website, 5 April 2005, at http://bit.ly/3bvz3iA.

59 M. Rosenthal and W. M. Stern, 'Deterring Nuclear Proliferation: The Importance of IAEA Safeguards', Brookhaven National Laboratory, United States, April 2019, at http://bit.ly/3sgoTG5, §9.2, p. 185.

60 Report of the IAEA Director General, IAEA doc. GOV/2006/15, 27 February 2006.

61 IAEA, 'IAEA and Iran: Chronology of Key Events', 2020, at http://bit.ly/3qN9vnA.

62 UN Security Council Resolution 1696, adopted by 14 votes to one (Qatar), fourth preambular para. and operative para. 2.

On 8 November 2011, the IAEA released a detailed safeguards report indicating that Iran's nuclear weapons programme, Project Amad, had been established in the late 1990s or early 2000s, although the bulk of the activity occurred between 2002 and 2003.[63] According to the Agency, Iran engaged in a range of activities 'relevant to the development of a nuclear explosive device'.[64] Prior to the end of 2003, development activities took place under a 'structured programme', but there were also indications that activities continued after 2003 and that, as of 2011, some might still be 'ongoing'.[65]

The report observed that 'although now declared and currently under safeguards, a number of facilities dedicated to uranium enrichment (the Fuel Enrichment Plant and Pilot Fuel Enrichment Plant at Natanz and the Fordow Fuel Enrichment Plant near Qom) were covertly built by Iran and only declared once the Agency was made aware of their existence by sources other than Iran'.[66] This, the IAEA declared, when considered in light of past efforts by Iran to conceal activities involving nuclear material, generated 'more concern about the possible existence of undeclared nuclear facilities and material in Iran'.[67] The Agency concluded that since Iran was not providing 'the necessary cooperation', it was 'unable to provide credible assurance about the absence of undeclared nuclear material and activities in Iran, and therefore to conclude that all nuclear material in Iran is in peaceful activities'.[68]

In November 2019, the IAEA reported finding uranium particles at a further site in Iran that had not been declared by the Iranian authorities.[69] This was followed by a report by the Agency fifteen months later that it had found further traces of uranium at two undeclared sites in Iran during snap inspections in 2020.[70] The authorities had yet to explain the presence at the sites of uranium: the sites had not been in operation for nearly two decades. An unnamed senior Iranian official told the Reuters news agency: 'We have nothing to hide. That is why we allowed the inspectors to visit those sites.' In fact, access had been blocked to the IAEA for several months. The agency suspects that one of the sites hosted uranium conversion work, a step in processing the source material before enrichment, while the other was used for explosive testing. Iran has persistently denied the existence of a clandestine nuclear weapons programme.[71]

IAEA Safeguards and Iraq's Nuclear Weapons Programme

Prior to 1991, Iraq had pursued a clandestine nuclear-weapons programme that was also not detected by the IAEA in the course of its safeguards work. Even though no nuclear

63 'Implementation of the NPT Safeguards Agreement and Relevant Provisions of Security Council Resolutions in the Islamic Republic of Iran', Report by the Director General of the IAEA, IAEA doc. GOV/2011/65, 8 November 2011, at https://bit.ly/2McHyX4, para. 20.

64 Ibid., para. 43.

65 Ibid., para. 45.

66 Ibid., para. 30.

67 Ibid.

68 Ibid., para. 53.

69 BBC, 'Iran Nuclear Deal: IAEA Finds Uranium Particles at Undeclared Site', 11 November 2019, at http://bbc.in/2ZFmTxW.

70 F. Murphy and J. Irish, 'Exclusive: IAEA Found Uranium Traces at Two Sites Iran Barred It From, Sources Say', Reuters, 19 February 2021, at https://reut.rs/3s9IURH.

71 Ibid.

explosive device was completed, in the 1980s especially, Saddam Hussein vigorously pursued a nuclear weapons programme that employed an estimated 7,000 scientists and 20,000 workers.[72] The programme included enrichment activities in buildings adjacent to facilities where the IAEA routinely conducted inspections under Iraq's Comprehensive Safeguards Agreement (specifically the Tuwaitha Research Centre) as well as at other, undeclared locations.[73]

In 1991, after the end of the Gulf War, Hans Blix told the US Senate Foreign Relations Committee that 'the IAEA safeguards inspection system should be given sharper teeth', citing the need for enhanced access to locations as well as access to additional information, including data obtained through national technical means, with satellite cameras and other intelligence-gathering activities.[74] The experience the IAEA gained in Iraq helped it develop a plan of action to strengthen safeguards under the Comprehensive Safeguards Agreement. This would lead to the elaboration and adoption of the Additional Protocol.

IAEA Safeguards and Libya's Nuclear Weapons Programme

Libya ratified the NPT in 1975, even though Muammar Gadhafi, who had come to power in a coup six years earlier, was already actively seeking to become a nuclear power. Libya imported 1,200 tons of uranium ore concentrate from mines in Niger without declaring it to the IAEA.[75] It cooperated with the Soviet Union (informing the IAEA of this cooperation), which resulted in the construction in 1979 of a research reactor in Tajoura. This offered Libya the opportunity to explore plutonium production technologies, which Libya did covertly, evading IAEA safeguards. By early 2002, the Pakistani nuclear scientist Abdul Qadeer Khan had provided Libya with the blueprint for a fission weapon.[76]

In October 2003, a German cargo ship, the *BBC China*, was intercepted at sea on its way to Tripoli and brought to an Italian port, where its cargo of components for one thousand high-speed centrifuges was confiscated. The parts had been made in Malaysia and shipped through the Middle East. The subsequent investigation by the IAEA resulted in a decision by Gaddafi to dismantle his nuclear programme.[77] On 19 December 2003, Libya agreed to eliminate all material and equipment involved in the production of nuclear weapons. In 2004, the United States and the United Kingdom dismantled Libya's nuclear weapons infrastructure with oversight from the IAEA.[78]

72 J. C. Davis and D. A. Kay, 'Iraq's Secret Nuclear Weapons Program', *Physics Today*, 1 July 1992, p. 21.

73 Rosenthal and Stern, 'Deterring Nuclear Proliferation: The Importance of IAEA Safeguards', para. 7.1.4, p. 142.

74 Cited in ibid.

75 K. Timmerman, 'Weapons of Mass Destruction: the Cases of Iran, Syria, and Libya', Simon Wiesenthal Center Middle East Defense News, August 1992, p. 89.

76 G. Kampani, 'Proliferation Unbound: Nuclear Tales from Pakistan', Center for Nonproliferation Studies, Monterey Institute of International Affairs, 2004.

77 L. Weiss, 'Turning a Blind Eye Again? The Khan Network's History and Lessons for U.S. Policy', *Arms Control Today*, 2005, at http://bit.ly/2Ny2pol.

78 Nuclear Threat Initiative (NTI), 'Libya: Nuclear', last updated January 2015, at https://bit.ly/2McL5og.

IAEA Safeguards and the Risk of Proliferation in Saudi Arabia

The original Small Quantities Protocol suspended the application of many provisions of a State's Comprehensive Safeguards Agreement. This is problematic in a number of States, but especially, as of this writing, in Saudi Arabia, which was described in January 2021 as 'the proliferation concern number one around the world'.[79] For although Saudi Arabia is party to a Comprehensive Safeguards Agreement with the IAEA, its old Small Quantities Protocol to that Agreement suspends most inspection and reporting requirements.[80] The Protocol in place with Saudi Arabia does not even allow the IAEA to verify whether the country meets the eligibility criteria for the Protocol, while Riyadh is not required to provide the IAEA with an initial report on all nuclear material which is subject to safeguards.[81] In October 2020, the IAEA Director General visited Saudi Arabia to discuss safeguards, including the possible adoption by Riyadh of an Additional Protocol.[82] None had been concluded as of this writing.

In April 2020, the US Government Accountability Office had reported that progress in US-Saudi nuclear cooperation was stalled over non-proliferation conditions.[83] The report noted that the United States 'promotes universal adoption of the Additional Protocol as a policy, but it is not a requirement for the conclusion of a nuclear cooperation agreement with the United States'.[84] The United States urged Saudi Arabia to conclude an Additional Protocol with the IAEA in a September 2019 letter from the Secretary of Energy to the Saudi Minister of Energy, Industry, and Mineral Resources. Saudi Arabia was said to have expressed 'an unwillingness' to do so.[85]

The IAEA Additional Protocol

Failures in Iraq and North Korea to detect an ongoing nuclear weapons programme threw into sharp relief the limitations of a Comprehensive Safeguards Agreement and led to the development of an Additional Protocol to the Agreement by the IAEA. The Additional Protocol, also a treaty under international law, grants the Agency additional inspection authority over a Comprehensive Safeguards Agreement, enabling its inspectorate to 'provide assurance about both declared and possible undeclared activities'.[86]

In particular, IAEA inspectors are guaranteed access to all parts of a contracting State's nuclear fuel cycle: uranium mines, fuel fabrication and enrichment plants, and nuclear waste sites, as well as any other location where nuclear material is or may be present.

79 'Nuclear Proliferation Is Not Fast, But It Is Frightening', *The Economist*, 31 January 2021.

80 Agreement between the Kingdom of Saudi Arabia and the International Atomic Energy Agency for the Application of Safeguards in Connection with the Treaty on the Non-proliferation of Nuclear Weapons, IAEA doc. INFCIRC/746, 16 February 2009, at https://bit.ly/39Utue4.

81 IAEA, *Safeguards Implementation Guide for States with Small Quantities Protocols*, Vienna, 2016, at https://bit.ly/3pTo3i1, p. 4.

82 'Saudi Arabia, IAEA Discuss Safeguards', Arms Control Today, October 2020, at https://bit.ly/3cMeh07.

83 US Government Accountability Office (GAO), 'U.S.-Saudi Nuclear Cooperation: Progress Is Stalled over Nonproliferation Conditions', Report to Congress, April 2020, at https://bit.ly/3aKBIpt.

84 Ibid., p. 5.

85 Ibid., p. 17.

86 IAEA, 'IAEA Safeguards Overview: Comprehensive Safeguards Agreements and Additional Protocols', 2020, at https://bit.ly/353kpLS.

Under a CSA alone, material in mining or ore processing activities (e.g., uranium at mines and mills) is not subject to the Agency's safeguards, as it is not yet suitable for enrichment.[87]

Reflecting the problems encountered in Iraq, under an Additional Protocol the IAEA is also accorded short-notice access to all buildings on a nuclear site. Access must be granted to assure the absence of undeclared nuclear material or to resolve questions or inconsistencies in information a State has provided about its nuclear activities. Activities carried out during complementary access can include examination of records, visual observation, environmental sampling, use of radiation detection and measurement devices, and the application of seals and other identifying and tamper-indicating devices. The IAEA may further collect environmental samples at locations beyond declared locations when it deems it necessary.[88]

Iran and the Additional Protocol

A key element to verify Iran's compliance with the 2015 Joint Comprehensive Plan of Action (JCPOA), which limited Iran's enrichment of uranium for an initial period of ten years, was Iran's provisional application of its Additional Protocol. Iran had signed the Protocol in December 2003 but never brought it into force. By 2015, however, Iran was operating 19,000 centrifuges at Natanz, had an enrichment site inside a mountain at Fordow, and its heavy-water reactor at Arak was complete.[89] Under the JCPOA, a politically binding agreement but not a treaty, Iran pledged never to develop or acquire any nuclear explosive devices.

Following the decision by the Trump administration to withdraw US compliance with the JCPOA, Iran progressively limited IAEA access to its nuclear sites while increasing its enrichment of uranium.[90] While hopes rose after the January 2021 presidential inauguration of Joe Biden that a resolution might be found, as of this writing, initial negotiations were proving difficult. In late February 2021, the IAEA reached an agreement with Iran to retain most of its access to nuclear sites throughout the country for the coming three months, providing space for wider political and diplomatic talks between Iran and the United States. While Iran was still planning to suspend compliance with the Additional Protocol, it still would voluntarily allow the inspectors to continue most of their work. The IAEA Director General declared there would be no reduction in the number of inspectors, and that 'not all' snap inspections would be banned. Iranian officials claimed that the verbal agreement would mean that the inspectors would have only 70 per cent of the access they previously enjoyed.[91]

87 GAO, 'U.S.-Saudi Nuclear Cooperation: Progress Is Stalled over Nonproliferation Conditions', p. 5.
88 Ibid.
89 G. Allison, 'The Iran Nuclear Deal, by the Numbers', Belfer Center for Science and International Affairs, Cambridge, MA, 4 April 2015, at http://bit.ly/2ZBOosm.
90 K. Robinson, 'What Is the Iran Nuclear Deal?', Backgrounder, Council on Foreign Relations, Washington, DC, last updated 4 January 2021, at http://on.cfr.org/37Crypo.
91 P. Wintour, 'IAEA and Iran Strike Three-Month Deal over Nuclear Inspections', *The Guardian*, 21 February 2021, at http://bit.ly/3pPFCli.

VERIFICATION OF DESTRUCTION OF NUCLEAR WEAPONS

The only global treaty to require the destruction of nuclear weapons by its States Parties is the 2017 Treaty on the Prohibition of Nuclear Weapons. No nuclear-armed State had adhered to the Treaty as of this writing and prospects for one to do so appeared remote. Article VI of the NPT obligates all States Parties to pursue negotiations in good faith on effective measures relating to nuclear disarmament, but these – should they ever occur – are expected to be conducted wholly outside the auspices of the Nuclear Non-proliferation Treaty. In 1996, the International Court of Justice declared unanimously in its Advisory Opinion on the legality of the threat or use of nuclear weapons that '[t]here exists an obligation to pursue in good faith and bring to a conclusion negotiations leading to nuclear disarmament in all its aspects under strict and effective international control'.[92] To date, no such initiative has been conducted. The closest the world has come was the abortive Baruch Plan in 1946[93] and, arguably, the Reykjavik Summit of 1986 between Ronald Reagan and Mikhail Gorbachev.

Nonetheless, the world still has significant experience in verifying the (limited) destruction of nuclear weapons by treaty. But that experience has been largely at bilateral rather than multilateral level, especially in treaties negotiated and adopted first between the Soviet Union and the United States, and later between the Russian Federation and the United States.[94]

A clear success story in terms both of the destruction programme and its verification regime – 'the first of its kind in the history of US-Soviet arms control'[95] – was the Treaty on the Elimination of Intermediate-Range and Shorter-Range Missiles.[96] More commonly known as the INF Treaty, this 1987 agreement effectively eliminated an entire class of weapons from Europe (and prevented their introduction anywhere else in the world by its States Parties). So successful were its verification provisions that the 1991 START I agreement to cut the strategic nuclear arsenals of the two superpowers by 40 per cent copied 'verbatim' the on-site inspection and verification language from the INF Treaty, whose 'thoroughness' would serve as a precedent for START.[97]

92 ICJ, *Legality of the Threat or Use of Nuclear Weapons*, Advisory Opinion, 8 July 1996, dispositif F.

93 See Chapter 3 for details of the Baruch Plan.

94 An exception might be the Document of the Stockholm Conference on Confidence- and Security-Building Measures and Disarmament in Europe, adopted on 19 September 1986 by participating States of the Conference on Security and Cooperation in Europe (CSCE). The Document granted each participating State the right to conduct a limited number of inspections on the territory of any other participating State within the zone of application for confidence- and security-building measures (CSBMs). Document of the Stockholm Conference on Confidence- and Security-Building Measures and Disarmament in Europe Convened in accordance with the Relevant Provisions of the Concluding Document of the Madrid Meeting of the Conference on Security and Co-operation in Europe, CSCE, Stockholm, 19 September 1986, at https://bit.ly/37C5VEX, para. 65.

95 M. Budjeryn and S. E. Steiner, 'Forgotten Parties to the INF', blog entry, Wilson Center, Washington, DC, 4 March 2019, at http://bit.ly/2Ny9R2L. The bipartisan Wilson Center was chartered by the US Congress in 1968 as the official memorial to President Woodrow Wilson.

96 Treaty on the Elimination of Intermediate-Range and Shorter-Range Missiles; signed at Washington, DC, 8 December 1987; entered into force 1 June 1988. The Treaty was defunct as of 2 August 2019.

97 Budjeryn and Steiner, 'Forgotten Parties to the INF'.

It was only several years after the intrusive verification obligations came to an end (in 2001) that the INF Treaty headed into stormy waters, with President Vladimir Putin declaring it no longer served Russian interests. Later, the two main parties exchanged accusations of non-compliance. This breakdown in trust culminated in formal withdrawal from the INF Treaty by first the United States and then Russia, and its effective demise *in toto* as an instrument of international law in 2019.

The INF Treaty's Verification Regime

The INF Treaty required the Soviet Union and the United States to eliminate all nuclear and conventional ground-launched ballistic and cruise missiles with ranges of between 500 and 5,500 kilometres, without exception. Article I thus obligated each Party to eliminate its intermediate-range missiles (defined as having a range of more than 1,000 and not more than 5,500 kilometres) and shorter-range missiles (with a range between 500 and 1,000 kilometres), to 'not have such systems thereafter', and to 'carry out the other obligations set forth' in the Treaty.

The Treaty required the weapons to be 'eliminated' (i.e., physically destroyed) – acts that were to be verified by extensive on-site inspections.[98] In this regard, Paragraph 1 of Article IX provided that '[f]or the purpose of ensuring verification of compliance with the provisions of this Treaty, each Party shall have the right to conduct on-site inspections. The Parties shall implement on-site inspections in accordance with this Article, the Protocol on Inspection and the Protocol on Elimination.' The Treaty required or permitted hundreds of on-site inspections at operational missile sites, repair facilities, storage depots, training sites, and former missile production or assembly facilities. Inspection teams carried out five types of inspections: baseline, elimination, portal monitoring, close-out, and short notice.[99]

As its name indicates, the purpose of the first type of inspection was to establish a baseline inventory. The United States was granted the right to send ten-strong inspection teams to 130 Soviet INF missile sites and missile-related facilities in Czechoslovakia and East Germany, as well as in the Soviet Union. The Soviet Union in turn had the right to send its on-site inspection teams to thirty-one US INF sites and facilities in Belgium, Italy, the Netherlands, the United Kingdom, and West Germany, as well as in the United States itself. At the end of the process, so-called close-out inspections at the missile operating bases and support facilities confirmed that all INF-specified equipment, support structures, and treaty-related activity had effectively ceased.

The United States declared it would eliminate a total of 846 INF missiles, as well as the launchers and associated equipment. These were grouped into three major weapons systems: the Pershing II (234 missiles) and Pershing IA (169 missiles), which were owned

[98] Most of the missiles were eliminated by detonation while they were unarmed, with their stages burnt, or else the missiles were cut in half and their wings and tail sections were severed.

[99] J. P. Harahan, 'On-Site Inspections Under The INF Treaty, A History of the On-Site Inspection Agency and Treaty Implementation, 1988–1991', US Government Printing Office, Washington, DC, 1993, at https://bit.ly/3qSOxDS, p. 9.

and operated by the US Army, and the 443 BGM-109 ground-launched cruise missiles belonging to the US Air Force. The Soviet Union declared it would eliminate a total of 1,846 INF missiles. Six types of Soviet ballistic and cruise missiles fell under the INF treaty prohibition, the most famous of which were the SS-20 Pioneers, deployed to East Germany and Czechoslovakia, as well to many sites in the Soviet Union (including in what are today Belarus and Ukraine). Six hundred and fifty-four SS-20 missiles were destroyed under the INF, most by detonation on the ground.

The Soviets designated eight elimination sites; the United States established four. All INF missile system eliminations and elimination inspections were to be completed within three years of the Treaty's entry into force. Two military bases in the east of the USSR, Kansk and Chita, served as elimination sites where SS-20 missiles were launched to destruction. The treaty permitted each party to destroy up to one hundred missiles in this way. Within the first six months following entry into force of the Treaty, the Soviets launched seventy-two SS-20 missiles from the two bases. Every launch was observed by American on-site inspection teams.[100]

Ambassador Steven Steiner, who from 1988 to 2002 served as head of the US delegation to the Special Verification Committee charged with negotiating the particulars of Treaty implementation, witnessed the destruction by detonation of the last two SS-20 missiles. He recalled later a 'very good inspection protocol' and a 'very positive atmosphere'.[101] Duly witnessed, the two (original) States Parties to the Treaty, the United States and the Soviet Union,[102] destroyed a total of 2,692 short- and intermediate-range missiles, with both nations meeting the Treaty-imposed deadline for completion of all disarmament of 1 June 1991.

In addition to witnessing the physical destruction of the missiles, both States were entitled to position on-site inspection teams of up to thirty inspectors at one former INF missile assembly plant or a former INF missile production facility to continuously monitor the entrance portals and perimeter. For a minimum of three years and a maximum of thirteen years (and thirty days) from entry into force, the Soviet Union and the United States were authorised to conduct these on-site 'portal monitoring' inspections.

The history by Joseph Harahan of the work of the United States' On-Site Inspection Agency (OSIA)[103] is perhaps the most authoritative version of the implementation of the INF Treaty and its verification from the US perspective.[104] Harahan recalled that during final treaty negotiations, the Soviets had declared that final assembly would proceed of a ground-launched ballistic missile that was 'outwardly similar' to a stage of an INF Treaty-prohibited

[100] Ibid., p. 103.

[101] Budjeryn and Steiner, 'Forgotten Parties to the INF'.

[102] Subsequently, Belarus, Kazakhstan, Russia, Turkmenistan, Ukraine, and Uzbekistan would succeed to the obligations of the INF Treaty as successor States to the defunct Soviet Union.

[103] In early 1988, President Reagan had directed the US Secretary of Defense to establish OSIA to perform the on-site inspection and escort responsibilities of the United States under the provisions of the Treaty. It was stipulated in the Treaty that all inspection teams had to be met and accompanied throughout the inspection by national escort teams.

[104] In the preface to his 1993 work, which outlined the organisation of the history, he recalled his thoughts turning occasionally to a saying by Dolly Parton: 'If you want to see the rainbow, you gotta put up with a little rain.'

missile but whose range was greater than 5,000 kilometres. For this reason, the United States was given the right to have resident on-site inspectors to monitor around the clock the portal and perimeter of the Votkinsk Machine Building Plant for up to thirteen years. While the inspectors could not physically enter the plant, the purpose of the inspections was to ensure that the Soviet Union did not assemble the illegal SS-20 missile under the guise of an SS-25 missile. A similar right was granted to the Soviets to place a team at the portals of the Hercules Plant No. I in Magna, Utah, where the Pershing II rocket motors had been produced.[105]

Inspection teams were also authorised to conduct annually, on short notice, a limited number of inspections of active missile operating bases or previously active (closed-out) missile sites, support facilities, or other production facilities. The purpose of these short-notice inspections was to determine if any INF missiles, support equipment. or declared items were present. During the first three years of the Treaty, each party had the right to conduct up to twenty short-notice on-site inspections annually. During the next five years, each side was allowed to conduct fifteen such inspections annually while during the final five years of the international verification regime's existence, a maximum of ten such inspections per year was permitted.

For both the United States and the Soviet Union, however, it was the Treaty eliminations that involved the deployment of the largest number of both inspectors and escorts. In the first three years, 129 OSIA on-site inspection teams and 64 OSIA escort teams participated in elimination inspections. Counting all types of inspections, the OSIA teams were involved in more than 600 inspections and escorts in the three years of destruction and elimination between 1988 and 1991.[106] While the authority to conduct on-site inspections formally ended on 31 May 2001, the use of surveillance satellites ('national technical means') was permitted to continue.

Verification of Compliance with the TPNW

Under the TPNW, verification of any future nuclear disarmament, with respect both to destruction of the weapons or other nuclear explosive devices belonging to a State Party and to the 'irreversible elimination of that State Party's nuclear-weapon programme, including the elimination or irreversible conversion of all nuclear-weapons-related facilities',[107] is to be entrusted to the 'competent international authority' that will be designated at some point by the States Parties to the Treaty.[108] A schematic proposal for the multiple tasks of such an authority, devised by Thomas Shea within the context of his thoughtful 2019 work on the creation of an International Disarmament Agency,[109] is included as an Annex to the *Nuclear Weapons Ban Monitor 2020*.[110] As of this writing, it

105 Harahan, 'On-Site Inspections under the INF Treaty: A History of the On-Site Inspection Agency and Treaty Implementation, 1988–1991', p. 10.

106 Ibid., p. 114.

107 Art. 4(2), TPNW.

108 Art. 4(6), TPNW.

109 T. Shea, *Verifying Nuclear Disarmament*, 1st ed., Routledge, United States, 2019.

110 G. Oestern (ed.), *Nuclear Weapons Ban Monitor 2020*, Norwegian People's Aid, Oslo, January 2021, Annex V.

seemed unlikely that such an authority would be so designated at the first Meeting of the States Parties, due to be held in Vienna in March 2022.

Once the requisite destruction of the weapons and elimination (or conversion) of the facilities have been completed, the IAEA will then become responsible for verifying the permanent peaceful nature of any nuclear programme in the State concerned. The Treaty specifies that an agreement must be negotiated with the IAEA and 'sufficient to provide credible assurance of the non-diversion of declared nuclear material from peaceful nuclear activities and of the absence of undeclared nuclear material or activities in the State as a whole'.[111] This means, at a minimum, the powers in both a CSA and an Additional Protocol. The negotiation must begin no later than the date upon which implementation of the elimination plan is completed with the agreement entering into force no later than eighteen months after the date of negotiations commence. That State Party 'shall thereafter, at a minimum, maintain these safeguards obligations, without prejudice to any additional relevant instruments that it may adopt in the future'.[112]

VERIFICATION OF DEPLOYED AND NON-DEPLOYED WEAPONS

As Chapter 5 described, the core of the 2010 New START Treaty[113] was the limit imposed on both Russian and US deployed strategic nuclear forces of an aggregate of 1,550 warheads and 700 'delivery vehicles' (aircraft, launchers, and submarines). New START effectively replaced both the 1991 Strategic Arms Reduction Treaty (START I),[114] which had expired four months earlier on 5 December 2009, along with its monitoring and verification regime, and the 2002 Moscow Treaty,[115] which had no verification measures and which expired upon entry into force of New START (namely, 5 February 2011).

While the START I Treaty had used the inspection regime developed under the INF Treaty to good effect, its overall verification regime was, like the provisions in START I itself, fiendishly complex. In addition to certain continuous monitoring activities, START I had provided for no fewer than twelve different types of inspections, including three forms of 'exhibition'.[116] These inspections covered more than seventy sites in Belarus,

[111] Art. 4(3), TPNW.

[112] Ibid.

[113] The Treaty between the United States of America and the Russian Federation on Measures for the Further Reduction and Limitation of Strategic Offensive Arms; signed at Prague, 8 April 2010; entered into force 5 February 2011.

[114] Treaty between the United States of America and the Union of Socialist Soviet Republics on Further Reduction and Limitation of Strategic Offensive Arms (START I); adopted at Moscow, 31 July 1991; entered into force 5 December 1994; expired 5 December 2009.

[115] Treaty between the United States of America and the Russian Federation on Strategic Offensive Reductions; signed at Moscow, 24 May 2002; entered into force 1 June 2003; expired, 5 February 2011.

[116] Article XI of START I addressed inspections as follows: baseline data inspections (Art. XI, para. 2); data update inspections (para. 3); new facility inspections (para. 4); suspect-site inspections (para. 5); re-entry vehicle inspections (para. 6); post-exercise dispersal inspections of deployed mobile launchers of ICBMs and their associated missiles (para. 7); conversion or elimination inspections (para. 8); close-out inspections (para. 9); formerly declared facility inspections (para. 10); technical characteristics exhibitions (para. 11); distinguishability exhibitions (para. 12); and baseline exhibitions (para. 13). Continuous monitoring activities were covered by Art. XI, para. 14.

Kazakhstan, the Russian Federation, and Ukraine.[117] While the use of exhibitions was maintained in the New START Treaty,[118] inspections were generally simplified and reduced to two main classifications, covering deployed and non-deployed weapons, respectively. Indeed, according to the Union of Concerned Scientists, one of New START's 'primary accomplishments' was its streamlining of the verification measures in the START I Treaty without sacrificing the collection of essential information, while adding 'the most intrusive verification system ever implemented for counting nuclear warheads'.[119]

Paul Nitze, a former US Deputy Secretary of Defense, had once observed that monitoring procedures must be good enough to detect cheating in time to do something about it – that is, before the cheating party gains a strategic advantage.[120] In a letter to the Senate Foreign Relations Committee in September 2010, US Secretary of Defense Robert Gates had concluded that Russia would not be able to achieve 'militarily significant cheating' under the New START Treaty given its verification regime.[121] Every year since then, the US Department of State has certified that Russia is in compliance with New START. Thus, in its January 2020 report on the Treaty (the most recent annual report, as of this writing), the US Department of State declared that 'based on the information available as of December 31, 2019, the United States certifies the Russian Federation to be in compliance with the terms of the New START Treaty.'[122]

Verification under New START

The verification regime under New START, which persists during the extended lifetime of the Treaty until 5 February 2026, comprises an array of means and mechanisms: national technical means (a combination of satellites, ground-based radars, and aircraft through which each party monitors the other's nuclear arsenal), on-site inspections, exhibitions, data exchanges and notifications, unique identifiers (UIDs), telemetric information, and a Bilateral Consultative Commission (BCC). Since New START's entry into force in February 2011, and as of late January 2021, the two parties had conducted a total of 328 on-site inspections; more than 21,400 notifications had been exchanged between them; 18 meetings of the BCC had been held; and 38 biannual data exchanges on strategic offensive arms subject to the Treaty had taken place.[123]

117 M. Donaldson, 'Verification of New START', Fact Sheet, Union of Concerned Scientists, Cambridge, MA, July 2010, at https://bit.ly/3cMWdQB.

118 According to Article XI of New START: 'Each Party shall conduct exhibitions and have the right to participate in exhibitions conducted by the other Party.' For instance, Russia offered to exhibit the new RS-26 'Avangard', which was tested to intercontinental range and would therefore be counted and captured in New START. R. Gottemoeller, 'The New START Verification Regime: How Good Is It?', *Bulletin of the Atomic Scientists*, 21 May 2020, at http://bit.ly/3qho209.

119 Donaldson, 'Verification of New START'.

120 Cited by Rose Gottemoeller: 'The New START Verification Regime: How Good Is It?'

121 R. Burns, 'Gates: Any Russian Arms Cheating Would Backfire', Associated Press, 9 September 2010.

122 US Department of State, Annual Report on Implementation of the New START Treaty, Washington, DC, January 2020, at https://bit.ly/3pJ94Ju, p. 4.

123 US Embassy in Russia, 'New START Treaty', accessed 24 February 2021, at http://bit.ly/3qQE1gj.

Reporting and Missile Identification

New START provides for ongoing data exchange on numbers, locations, and technical characteristics of weapons systems and facilities. Scheduled data exchange, which occurs twice a year, concerns facilities, the number and location of strategic offensive arms, and the aggregate number of warheads. Among the forty-three 'as required' notifications are the movement of strategic offensive arms, missile flight tests, inspections, and new types of strategic offensive arms that are developed.

Each State was obligated under the Treaty to place a unique identifier tag – a UID – on each of its missiles, associated launchers, and bombers. Each party must further specify the number of warheads incorporated in each individual missile, which can then be verified by inspections. This was an especially important issue for the Americans as the last data exchange under START I in July 2009 had reported the United States as deploying more than 5,900 warheads, whereas the Pentagon said that the number was actually under the 2,200 limit that had been imposed by the 2002 Moscow Treaty.[124] As an example, while US SLBMs could carry eight warheads each (the figure registered under START I), the United States had downloaded its SLBM force, so actual warhead deployments on each missile were sometimes only four. As a result, the START I database showed higher numbers of US submarine warheads than were actually on the missiles. At the same time, there was a possible undercounting of Soviet deployment of its nuclear arsenal: Rose Gottemoeller thus noted that, under START I, the Soviet SS-18 missile was determined based on telemetric data (see below) to have ten warheads, although its carrying capacity is much greater, 'by some reckoning 14 or even more'.[125]

Each party to New START is also required to give the other forty-eight hours' notice of a newly produced missile falling within the ambit of the Treaty leaving a factory. This allows national technical means of verification to be brought to bear. Continuous monitoring of Russia's mobile missile production plant at Votkinsk had ended with the expiry of the START I Treaty and Russia rebuffed US efforts to restore it under New START.[126] This was one of the issues of concern raised during the ratification process in the US Senate.

To avoid provoking concern among the other's military forces, each party must provide notification, at least two weeks in advance, of any major strategic exercise involving heavy bombers. It must further notify the other party within two days of the exercise's conclusion.

Telemetric Data

Telemetry is the technical data that a missile sends back about its operation during a flight test. Telemetric data was critical to verification of START I since, as noted above, that Treaty did not provide for direct verification of the number of warheads a missile carried, but rather counted each type of missile as carrying the maximum number of warheads it had carried in tests. This number was determined in part by telemetry. Telemetry was also used to verify that tests were not being used to develop new types of missiles that were banned under the treaty.[127]

124 Donaldson, 'Verification of New START', July 2010.
125 Gottemoeller: 'The New START Verification Regime: How Good Is It?'
126 Donaldson, 'Verification of New START', July 2010.
127 Ibid.

Since New START counts actual warheads and does not impose limits on new missile types, telemetry was not needed for its verification. Nonetheless, its importance was 'hotly debated' during the course of the negotiations.[128] Ultimately, the limited telemetry exchanges required between the parties to New START were considered an additional – and valuable – confidence-building measure between the two States.[129]

Inspections

New START has only two types of inspections in addition to exhibitions, one dealing with deployed weapons and the other concerning non-deployed weapons. 'Type One' inspections verify declared data at ICBM bases, submarine bases, and air bases, as well as the number of warheads on deployed ICBMs and SLBMs and the number of nuclear arms associated with deployed heavy bombers. Type One inspections can be conducted a maximum of ten times each year. Type Two inspections, which can be conducted up to eight times each year, verify data regarding non-deployed strategic offensive arms at other locations.[130]

Owing to cooperative efforts following the break-up of the Soviet Union, many facilities formerly associated with strategic offensive arms under START I had been closed by the time New START was being negotiated. Inspectors under New START were thus only concerned with 35 Russian facilities, a drop of one half compared to START I, which had included sites in three other States of the former USSR that were party to that treaty (Belarus, Kazakhstan, and Ukraine).

One of the challenges for the inspectors was how to confirm the exact number of warheads that the parties declared on an individual missile without effectively being given access to confidential technical information. This was accomplished through on-site inspection of re-entry vehicles but with concealment of the items therein themselves. Thus, as Gottemoeller explains, inspectors were given the opportunity to count objects on the front ends of missiles, which would be opened but then covered 'with a soft or pliable cover so that objects could be counted without revealing their technical characteristics'.[131] The further problem of differentiating nuclear warheads from other non-nuclear objects present on the front end of a missile (e.g., penetration aids, chaff dispensers, or decoys to spoof missile defences) was overcome by the use of radiation detection devices.[132]

THE OPEN SKIES TREATY

The 1992 Treaty on Open Skies[133] establishes general confidence and security-building measures among Member States of the Organization for Security and Co-operation in Europe (OSCE). The Treaty allows States Parties – all but one of which (Canada) were in

[128] Gottemoeller: 'The New START Verification Regime: How Good Is It?'
[129] Donaldson, 'Verification of New START', July 2010; and Gottemoeller: 'The New START Verification Regime: How Good Is It?'
[130] Donaldson, 'Verification of New START', July 2010.
[131] Gottemoeller, 'The New START Verification Regime: How Good Is It?'
[132] Ibid.
[133] Treaty on Open Skies; signed, 24 March 1992; entered into force 1 January 2002.

Europe – to conduct short-notice, unarmed reconnaissance flights over other parties' entire territories to collect data on military forces and activities. The treaty allows participation in overflights by other States than the overflying State. All of a State Party's territory can be overflown and no territory can be declared off-limits by the host nation.

In its last treaty withdrawal, the Trump administration formally withdrew the United States from the 1992 Treaty on 22 November 2020.[134] In January 2021, Russia announced that it would follow suit and withdraw from the Treaty.[135] Whether the Biden administration would rejoin the Treaty[136] and whether this would prompt Russia to reverse its decision was unknown as of this writing. Leonid Slutsky, the head of the foreign affairs committee in the lower house of the Russian parliament, had said in January 2021 that Russia could review its decision to withdraw if the United States decided to return to the Treaty, but acknowledged that the prospect looked 'utopian'.[137]

CONCLUDING REMARKS

Writing in February 2021, two US security experts declared that New START might be the last nuclear arms control agreement between the Russian Federation and the United States, arguing that there was 'virtually no chance' that another negotiated treaty 'will be waiting to succeed' New START when it expires in February 2026.[138] They arrived at this stance on the basis of the pursuit by both nations of high-precision long-range conventional weapons and cyber and artificial intelligence (AI) capabilities: 'the kind of weapons whose stealthy and destructive potential matters far more than quantity'. New technologies, they observe, are 'blurring the lines between conventional and nuclear weapons', with certain cyber and AI capabilities being 'extremely difficult, if not impossible, to verify'. If the arms control relationship between Russia and the United States is to 'continue and remain meaningful', they conclude, 'both sides will need to come up with new approaches beyond negotiated treaties and intrusive verification regimes'.[139]

134 K. Reif and S. Bugos, 'U.S. Completes Open Skies Treaty Withdrawal', Arms Control Today, December 2020, at http://bit.ly/3bDKfd7.

135 V. Isachenkov, 'Russia Follows US in Withdrawal from Open Skies Treaty', Associated Press, 15 January 2021, at https://bit.ly/2ZKIJAb.

136 US scholars dispute whether President Biden can rejoin the Treaty without the need for renewed Senate consent by supermajority (67 affirmative votes). The better view is that he can. Thus, Jean Galbraith wrote in early February 2021, 'President Biden has the authority to rejoin the United States to the treaty in reliance on the Senate's original resolution of advice and consent. Neither Congress nor the Senate has overridden this resolution. What President Trump has unmade unilaterally, President Biden should similarly have the power to remake.' J. Galbraith, 'The President's Authority to Rejoin the Open Skies Treaty', blog entry, Lawfare, 8 February 2021, at http://bit.ly/3khNXg8. For a contrary advice on the Lawfare website, to which Professor Galbraith was responding, see S. Rademaker, 'Are There Shortcuts for the U.S. to Rejoin the Open Skies Treaty?', blog entry, Lawfare, 15 January 2021, at http://bit.ly/3uvEEya. See also S. Pifer, 'Saving the Open Skies Treaty', The Brookings Institution, 27 January 2021, at http://brook.gs/3pLa7c1.

137 Ibid. See also TASS, 'US Unlikely to Be Back in Open Skies Treaty under Biden Administration – Russian Diplomat', 15 January 2021, at http://bit.ly/37Ij1k2.

138 E. Rumer and R. Sokolsky, 'Why the New START Extension Could Be the End of Arms Control as We Know It', Opinion Editorial, Politico, 7 February 2021, at http://politi.co/37GbthQ.

139 Ibid.

While their conclusion may be true with respect to agreements with respect to other weapons and technologies, it is slightly beside the point. Not only does it not preclude the negotiation of an agreement to secure further reductions in nuclear weapons and to verify that agreement; it even reinforces it. The duty to pursue negotiations in good faith on effective measures relating to nuclear disarmament remains as relevant – and as important – as ever.

8

Use and Testing of Nuclear Weapons under International Law

General international law does not prohibit all and any use of nuclear weapons. This affirmation is made notwithstanding the fact that as set out in the preamble to the 2017 Treaty on the Prohibition of Nuclear Weapons every State Party to the TPNW – totalling fifty-four as of this writing – considers that 'any use of nuclear weapons would be contrary to the rules of international law applicable in armed conflict, in particular the principles and rules of international humanitarian law'.[1]

It is true that, as this chapter describes, the use of nuclear weapons is heavily circumscribed by a number of branches of international law. But the conclusion of the International Court of Justice in 1996 that customary international law does not comprehensively and universally prohibit the use of nuclear weapons 'as such'[2] remains valid today. There remain conceivable circumstances in a situation of international armed conflict, however remote they may be, in which a particular use of nuclear weapons would not be violative of extant international law.

In contrast, general international law dictates that explosive nuclear testing is no longer permissible under any circumstances. The rule constrains a test detonation underground within even one of the five nuclear-weapon States designated as such by the Treaty on the Non-proliferation of Nuclear Weapons (NPT).[3] Under Article I of the Comprehensive Nuclear-Test-Ban Treaty (CTBT), each State Party 'undertakes not to carry out any nuclear weapon test explosion or any other nuclear explosion'.[4] This fundamental rule, which encapsulates the object and purpose of the CTBT, applies to any such detonation carried out underwater, underground, in the atmosphere, or in outer space.

The treaty prohibition on explosive nuclear testing has crystallised as a customary norm of arms control law. This is on the basis that it has become a 'general practice accepted as law', as Chapter 4 argues. It is so, even though the CTBT itself has not entered into force as

1 Treaty on the Prohibition of Nuclear Weapons; adopted at New York, 7 July 2017; entered into force 22 January 2021, tenth preambular para.

2 International Court of Justice, *Legality of the Threat or Use of Nuclear Weapons*, Advisory Opinion, 8 July 1996 (hereinafter, ICJ Advisory Opinion on Nuclear Weapons), para. 105(2), dispositif B, passed by eleven votes to three.

3 Art. IX(3), Treaty on the Non-proliferation of Nuclear Weapons; opened for signature at London, Moscow, and Washington, DC, 1 July 1968; entered into force 5 March 1970.

4 Art. I(1), Comprehensive Nuclear-Test-Ban Treaty; adopted at New York, 10 September 1996; not yet in force.

a legally binding instrument of international law. While the customary prohibition does not encompass and outlaw subcritical nuclear testing, no State may lawfully detonate a nuclear explosive device, however small its explosive yield, either to verify it functions as intended or for a 'peaceful purpose'.

INTERNATIONAL LAW GOVERNING THE USE OF NUCLEAR WEAPONS

The branches of international law that govern the use of nuclear weapons, specifically or generally, are, predominantly, *jus ad bellum* and *jus in bello*. While the use of a nuclear weapon outside a situation of armed conflict is, in theory, possible, this would be unequivocally unlawful, amounting in all likelihood to a crime against humanity and possibly, depending on the situation, even an act of genocide. This is implicit in the World Court's holding that it could not conclude 'definitively whether the threat or use of nuclear weapons would be lawful or unlawful in an extreme circumstance of self-defence, in which the very survival of a State would be at stake'.[5]

Jus ad bellum

This 'extreme circumstance of self-defence' referred to by the International Court of Justice is a manifestation of the law on inter-State use of force. Contemporary *jus ad bellum* is found primarily in the 1945 Charter of the United Nations[6] and in customary international law. A general prohibition on inter-State use of force is set forth in the Charter whereunder all UN member States 'shall refrain in their international relations from the threat or use of force against the territorial integrity or political independence of any State, or in any other manner inconsistent with the Purposes of the United Nations'.[7] An identical customary rule applies to every State, whether or not it is a member of the United Nations. While the rule does not address the use of force on a State's own sovereign territory to suppress a domestic armed insurrection or rebellion, it otherwise restricts when one State may lawfully use force against or on the territory of another.

An act of aggression is a serious violation of the prohibition on inter-State use of force – 'the most serious and dangerous form of the illegal use of force' in the words of the UN General Assembly – and one that is, it observed, 'fraught, in the conditions created by the existence of all types of weapons of mass destruction, with the possible threat of a world conflict'.[8] The prohibition of aggression in international law is a peremptory norm (*jus cogens*).[9] In 1974, in its Resolution 3314 (XXIX), the Assembly confirmed, lest there be

5 ICJ Advisory Opinion on Nuclear Weapons, para. 105(2), dispositif E, passed by seven votes to seven, by the President's casting vote.

6 Charter of the United Nations; signed at San Francisco, 26 June 1945; entered into force 24 October 1945 (hereinafter, UN Charter).

7 Art. 2(4), UN Charter.

8 UN General Assembly Resolution 3314 (XXIX); adopted without a vote on 14 December 1974, Annex: 'Definition of Aggression' (hereinafter, UN Definition of Aggression), fifth preambular para.

9 International Law Commission, *Report of the International Law Commission*, Seventy-first session, UN doc. A/74/10, 2019, Chap. V, Annex, para. (a).

doubt, that aggression included bombardment by the armed forces of a State against the territory of another State or the use of any weapons by a State against the territory of another State.[10] The use of any nuclear weapon in an act of aggression would further aggravate the commission of the 'supreme' international crime.[11]

Two main exceptions pertain to the general prohibition on the inter-State use of force: an authorisation to use force on the territory of any State that is granted by the UN Security Council under Chapter VII of the UN Charter and whose parameters are duly observed, and use of force in individual or collective self-defence. That the Security Council might authorise the use of nuclear weapons is fanciful. That a State might choose to use nuclear weapons in self-defence is markedly less so.

The 'inherent' right of self-defence – meaning that the right of any State to defend itself is of a customary nature – is codified in Article 51 of the UN Charter. It is also a rule of general international law that this right may be exercised by any State if an armed attack occurs against it. For this purpose, an armed attack is deemed to be underway not only when its impact is felt but also when missiles are launched by or from one State against another. In such circumstances, if it is certain that missiles are going to hit the territory or forces of a State, that State is entitled to intercept and destroy them in flight as well as to prevent further launches by force.[12] The notion of 'interceptive' self-defence advocated by Yoram Dinstein[13] is in keeping with the letter and spirit of both Article 51 of the Charter and customary law. But there is no room for mistake. A computer failure which wrongly identifies that an attack is incoming will lead to aggression by the mistakenly 'intercepting' State.

While *jus ad bellum* is not, as a general rule, weapon specific, in its 1996 Advisory Opinion, the International Court of Justice agreed unanimously that a use of force by means of nuclear weapons that is contrary to Article 2(4) of the UN Charter and which fails to meet all the requirements of Article 51 is unlawful. In contentious jurisprudence before it, as well as in the Advisory Opinion itself, the Court has determined that customary law demands that any use of force in self-defence be both necessary in the circumstances and proportionate. These twin requirements of necessity and proportionality were first detailed in 1986 in the Court's judgment on the merits in the *Nicaragua* case and have been reiterated consistently thereafter.[14] Seemingly, an additional requirement – that the target

[10] UN Definition of Aggression, Art. 3(b).

[11] Judgment of the Nuremberg Tribunal in *Trial of the Major War Criminals Before the International Military Tribunal*, Vol. I, Nuremberg, 1947, available at https://bit.ly/3knUMgf, p. 186: 'To initiate a war of aggression, therefore, is not only an international crime; it is the supreme international crime differing only from other war crimes in that it contains within itself the accumulated evil of the whole.'

[12] S. Casey-Maslen, *Jus ad Bellum: The Law on Inter-State Use of Force*, Hart Publishing, Oxford, 2020, p. 67.

[13] Y. Dinstein, *War, Aggression and Self-defence*, 6th ed., Cambridge University Press, Cambridge, 2017, paras. 598, 606–10.

[14] International Court of Justice, *Case Concerning Military and Paramilitary Activities in and against Nicaragua (Nicaragua v. United States of America)*, Judgment (Merits), 27 June 1986 (hereinafter, ICJ *Nicaragua* judgment), para. 194. See further ICJ Advisory Opinion on Nuclear Weapons, para. 41; and International Court of Justice, *Case Concerning Oil Platforms (Islamic Republic of Iran v. United States of America)* Judgment, 6 November 2003 (hereinafter, ICJ *Oil Platforms* judgment), para. 73.

of the use of force in self-defence be a lawful military objective – was set forth in its 2003 judgment in the *Oil Platforms* case.[15] This specific criterion is a contentious holding.

Necessity *ad bellum*

According to the principle of necessity, it must be objectively and strictly necessary, 'leaving no room for any "measure of discretion"' in the words of the International Court of Justice, that force be used to respond to an armed attack.[16] This means that no reasonable avenue for peaceful resolution of the dispute exists in the prevailing circumstances[17] and that the victim State is both certain and correct as to the identity of the attacker. No margin for error is imparted to a decision to use force.[18] In most conceivable cases involving an armed attack through the use of nuclear weapons, this threshold would not impose a legal obstacle to an immediate forcible response. But the perpetrator of a detonation of a single nuclear explosive device on the territory of a State might be either unknown or his identity uncertain. After all, in the aftermath of the Madrid train bombings of 11 March 2004, the UN Security Council adopted Resolution 1530 by unanimous vote in which it condemned the separatist group ETA (Euskadi Ta Askatasuna: 'Basque Homeland and Liberty') for its deadly actions.[19] In fact, the bombings (using conventional explosives) had been carried out not by ETA, as the resolution had expressly determined, but by al-Qaeda operatives.[20]

Proportionality *ad bellum*

When the use of force is necessary in self-defence and therefore legitimate, such force as is reasonably necessary to halt and repel the attack will not be disproportionate.[21] Proportionality understood thus is linked to the aim of the use of force, assessed objectively, rather than purely in relation to the scale of the armed attack. Accordingly, as the Independent International Fact-Finding Mission on the Conflict in Georgia stated in 2009: an operation needed to halt and repel the attack 'may well have to assume dimensions much greater than the attack suffered, and may still be proportionate to the objective of countering the attack'.[22] Neither regime change nor the annihilation of the enemy's forces, however, (much less its civilian population), is a lawful aim.

An obvious interpretation of the International Court of Justice's holding that the use of nuclear weapons might be allowable in an 'extreme circumstance of self-defence' in which a State's very survival would be at stake is that short of that circumstance no such use would

[15] ICJ *Oil Platforms* judgment, para. 51.

[16] Ibid., para. 73.

[17] T. Ruys, *'Armed Attack' and Article 51 of the UN Charter: Evolutions in Customary Law and Practice*, Cambridge University Press, Cambridge, 2010, p. 98.

[18] Casey-Maslen, *Jus ad Bellum: The Law on Inter-State Use of Force*, pp. 71–72.

[19] UN Security Council Resolution 1530, adopted by unanimous vote on 11 March 2004, para. 1.

[20] T. O'Donnell, 'Security Council Resolution 1530, Evidence and the United Nations Security Council', *Proceedings of the Annual Meeting* (American Society of International Law), 29 March–1 April 2006, Vol. 100 (2006), 47–51, at https://bit.ly/3qUSlnQ.

[21] C. Gray, *International Law and the Use of Force*, 4th ed., Oxford University Press, Oxford, 2018, p. 159.

[22] Independent International Fact-Finding Mission on the Conflict in Georgia, Report, Vol. II, September 2009, p. 249.

be permissible. While the Court seemingly had in mind a massive exchange of nuclear weapons between the two superpowers, other scenarios may be envisaged. In 2019, nuclear-armed States India and Pakistan engaged in a short-lived armed conflict in which the use of nuclear weapons was mooted on both sides. Had one of the parties targeted a city on the other's territory with a single nuclear weapon, the severity of the practical consequences that would have followed are in no doubt.[23] But how would such a reaction be adjudged under international law? Would a forcible response by means of nuclear attack automatically or potentially be ruled out?

Furthermore, even if the use of nuclear weapons were potentially lawful, would an attack on a city in the ostensible exercise of self-defence be illegal? Or would their use be limited to 'a legitimate military target open to attack in the exercise of self-defence' in accordance with the International Court's dictum in its judgment in the *Oil Platforms* case?[24] If the aim is to repel the attack, in all likelihood this would be better achieved by targeting the enemy's armed forces and in particular any nuclear-tipped missiles or nuclear bombs. The existence of a submarine equipped with ballistic missiles would be an obvious target, which might require the use of nuclear weapons to be effective. It is, however, very hard to see what lawful purpose could be achieved from a further occasioning of mass killing by hitting a populated area. Certainly, the targeting of cities during the Second World War did not prevent similar reciprocal actions, while, arguably, the atomic weapons dropped on Hiroshima and Nagasaki did not bring the war to an end, as is often claimed.[25]

In its 1996 Advisory Opinion, the International Court of Justice had stated that a 'use of force that is proportionate under the law of self-defence, must, in order to be lawful, also meet the requirements of the law applicable in armed conflict which comprise in particular the principles and rules of humanitarian law'.[26] Thus described, compliance with international humanitarian law in targeting was not seen as a distinct requirement but was more logically subsumed within the principle of proportionality.

International Humanitarian Law

The mainstay of *jus in bello* is the law of armed conflict, more popularly referred to as international humanitarian law (IHL).[27] In its 1996 Advisory Opinion, the International Court of Justice noted that the nuclear-weapon States appearing before it 'either accepted,

[23] In April 2019, Indian Prime Minister Narendra Modi said publicly: 'We have the mother of nuclear bombs. I decided to tell [Pakistan], do whatever you want to do but we will retaliate.' C. McGrath, 'Modi Warns Pakistan against "Threats"', *Express*, 18 April 2019, at http://bit.ly/2ZrqCl2.

[24] ICJ *Oil Platforms* judgment, para. 51. Possibly, the dictum in this contentious case could be distinguished on the basis that the *Oil Platforms* case concerned alleged attacks on US military assets by Iran not on US civilians or civilian objects. But this does not apply to the corresponding claim in the earlier Advisory Opinion cited below.

[25] On this issue, see W. Wilson, 'Did Nuclear Weapons Cause Japan to Surrender?', Carnegie Council for Ethics in International Affairs, 2021, at http://bit.ly/3uumywg.

[26] ICJ Advisory Opinion on Nuclear Weapons, para. 22.

[27] S. Casey-Maslen and S. Weill, 'The Use of Weapons in Armed Conflict', chapter 8 in S. Casey-Maslen (ed.), *Weapons under International Human Rights Law*, Cambridge University Press, Cambridge, 2014, p. 240.

or did not dispute, that their independence to act was indeed restricted by the principles and rules of international law, more particularly humanitarian law', as indeed did the other States which took part in the proceedings.[28] The Court held, unanimously, that any use of nuclear weapons should be 'compatible with the requirements of the international law applicable in armed conflict, particularly those of the principles and rules of international humanitarian law'.[29] While the Court's choice of wording – 'compatible' – is unfortunate (and is by no means the only instance of such loose language in the Advisory Opinion), the underlying principle is that nuclear weapons, should their use comply with *jus ad bellum* rules, must also fully comply with the rules of *jus in bello*.

The legality of the use of nuclear weapons *in bello* falls to be considered by the IHL rules governing the conduct of hostilities. These rules govern decisions by parties to an armed conflict on targeting as well as the legality of the means and methods of warfare they employ against those targets. In its 1996 Advisory Opinion, the Court concluded, though only on the basis of the President's casting vote, that the use of nuclear weapons 'would generally be contrary to the rules of international law applicable in armed conflict, and in particular the principles and rules of humanitarian law'.[30] This holding, however narrowly it was passed at the time within the Court, remains legally robust today.

The Principle of Distinction

With respect to targeting, the basic IHL rule of distinction (also termed a principle, to reflect its fundamental nature) dictates that parties to an armed conflict must at all times distinguish between civilians and combatants. 'Attacks may only be directed against combatants. Attacks must not be directed against civilians.'[31] This is a customary rule applicable in all armed conflicts.[32] It is also a peremptory norm of international law (*jus cogens*).[33]

In addition to direct attacks on civilians, the principle of distinction also prohibits 'indiscriminate attacks'.[34] An indiscriminate attack is of a nature 'to strike military objectives and civilians or civilian objects without distinction'. This is because the attack is not directed at a specific military objective or on the basis that it uses a means or method of warfare that either cannot be directed at a specific military objective or whose effects cannot be limited as

[28] ICJ Advisory Opinion on Nuclear Weapons, para. 42.

[29] Ibid., para. 105(2), dispositif D.

[30] Ibid., para. 105(2), dispositif E.

[31] International Committee of the Red Cross (ICRC), Customary IHL Rule 1: 'The Principle of Distinction between Civilians and Combatants', at http://bit.ly/32rIERo.

[32] In its 1996 Advisory Opinion, the Court explicitly did not address the use of nuclear weapons by a State in a non-international armed conflict 'within its own boundaries'. In its Opinion, the Court contented itself to observe that this particular aspect was not dealt with by any of the States which addressed the Court orally or in writing in the proceedings at hand, finding that it was 'not called upon to deal with an internal use of nuclear Weapons'. ICJ Advisory Opinion on Nuclear Weapons, para. 50.

[33] See, e.g., International Law Commission, *Report of the International Law Commission*, Seventy-first session, UN doc. A/74/10, 2019, Chap. V, Annex, para. (d). See also ICJ Advisory Opinion on Nuclear Weapons, para. 79, in which the International Court of Justice describes the rule of distinction as an 'intransgressible' principle of customary international law.

[34] ICRC, Customary IHL Rule 11: 'Indiscriminate Attacks', at http://bit.ly/2kmcrdT.

required by IHL.[35] It is further prohibited to conduct an attack by bombardment 'by any method or means which treats as a single military objective a number of clearly separated and distinct military objectives located in a city, town, village or other area containing a similar concentration of civilians or civilian objects'.[36] As Yoram Dinstein explains, in contrast to a direct attack on a civilian or civilian object, in an indiscriminate attack any civilian harm is 'merely' a matter 'of no concern' to the attacking party.[37]

The 'cardinal' principle of distinction in IHL means that States must never use weapons that are incapable of distinguishing between civilians and military targets – such weapons are 'inherently' indiscriminate.[38] This notion pertains both to the accuracy of the weapon in its targeting and to the breadth of its effects once used. With respect to the latter, a biological weapon is generally accepted to be a means of warfare whose effects cannot be limited as required by IHL. Indeed, already in the US Air Force's 1976 manual on international law, biological weapons were cited as a 'universally agreed illustration of . . . an indiscriminate weapon'. The document observed that the uncontrollable effects from such weapons 'may include injury to the civilian population of other states as well as injury to an enemy's civilian population'.[39] These uncontrolled effects exist not only spatially but also over time.

The same applies to poison; as the ICRC has observed, 'poison is unlawful in itself, as would be any weapon which would, by its very nature, be so imprecise that it would inevitably cause indiscriminate damage'.[40] The huge emission of poisonous radiation by the detonation of a high-yield nuclear weapon, and especially a 'salted' bomb in which the device is surrounded by cobalt-60 or gold-198 to enhance radioactive dissemination, would likely also violate this prohibition.[41] The United States ordinarily rejects the notion that radioactivity and subsequent fallout render nuclear weapons unlawful as they are not its primary intended effects (which are rather the power of the blast and intense heat). On the specific issue of poison, in its written statement to the Court in 1995 in the context of the Advisory Opinion, the United States declared:

> This prohibition was established with particular reference to projectiles that carry poison into the body of the victim. It was not intended to apply, and has not been applied, to weapons that are designed to injure or cause destruction by other means, even though they also may create toxic byproducts. For example, the prohibition on poison weapons does not prohibit conventional explosives or incendiaries, even though they may produce dangerous fumes. By the same token, it does not prohibit nuclear weapons, which are

35 ICRC, Customary IHL Rule 12: 'Definition of Indiscriminate Attacks', at http://bit.ly/2lJ2V4y.

36 ICRC, Customary IHL Rule 13: 'Area Bombardment', at http://bit.ly/3aSlHxL.

37 Y. Dinstein, *The Conduct of Hostilities under the Law of International Armed Conflict*, 3rd ed., Cambridge University Press, Cambridge, 2016, para. 393.

38 ICJ Advisory Opinion on Nuclear Weapons, para. 78.

39 See US Department of the Air Force, *International Law – The Conduct of Armed Conflict and Air Operations*, Air Force Pamphlet 110–31, 1976, §6–3(c).

40 Commentary on Article 35 of the 1977 Additional Protocol I, in Y. Sandoz, C. Swinarski, and B. Zimmermann (eds.), *Commentary to the Additional Protocols of 8 June 1977 to the Geneva Conventions of 12 August 1949*, ICRC/Martinus Nijhoff, Geneva, 1987, para. 1402.

41 S. Casey-Maslen with S. Haines, *Hague Law Interpreted: The Conduct of Hostilities under the Law of Armed Conflict*, Hart Publishing, Oxford, 2018, p. 155.

designed to injure or cause destruction by means other than poisoning the victim, even though nuclear explosions may also create toxic radioactive byproducts.[42]

In its Advisory Opinion, the Court did not find that any particular nuclear weapon, much less every nuclear weapon, was inherently indiscriminate. Among earlier variants of nuclear weapons, however, the Polaris submarine-launched ballistic missile (SLBM) stands out as a possible candidate. Polaris, the first variant of which was operationally deployed by the US Navy in 1960, appears to be the epitome of an inherently indiscriminate weapon. This is so, at least according to modern understandings of the term, on the basis that the missile could not be targeted reliably to within 1 kilometre of its target and had a warhead yield of 0.2 MT.[43] Indeed, Polaris missiles were considered too inaccurate by the United Kingdom and the United States to be aimed at Soviet missile sites and were reserved for retaliatory strikes against Soviet cities in the event of a first nuclear strike being launched against American or British assets.

More recently, the legal basis for a massive retaliatory nuclear strike appears to rest on the basis of a belligerent reprisal. While, as discussed below, belligerent reprisals against the civilian population are explicitly outlawed under the 1977 Additional Protocol I,[44] two of the nuclear-armed powers that are party to the Protocol (France and the United Kingdom) have expressly entered a reservation as to the provision while more broadly a number of nuclear-armed powers, particularly the United States, negotiated the Protocol on the basis that it would not apply *in toto* to nuclear weapons. Referring to this debate, the International Court of Justice stated that it had no need to elaborate on the question of the applicability of the Additional Protocol to nuclear weapons on the basis that the Protocol 'in no way replaced the general customary rules applicable to all means and methods of combat including nuclear weapons' and that the relevant rules in the Protocol, 'when adopted, were merely the expression of the pre-existing customary law'.[45] While this is true with respect to the principle of distinction and the prohibition of weapons of a nature to cause superfluous injury, the same cannot be said to be the case with respect to the principle of proportionality (discussed below), whose definition was, at the time, a progressive development of international law rather than a codification of existing custom.[46]

[42] Written Statement of the Government of the United States of America, 20 June 1995, ICJ, Request by the United Nations General Assembly for an Advisory Opinion on the Legality of the Threat or Use of Nuclear Weapons, p. 24.

[43] Casey-Maslen with Haines, *Hague Law Interpreted: The Conduct of Hostilities under the Law of Armed Conflict*, pp. 113–14.

[44] Art. 51(6), Protocol Additional to the Geneva Conventions of 12 August 1949, and relating to the Protection of Victims of International Armed Conflicts; adopted at Geneva, 8 June 1977; entered into force 7 December 1978 (hereinafter, 1977 Additional Protocol I).

[45] ICJ Advisory Opinion on Nuclear Weapons, para. 78.

[46] Indeed, at the Diplomatic Conference that negotiated the Additional Protocols, France had voted against the adoption of the provisions pertaining to proportionality in Article 51 because it deemed that by their 'very complexity' they would 'seriously hamper the conduct of defensive military operations against an invader and prejudice the inherent right of legitimate defence'. France, Statement at the Diplomatic Conference of Humanitarian Law, Official Records, Vol. VI, CDDH/SR.41, 26 May 1977, p. 163, para. 118.

A further, long-standing rule of IHL concerning attacks on populated areas stipulates that the 'attack or bombardment of towns, villages, habitations or buildings which are not defended, is prohibited'. This was at issue in the *Shimoda* case before the Tokyo District Court in 1963. The case concerned the legality of the use of nuclear weapons against the Japanese cities of Hiroshima and Nagasaki in 1945 (and the decision by the Japanese government to drop all claims against the United States for that use). The multiple plaintiffs – residents of the two cities at the time of the bombing – argued that the dropping of the two bombs had breached international law prevailing at the time. The District Court held that while nuclear weapons were not expressly prohibited by international law, their use against an undefended city breached customary rules of warfare applicable in 1945.[47] The court further declared that the principle of distinction between military objectives and civilians had not been nullified by the adoption by the belligerents of the doctrine of 'total war'.[48]

Belligerent Reprisals

Belligerent reprisals are acts that would ordinarily be violations of IHL but which, exceptionally, are lawful in so far as they respond to and seek to bring an end to serious violations by the opposing party to an armed conflict. The US Department of Defense describes reprisals in the latest (December 2016) version of its *Law of War Manual* as 'extreme measures of coercion used to help enforce the law of war by seeking to persuade an adversary to cease violations'.[49]

For those reprisals that are not explicitly outlawed, either by treaty or as a matter of custom, they are subject to six conditions, all of which must be fulfilled:[50]

1. An act of reprisal by one party must be in response to a prior unlawful act by an adverse party.
2. The act of reprisal must be in response to serious violations of the law of armed conflict.
3. Recourse to a reprisal must be necessary in the circumstances.
4. The primary intent of the reprisal must be to end the adverse party's serious violations of the law of armed conflict.
5. The act of reprisal must be proportionate to those serious violations.
6. Reprisals must not be committed against prohibited targets.

Reprisals against civilians are, in the words of the International Criminal Tribunal for the former Yugoslavia (ICTY) in the *Kupreškić* case, 'inherently a barbarous means of seeking compliance with international law'.[51] But it is not certain that they are unlawful as a matter

47 Tokyo District Court, *Shimoda et al.* v. *The State*, Decision, 7 December 1963, decision translated in *The Japanese Annual of International Law*, Vol. 8 (1964), 231.

48 ICRC, 'Shimoda case (Compensation claim against Japan brought by the residents of Hiroshima and Nagasaki), Tokyo District Court, 7 December 1963', National Implementation of IHL database, at http://bit.ly/3bDyq6z.

49 US Department of Defense, *Law of War Manual*, Updated December 2016, Washington, DC, 2016, §18.18.

50 See Casey-Maslen with Haines, *Hague Law Interpreted: The Conduct of Hostilities under the Law of Armed Conflict*, pp. 337–42.

51 ICTY, *Prosecutor* v. *Zoran Kupreškić and others*, Judgment (Trial Chamber) (Case No. IT-95–16-T), 14 January 2000, para. 528.

of general international law. This is specifically the case with respect to the use of nuclear weapons against civilians and civilian objects in enemy territory during the conduct of hostilities.

Article 51(6) of the 1977 Additional Protocol I simply stipulates that '[a]ttacks against the civilian population or civilians by way of reprisals are prohibited'. In its 1987 commentary on this provision, the ICRC asserted that this prohibition 'is not subject to any conditions and it therefore has a peremptory character; in particular it leaves out the possibility of derogating from this rule by invoking military necessity'.[52] But the ICRC overstates the case for the 'peremptory character' of the prohibition on reprisals. The provision was much debated during the negotiations and remains opposed by a small number of States. The United States, for instance, has expressed the view that the provisions in the 1977 Additional Protocol I on reprisals are 'counterproductive', and that 'they remove a significant deterrent that protects civilians and war victims on all sides of a conflict'.[53] In 1998, the UK attached the following 'understanding' to its ratification of the Protocol, which clarifies its position with regard to reprisals more generally:

> If an adverse party makes serious and deliberate attacks, in violation of Article 51 or Article 52 against the civilian population or civilians or against civilian objects, ... the United Kingdom will regard itself as entitled to take measures otherwise prohibited by the Articles in question to the extent that it considers such measures necessary for the sole purpose of compelling the adverse party to cease committing violations under those Articles, but only after formal warning to the adverse party requiring cessation of the violations has been disregarded and then only after a decision taken at the highest level of government. Any measures thus taken by the United Kingdom will not be disproportionate to the violations giving rise thereto and will not involve any action prohibited by the Geneva Conventions of 1949 nor will such measures be continued after the violations have ceased.[54]

In addition, Egypt, Germany, and Italy have reserved the right to react to serious violations of the Protocol with any means permitted by international law to prevent further violations.

In 2005, the ICRC Study of Customary IHL concluded with respect to the legality of reprisals:

> Because of existing contrary practice, albeit limited, it is difficult to conclude that there has yet crystallized a customary rule specifically prohibiting reprisals against civilians during the conduct of hostilities. Nevertheless, it is also difficult to assert that a right to resort to such reprisals continues to exist based on the practice of only a limited number of States, some of which is also ambiguous. Hence, there appears, at a minimum, to exist a trend in favour of prohibiting such reprisals.

52 Sandoz, Swinarski, and Zimmermann (eds.), *Commentary to the Additional Protocols of 8 June 1977 to the Geneva Conventions of 12 August 1949*, para. 1984.

53 'The Position of the United States on Current Law of War Agreements: Remarks of Judge Abraham D Sofaer, Legal Adviser, US Department of State, 22 January 1987', *American University Journal of International Law and Policy*, Vol. 2 (1987), 460, at p. 469.

54 Declaration of the United Kingdom of 28 January 1998, point (m), at http://bit.ly/2PCocrS.

In fact, as Louise Doswald-Beck, formerly the Head of the ICRC's Legal Division, has suggested, in the case of belligerent reprisals against civilian populations in the opposing party's own territory, there may simply be no customary rule at all.[55] Thus, as the International Court of Justice implied, it might not be unlawful under IHL to use nuclear weapons in 'an extreme circumstance of self-defence'. Despite the Court's apparent claims to the contrary,[56] this could be as a belligerent reprisal against a prior unlawful use of nuclear weapons *in bello*. Such use, where it was purely or primarily retaliatory in nature, however, would amount to a serious violation of IHL and a war crime.

The Principle of Proportionality

The second fundamental principle of IHL governing the conduct of hostilities is the principle of proportionality in attack. While in the 1977 Additional Protocol I to the Geneva Conventions, proportionality is articulated as a form of indiscriminate attack,[57] it is better – and generally – understood as an autonomous principle. This is the case under general international law. Thus the ICRC determined that a distinct customary rule provides: 'Launching an attack which may be expected to cause incidental loss of civilian life, injury to civilians, damage to civilian objects, or a combination thereof, which would be excessive in relation to the concrete and direct military advantage anticipated, is prohibited.'[58] In its 1996 Advisory Opinion, the International Court of Justice did not address the principle of proportionality *in bello*, other than to make a passing reference in relation to the protection of the environment during armed conflict and in the context of belligerent reprisals (which it declined to consider).[59] This is surprising to say the least, given that the rule of proportionality in attack would, in most cases, dictate that the use of a nuclear weapon would be unlawful. Modern nuclear weapons can, as a general rule, be targeted at a military objective with the level of accuracy demanded by IHL. But, were they to be used other than, for instance, in a remote desert area against a conveniently massed grouping of combatants or against a warship or submarine on the high seas, the catastrophic humanitarian effects they would wreak on civilians and civilian objects would far outweigh any notion of concrete and direct military advantage that might be anticipated.

The Superfluous Injury Principle

One of the longest existing principles of the law of war/IHL was first expounded in the preamble to the 1868 St Petersburg Declaration.[60] The Declaration, a treaty that prohibited the use in warfare of exploding bullets, stated that the 'only legitimate object which

55 Remarks to experts meeting, Oslo, 17 June 2013; author's notes.
56 ICJ Advisory Opinion on Nuclear Weapons, para. 46.
57 'Among others, the following types of attacks are to be considered as indiscriminate: . . . an attack which may be expected to cause incidental loss of civilian life, injury to civilians, damage to civilian objects, or a combination thereof, which would be excessive in relation to the concrete and direct military advantage anticipated.' Art. 51(5)(b), 1977 Additional Protocol I.
58 ICRC, Customary IHL Rule 14: 'Proportionality in Attack', at http://bit.ly/2k9mrHh.
59 ICJ Advisory Opinion on Nuclear Weapons, paras. 30 and 46, respectively.
60 Declaration Renouncing the Use, in Time of War, of Explosive Projectiles Under 400 Grammes Weight; adopted and signed at St Petersburg, 11 December 1868; entered into force the same day.

States should endeavour to accomplish during war is to weaken the military forces of the enemy' and that this object 'would be exceeded by the employment of arms which uselessly aggravate the sufferings of disabled men, or render their death inevitable'.[61] In 1899, the Regulations annexed to the Hague Convention II on Land Warfare stipulated that it was 'especially prohibited' to 'employ arms, projectiles, or material of a nature to cause superfluous injury'.[62] This has become a customary rule applicable in all armed conflict in the following terms: 'The use of means and methods of warfare which are of a nature to cause superfluous injury or unnecessary suffering is prohibited.'[63]

In its 1996 Advisory Opinion, the International Court of Justice deemed the prohibition on using weapons that cause unnecessary suffering to combatants to be an 'intransgressible' principle of customary international law.[64] It is thus a peremptory norm of international law (*jus cogens*). It did not, however, deem nuclear weapons to fall within the scope of the prohibition.

The US Department of the Navy's *Annotated Supplement to the Commander's Handbook on the Law of Naval Operations*, published in 1989, confirmed the customary nature of the prohibition 'of weapons calculated to cause unnecessary suffering' but noted that the 'humanitarian considerations are offset by a due regard for the military interests at stake'.[65] This understanding was reflected seven years later by the International Court of Justice, which defined unnecessary suffering as 'a harm greater than that unavoidable to achieve legitimate military objectives'.[66]

'Nuclear weapons can', the US Department of the Navy declared, 'be selectively directed against military targets'. It concluded that '[i]n the context of this balance, it is not clear that the use of nuclear weapons necessarily violates international law'.[67] The ICRC declared in the context of its study of customary IHL that given the World Court's Advisory Opinion it 'deemed it not appropriate' to engage in a similar assessment of the legality of nuclear weapons.[68] That said, it recalled that a number of States had declared to the Court their view that nuclear weapons cause unnecessary suffering (Ecuador, Egypt, India, Iran, Japan, Lesotho, the Marshall Islands, Samoa, the Solomon Islands, Sweden, and Zimbabwe), but did not either endorse or contradict that view.[69]

In 2014, Simon O'Connor, a Senior Legal Adviser at the Norwegian Red Cross, addressed the superfluous injury/unnecessary suffering rule in some detail. He recalled

61 Ibid., second and fourth preambular paras.

62 Art. 25(e), Regulations concerning the Laws and Customs of War on Land annexed to Convention (II) with Respect to the Laws and Customs of War on Land; adopted at The Hague, 29 July 1899; entered into force 4 September 1900.

63 ICRC, Customary IHL Rule 70: 'Weapons of a Nature to Cause Superfluous Injury or Unnecessary Suffering', at http://bit.ly/2CyqlPC.

64 ICJ Advisory Opinion on Nuclear Weapons, paras. 78, 79.

65 US Department of the Navy, *Annotated Supplement to the Commander's Handbook on the Law of Naval Operations*, Doc. NWP 9 (REV. A)/FMFM 1–10, Washington, DC, 1989, at https://bit.ly/3uwAlT7, pp. 10–12.

66 ICJ Advisory Opinion on Nuclear Weapons, para. 78.

67 US Department of the Navy, *Annotated Supplement to the Commander's Handbook on the Law of Naval Operations*, pp. 10–12.

68 ICRC, 'Nuclear Weapons', Customary IHL Study, at http://bit.ly/3ssAiGc.

69 ICRC, Customary IHL Rule 70: 'Weapons of a Nature to Cause Superfluous Injury or Unnecessary Suffering'.

the horrific blast and burn injuries nuclear weapons would inflict on hundreds of thousands of people across a huge area in the instant following detonation, which would be dramatically enhanced by the lethal doses of radiation that would kill in the ensuing days and weeks. The long-term impact of nuclear weapons, he further recalled, also means a significantly increased risk of cancer mortality throughout the life of the survivors. 'Even if', he concluded, 'the unnecessary suffering rule … does not operate as an absolute standard, it is almost impossible to conceive of circumstances when engendering such injuries and suffering, even among those engaged in combat, could be deemed truly necessary'.[70]

International Human Rights Law

In terms of adjudging the legality of the use of nuclear weapons in the context of an international armed conflict, the view of the International Court of Justice is that international human rights law does not materially affect the applicable rules. In its Advisory Opinion, the Court confirmed that the right to life, and specifically its *jus cogens* prohibition on arbitrary deprivation of life as codified in the 1966 Covenant on Civil and Political Rights,[71] would indeed apply to such a use of nuclear weapons. But in a famous, oft-quoted passage, the Court held that the test of what is an arbitrary deprivation of life falls to be determined by 'the law applicable in armed conflict which is designed to regulate the conduct of hostilities'.[72] Thus, the Court observed, 'whether a particular loss of life, through the use of a certain weapon in warfare, is to be considered an arbitrary deprivation of life contrary to Article 6 of the Covenant, can only be decided by reference to the law applicable in armed conflict and not deduced from the terms of the Covenant itself'.[73]

Accordingly, should the IHL rules of distinction or proportionality in attack or the superfluous injury or unnecessary rule be violated by the use of nuclear weapons, a violation will also have occurred of the right to life. In its General Comment No. 36 on the right to life under the Covenant on Civil and Political Rights, the Human Rights Committee, which is the formal treaty body overseeing the implementation of the Covenant, stated that 'the threat or use of weapons of mass destruction, in particular nuclear weapons, which are indiscriminate in effect and are of a nature to cause destruction of human life on a catastrophic scale, is incompatible with respect for the right to life and may amount to a crime under international law'.[74] At the same time, the Committee

[70] S. O'Connor, 'Nuclear Weapons and the Unnecessary Suffering Rule', chapter 5 in G. Nystuen, S. Casey-Maslen, and A. G. Bersagel (eds.), *Nuclear Weapons under International Law*, Cambridge University Press, Cambridge, 2014, p. 147.

[71] Art. 6(1), Covenant on Civil and Political Rights; adopted at New York, 16 December 1966; entered into force 23 March 1976.

[72] ICJ Advisory Opinion on Nuclear Weapons, para. 25.

[73] Ibid.

[74] Human Rights Committee, General Comment No. 36: Article 6: right to life, UN doc. CCPR/C/GC/36, 3 September 2019 (hereinafter, Human Rights Committee General Comment 36 on the right to life), para. 66.

determined that the 'use of lethal force consistent with international humanitarian law and other applicable international law norms is, in general, not arbitrary'.[75]

The Law of Neutrality

The law of neutrality covers legal issues that are both applicable *ad bellum* and *in bello*.[76] In its Advisory Opinion, the Court cited directly from one of the written statements whereby it was affirmed that the principle of neutrality applies 'to the transborder damage caused to a neutral State by the use of a weapon in a belligerent State'.[77] In endorsing this claim, the Court added that it was also 'an established part of the customary international law'.[78]

But after declaring that the applicability of the principle of neutrality to nuclear weapons was 'hardly disputed', the Court noted that the 'conclusions to be drawn from this applicability are, on the other hand, controversial'.[79] Despite claims by certain States that the principle would 'rule out the use of a weapon the effects of which simply cannot be contained within the territories of the contending States', the Court did not consider that it had 'a sufficient basis for a determination on the validity of this view'.[80] Materially, the law of neutrality does not affect the legality of the use of nuclear weapons in a situation of international armed conflict.

International Environmental Law

Any use of nuclear weapons would certainly inflict a significant environmental impact. Thus the Court observed in its Advisory Opinion that ionizing radiation has the potential to damage the future environment, affect food and the global marine ecosystem, and cause genetic defects and illness in future generations.[81] In the preamble to the TPNW, States Parties similarly note that 'the catastrophic consequences of nuclear weapons' posed 'grave implications' for the environment.[82]

But despite the legitimate, and growing, concern for the environment, it might seem perverse to many were a use of a nuclear weapon in a populated area that killed tens of thousands or more deemed somehow not to violate fundamental rules of IHL, but for that act to be somehow unlawful on the basis of either international environmental law or the environmental provisions laid down by IHL. The Court, however, rejected such a far-fetched possibility, again deferring to the fundamental rules of *jus ad bellum* and *jus in bello*.

75 Human Rights Committee General Comment 36 on the right to life, para. 64.
76 For a detailed discussion of these issues see chapter 5 in Casey-Maslen, *Jus ad Bellum: The Law on Inter-State Use of Force*, 2020.
77 ICJ Advisory Opinion on Nuclear Weapons, para. 88, citing the Written Statement of Nauru (I), p. 35, §IV E.
78 ICJ Advisory Opinion on Nuclear Weapons, para. 88.
79 Ibid., para. 90.
80 Ibid., paras. 93, 94.
81 Ibid., para. 35.
82 TPNW, fourth preambular para.

A commonly cited principle of environmental law – also forming part of the corpus of contemporary general international law – is Principle 21 of the 1972 Stockholm Declaration and Principle 2 of the 1992 Rio Declaration. These express the duty on States to 'ensure that activities within their jurisdiction or control do not cause damage to the environment of other States or of areas beyond the limits of national jurisdiction'. This principle applies to atmospheric testing of nuclear weapons as it does to their use. That said, as the Court recalled, Principle 24 of the Rio Declaration provided that since warfare is inherently destructive of sustainable development, States shall 'respect international law providing protection for the environment in times of armed conflict and cooperate in its further development, as necessary'.

The IHL provisions on the environment – whose very application as a matter of customary or conventional law to nuclear weapons remains contested – were not deemed by the Court to be 'obligations of total restraint during military conflict'.[83] Rather, it said, States 'must take environmental considerations into account when assessing what is necessary and proportionate in the pursuit of legitimate military objectives'. Respect for the environment is 'one of the elements' that contribute to an assessment of the principle of proportionality.[84]

RESPONSIBILITY UNDER INTERNATIONAL LAW FOR UNLAWFUL USE OR TESTING OF NUCLEAR WEAPONS

Both States and individuals are responsible for any unlawful use or testing of nuclear weapons or other nuclear explosive devices. States are responsible under general international law for internationally wrongful acts they commit or assist, including with respect to nuclear weapons. Individuals are criminally responsible under international criminal law should they perpetrate or assist the commission of an international crime involving nuclear weapons. These differing forms of accountability are addressed in turn.

State Responsibility

States are first and foremost responsible for the violations of international law they commit. The notion of State responsibility thus articulates the circumstances and consequences for a State that violates a primary rule of international law. The central reference in this regard is the International Law Commission's Draft Articles on Responsibility of States for Internationally Wrongful Acts, which it concluded in 2001.[85] Article 1 of the 2001 Draft Articles on State Responsibility simply provides that 'every internationally wrongful act of

83 ICJ Advisory Opinion on Nuclear Weapons, para. 30.
84 Ibid.
85 Draft articles on Responsibility of States for Internationally Wrongful Acts, with commentaries, 2001; text adopted by the International Law Commission (ILC) at its fifty-third session, in 2001, and submitted to the UN General Assembly as a part of the Commission's report covering the work of that session, in UN doc. A/56/10, at http://bit.ly/32A30cT.

a State entails the international responsibility of that State'. The Draft Articles reflect general international law applicable to all States.

An 'internationally wrongful act' is, simply put, a violation of a rule of international law by a State that it binds. The rule may be demarcated in a treaty; it may be customary in nature; it may originate in a general principle of law; or it may be a rule discerned by a competent judicial body, such as the International Court of Justice, a regional human rights court, or a domestic court. It must, however, be applicable to the State in question. As Article 13 of the 2001 Draft Articles on State Responsibility provides: 'An act of a State does not constitute a breach of an international obligation unless the State is bound by the obligation in question at the time the act occurs.'

The term 'act' can also encompass an omission.[86] Thus, for example, beyond responsibility for any use or testing of nuclear weapons a State may conduct, the failure to pursue negotiations in good faith on effective measures relating to nuclear disarmament can also engage the responsibility of a State. The challenge of course is identifying a judicial or quasi-judicial forum within which a State may be held accountable. On 24 April 2014, the Republic of the Marshall Islands filed applications before the International Court of Justice against the nine nuclear-armed States, accusing them of not fulfilling their obligations under international law to pursue nuclear disarmament. While the nine applications all related to the same matter, the Marshall Islands distinguished between the three States – India, Pakistan, and the United Kingdom – that had recognised the compulsory jurisdiction of the Court pursuant to Article 36(2) of its Statute, and the six others, for which the consent to the jurisdiction of the Court had to be expressly given (and was not in this case).

The Marshall Islands alleged specifically that the United Kingdom had violated Article VI of the NPT, a Treaty to which they were (and are) both party. In its Memorial to the Court, the Marshall Islands recalled the Practical Steps agreed upon by consensus at the 2000 NPT Review Conference, which included an 'unequivocal undertaking by the nuclear-weapon States to accomplish the total elimination of their nuclear arsenals leading to nuclear disarmament, to which all States parties are committed under article VI'.[87] The United Kingdom has breached its Article VI obligation, the Memorial argued, 'in the first place' by failing to pursue negotiations on nuclear disarmament. 'No such negotiations exist or have existed', and the United Kingdom had 'failed to seek to bring them into existence'. Indeed, it observed, the United Kingdom has 'actively opposed' the initiation of such negotiations as well as the UN General Assembly's effort to facilitate their commencement.[88] Forty-five years after the entry into force of the NPT, the United Kingdom's delay in fulfilling its obligation to pursue negotiations on nuclear disarmament was, the Memorial concluded, 'manifestly unreasonable'.[89] The Marshall Islands recalled the 2001 Draft Articles on State Responsibility, and specifically

86 Commentary, para. 8, on Draft Article 1, 2001 Draft Articles on State Responsibility.
87 Memorial of the Marshall Islands, *Obligations Concerning Negotiations Relating to Cessation of the Nuclear Arms Race and to Nuclear Disarmament* (*Marshall Islands* v. *United Kingdom*), 16 March 2015, at https://bit.ly/3dQ9Rpx, para. 165.
88 Ibid., para. 210.
89 Ibid., para. 213.

Article 12, which provides: 'There is a breach of an international obligation by a State when an act of that State is not in conformity with what is required of it by that obligation, regardless of its origin or character.'[90] The Marshall Islands formally requested the Court to adjudge and declare 'that the United Kingdom has violated and continues to violate its international obligations under the NPT, more specifically under Article VI of the Treaty, by failing to pursue in good faith and bring to a conclusion negotiations leading to nuclear disarmament in all its aspects under strict and effective international control'.[91] With respect to India and Pakistan, who were not parties to the NPT, the Marshall Islands contended that the relevant obligations applied to all States as a matter of customary international law. All three States, however, objected to the jurisdiction of the Court, which prevented the consideration of any of the merits of the applications prior to the resolution of the jurisdictional issue. On 5 October 2016, the Court delivered its judgment in each case, upholding the preliminary objection raised by the three respondent States, based on the absence of a 'dispute' between the parties at the time the applications were filed.

In its judgment on the Preliminary Objections by the United Kingdom, the Court summarised the position of the United Kingdom as contending that customary international law requires a State intending to invoke the responsibility of another State to give specific and direct notice of its claim to that State. The United Kingdom had claimed that this principle was reflected in Article 43 of the 2001 Draft Articles on State Responsibility.[92] In response, the Marshall Islands contested the existence of such a principle with respect to proceedings before the International Court of Justice (citing the commentary on Article 44 of the Draft Articles, whereby it was stated that the Articles were 'not concerned with questions of the jurisdiction of international courts and tribunals, or in general with the conditions for the admissibility of cases'). The Marshall Islands further observed that, in any event, it had given due notice of its claim by means of its Application to the Court.[93]

The Court noted that the Marshall Islands, 'by virtue of the suffering which its people endured as a result of it being used as a site for extensive nuclear testing programs', had 'special reasons for concern about nuclear disarmament'.[94] It acknowledged that, at a conference on the humanitarian consequences of nuclear weapons held in Nayarit in Mexico in February 2014, the Marshall Islands had delivered a statement in which it affirmed that 'States possessing nuclear arsenals are failing to fulfil their legal obligations' under Article VI of the NPT and customary international law. However, the Court observed, the United Kingdom was not present at the conference and, moreover, the conference was not directly concerned with nuclear disarmament.[95] In all the circumstances, the Court concluded, it 'cannot be said that the United Kingdom was aware, or

90 Ibid., para. 207.

91 Ibid., para. 239(a).

92 International Court of Justice, *Obligations Concerning Negotiations Relating to Cessation of the Nuclear Arms Race and to Nuclear Disarmament* (*Marshall Islands* v. *United Kingdom*), Judgment (Preliminary Objections), 5 October 2016, para. 27.

93 Ibid., para. 34.

94 Ibid., para. 44.

95 Ibid., para. 50.

could not have been unaware, that the Marshall Islands was making an allegation that the United Kingdom was in breach of its obligations'.[96]

The Court upheld, by eight votes to eight, by the President's casting vote, the preliminary objection to jurisdiction raised by the United Kingdom and further, by nine votes to seven, found that it could not proceed to the merits of the case.[97] To ensure that a similar case may not be brought against it, in its 2017 declaration accepting the compulsory jurisdiction of the International Court, the United Kingdom excluded 'any claim or dispute that arises from or is connected with or related to nuclear disarmament and/or nuclear weapons, unless all the other nuclear-weapon States Party to the Treaty on the Non-proliferation of Nuclear Weapons have also consented to the jurisdiction of the Court and are party to the proceedings in question'.[98]

In his dissenting opinion in the case, Judge Crawford noted that the Court had earlier held that it must 'objectively determine whether there is a dispute based on "an examination of the facts"'.[99] He further observed that the Court in the case at hand had discarded its 'tradition of flexibility'.[100] Judge Crawford affirmed, correctly in the view of the present author, that there was 'an incipient dispute between the Marshall Islands and the nuclear-weapon States at the time of Nayarit. This was not an accidental development, but the expression of a real underlying disagreement of a legal character as to the trajectory of Article VI.'[101] The 'fact' of a conflict over Article VI was, he concluded, 'public knowledge, to which the Court need not be blind'.[102]

In his passionate dissenting opinion, Judge Cançado Trindade criticised the Court for being '[a]lways attentive and over-sensitive to the position of nuclear-weapon States', as well as for its 'entirely formalistic reasoning' in the case.[103] In his perception, the threshold imposed by the Court 'unduly creates a difficulty for the very access to justice (by applicants) at [the] international level, in a case on a matter of concern to the whole of humankind'. This was, he observed, 'most regrettable'.[104]

More successful, at least in terms of outcome, was the application of Australia and New Zealand to the Court against continued atmospheric nuclear testing in the Pacific by France in the 1970s. That said, as Judge Cançado Trindade observed, the Court avoided issuing a declaratory judgment that atmospheric nuclear tests were contrary to international law. It did so on the basis that France had discontinued its atmospheric tests and that the President of the French Republic had made a legally binding unilateral declaration to this effect 'to the international community to which his words were

96 Ibid., para. 52.
97 Ibid., para. 59, dispositives 1 and 2.
98 Declaration recognizing the jurisdiction of the Court as compulsory by the United Kingdom of Great Britain and Northern Ireland, 22 February 2017, at http://bit.ly/37O2yv2, para. 1(vi).
99 International Court of Justice, *Marshall Islands* v. *United Kingdom*, Judgment (Preliminary Objections), Dissenting Opinion of Judge Crawford, para. 5.
100 Ibid., para. 10.
101 Ibid., para. 26.
102 Ibid., para. 30.
103 International Court of Justice, *Marshall Islands* v. *United Kingdom*, Judgment (Preliminary Objections), Dissenting Opinion of Judge Cançado Trindade, paras. 27, 28.
104 Ibid., para. 30.

addressed'.[105] The Court held therefore that the claims of Australia and New Zealand no longer had 'any object'.[106]

The consequences for a State of being found responsible for an internationally wrongful act are potentially manifold. The 2001 Draft Articles identify a number of these legal consequences. In particular, a 'responsible' State is obligated to make 'full reparation for the injury caused by the internationally wrongful act'.[107] Reparation comprises both material and moral damage.[108] Material damage concerns damage to property or other interests of the State and its nationals that is assessable financially. Moral damage includes pain and suffering and the loss of loved ones.[109] As the Draft Articles further clarify: 'Full reparation for the injury caused by the internationally wrongful act shall take the form of restitution, compensation and satisfaction, either singly or in combination.'[110]

Depending on the character and content of the obligation and on the circumstances of the breach, the responsible State may, according to the Draft Articles, be obligated to another State, several States, or the international community as a whole.[111] The reference to several States includes the case in which a breach affects all the other States Parties to a treaty.[112] Should a State be responsible for a violation of international law involving nuclear weapons, the rights of those persons affected by that violation will also have been violated, giving rise to the right to a remedy. This concerns especially the right to life. Thus the Human Rights Committee declared that States must 'afford adequate reparation to victims whose right to life has been or is being adversely affected by the testing or use of weapons of mass destruction, in accordance with principles of international responsibility'.[113]

In this regard, the Committee referred to its Concluding Observations on the fifth periodic report of France under the Covenant. Therein it addressed the issue of compensation for the victims of French nuclear tests, expressing its concern about the fact that, as of 1 March 2015, the Nuclear Test Victims Compensation Committee had dismissed 98.3 per cent of claims made for compensation. The Committee called on France to 'take all the necessary steps to ensure the effective recognition and compensation of all the victims of French nuclear tests, especially the local population'.[114]

Individual Criminal Responsibility

In the words of the International Military Tribunal at Nuremberg, 'Crimes against international law are committed by men, not by abstract entities, and only by punishing

105 International Court of Justice, *Nuclear Tests Case* (*Australia* v. *France*), Judgment, 20 December 1974, para. 51.
106 Ibid., para. 62.
107 Art. 31(1), 2001 Draft Articles on State Responsibility.
108 Art. 31(2), 2001 Draft Articles on State Responsibility.
109 Commentary, para. 5, on Draft Article 31, 2001 Draft Articles on State Responsibility.
110 Art. 34, 2001 Draft Articles on State Responsibility.
111 Art. 33(1), 2001 Draft Articles on State Responsibility.
112 Commentary, para. 2, on Draft Article 33, 2001 Draft Articles on State Responsibility.
113 Human Rights Committee General Comment 36 on the right to life, para. 66.
114 Human Rights Committee, Concluding observations on the fifth periodic report of France, UN doc. CCPR/C/FRA/CO/5, 17 August 2015, para. 21.

individuals who commit such crimes can the provisions of international law be enforced.'[115] Individuals are personally responsible under international criminal law for perpetrating or assisting the commission of an international crime, which would include one that involves the use of nuclear weapons. Such a crime could be, depending on the situation, a crime against humanity, an act of genocide, or a war crime, as well as the crime of aggression.

Each of these crimes is potentially within the jurisdiction of the International Criminal Court, which has operated since July 2002. The Court may exercise its jurisdiction with respect to a senior figure who is a national of a State Party or whose criminal acts are committed on the territory of a State Party to the 1998 Rome Statute of the International Criminal Court.[116] Alternatively, the UN Security Council, acting under Chapter VII of the UN Charter, may refer a situation to the Court for possible prosecution of any international crimes committed in that context.[117]

It is important to bear in mind also that irrespective of the international crime being prosecuted there are always two elements to any international crime that must be successfully established for a conviction to be secured: a culpable act (known by its Latin moniker, *actus reus*) and a culpable state of mind (*mens rea*). This is the same as routinely occurs in domestic law. Thus, for example, under the law in force in England and Wales, murder is where one person kills another (the *actus reus* element) with the intention to cause either death or serious injury unlawfully (the *mens rea* element).[118] With respect to the use of nuclear weapons, while we would likely be talking about a charge of mass murder on an unparalleled scale, this would not affect the need for sufficient proof beyond reasonable doubt of these two fundamental elements of criminal law.

Use of Nuclear Weapons as a Crime of Aggression

A serious violation of the prohibition of inter-State use of force under *jus ad bellum* is an act of aggression, which is now capable of being prosecuted by the International Criminal Court when perpetrated by a senior State official. Such prosecutions are, in practice, extremely unlikely.[119] The last time an international tribunal successfully prosecuted 'crimes against peace' was in the trials of Nazi war criminals at Nuremberg after the end of the Second World War.[120] Whether or not it was a progressive development of the law –

115 *Trial of the Major War Criminals before the International Military Tribunal*, Vol. I, Nuremberg, 1947, 223.

116 Rome Statute of the International Criminal Court; adopted at Rome, 17 July 1998; entered into force 1 July 2002 (hereinafter, Statute of the International Criminal Court).

117 Art. 13(b), Statute of the International Criminal Court. This it has done in the case of Libya and Sudan (Darfur). See generally, e.g., A. S. Galand, *UN Security Council Referrals to the International Criminal Court: Legal Nature, Effects and Limits*, Leiden Studies on the Frontiers of International Law, Vol. 5, Brill, Leiden, 2019.

118 See, e.g., Crown Prosecution Service, 'Homicide: Murder and Manslaughter', Updated 18 March 2019, at http://bit.ly/308Wrqh.

119 See, e.g., D. Ferencz, *'The Nuremberg Legacy and the Crime of Aggression: A Promise Betrayed or Merely Delayed?'*, blog entry, Centre for Criminology, University of Oxford, 13 February 2015, at http://bit.ly/365tKVg.

120 Global Institute for the Prevention of Aggression, 'The Crime of Aggression – a Brief History', at http://bit.ly/3c7DO3E.

views among even the prosecutors differed at the time[121] – the 1945 Charter of the International Military Tribunal provided that crimes against peace were the 'planning, preparation, initiation or waging of a war of aggression, or a war in violation of international treaties, agreements or assurances, or participation in a common plan or conspiracy for the accomplishment of any of the foregoing'.[122]

Under the amended Statute of the International Criminal Court, the crime of aggression is specified to be 'the planning, preparation, initiation or execution, by a person in a position effectively to exercise control over or to direct the political or military action of a State, of an act of aggression which, by its character, gravity and scale, constitutes a manifest violation of the Charter of the United Nations'.[123] An 'act of aggression' means, in turn, 'the use of armed force by a State against the sovereignty, territorial integrity or political independence of another State, or in any other manner inconsistent with the Charter of the United Nations'.[124] In the corresponding 'elements' of the crime of aggression, it is stated that there is no requirement to prove that either the perpetrator had made a legal evaluation as to whether the use of armed force was inconsistent with the UN Charter or that he or she had made a legal evaluation as to the 'manifest' nature of that violation.[125] That said, it was made explicit in the 1974 UN Definition of Aggression that '[t]he first use of armed force by a State in contravention of the Charter shall constitute prima facie evidence of an act of aggression'.[126]

One of the acts that might constitute an act of aggression by use of a nuclear weapon is the 'ombardment by the armed forces of a State against the territory of another State or the use of any weapons by a State against the territory of another State'.[127] Potentially also relevant in the case of nuclear weapons would be the 'action of a State in allowing its territory, which it has placed at the disposal of another State, to be used by that other State for perpetrating an act of aggression against a third State'.[128] Five NATO allies of the United States accept the stationing of nuclear weapons on their territory: Belgium, Germany, Italy, the Netherlands, and Turkey. Conceivably also a State could decide to send an armed group to carry out an act of armed force against another State of significant gravity to constitute an act of aggression, such as by the group's placement and detonation of a nuclear explosive device on that target State's territory.[129]

In March 2006, the United Kingdom's House of Lords unanimously decided in *R* v. *Jones (Margaret)*, in the context of the unlawful invasion of Iraq in 2003, that although the crime of aggression existed under customary international law, there was no such crime under the law of England and Wales, as it had not been incorporated into domestic law

[121] For a brief discussion of the views at the time, see Casey-Maslen, *Jus ad bellum: Law on the Inter-State Use of Force*, pp. 130–32.

[122] Art. 6(a), Charter of the International Military Tribunal, Annex to the Agreement for the Prosecution and Punishment of the Major War Criminals of the European Axis; signed at London, 8 August 1945.

[123] Art. 8 *bis* (1), Statute of the International Criminal Court.

[124] Art. 8 *bis* (2), Statute of the International Criminal Court.

[125] Elements of Crimes, Article 8 *bis*: Crime of aggression, at http://bit.ly/2OFt14t, Introduction, paras. 2 and 4.

[126] Art. 2, 1974 UN Definition of Aggression.

[127] Art. 8 *bis* (2)(b), Statute of the International Criminal Court.

[128] Art. 8 *bis* (2)(f), Statute of the International Criminal Court.

[129] Art. 8 *bis* (2)(f), Statute of the International Criminal Court.

(the United Kingdom being a dualist State under international law).[130] The United Kingdom has not ratified the amendment to the Statute pertaining to the crime of aggression under Article 8*bis*, but forty other States Parties to the Rome Statute had done so as of this writing. This included numerous allies of the United Kingdom within the North Atlantic Treaty Organization (NATO) alliance: Belgium (where NATO is headquartered), Croatia, Czechia, Estonia, Germany, Iceland, Lithuania, Luxembourg, the Netherlands, North Macedonia, Poland, Portugal, Slovakia, Slovenia, and Spain.

In practical and legal terms, a person 'in a position effectively to exercise control over or to direct the political or military action of a State' would be the head of the armed forces; the minister of defence; the prime minister (in a parliamentary democracy); and/or the king, queen, or president (where the title was not ceremonial but executive). A member of the armed forces who actually launched the weapon under instruction from his or her commander in the armed forces would not be held responsible by the International Criminal Court for the crime of aggression.

In the United States, where the president is also the commander in chief of the armed forces, it is a misconception that he or she has a nuclear 'button' that launches the weapons. The 'nuclear football' is an authorisation to launch, not a means by which weapons are launched. If the president were to order a strike, he would use the codes[131] – known bizarrely as the 'biscuit' – to identify himself to the military who would then, in the ordinary scheme of things, take the required action.[132]

In November 2017, for the first time in forty years, Congress examined the president's authority to launch a nuclear attack. One of the experts summoned to testify was Claude Robert Kehler, the commander of US Strategic Command in 2011–13 and a retired general. General Kehler told a congressional committee that, as trained, he would follow the president's nuclear order, but only if it were legal. Under certain circumstances, he explained, 'I would have said "I'm not ready to proceed."' One senator asked him, 'Then what happens?' Kehler admitted, 'I don't know.'[133]

As of this writing, discussion was underway in Congress as to whether the sole power of the US President to launch nuclear weapons should be replaced with some form of dual control. Giving one person such authority 'entails real risks', according to a letter in February 2021 endorsed by thirty-one Democratic members of the House of Representatives. 'Past presidents have threatened to attack other countries with nuclear

[130] House of Lords, *R* v. *Jones (Margaret)* [2007] 1 AC 136.

[131] It was alleged that the codes to be used by President Clinton to launch a nuclear strike were mislaid for several months around the year 2000. BBC, 'US Presidential Nuclear Codes "Lost for Months"', 21 October 2010, at http://bbc.in/3stNQkH.

[132] The president passes his order to the Chairman of the Joint Chiefs of Staff, the highest-ranking US military officer under the Commander in Chief. His order then goes to the US Strategic Command HQ in Offutt Airbase, Nebraska, which passes it to 'on the ground' teams who may be at sea or underwater. The order to fire is transmitted via codes, which must match codes locked in the launch team's safes. BBC, 'Does Donald Trump Have a Nuclear Button?', 3 January 2018, at http://bbc.in/2P8qmTE.

[133] Ibid.

weapons or exhibited behavior that causes other officials to express concerns about the president's judgment', the letter stated.[134]

Were two people in a State required to authorise a use of nuclear weapons, naturally that would not preclude their both being held responsible for an act of aggression falling within the jurisdiction of the International Criminal Court. A footnote to the elements of crimes adopted by the States Parties to the Rome Statute makes it explicit that, with respect to an act of aggression, more than one person may be in a position to meet the requisite criteria.[135]

Use of Nuclear Weapons as a War Crime

At the same time and indeed through the very same conduct that constituted an act of aggression (through use of a nuclear weapon), a war crime could also be committed. A single act could thus serve to ground a prosecution for two different international crimes. Equally, of course, the use of nuclear weapons as a war crime could be unrelated to any alleged act of aggression.

War crimes are serious violations of IHL, whose commission in the context of an armed conflict is criminalised.[136] There is a duty under international law to prosecute, or to hand over to another State or international court for prosecution, anyone who is reasonably suspected to have committed a war crime.[137] This is so, whether they acted as perpetrators or under other modes of liability, such as ordering the crime to be committed or aiding and abetting its commission.[138] For a prosecution of an alleged war crime to be successful, there must be a direct connection – a nexus – to a specific armed conflict.

The Statute of the International Criminal Court does not provide for the prosecution of the use of a nuclear weapon per se. This is in contrast to the use of biological or chemical weapons, both of which fall within the Statute in all armed conflict. Efforts were made during the negotiation of the Statute to accord the Court jurisdiction over the war crime of using a nuclear weapon but they were unsuccessful.[139] More recently, in 2009, Mexico sought to 'reassert its amendment proposal' to Article 8 of the Rome Statute to criminalise 'the use or threat of use of nuclear weapons as a war crime' in international armed conflict. The proposed amendment was to add to Article 8(2)(b) of the Statute the following crime:

134 S. Herman, 'Democrats Want Biden to Relinquish Sole Authority for Nuclear Launches', *Voice of America*, 25 February 2021, at http://bit.ly/2PlbaTz.

135 Elements of Crimes, Article 8*bis*: Crime of aggression, Elements, para. 2, note 1.

136 'War Crimes', *How does Law Protect in War?* International Committee of the Red Cross (ICRC), at http://bit.ly/39ay33m.

137 ICRC Customary IHL Rule 158: 'Prosecution of War Crimes', at http://bit.ly/37FdYin.

138 See Art. 25(3), Rome Statute of the International Criminal Court; adopted at Rome, 17 July 1998; entered into force 1 July 2002 (Statute of the International Criminal Court). As of 1 January 2021, 123 States were party to the Statute.

139 See, e.g., P. Kirsch and J. T. Holmes, 'The Rome Conference on an International Criminal Court: The Negotiating Process', *American Journal of International Law*, Vol. 93, No. 1 (January 1999), 2–12; and M. C. Bassiouni, 'Negotiating the Treaty of Rome on the Establishment of an International Criminal Court', *Cornell International Law Journal*, Vol. 32, No. 3 (1999), Symposium Article 3, at https://bit.ly/3pZKqnZ.

'Employing nuclear weapons or threatening to employ nuclear weapons.'[140] This has not been incorporated in the Statute.

That does not mean that an unlawful use of nuclear weapons in armed conflict could not be prosecuted as a war crime by the Court. Deliberately attacking civilians in the conduct of hostilities is one of a number of war crimes perpetrated against the civilian population. In its detailed study of customary IHL, published in 2005, the International Committee of the Red Cross (ICRC) identified a number of war crimes under customary law that concern the targeting of civilians, including the two following crimes:[141]

- making the civilian population or individual civilians, not taking a direct part in hostilities, the object of attack; and
- launching an indiscriminate attack resulting in loss of life or injury to civilians.

These war crimes are applicable in all armed conflict and may be committed by members of State armed forces as well as by members of organised armed groups (and even potentially by individual civilians).

The Rome Statute gives the International Criminal Court jurisdiction over the war crime of 'intentionally directing attacks against the civilian population as such or against individual civilians not taking direct part in hostilities' in both international and non-international armed conflict.[142] The elements of this war crime in international armed conflict demand that the Court be satisfied as to the following five cumulative requirements:

ARTICLE 8 (2) (B) (I): WAR CRIME OF ATTACKING CIVILIANS.

Elements

1. the perpetrator directed an attack.
2. the object of the attack was a civilian population as such or individual civilians not taking direct part in hostilities.
3. the perpetrator intended the civilian population as such or individual civilians not taking direct part in hostilities to be the object of the attack.
4. the conduct took place in the context of and was associated with an international armed conflict.
5. the perpetrator was aware of factual circumstances that established the existence of an armed conflict.

Elements 1 and 2 are the actus reus elements of the war crime of attacking civilians. Elements 3 and 5 are the mens rea elements of the war crime of attacking civilians.[143] The nexus to armed conflict, which the prosecution must also prove, is covered by Element 4.

140 See ICRC, 'Mexico: Practice Relating to Nuclear Weapons', accessed 1 February 2021, at http://bit.ly/3spt8Cu.

141 ICRC, Customary IHL Rule 156: 'Definition of War Crimes' at http://bit.ly/32HjZb2.

142 Art. 8(2)(b)(i) and (e)(i), Rome Statute of the International Criminal Court.

143 The fifth element does not require that the perpetrator understand from a legal perspective whether an armed conflict exists, just the facts that underpin the existence of that armed conflict.

The Rome Statute does not specifically provide for prosecution of indiscriminate attacks in any armed conflict.[144] In its 2019 judgment in the *Ntaganda* case, however, a Trial Chamber of the International Criminal Court held that the crime under the Statute of attacking civilians 'may encompass attacks that are carried out in an indiscriminate manner, that is by targeting an area, as opposed to specific objects, or not targeting specific military objects or persons taking a direct part in hostilities, … so long as the perpetrator was aware of the presence of civilians in the relevant area'.[145] The Trial Chamber further held that the crime 'may also include attacks that are launched without taking necessary precautions to spare the civilian population or individual civilians'.[146] Clearly, therefore, the use of a nuclear weapon against a city that contained lawful military objectives could constitute a direct attack on civilians that is potentially within the remit of the Court.

Robert Forsyth, a British submarine commander who served in the submarine service in 1961–81, was the executive officer and was in command of the Polaris-armed submarine *HMS Repulse*.[147] He has expressed concern as to the legal jeopardy that might attach to the 'last in the line military commander who has the ability to withhold fire'. In the case of the United Kingdom, this would be the nuclear-missile-firing submarine captains who have a physical key they must insert in a control panel, turn, and say, 'You have my permission to fire.' He fears that, to avoid possible prosecution for a war crime, the Commanding Officer must know that he is not blindly obeying an order that is manifestly unlawful given that 'on distant patrol and submerged, he does not have that knowledge'.[148]

Commander Forsyth refers to Article 33 of the Rome Statute, which stipulates, in part, the following:

> The fact that a crime within the jurisdiction of the Court has been committed by a person pursuant to an order of a Government or of a superior, whether military or civilian, shall not relieve that person of criminal responsibility unless:
>
> (a) The person was under a legal obligation to obey orders of the Government or the superior in question;
> (b) The person did not know that the order was unlawful; and
> (c) The order was not manifestly unlawful.[149]

This dictates that the military officer must not *know* that the order was unlawful not that he must ensure that it *was* lawful. Obedience to orders is the fundamental tenet of any armed

144 Art. 8(2)(b)(iv) covers serious violations of the principle of proportionality: 'Intentionally launching an attack in the knowledge that such attack will cause incidental loss of life or injury to civilians or damage to civilian objects or widespread, long-term and severe damage to the natural environment which would be clearly excessive in relation to the concrete and direct overall military advantage anticipated.'

145 International Criminal Court, *Prosecutor* v. *Bosco Ntaganda*, Judgment (Trial Chamber) (Case No. ICC-01/04–02/06), 8 July 2019, para. 921.

146 Ibid.

147 For a presentation by Commander Forsythe on his military naval service, see http://bit.ly/3pXANGA.

148 Email from Commander Robert Forsythe to the author, 14 February 2020.

149 Art. 33(1), Statute of the International Criminal Court.

force. The Statute further points out, however, that orders to commit genocide or crimes against humanity are ipso facto manifestly unlawful.[150]

Although the Commander's fears of a prosecution for war crimes would not be realised – as a submarine commander would in all likelihood not be specifically instructed to engage in a wanton massacre and would not be in a position to know that an order he or she was following was to carry out an illegal act – further up the military chain of command, the same cannot be said. Were it the case that an officer in the similar position of General Kehler was given a nuclear order by the commander-in-chief of the armed forces, and he knew that the order was to carry out an international crime, either because it amounted to an act of aggression or a war crime (or both), an asserted defence of superior orders would fail.

Use of Nuclear Weapons as a Crime against Humanity

A crime against humanity can certainly be committed by the use of nuclear weapons. In December 2020, by a large majority, the UN General Assembly reaffirmed earlier resolutions which declared that any use of nuclear weapons would amount to a crime against humanity.[151]

Crimes against humanity are punishable before the International Criminal Court where acts of violence are perpetrated 'as part of a widespread or systematic attack directed against any civilian population, with knowledge of the attack'.[152] The essence of crimes against humanity is therefore an attack that is made against civilians. Crimes against humanity may be committed in a situation of armed conflict or during peacetime.[153] When committed in connection with an armed conflict, the same act may be a war crime as well as a crime against humanity. The perpetrator may be a State official or a member of an armed group where there is a governmental or organisational policy to commit such an attack.

An attack is widespread if it is conducted on a large scale and results in many victims,[154] although there is no specific 'numerical threshold'.[155] The ICTY defined 'systematic' as 'the organised nature of the acts of violence and the improbability of their random occurrence'[156] and found that evidence of a pattern or a methodical plan establishes that an attack was systematic.[157] A single nuclear strike against a populated area would,

150 Art. 33(2), Statute of the International Criminal Court.

151 UN General Assembly Resolution 75/75 ('Convention on the Prohibition of the Use of Nuclear Weapons'), adopted on 7 December 2020 by 120 votes to 50 with 14 abstentions, sixth preambular para. In legal terms, however, this would not necessarily be the case. A nuclear strike on a submarine that was about to target a populated area with a nuclear weapon would be preventing, not committing, a crime against humanity.

152 Art. 7(1), Statute of the International Criminal Court.

153 ILC, Draft articles on Prevention and Punishment of Crimes Against Humanity, with commentaries, in UN doc. A/74/10, 2019, at https://bit.ly/30dgLXD, para. 45, commentary para. 1. When a crime against humanity is committed during an armed conflict, the same acts may also amount to war crimes.

154 ICTY, *Prosecutor* v. *Blaškić*, Judgment (Trial Chamber) (Case No. IT-95-14-T), 3 March 2000, para. 206.

155 C. Stahn, *A Critical Introduction to International Criminal Law*, Cambridge University Press, Cambridge, 2019, p. 57.

156 ICTY, *Prosecutor* v. *Mrkšić*, Judgment (Trial Chamber) (Case No. IT95-13/1-T), 27 September 2007, para. 437.

157 ICTY, *Prosecutor* v. *Kunarac*, Judgment (Appeals Chamber) (Case Nos. IT-96-23 & IT-96–23/1-A), 12 June 2002, para. 94.

however, be sufficient to constitute a crime against humanity. In 2010, a Pre-trial Chamber of the International Criminal Court reaffirmed that a widespread attack may be the 'cumulative effect of a series of inhumane acts or the singular effect of an inhumane act of extraordinary magnitude'.[158]

The core elements of 'a widespread or systematic attack directed against any civilian population, with knowledge of the attack' and the associated crimes are part of customary law. There is, however, no specific treaty that exists to prevent and repress crimes against humanity as there is for genocide. Nonetheless, it is accepted custom that an array of acts may be prosecuted as crimes against humanity, which include murder, extermination, and other inhumane acts intentionally causing great suffering or serious bodily injury.[159]

The frequent link between acts carried out with a view to terrorise civilians, such as bombardment, and crimes against humanity has been widely seen in Syria. In 2014, the UN Commission of Inquiry on Syria found that the government had employed a military strategy targeting the civilian population, combining long-lasting sieges with continuous air and ground bombardment. In neighbourhoods around Damascus, civilians were targeted on the basis of their perceived opposition to the government. Innocent civilians would be attacked for merely residing in or originating from these neighbourhoods.[160] The Commission concluded that the Syrian regime 'has carried out a widespread and systematic attack against the civilian population of Aleppo to punish and terrorize civilians for supporting or hosting armed groups, in an apparent strategy to erode popular support for those groups'.[161]

Use of Nuclear Weapons as an Act of Genocide

Genocide, known as the 'crime of crimes', was formally outlawed by the 1948 Genocide Convention.[162] Genocide is also punishable as an international crime before the International Criminal Court. It is the act of killing or seriously injuring or starving members of a minority where the act is committed 'with intent to destroy, in whole or in part' that group.[163] As is the case with crimes against humanity, genocide may be committed in a situation of armed conflict or in peacetime.

In 2004, the ICTY issued its judgment on appeal in the *Krstić* case, terming the killings in the aftermath of the fall of the Bosnian Muslim enclave of Srebrenica 'genocide'.[164] The

158 International Criminal Court Pre-trial Chamber, 'Situation in the Republic of Kenya, Decision Pursuant to Article 15 of the Rome Statute on the Authorization of an Investigation into the Situation in the Republic of Kenya', Doc. ICC-01/09–19, 31 March 2010, para. 95.

159 See Art. 7(1)(a), (b), and (k), Statute of the International Criminal Court.

160 Report of the Independent International Commission of Inquiry on the Syrian Arab Republic, UN doc. A/HRC/27/60, 13 August 2014, para. 104.

161 Ibid.

162 Convention on the Prevention and Punishment of the Crime of Genocide; adopted at Paris, 9 December 1948; entered into force 12 January 1951 (hereinafter, 1948 Genocide Convention). As of 1 January 2021, 152 States were party to the Convention.

163 Art. 6, Statute of the International Criminal Court. See also Art. 2, 1948 Genocide Convention.

164 ICTY, *Prosecutor* v. *Krstić*, Judgment (Appeals Chamber) (Case No. IT-98-33-A), 19 April 2004, paras. 37–38.

Appeals Chamber accepted that genocide could occur in a localised area and with respect to a small percentage of the population of a national minority.[165] Thus even a low-yield nuclear weapon that was targeted at a minority with the requisite intent (*dolus specialis*) could amount to genocide.

165 Stahn, *A Critical Introduction to International Criminal Law*, p. 40.

Concluding Remarks on the Future of Nuclear Arms Control and Disarmament

In its declaration submitted in accordance with Article 2 of the Treaty on the Prohibition of Nuclear Weapons,[1] Kazakhstan expressed the 'collective' hope that by the one-hundredth anniversary of the United Nations in 2045, nuclear weapons would have been eliminated.[2] But at the time of the declaration's submission in February 2021, the prospects for global nuclear arms control and, a fortiori, nuclear disarmament appeared bleak.

While the absence of an effective forum to negotiate such instruments – given the twenty-five-year-long impasse in the Conference on Disarmament – could be overcome, the will to do so among nuclear-armed States (as well as among those seeking the protection of their nuclear forces) is largely absent. The extension of New START averted the risk of the bilateral legal landscape being completely barren in February 2021, but the disappearance of the 1989 Intermediate Nuclear Forces (INF) Treaty has left a legal gap that the introduction of short- and intermediate-range missiles in Asia and Europe may fill.

The United States' Creating an Environment for Nuclear Disarmament (CEND) initiative, which had manifested itself as little more than a diversionary tactic, seemed moribund following the downfall of the Trump administration. The Swedish 'Stepping Stones' initiative,[3] endorsed by Argentina, Canada, Finland, Germany, Indonesia, Japan, Jordan, Kazakhstan, the Netherlands, New Zealand, Norway, South Korea, Spain, Sweden, and Switzerland, while well-intentioned, offered little of substance that was new. More critically, despite its moniker, there was no indication as to how desirable outcomes – the entry into force of the Comprehensive Nuclear-Test-Ban Treaty and the negotiation of a treaty prohibiting fissile material production, among others – would be achieved. Calls to 'Nuclear-Weapon States and Nuclear Possessor States to show leadership to unblock negotiations' on such a Treaty merely served to highlight the lack of any concrete strategy.

[1] Treaty on the Prohibition of Nuclear Weapons; adopted at New York, 7 July 2017; entered into force 22 January 2021.

[2] TPNW Article 2 Declaration of Kazakhstan, Deputy Prime Minister and Minister of Foreign Affairs of Kazakhstan, 18 February 2021, at https://bit.ly/2MtrpN1, first and third preambular paras.

[3] Mission of Sweden in Geneva, 'Ministerial Meeting of the Stockholm Initiative for Nuclear Disarmament', 27 February 2020, at http://bit.ly/3stJpXb.

In a speech by Germany's Federal Foreign Minister Heiko Maas to the Conference on Disarmament, the year 2021 was described as a 'watershed year for arms control'.[4] The minister's remarks included a reference to the Stockholm Initiative and its 'roadmap to advance nuclear disarmament', and he noted that the practical steps remained 'on the table'. There was not even a call upon the United States to ratify the Comprehensive Nuclear-Test-Ban Treaty (CTBT), the preamble to which had recognised that the 'cessation of all nuclear weapon test explosions and all other nuclear explosions' was 'an effective measure of nuclear disarmament and non-proliferation in all its aspects'.[5]

The headline on the front cover of The Economist's 30 January 2021 issue had asked, 'Who will go nuclear next?'[6] The associated article considered the possible emergence of Iran, Saudi Arabia, and Turkey as new nuclear-armed States. While the piece tempered the likelihood that of further proliferation occurring in the short term, the fact that the question was even being seriously posed demonstrates the cracks that have appeared in the nuclear non-proliferation regime.

Moving forward, the chance of trilateral negotiations between China, Russia, and the United States even beginning, let alone coalescing in a replacement for the New START Treaty, in 2026 is minimal. Any such replacement will be down to Russia and the United States, and to them alone. It has been suggested that the two nuclear superpowers revisit proposals from earlier treaties, such as a prohibition or at least greater curbs on land-based MIRVed missiles, as had been set forth in the 1993 START II Treaty.[7] This could ease the pressure to launch land-based ICBMs early in a crisis. That said, Russia considers MIRVed land-based missiles to be a part of its response to US ballistic missile defences and is unlikely to accept such a proposal unless the United States yields on its planned missile defence systems.[8]

A path to both effective cessation of the nuclear arms race and to nuclear disarmament is, nonetheless, possible. Limited missile defence against rogue nations, such as North Korea, could be achievable by the United States, in consultation with others, especially but not only the Russian Federation, without provoking further vertical proliferation. This could and should be codified in new international law. But it would require statesmanship on a level that has been largely absent from the leaders of the major military powers. Even deeply flawed human beings like Richard Nixon and Leonid Brezhnev were able to reduce tensions and limit missile defence in the two superpowers by negotiation. Joe Biden is more knowledgeable about nuclear weapons than most if not all of the fourteen 'nuclear' US presidents who preceded him. But is he a true statesman? By November 2024, the world will know.

4 German Ministry of Foreign Affairs, 'Speech by Federal Foreign Minister Heiko Maas at the Geneva Conference: "A watershed year for arms control"', Geneva, 22 February 2021, at https://bit.ly/37T8fI2.

5 Comprehensive Nuclear-Test-Ban Treaty; adopted at New York, 10 September 1996; not yet in force, fifth preambular para.

6 At http://econ.st/39BaWiP.

7 D. S. Rudesill, 'MIRVs Matter: Banning Hydra-Headed Missiles in a New START II Treaty', *Stanford Journal of International Law*, Vol. 54, No. 1 (Winter 2018), 83–115.

8 A. F. Woolf, 'The New START Treaty: Central Limits and Key Provisions', Congressional Research Service, Washington, DC, updated 3 February 2021, at https://bit.ly/2ZfR2Ug, p. 42.

General Omar Bradley famously declared on Armistice Day (11 November) in 1948 that '[t]he world has achieved brilliance without wisdom, power without conscience. Ours is a world of nuclear giants and ethical infants'.[9] Three-quarters of a century later, his words are as true now as they were then.

[9] No. 8126, in R. Andrews, M. Biggs, and M. Seidel (eds.), *The Columbia World of Quotations*, Columbia University Press, New York, 1996, quotation available online at http://bit.ly/2TRWFWI.

Select Bibliography

BOOKS

R. C. Avenhaus, V. Kremenyuk, and G. Sjöstedt (eds.), *Containing the Atom*, New York: Lexington Books, 2002.

P. Ball, *Serving the Reich: The Struggle for the Soul of Physics under Hitler*, Chicago: University of Chicago Press, 2014.

G. Barass, *The Great Cold War: A Journey through the Hall of Mirrors*, Stanford: Stanford University Press, 2009.

M. Beschloss, *Presidents of War: The Epic Story, from 1807 to Modern Times*, New York: Broadway Books, 2019.

J. L. Black-Branch, *The Treaty on the Prohibition of Nuclear Weapons: Legal Challenges for Military Doctrines and Deterrence Policies*, Cambridge: Cambridge University Press, 2021.

R. Braithwaite, *Armageddon and Paranoia: The Nuclear Confrontation*, London: Profile Books, 2019.

H. G. Brauch (ed.), *Military Technology, Armaments Dynamics and Disarmament: ABC Weapons, Military Use of Nuclear Energy and of Outer Space and Implications for International Law*, London: Palgrave Macmillan, 1989.

S. Breyman, *Why Movements Matter: The West German Peace Movement and U.S. Arms Control*, New York: SUNY Press, 2001.

W. Burr and J. Kimball (eds.), *Nuclear Weapons, the Vietnam War, and the 'Nuclear Taboo'*, reproduced in National Security Archive Electronic Briefing Book No. 195.

W. E. Burrows and R. Windrem, *Critical Mass: The Dangerous Race for Superweapons in a Fragmenting World*, New York: Simon & Schuster, 1994.

S. Casey-Maslen, *Jus ad Bellum: The Law on Inter-State Use of Force*, Oxford: Hart Publishing, 2020.

S. Casey-Maslen (ed.), *Weapons under International Human Rights Law*, Cambridge: Cambridge University Press, 2014.

S. Casey-Maslen with S. Haines, *Hague Law Interpreted: The Conduct of Hostilities under the Law of Armed Conflict*, Oxford: Hart Publishing, 2018.

T. B. Cochran, W. M. Arkin, and M. M. Hoenig, *Nuclear Weapons Databook, Vol. I: U.S. Nuclear Forces and Capabilities*, Cambridge, MA: National Resources Defense Council, 1984.

T. B. Cochran, R. S. Norris, and O. A. Bukharin, *Making the Russian Bomb: From Stalin to Yeltsin*, Boulder: Westview Press, 1995.

G. DeGroot, *The Bomb: A Life*, London: Jonathan Cape, 2004.

T. Downing, 1983: *The World at the Brink*, London: Little, Brown, 2018.

Y. Dinstein, *The Conduct of Hostilities under the Law of International Armed Conflict*, 3rd ed., Cambridge: Cambridge University Press, 2016.

Y. Dinstein, *Non-international Armed Conflicts in International Law*, 2nd ed., Cambridge: Cambridge University Press, 2021.
Y. Dinstein, *War, Aggression and Self-Defence*, 6th ed., Cambridge: Cambridge University Press, 2017.
W. Epstein, *The Last Chance: Nuclear Proliferation and Arms Control*, New York: Free Press, 1976.
F. FitzGerald, *Way Out There in the Blue: Reagan, Star Wars, and the End of the Cold War*, New York: Touchstone, 2001.
J. Goldblat, *Arms Control: The New Guide to Negotiations and Agreements*, Thousand Oaks: Sage, 2002.
M. Gorbachev, *Memoirs*, New York: Doubleday, 1995.
R. Gottemoeller, *Negotiating the New START Treaty*, New York: Cambria Press, 2021.
C. Gray, *International Law and the Use of Force*, 4th ed., Oxford: Oxford University Press, 2018.
P. Ham, *Hiroshima Nagasaki*, London: Transworld Publishers, 2013.
D. Holloway, *Stalin and the Bomb: The Soviet Union and Atomic Energy, 1939–1956*, New Haven: Yale University Press, 1996.
D. Irving, *The German Atomic Bomb*, New York: Simon & Schuster, 1967.
H. K. Jacobson and E. Stein, *Diplomats, Scientists, and Politicians: The United States and the Nuclear Test Ban Negotiations*, Ann Arbor: University of Michigan Press, 1966.
R. Jungk, *Brighter than 1000 Suns*, trans. J. Cluegh, London: Penguin Books, 1980.
J. Keegan (ed.), *The Times Atlas of the Second World War*, 1st ed., London: Times Books, October 1989.
P. R. Lavoy, S. D. Sagan, and J. J. Wirtz (eds.), *Planning the Unthinkable: How Powers Will Use Nuclear, Biological and Chemical Weapons*, Ithaca: Cornell University Press, 2000.
E. Louka, *Nuclear Weapons, Justice and the Law*, Cheltenham: Edward Elgar, 2011.
D. McCullough, *Truman*, New York: Simon & Schuster, 1992.
G. Nystuen, S. Casey-Maslen, and A. G. Bersagel (eds.), *Nuclear Weapons under International Law*, Cambridge: Cambridge University Press, 2014.
P5 Working Group on the Glossary of Key Nuclear Terms, *P5 Glossary of Key Nuclear Terms*, 1st ed., Beijing: China Atomic Energy Press, 2015.
I. Pogany (ed.), *Nuclear Weapons and International Law*, Aldershot: Avebury, 1987.
T. Powers, *Heisenberg's War: The Secret History of the German Bomb*, London: Jonathan Cape, 1993.
B. Pullman, *The Atom in the History of Human Thought*, Oxford: Oxford University Press, 1998.
T. C. Reed and D. B. Stillman, *The Nuclear Express: A Political History of the Bomb and Its Proliferation*, Minneapolis: Zenith Press, 2009.
R. Reeves, *President Nixon, Alone in the White House*, New York: Simon & Schuster, 2001.
E. Reischauer, *My Life between Japan and America*, New York: Harper Collins, 1986.
P. L. Rose, *Heisenberg and the Nazi Atomic Bomb Project, 1939–1945: A Study in German Culture*, Berkeley: University of California Press, 2001.
T. Ruys, *'Armed Attack' and Article 51 of the UN Charter: Evolutions in Customary Law and Practice*, Cambridge: Cambridge University Press, 2010.
Y. Sandoz, C. Swinarski, and B. Zimmermann (eds.), *Commentary to the Additional Protocols of 8 June 1977 to the Geneva Conventions of 12 August 1949*, Geneva: ICRC/Martinus Nijhoff, 1987.
M. I. Shaker, *The Nuclear Non-proliferation Treaty. Origins and Implementation 1959–1979*, 3 vols., London/Rome/New York: Oceana Publications, March 1980.
G. P. Shultz, *Turmoil and Triumph: Diplomacy, Power, and the Victory of the American Ideal*, New York: Charles Scriber's Sons, 1993.
E. Schlosser, *Command and Control*, New York: Penguin, 2014.
S. I. Schwartz (ed.), *Atomic Audit: The Costs and Consequences of U.S. Nuclear Weapons Since 1940*, Washington, DC: The Brookings Institution, 1998.
T. Shea, *Verifying Nuclear Disarmament*, 1st ed., New York: Routledge, 2019.

C. Stahn, *A Critical Introduction to International Criminal Law*, Cambridge: Cambridge University Press, 2019.

T. Skylark, *Final Months of the Pacific War*, Washington, DC: Georgetown University Press, 2002.

A. Speer, *Inside the Third Reich*, London: Weidenfeld & Nicholson, 2003.

A. Summers, *The Arrogance of Power: The Secret World of Richard Nixon*, London: Orion Books, 2000.

S. Weart and G. Szilard, *Leo Szilard: His Version of the Facts*, Cambridge, MA: MIT Press, 1978.

S. Weintraub, *MacArthur's War: Korea and the Undoing of an American Hero*, New York: Free Press, 2000.

H. G. Wells, *The World Set Free*, n.p., 1914.

R. K. Wilcox, *Japan's Secret War*, 3rd rev. ed., New York: Permuted Press, 2019.

M. Wolverton, *Burning The Sky: Operation Argus and the Untold Story of the Cold War Nuclear Tests in Outer Space*, New York: Abrams Press, 2018.

S. J. Zaloga, *The Kremlin's Nuclear Sword: The Rise and Fall of Russia's Strategic Nuclear Forces, 1945–2000*, Washington, DC: Smithsonian Books, 2002.

ARTICLES, BOOK CHAPTERS, MONOGRAPHS, AND REPORTS

T. B. Allen and N. Polmar, 'The Radio Broadcast That Ended World War II', *The New Atlantic*, 7 August 2015.

D. M. Allison and S. Herzog, '"What about China?" and the Threat to US–Russian Nuclear Arms Control', *Bulletin of the Atomic Scientists*, Vol. 76, No. 4 (2020), 200–5.

J. V. Anderson and A. J. Nelson, 'The INF Treaty: A Spectacular, Inflexible, Time-Bound Success', *Strategic Studies Quarterly*, Summer 2019, 90–122.

A. Arimuko, E. Sujarwanto, and A. Marsono, 'Measurements of Earthquake Moment Magnitude (Mw) to Estimate Detonation Energy of a Nuclear Bomb as Plutonium-240', *Journal of Physics Conference Series*, March 2020.

K.-H. Barth, 'The Politics of Seismology: Nuclear Testing, Arms Control, and the Transformation of a Discipline', *Social Studies of Science*, Vol. 33, No. 5 (October 2003), 743–81.

M. C. Bassiouni, 'Negotiating the Treaty of Rome on the Establishment of an International Criminal Court', *Cornell International Law Journal*, Vol. 32, No. 3 (1999), Symposium Article 3.

H. A. Bethe, 'The Hydrogen Bomb', *Bulletin of the Atomic Scientists*, Vol. 6, No. 4 (April 1950), 99–104.

H. Blix, 'Safeguards and Non-proliferation: The IAEA and Efforts to Counteract the Spread of Nuclear Weapons', *IAEA Bulletin*, Summer 1985.

N. Bohr and J. A. Wheeler, 'The Mechanism of Nuclear Fission', *Physical Review*, Vol. 56 (1 September 1939), 426–50.

D. Bourantonis, 'The Negotiation of the Non-proliferation Treaty, 1965–1968: A Note', *International History Review*, Vol. 19, No. 2 (May 1997), 347–57.

Centre for Science and Security Studies of King's College London and the European Leadership Network, The P5 Process: Opportunities for Success in the NPT Review Conference, London, June 2020.

S. Charap, 'The Demise of the INF: Implications for Russia-China Relations', RAND Corporation, Document submitted on 9 April 2019, to the US-China Economic and Security Review Commission as a statement for the record for the hearing on 21 March 2019.

M. Clarke, 'Does My Bomb Look Big in This?', *International Affairs*, Vol. 80, No. 1 (2004).

A. Cohen, 'Most Favored Nation', *Bulletin of the Atomic Scientists*, Vol. 51, No. 1 (January–February 1995), 44–53.

'Conscience, Arrogation and the Atomic Scientists', *Journal of the Federation of American Scientists*, Vol. 47, No. 4 (July/August 1994).

A. D'Amato, 'Legal Aspects of the French Nuclear Tests', *American Journal of International Law*, Vol. 61, No. 1 (January 1967), 66–77.
J. W. De-Villiers, R. Jardine, and M. Reiss, 'Why South Africa Gave Up the Bomb', *Foreign Affairs*, Vol. 72, No. 5 (November/December 1993), 98–109.
E. Eaves, 'Why Is America Getting a New $100 Billion Nuclear Weapon?', *Bulletin of the Atomic Scientists*, 8 February 2021.
A. S. Eddington, 'The Internal Constitution of the Stars', *The Scientific Monthly*, Vol. 11, No. 4 (October 1920), 297–303.
J. Enkhsaikhan, 'Mongolia's Nuclear-Weapon-Free Status: Concept and Practice', *Asian Survey*, Vol. 40, No. 2 (2000).
M. Field, 'As the US, China, and Russia Build New Nuclear Weapons Systems, How Will AI Be Built In?', *Bulletin of the Atomic Scientists*, 20 December 2019.
M. Field, 'Strangelove Redux: US Experts Propose Having AI Control Nuclear Weapons', *Bulletin of the Atomic Scientists*, 30 August 2019.
E. B. Firmage, 'The Treaty on the Non-proliferation of Nuclear Weapons', *American Journal of International Law*, Vol. 63, No. 4 (October 1969), 711–46.
B. French, S. Funamoto, H. Sugiyama, R. Sakata, J. Cologne, H. M. Cullings, K. Mabuchi, and D. L. Preston, 'Measurement and Impact on Radiation Risk Estimates in the Life Span Study of Atomic Bomb Survivors', *American Journal of Epidemiology*, Vol. 187, No. 8 (August 2018), 1623–29.
F. Joliot, 'Chemical Evidence of the Transmutation of Elements', Nobel Lecture, 12 December 1935.
B. Goldschmidt, 'The Negotiation of the Non-proliferation Treaty (NPT)', *IAEA Bulletin*, Vol. 22, Nos. 3/4 (August 1980), 73–80.
R. Gottemoeller, 'The New START Verification Regime: How Good Is It?', *Bulletin of the Atomic Scientists*, 21 May 2020.
R. Grant, 'Dien Bien Phu', *Air Force Magazine*, Vol. 87, No. 8 (August 2004).
B. I. Gusev, Z. N. Abylkassimova, and K. N. Apsalikov, 'The Semipalatinsk Nuclear Test Site: A First Assessment of the Radiological Situation and the Test-Related Radiation Doses in the Surrounding Territories', *Radiation Environmental Biophysics*, Vol. 36, No. 3 (September 1997), 201–4.
M. H. Halperin, 'Nuclear Weapons and Limited War', *Journal of Conflict Resolution*, Vol. 5, No. 2 (June 1961), 146–66.
J. P. Harahan, 'On-Site Inspections under the INF Treaty, A History of the On-Site Inspection Agency and Treaty Implementation, 1988–1991', Washington, DC: US Government Printing Office, 1993.
J. R. Harvey and S. Michalowski, 'Nuclear Weapons Safety: The Case of Trident', *Science & Global Security*, Vol. 4, No. 3 (1994), 261–337.
S. Hill, 'NATO and the Treaty on the Prohibition of Nuclear Weapons', Research Paper, Chatham House, London, January 2021.
M. S. Holmes, 'Spies Who Spilled Atomic Bomb Secrets', *Smithsonian Magazine*, 19 April 2009.
Independent International Fact-Finding Mission on the Conflict in Georgia, Report, Vol. II, September 2009.
International Law Commission (ILC) Draft articles on Responsibility of States for Internationally Wrongful Acts, with commentaries, 2001; text adopted by the ILC at its fifty-third session, in 2001, and submitted to the UN General Assembly as a part of the Commission's report covering the work of that session, in UN doc. A/56/10.
IPPNW, *Radioactive Heaven and Earth: The Health and Environmental Effects of Nuclear Weapons Testing in, on, and above the Earth*, New York: Apex Press, 1991.
F. L. Kirgis, 'North Korea's Withdrawal from the Nuclear Nonproliferation Treaty', *ASIL Insights*, Vol. 8, No. 2 (24 January 2003).

P. Kirsch and J. T. Holmes, 'The Rome Conference on an International Criminal Court: The Negotiating Process', *American Journal of International Law*, Vol. 93, No. 1 (January 1999), 2–12.

W. L. Kohl, 'Nuclear Sharing in Nato and the Multilateral Force', *Political Science Quarterly*, Vol. 80, No. 1 (March 1965), 88–109.

H. M. Kristensen, R. S. Norris, and J. Diamond, 'Pakistani Nuclear Forces, 2018', *Bulletin of the Atomic Scientists*, Vol. 74, No. 5 (2018), 348–58.

H. M. Kristensen and R. S. Norris, 'Russian Nuclear Forces, 2018', *Bulletin of the Atomic Scientists*, Vol. 74, No. 3 (2018), 185–95.

H. M. Kristensen and M. Korda, 'Chinese Nuclear Forces, 2020', *Bulletin of the Atomic Scientists*, Vol. 76, No. 6 (November–December 2020), 443–57.

H. M. Kristensen and M. Korda, 'French Nuclear Forces, 2019', *Bulletin of the Atomic Scientists*, Vol. 75, No. 1 (2019), 51–55.

R. McDermott, 'Russia's Aerospace Forces Prepare Training for Kinzhal Hypersonic Missiles', *Eurasia Daily Monitor*, Vol. 17, No. 67 (May 2020).

J. C. McDowell, 'The Edge of Space: Revisiting the Karman Line', *Acta Astronautica*, Vol. 151 (October 2018), 668–77.

L. Meitner and O. R. Frisch, 'Disintegration of Uranium by Neutrons: a New Type of Nuclear Reaction', Letter, *Nature*, Vol. 143 (1939), 239–40.

C. Mills, 'Replacing the UK's Nuclear Deterrent: Progress of the Dreadnought Class', Research Paper, House of Commons Library, 11 February 2020.

M. S. Minor, 'China's Nuclear Development Program', *Asian Survey*, Vol. 16, No. 6 (June 1976), University of California Press, 571–79.

P. H. Nitze, 'The Vladivostok Accord and SALT II', *The Review of Politics*, Vol. 37, No. 2 (April 1975), 147–60.

I. Noddack, 'Über das Element 93', *Angewandte Chemie*, Vol. 47, No. 37 (15 September 1934), 653–55.

R. S. Norris and H. M. Kristensen, 'Global Nuclear Weapons Inventories, 1945–2010', *Bulletin of the Atomic Scientists*, Vol. 66, No. 4 (2010), 77–83.

T. O'Donnell, 'Security Council Resolution 1530, Evidence and the United Nations Security Council', *Proceedings of the Annual Meeting* (American Society of International Law), 29 March–1 April 2006, Vol. 100 (2006), 47–51.

G. Oestern (ed.), *Nuclear Weapons Ban Monitor 2020*, Oslo: Norwegian People's Aid, January 2021.

A. Persbo, 'A Reflection on the Current State of Nuclear Non-proliferation and Safeguards', Non-proliferation Papers, No. 8 (February 2012), European Union (EU) Non-proliferation Consortium.

S. Pivot, M. Baroni, E. Bard, and X. Giraud, 'A Comparison of 36Cl Nuclear Bomb Inputs Deposited in Snow From Vostok and Talos Dome, Antarctica, Using the 36Cl/Cl− Ratio', *Journal of Geophysical Research*, Vol. 124, No. 20 (27 October 2019).

K. Reif and S. Bugos, 'U.S., Russia Hit Impasse on New START', *Arms Control Today*, October 2020.

Report by the Maralinga Rehabilitation Technical Advisory Committee (MARTAC) on the Rehabilitation of Former Nuclear Test Sites at Emu and Maralinga (Australia), 2003.

Report of the Independent International Commission of Inquiry on the Syrian Arab Republic, UN doc. A/HRC/27/60, 13 August 2014.

D. A. Rosenberg, 'American Atomic Strategy and the Hydrogen Bomb Decision', *Journal of American History*, Vol. 66, No. 1 (1 June 1979), 62–87.

D. S. Rudesill, 'MIRVs Matter: Banning Hydra-Headed Missiles in a New START II Treaty', *Stanford Journal of International Law*, Vol. 54, No. 1 (Winter 2018), 83–115.

P. H. Sand, 'Diego Garcia: British–American Legal Black Hole in the Indian Ocean?', *Journal of Environmental Law*, Vol. 21, No. 1 (1 January 2009), 113–37.

T. S. Sechser, 'Sharing the Bomb: How Foreign Nuclear Deployments Shape Nonproliferation and Deterrence', *Nonproliferation Review*, Vol. 23, Nos.3–4 (2016), 443–58.

D. Shapley, 'Nuclear Weapons History: Japan's Wartime Bomb Projects Revealed', *Science*, Vol. 199, No. 4325 (13 January 1978), 152–57.

'The Position of the United States on Current Law of War Agreements: Remarks of Judge Abraham D Sofaer, Legal Adviser, US Department of State, 22 January 1987', *American University Journal of International Law and Policy*, Vol. 2 (1987), 460.

G. Thielmann, 'The Missile Gap Myth and Its Progeny', *Arms Control Today*, May 2011.

J. Trebes and T. Lavietes, 'Monitoring a Nuclear Weapon from the Inside', 'Monitoring a Nuclear Weapon from the Inside', *Science & Technology Review*, July/August 2008, Lawrence Livermore National Laboratory, 12–19.

United States Department of the Air Force, *International Law – The Conduct of Armed Conflict and Air Operations*, Air Force Pamphlet 110–31, 1976.

United States Department of Defense, *Law of War Manual*, updated December 2016, Washington, DC, 2016.

United States Department of the Navy, *Annotated Supplement to the Commander's Handbook on the Law of Naval Operations*, Doc. NWP 9 (REV. A)/FMFM 1–10, Washington, DC, 1989.

K. Young, 'The Skybolt Crisis of 1962: Muddle or Mischief?', *Journal of Strategic Studies*, Vol. 27, No. 4 (2004), 614–35.

J. S. Walker, 'Recent Literature on Truman's Atomic Bomb Decision: A Search for Middle Ground', *Diplomatic History*, Vol. 29, No. 2 (April 2005), 311–34.

M. Willrich, 'The Treaty on the Non-proliferation of Nuclear Weapons', *The Yale Law Journal*, Vol. 77, No. 8 (July 1968), 1447–519.

A. F. Woolf, 'The New START Treaty: Central Limits and Key Provisions', Congressional Research Service, Washington, DC, updated 3 February 2021.

A. F. Woolf, 'Strategic Arms Control After START: Issues and Options', Congressional Research Service, Washington, DC, updated 6 May 2010.

C. M. Wright and L.-E. De Geer, 'The 22 September 1979 Vela Incident: The Detected Double-Flash', *Science & Global Security*, Vol. 25, No. 3 (2017), 95–124.

C. M. Wright and L.-E. De Geer, 'The 22 September 1979 Vela Incident: Radionuclide and Hydroacoustic Evidence for a Nuclear Explosion', *Science & Global Security*, Vol. 26, No. 1 (2018), 1–35.

Index

Ababeel (missiles), 44
Able Archer 83 (exercise), 33, 34, 60
ABM Treaty, 47
  withdrawal from, 47
actus reus, 217
acute radiation syndrome, 166
Addis Ababa, 152
Additional Protocol (to an IAEA Comprehensive Safeguards Agreement), 84, 180, 185, 186
Additional Protocol I (1977), 205, 208
AFCONE, 152
Afghanistan
  Soviet invasion of, 134
African Union, 151
aggression, 43, 71, 161, 217
aggression, crime of, 217
aggression, prohibition of, 199
Agni-V (ICBM), 43
Air Force One, 33
Alavi, Mahmoud, 2
Albania, 71
Aleppo, 224
Algeria, 103, 108
Almaty Declaration (1997), 153
American University in Washington, 108
Americium, 168
Andropov, Yuri, 31, 32
Anschluss, 18
Antarctic, 105
Antarctic Treaty (1959), 73, 105, 142
Anti-Ballistic Missile (ABM) Treaty, 118, 130
  US withdrawal, 119
anti-ballistic missile defence, 34, 129
Antigua and Barbuda, 165, 171
anti-satellite weapons, 143
Antonov, Anatoly, 120
Apartheid, 45
Arak, 183, 187
Arakatsu, Bunsaku, 22
Argentina, 41, 78, 105, 183
Arihant Class submarines, 43
Aristotle, 105
Arkhipov, Vasili, 61
armed conflict, 159
  India and Pakistan (2019), 44
  International, 78
arms race, 1, 7, 27, 31, 90, 93, 119
artificial intelligence, 7, 51, 196
ASEAN, 150
assistance, prohibition of, 78
  non-nuclear-weapon States Parties to the NPT, 81
atmospheric tests, 215
Atomic Energy Act (US), 16, 36, 73
Atomic Energy Commission (US), 16
Atomic Energy Organisation of Iran, 183
atomic scientists, 7
Atomic Weapons Establishment (UK), 77
Atoms for Peace speech, 82
Attorney-General (UK), 91, 93
Australia, 42, 105, 112, 176, 215
Austria, 171, 172
autonomous weapons, 7

B-29 bombers, 62
B-61 (bombs), 77
B61-12 (bomb), 49
Babur-3 (SLCM), 44
Backfire (bomber), 133
Bahrain, 156
Bangkok Treaty, 150, 160
  Annex, 151
Bangladesh, 165, 171
barium, 10
Baruch, Bernard, 67
Baruch Plan, 67, 188
Bay of Pigs invasion, 60
BBC, 167
BBC China, 185
BBC Home Service, 56
Belarus, 2, 7, 45, 74, 131, 135, 136, 190, 192, 195

Belgium, 19, 77, 86, 105, 112, 189, 218, 219
belligerent reprisals, 205, 206
Ben-Gurion, David, 40
Benin, 165
Beria, Lavrentiy, 24
Beryllium, 16
Bevin, Ernest, 36
BGM-109, 190
Bhutan, 112
Bhutto, Zulfikar Ali, 43
Biden, Joe, 49, 85, 121, 227
Bikini atoll, 26, 100
Billingslea, Marshall, 125
bin Salman, Mohammed, 78
binding energy, 8
biological weapons, 204
Biological Weapons Convention, 159
Blinken, Antony, 3
Blix, Hans, 84, 182, 185
Blue Streak, 36
Bockscar, 56
Bohr, Niels, 10, 16, 21
Bolivia, 144
boosted (nuclear weapons), 30
Bosnia and Herzegovina, 142
Bothe, Walther, 19
Botswana, 171
Bourantonis, Dimitris, 72
Bouteflika, Abdelaziz, 86
Bradley, Omar, 228
Brazil, 71, 79, 144, 146
break-out time, 2
Brezhnev, Leonid, 126, 134
broken arrows, 64
Brookings Institution, 131, 139
Budapest, 136
Bulletin of the Atomic Scientists, 49, 176
Burg, Avraham, 40
Burundi, 151
Bush, George H. W., 46, 101, 135, 137
Bush, George W., 46, 131, 138
Byrnes, James, 25, 36, 53

caesium, 166
Cairncross, John, 24
Canada, 67
Cançado Trindade, Antônio Augusto, 215
cancer, 103
Carolinum, 8
Carter, Jimmy, 31, 134
Casey, William, 126
Castle Bravo (test), 100
CEND (Initiative), 87
Centers for Disease Control and Prevention (CDC), 166
centrifuge, 12
Chadwick, James, 9
chain reaction, 13, 15, 21, 114
Charter of the International Military Tribunal (1945), 218
Chemical Weapons Convention (1992), 68, 112, 159, 162
Chernenko, Konstantin, 34
Chernobyl, 34, 86
Chevalier, Haakon, 13
Chicago Pile-1, 9, 13
Chile, 105, 144, 155
China, 3, 7, 23, 27, 42, 47, 50, 62, 67, 69, 71, 74, 89, 90, 94, 96, 98, 109, 113, 115, 116, 121, 122, 132, 139, 143, 153, 155
  nuclear weapons programme, 39
Chita, city of, 190
chlorine-36, 107
Christmas Island, 103, 167
Churchill, Winston, 20, 25, 36
civilian objects, 207
civilians, 207
Cleverly, James, 91
Clinton Engineering Works, 13
Clinton, Bill, 101, 112, 137
Clinton, Hillary, 121
Cobalt-60, 204
Cold War, 1, 2, 27, 33, 47, 50, 51, 52, 59, 65, 90, 105, 112, 135, 139, 154, 167
Collective Security Treaty (1992), 154, 161
Columbia University, 10, 11
Commission for International Control of Atomic Weapons, 67
Commission for the Southeast Asia Nuclear Weapon-Free Zone, 151
Commission on Disarmament, 69
Comoros, 112
Comprehensive Safeguards Agreement, 83, 171, 180
concrete dome, 168
Conference on Disarmament, 42, 89, 91, 112, 143, 226
Conference on the Discontinuance of Nuclear Weapon Tests, 107
Congo, 13
Conrad, David, 114
continuous at-sea deterrent, 37
Convention on the Law of the Sea, 161
Cook Islands, 72, 148
COPREDAL, 145
Costa Rica, 144, 157, 165, 171
Cotton, Tom, 127
counterstrike weapon, 32, 37
Countryman, Thomas, 49
Covenant on Civil and Political Rights (1966), 210
COVID-19, 155
Crawford, James, 215

Creating an Environment for Nuclear Disarmament (CEND), 226
crime against humanity, 33, 217, 223
critical mass, 15, 21, 115
Croatia, 219
Crockcroft, John, 36
cruise missile, 1, 28, 31
CTBT, 3, 38, 42, 60, 80, 89, 98, 99, 104, 110, 112, 153, 158, 159, 166, 175, 177, 198, 226, 227
  Annex 2 States, 113, 117
  International Monitoring System, 113, 175, 177
  on-site inspections, 179
  protocol on on-site inspections, 179
  verification regime, 177
CTBTO, 99, 114, 177
  Executive Council, 179
Cuba, 30, 71, 112, 115, 146, 164, 165, 171
Cuban Missile Crisis, 30, 52, 60, 68, 107, 176
customary international law, 78, 80, 92, 109, 115, 143, 160, 172, 198, 199, 205, 214, 218
cyber operations, 7, 50, 196
cyclotron, 17, 22
Czechia, 106, 219
Czechoslovakia, 19, 189, 190
Czechoslovakia, invasion of, 129

Davy Crockett, 28
de Gaulle, Charles, 38
De Geer, Lars-Erik, 176
de Klerk, F. W., 45
decapitation (strike), 31
DEFCON, 61
De-MIRV-ing Agreement, 32
Democratic People's Republic of Korea. *See* North Korea
Democritus, 8
Demon core, 16
Depositary States, 109, 111, 142
destroy and join, 169
deuterium, 15, 19, 30
Deutsche Welle, 92
development (of nuclear weapons), 7, 23, 67
  Regulation under the NPT, 80
DF-41 (ICBM), 40
Diego Garcia, 153
Dien Bien Phu, Battle of, 38, 63
Dimona, 40, 41
Dinstein, Yoram, 200, 204
directed-energy weapons, 34
Dirty Harry (test), 100
disarmament, 2, 35, 67, 68, 159, 213
Disarmament Committee, 69, *See also* Conference on Disarmament
Disarmament Committee, Conference of the, 70
disarmament obligations, 169
discriminatory (instrument), 74
dolus specialis, 225
Donne, John, 14
Doomsday Clock, 13
Doomsday Machine, 51
Dr Strangelove, 27, 51, 54
Dragon's tail, 15
Dreadnought Class submarines, 37
drones, 128
dualist State, 219
dual-key (control), 77
Dulles, Allen, 107
Duma, 132

East Berlin, 108
East Germany, 33, 189, 190
Eastwood, Clint, 100
The Economist, 6, 227
Ecuador, 114, 144, 171
Eddington, Arthur, 8
Egypt, 41, 61, 81, 113, 156, 207
Einstein, Albert, 7, 11, 16
Eisenhower, Dwight D., 60, 62, 82, 107
Eisenhower administration, 29
El Salvador, 146
ElBaradei, Mohamed, 183
The Elders, 92
electro-magnetic pulse (EMP), 101
Emperor Hirohito, 53, 57
Emu Field, 103
Enewetak atoll, 26, 100, 168
Enola Gay, 55
environmental remediation, 65, 167
Epstein, William, 1, 72, 78
espionage. *See also* Spy
Estonia, 219
ET.317 (warhead), 75
ETA, 201
evil empire (quote), 33
Exercise Desert Rock I, 101
expenditure (on nuclear arms), 1
explosive yield, 15, 39, 43, 44, 46, 56, 77, 99, 104, 111

Fallout (radioactive), 168, 204
Fangataufa atoll, 103
Fat Man (bomb), 14, 56
Federation of American Scientists, 90, 133, 134
Fermi, Enrico, 9, 26
F-Go (programme), 22
Fiji, 103, 165, 171
Financing, 162
Finland, 27, 33, 87
firebombing of Tokyo, 54
Firmage, Edwin Brown, 77
First World War, 9

fission, 8, 10
  device, 57
fission bomb, 7
Fitzpatrick, Mark, 84, 92
Flyorov, Georgy Nikolayevich, 24
Forsyth, Robert, 222
France, 7, 19, 23, 38, 67, 71, 74, 86, 90, 98, 103, 105, 108, 109, 115, 149, 153, 205, 215, 216
  nuclear weapons programme, 38
French armed forces, 63
French Far East Expeditionary Corps, 63
Fromm, Friedrich, 20
Fuchs, Klaus, 16, 24, 25
fusion, 8, 26
fusion bomb. *See also* Thermonuclear

Gadget (bomb), 15
Gadhafi, Muammar, 185
The Gambia, 171
gamma rays, 110, 176
García-Margallo, José Manuel, 65
gaseous diffusion, 12
Gates, Robert, 193
general international law, 198, *See also* customary international law
Geneva, 129
genocide, 26, 217, 224
Gerasimov, Valery, 48
Gerboise bleue, 103
Germany, 33, 42, 77, 86, 87, 126, 185, 207, 218, 219
Glossary of Nuclear Weapons Terms, 73
Gobi desert, 104
gold-198, 204
Goldblat, Jozef, 80
Goldschmidt, Bertrand, 72, 88
good faith, 90, 92, 93
  duty of, 88
Gorbachev, Mikhail, 34, 126, 135, 188
Gottemoeller, Rose, 120, 125, 195
Grand Forks, 131
Graphite, 19
Grapple X (test), 103
Grapple Y (test), 103
Greece, 33
Greenpeace, 38
Grossi, Rafael, 85
Ground Zero, 55
Ground-Based Strategic Deterrent (GBSD) programme, 49
Groves, Leslie, 12, 13, 16, 19
Guam, 55

Hague Convention II (1899), 209
Hahn, Otto, 10
Hanford, 14
  site clean-up, 14
Harahan, Joseph, 190
heavy bomber, 123, 124
heavy water, 17, 19, 30, 40, 183
heavy-water reactor, 187
Heisenberg, Werner, 17, 20
Helms, Richard, 41
Hercules Plant No. I, 191
hibakusha, 167
Hiroshima, 21, 23, 53, 55, 206
HMS Repulse, 222
Holy See, 171
Honduras, 171
Houtermans, Fritz, 9
Human Rights Committee, 210, 216
Hungarian complex, 31
Hussein, Saddam, 185
Hyde Park Agreement, 35
Hydro, 19
hydrodynamic yield measurement, 111
hydrogen, 8, 9, 26
hydrogen, heavy, 26
Hydro-nuclear testing, 115

IAEA, 45, 46, 79, 82, 83, 145, 149, 150, 152, 164, 169, 171, 174, 183, 192
  Additional Protocol, 171
  routine inspections, 182
  Safeguards. *See also* Comprehensive Safeguards Agreement; Additional Protocol
  Safeguards agreements, 171
  safeguards regime, 180
ICBM, 1, 2, 28, 29, 122, 125, 143
  bases, 195
  launchers, 134
Iceland, 219
ICRC, 162, 204, 207, 208
  Study of Customary IHL, 207
ICTY, 206
  Krstić case, 224
  Kupreškić case, 206
Il Sung, Kim, 46
Imperial Japan, 7
inalienable (right), 160
Independent International Fact-Finding Mission on the Conflict in Georgia, 201
India, 1, 7, 23, 71, 72, 79, 88, 95, 96, 99, 112, 113, 116, 132, 202, 214
  nuclear weapons programme, 42
Indiscriminate attack, notion of, 203
individual criminal responsibility, 216
Indochina, 52
Indonesia, 88, 150, 155, 162
Indo-Pakistani war (1971), 44

INF Treaty, 2, 31, 35, 118, 126, 139, 226
US withdrawal, 127
verification regime, 188, 189
violation, 127
Innocent passage, right of, 161
Inspections
on-site, 108, 136, 174, 178
Institute of Physics and Atomic Energy (Beijing), 39
Interim Committee, 54
intermediate-range nuclear missiles, 2
International Atomic Energy Agency. *See* IAEA
International Committee of the Red Cross. *See* ICRC
international cooperation and assistance, 170
International Court of Justice, 88, 93, 104, 198, 201, 204, 208, 209, 213, 214
Nicaragua case, 200
Nuclear Weapons Advisory Opinion, 88, 200, 202, 208, 211
Oil Platforms case, 201, 202
International Criminal Court, 217, 218, 220, 222
international criminal law, 212
International Criminal Tribunal for the former Yugoslavia. *See* ICTY
international environmental law, 211
International Geophysical Year of 1957–58, 105
international human rights law, 166, 210
international humanitarian law, 166, 202
environmental protection, 212
principle of proportionality, 208
principle of superfluous injury, 208
International Law Commission, 212
International Military Tribunal at Nuremburg, 216
international organisations
nature of, 180
internationally wrongful act, 213
iodine, 166
Iran, 2, 44, 84, 113, 117, 140, 156, 182, 227
IAEA Additional Protocol, 187
Minister of Intelligence, 2
nuclear weapons programme, 182
Iraq, 84, 86, 182
nuclear weapons programme, 184
Ireland, 68, 171
Iskander-K, 127
Israel, 1, 7, 23, 41, 72, 96, 98, 113, 144, 156, 176
nuclear weapons programme, 40
Italy, 77, 189, 207, 218
Ivy Mike, 26
Iwo Jima, 53

Jamaica, 171
Japan, 51, 52, 83, 105
nuclear weapons programme, 22
JCPOA, 2, 84, 187
Jin-class submarines, 40
Joachimstal, 19
Johnson, Boris, 94
Johnson, Lyndon, 16, 41, 64, 83, 129
Johnston atoll, 100
join and destroy, 169
Joliot-Curie, Frédéric, 9
Jong Un, Kim, 47
Joyner, Dan, 80, 89
Jungk, Robert, 14, 16, 18, 53
Jupiter missiles, 61
jurisdiction, 82, 83, 113, 166
jus ad bellum, 199
principle of necessity, 201
principle of proportionality, 201
jus cogens, 161, 199, 203, 207, 209, 210
jus in bello, 199

Kahn, Herman, 27
Kaiser-Wilhelm Institute, 17
Kansk, 190
Kazakhstan, 2, 7, 45, 58, 59, 74, 101, 131, 135, 136, 153, 154, 158, 163, 167, 171, 193, 195, 226
Soviet arsenal, 74
Keegan, John, 53
Kehler, Claude Robert, 219
Keitel, Wilhelm, 12
Kennedy, John F., 13, 29, 38, 60, 68, 108
Kennedy, Robert F., 28, 60
Kennedy, Ted, 34
Kerry, John, 65
Khamenei, Ali, 2
Khan, A. Q., 44, 185
Khrushchev, Nikita, 27, 39, 60, 107
Ki-moon, Ban, 68
Kinzhal, 48
Kiribati, 103, 167
Kiritimati, 103
Kissinger, Henry, 64
Kokura, 53, 55
Korda, Matt, 41
Korean Air, 33
Korean War, 29, 52, 62
Kosygin, Alexei, 71
Kristensen, Hans, M., 41, 75
Kuala Lumpur, 150
Kubrick, Stanley, 27
Kurchatov, Igor, 24
Kvashnin, Anatoly, 132
Kyoto, 53
Kyrgyzstan, 153

Laboratory No. 2, 24
landmine (nuclear), 28
launch on warning, 50, 126
Lavrov, Sergei, 121

law of neutrality, 211
Lebanon, 112
legal person. *See also* private company
LeMay, Curtis, 54, 62, 63
Lenard, Philipp, 18
Lesotho, 171
Leucippus, 8
Lewis, Robert, 56
Libya, 44, 84, 112, 182
  nuclear weapons programme, 185
Lisbon Protocol (1992), 136
lithium, 27
Lithuania, 219
Little Boy (bomb), 15, 55
Lockheed X-17, 105
London, 20
Lop Nur, 104
  test site, 39
López Mateos, Adolfo, 144
Los Alamos, 12, 13, 110, 176
Lucky Dragon Number 5, 100
Luxembourg, 219

Maas, Heiko, 92, 93, 227
MacArthur, Douglas, 62
Macmillan, Harold, 36, 68, 107, 109
Macron, Emmanuel, 39
Magna, Utah, 191
Mahabharata, 15
Malaysia, 150
Malden Island, 103
Malta, 147, 171
Mandela, Nelson, 92
Manhattan Project, 7, 11, 52
  press agency, 15
manufacture, 82
manufacture, prohibition on. *See also* Production
Mao Tse Tung, 39
Maralinga, 103
Mark 41 Vertical Launch System, 128
Marshall Islands, 26, 100, 168, 213, 214
Marshall, George, 19
MAUD Committee, 11, 20, 35
MAUD Report, 11
Mauritius, 112
McCloy, John J., 13
McMahon Act. *See* Atomic Energy Act
McNamara, Robert, 28, 30, 36
Medvedev, Dmitry, 120
megadeath, 27
Meir, Golda, 41
Meitner, Lise, 10, 18
Memorandum of Understanding (1997), 131
Mendès France, Pierre, 38
mens rea, 217
Mexico, 70, 144, 171, 214, 220
Mexico City, 144
Middle East
  proposed nuclear-weapon-free zone, 155
Milch, Erhard, 20
Military preparations for use, 162
Minuteman III (missiles), 49, 61, 140
MIRV, 1, 30, 32, 37, 40, 47, 132, 136, 137, 227
missile defence, 227, *See also* Star Wars
missile technology, 82
Mitsubishi Steel and Arms Factory, 56
moderator, 19
Modernisation (of nuclear weapons), 2, 89, 139
Mongolia, 153, 155
  Nuclear-weapon-free status, 154
Monte Bello Islands, 36, 103
Moon, 111, 143
Morocco, 87
Moruroa atoll, 103
Moscow, 131
Moscow Treaty. *See SORT Treaty*
Multilateral force (MLF), 70
mushroom cloud, 26
mutual assured destruction (MAD), 30
MX (Missile Experimental), 32

Nagasaki, 14, 56, 206
Namibia, 171
Napoleon Bonaparte, 11
Natanz, 183, 184, 187
National Council of Resistance of Iran, 183
NATO, 29, 39, 69, 70, 77, 108, 126, 128, 133, 162, 218, 219
  Strategic Concept, 162
Nazi Germany, 7, 9, 11, 17, 21
Nazi Germany and the bomb, 16
negative (security) assurances, 71
Nehru, Jawaharlal, 42, 107
neptunium, 18
the Netherlands, 77, 87, 159, 161, 189, 218, 219
neutron, 9, 14, 110, 176
neutron bomb, 31
Nevada Test Site, 100, 101, 103
New Mexico, 13, 15
New START Treaty, 2, 37, 118, 119, 138, 227
  aggregate limits, 122
  Annex on Inspection Activities, 125
  extension, 121
  negotiation, 119
  on-site inspections, 195
  Protocol, 125
  verification regime, 192, 193
new technologies, 47
The New York Times, 106
New Zealand, 72, 103, 105, 165, 171, 215
Nicaragua, 171

Nichols, Kenneth D., 12
Nigata, 53
Niger, 185
Nigeria, 171
Ni-Go (programme), 22
Nishina, Yoshio, 22
nitrogen, 9
Nitze, Paul, 193
Niue, 72
Nixon, Richard, 29, 37, 61, 63, 64, 126, 129
NKVD, 24
No First Use policy, 43
Nobel Peace Prize, 119
Nobel Prize, 9, 18, 36
Noddack, Ida, 9
Non-Aligned Movement (NAM), 70, 88
non-nuclear weapon States, 3, 68, 69, 71, 74, 112
  provision of nuclear material to NPT nuclear-weapon State, 82
non-nuclear-weapon States Parties (to the NPT)
  Obligations under the NPT, 80
North Carolina, 64
North Korea, 22, 23, 44, 72, 73, 88, 95, 96, 99, 113, 116, 140, 178, 227, *See also* Democratic People's Republic of Korea
  nuclear weapons programme, 45
North Macedonia, 219
North Vietnam, 62, 64
Northrop Grumman, 49
Norway, 27, 33, 105
Norwegian Hydro-Electric Company, 19
Norwegian People's Aid, 164
Norwegian Red Cross, 209
Novator 9M729, 128
Novaya Zemlya, 27, 101, 102
NPT, 1, 3, 37, 42, 45, 46, 59, 67, 141, 146, 156, 158, 159, 188, 198
  application in armed conflict, 78
  Article VI, 86, 91, 130, 139, 188, 215
  definition of a nuclear weapon, 73, 75
  Depositary States, 72
  entry into force, 72
  extension of duration, 90
  national implementation clause, absence of, 82
  negotiation of, 69
  obligations of the nuclear-weapon States Parties, 74
  prohibition on transfer, 75
  Review and Extension Conference (1995), 90, 94, 155
  Review Conference, 3
  Review Conference (1975), 94
  Review Conference (1995), 89
  Review Conference (2000), 60, 79, 82, 95, 155
  Review Conference (2015), 69, 95, 155
  Review Conference (2021), 87, 95, 140
  review conferences, 94
  safeguards, 180
  three pillars, 68
  verification of, 82
  verification regime, 181
  withdrawal from, 46, 73
Ntaganda case, 222
nth country problem, 68, 107
nuclear arsenal, 26, 28
nuclear disarmament
  Duty to pursue, 86
nuclear energy, 81
  generation of electricity, 86
  peaceful use of, 68, 85
Nuclear Explosions for the National Economy (programme), 58
nuclear football, 219
Nuclear Nonproliferation Act (1978), 176
Nuclear Posture Review (2001), 138
nuclear sword of Damocles, 60
Nuclear Test Victims Compensation Committee (France), 216
Nuclear Threat Initiative (NTI), 50, 136, 151
nuclear triad, 43
Nuclear Weapons Ban Monitor 2020, 164, 191
Nuclear Yalta, 96
nuclear-weapon free zones, 141
nuclear-weapon States, 1, 74, 116
  definition, 74

O'Connor, Simon, 209
O'Neill, Paul, 92
Oak Ridge, 13, 23
OAU, 152
Obama, Barack, 48, 119
Oestern, Grethe, 77, 165
Okinawa, 53, 62
Oliphant, Mark, 26
OPANAL, 147, 155
Open Skies Treaty, 195
Open-Ended Working Group, 157
Operation 59–6, 39, 104
Operation Alsos III, 19
Operation Anadyr, 60
Operation Argus, 105
Operation Bravo, 26
Operation Desert Rock, 101
Operation Duck Hook, 64
Operation First Lightning, 25
Operation Fracture Jaw, 63
Operation Grapple, 103
Operation Hurricane, 36
Operation Linebacker, 64
Opération Satanique, 38
Operation Second Lightning, 25

Operation Shakti, 42
Operation Upshot-Knothole, 100
Operation Vulture, 63
Oppenheimer, Robert, 12, 15, 26
Organization of American States (OAS), 144
OSCE, 195
Outer Space Treaty (1966), 73, 110, 142
oxygen, 9

Pacific Islands Forum, 148
Pacific Proving Grounds, 100
pacta sunt servanda. *See* good faith
Pakistan, 7, 23, 42, 72, 88, 95, 96, 99, 113, 132, 202, 214
  nuclear weapons programme, 43
Palau, 171
Palestine, 72
Palomares, 65, 167
Panama, 171
Panama Canal, 58
Paraguay, 171
Partial Test-Ban Treaty, 38, 41, 59, 73, 107, 143, 159, 175
peaceful nuclear explosions, 42, 52, 57, 79, 146
Peaceful Nuclear Explosions Treaty (1976), 59, 118
peaceful purposes, 81
Peacekeeper (missile), 32
Pelindaba Treaty, 151, 160
  Protocol I, 153
the Pentagon, 12
Pentetic acid, 167
People's Mujahedin Organisation of Iran, 183
Pereira, Fernando, 38
Perrin, Francis, 21
Perry, Rick, 78
Persbo, Andreas, 81
Pershing IA, 189
Pershing II, 31, 189, 191
persistent objector status, 115
Peskov, Dmitry, 93
Petrov, Stanislav, 51, 62
the Philippines, 150
Pifer, Steven, 138
pitchblende, 9
plutonium, 12, 14, 16, 18, 25, 36, 65, 104, 168
poison, 204
Pokhran I, 42, 79
Pokhran II, 42
Poland, 33, 68, 219
Polaris, 36, 75, 205, 222
Polynesia, 104
Polyus spacecraft, 35
populated areas, attacks on, 206
Portugal, 219
positive (security) assurances, 71
potassium iodide, 166
Powers, Thomas, 21
Prague, 119
Prague Declaration, 106
Princess Elizabeth Land, 107
principle of distinction (IHL), 203
Principle of irreversibility, 90
private companies, 78
  regulation of, 75
private individuals
  regulation of acts of, 75
Private Ownership of Special Nuclear Materials Act (US), 16
production, 28
Prohibition of Nuclear Weapons Act (2019), 165
Project Alberta, 55
Project Amad, 184
Project Gasbuggy, 58
Project Plowshare, 45
Project Vela, 110, 175
Project Vela Uniform, 110, 175, 176
proliferation
  horizontal, 68
  origin of term, 68
  vertical, 68
Punggye-ri, 46
Putin, Vladimir, 47, 127, 132, 138, 189

Qom, 184
Quantum mechanics, 17

R-7 (rocket), 29
R-12 (rocket), 30
Radford, Arthur, 62
radioactive waste, 142
radioactivity, 9
radionuclide laboratories, 178
Rainbow Warrior, 38
Ramanna, Raj, 42, 79
RAND Corporation, 126
Rarotonga, 148
RDS-1, 25
RDS-2, 25
RDS-3, 26
RDS-37, 27
RDS-6s, 27
RDS-220, 27
Reagan, Ronald, 30, 31, 33, 126, 135, 188, 190
Red Army, 23, 102
Reischauer, Edwin, 53
reparation, 216
Reuters, 184
Reykjavik Summit (1986), 35, 188
Richard, Charles, 3, 37
Rio Declaration (1992), 212
Robinson, Mary, 92
Romania, 71

Rome Statute of the International Criminal Court, 217
Rongelap atoll, 100
Roosevelt, Franklin D., 11, 16, 54
Rosatom State Atomic Energy Corporation, 102
Rose, Frank, 139
Rosenberg, Julius and Ethel, 16
Royal Air Force, 37
RS-24 Yars (ICBM), 47
RS-26 Avangard, 193
Rubio, Marco, 127
Runit island, 168
RUSI, 77, 92
Rusk, Dean, 78
Russia, 2, 3, 23, 50, 58, 74, 89, 90, 93, 109, 116, 118, 119, 135, 143, 153, 154, 155, 161, 174, *See also* Soviet Union; Russian Federation
  Ministry of Foreign Affairs, 50
Russian Federation, 193
Rutherford, Ernest, 9, 21
Ryabkov, Sergei, 2

Sachs, Alexander, 11
Sahara, 103
Sahrawi Arab Democratic Republic, 151
Saint Kitts and Nevis, 171
Sakharov, Andrei, 27
SALT I Treaty, 119, 130, 132
  expiry, 133
SALT II Treaty, 133, 135
  aggregate limits, 134
  controversy, 133
salted (bomb), 204
Saransk, 25
Saturday Night Massacre, 61
Saudi Arabia, 78, 84, 156, 227
  risk of proliferation, 186
  Minister of Energy, Industry, and Mineral Resources, 186
  Small Quantities Protocol, 85
Savitsky, Valentin, 61
Schlesinger, James, 61
Schmitt, Helmut, 126
Scottish Campaign for Nuclear Disarmament, 37
Sea-Bed Treaty, 147
Second World War, 7, 13, 16, 23, 217
  bombing of cities, 202
Seismic monitoring, 111
Seismology, 177
self-defence, right of, 200
Semipalatinsk, 25, 153
Semipalatinsk Test Site, 59, 101, 167
Shaffer, Alan, 37
Shagan, 59
Shea, Thomas, 191
Shimoda case, 206
Short-range nuclear missiles, 2
Shultz, George, 35
Singapore, 50, 150, 159, 161
Six-Day War, 41
Skaar lawsuit, 66
Skybolt, 36
SLBM, 28, 29, 39, 47, 49, 122, 194, 205
SLCM, 44
Slotin, Louis, 15
Slovakia, 219
Slovenia, 106, 219
Slutsky, Leonid, 196
Small Quantities Protocol (SQP), 84, 180
  problems with, 186
Smiling Buddha, 42
Solid-fuel rockets, 82
SORT Treaty, 119, 121, 138
Source material, 83
  definition, 181
South Africa, 7, 41, 105, 152, 158, 163, 164, 171, 176
  Atomic Energy Corporation, 45
  nuclear weapons programme, 45
South Carolina, 65, 167
South Korea, 46, 51, 87
South Sudan, 72
South Vietnam, 63
Soviet Threat Reduction Act (1991), 135
Soviet Union, 1, 12, 23, 27, 29, 33, 39, 45, 52, 57, 58, 61, 67, 68, 69, 70, 74, 77, 81, 83, 98, 105, 108, 111, 119, 142, 147, 154, 174, 185, 189
  collapse of, 135
  nuclear weapons programme, 23
Spain, 153, 167, 219
special fissionable material, 83
  definition, 181
Special Relationship, 36
special theory of relativity, 7
specially affected States, 115
Speer, Albert, 20
splitting the atom, 9
Sputnik, 29
spy, 16, 24
Sri Krishna, 15
SS-18 Satan, 48, 124, 194
SS-19, 30
SS-20, 31, 33, 126, 190
SS-25, 191
SS-27, 124
St Petersburg Declaration (1868), 208
Stalin, 24, 25
Star Wars, 34, 35, 126, 140
Starfish Prime (test), 100
Stark, Johannes, 18
START I Treaty, 35, 119, 120, 135, 188, 192

START II Treaty, 32, 132, 135, 136
  denunciation, 137
START III Treaty, 132, 135, 137
State responsibility, 212
Steiner, Steven, 190
Stepping Stones initiative, 226
Stimson, Henry L., 53
Stockholm Declaration (1972), 212
Stockholm Initiative, 227
stockpile destruction, 124, 126, 136
  verification of, 174, 188
stockpiling, 123
Storax Sedan, 58
Strassmann, Fritz, 10
Strategic Arms Limitation Talks (SALT), 119, 129
Strategic Defense Initiative. *See* Star Wars
strategic nuclear arsenal, 2
Submarine (on the high seas), 208
Suez Crisis, 40
The Sunday Times, 41
superpowers, 7, 79, 118, 127, 188
Sweden, 226
Switzerland, 86
Syria, 41, 112
Szilard, Leo, 8, 9, 10, 52

Taiwan, 86
Tajikistan, 153
Tanzania, 71, 112
Taylor, Maxwell D., 28
Tehran Research Reactor, 182
telemetry, 120, 136, 194
Teller, Edward, 15, 26, 27, 34
test detonations, 52
testing, 98
  atmospheric, 99
    unilateral moratorium, 108
  China, 104
  customary international law, 115
  France, 103
  Soviet Union, 101
  sub-critical, 114
  thermonuclear, 15
  United Kingdom, 103
  United States, 99
  verification, 174, 175
Thailand, 150, 171
Thallium, 167
thousand suns, 15
Threshold Test-Ban Treaty, 111, 118
Tinian island, 55
Tito, Josip Broz, 70
TNT, 26, 56, 99
Tokyo District Court, 206
Totskoye (village), 102
transfer, 69
  NPT prohibition, 74
  of control over nuclear weapons, 77
transit, 161
Treaty of Rarotonga, 148, 160
  Protocol I, 149
  Protocol II, 149
  Protocol III, 149
Treaty of Semipalatinsk, 153, 160
Treaty of Tlatelolco (1967), 79, 144
  Additional Protocol I, 146
  OPANAL, 79
Treaty on the Prohibition of Nuclear Weapons, 3, 114, 117, 141, 154, 156, 175, 198
  Article 2 Declaration, 163
  disarmament obligations, 169
  duty to promote the universalisation of, 165
  First Meeting of States Parties, 169, 172
  verification regime, 179
Trident, 37, 75, 124
Trinity test, 14, 55
tritium, 30
Truman, Harry, 25, 54, 57, 62
Trump, Donald, 47, 48, 121
Tsar Bomba, 27, 102
Tube Alloys Directorate, 20
Tube Alloys Project, 35
Turkey, 61, 218, 227
Turkmenistan, 2, 58, 153
Tuwaitha Research Centre, 185

U Thant, 147
U-2 (spy plane), 29, 61
U-boat, 23
UID, 194
Ukraine, 2, 7, 45, 58, 74, 86, 90, 131, 135, 136, 190, 193, 195
  Soviet arsenal, 74
Union Minière du Haut-Katanga, 13
Union of Concerned Scientists, 193
United Arab Emirates, 156
United Arab Republic. *See* Egypt
United Kingdom, 1, 7, 16, 23, 35, 67, 74, 75, 76, 90, 94, 98, 105, 142, 147, 149, 153, 185, 189, 205, 207, 213, 214
  decision to increase nuclear arsenal cap, 91
  Foreign, Commonwealth and Development Office, 91
  House of Lords, 218
United Nations
  Atomic Energy Commission, 67
  Charter, 143, 147, 199
  Commission of Inquiry on Syria, 224
  Forces, 62

General Assembly, 42, 60, 68, 70, 79, 110, 144, 147, 148, 156
Resolution 1911 (XVIII), 144
Resolution 2222 (XXI), 142
Resolution 2373 (XXII), 71
Resolution 55/33S, 155
Resolution 71/258, 157
Resolution 75/33, 156
Resolution 75/35, 144
High Commissioner for Human Rights, 92
Office for Disarmament Affairs (UNODA), 73, 155
Secretary-General, 91, 145
Security Council, 67, 71, 73, 117, 217
Resolution 255, 71
Resolution 1172, 43, 116
Resolution 1530, 201
Resolution 1696, 183
Resolution 2310, 117
Resolution 2375, 47
United States, 1, 2, 3, 16, 18, 23, 26, 29, 52, 57, 59, 63, 67, 68, 70, 75, 76, 77, 78, 80, 81, 86, 87, 89, 90, 92, 95, 98, 105, 111, 113, 116, 118, 142, 143, 144, 147, 149, 156, 174, 177, 183, 185, 189, 196, 204, 205, 207, 219, 226, 227
Air Force Institute of Technology, 51
Army Corps of Engineers, 12
Army Counter-Intelligence, 12
Atomic Energy Commission, 110, 176
Central Intelligence Agency (CIA), 60, 126
Congress, 133
Defense Intelligence Agency, 90
Department of Defense, 37, 48, 65, 110, 143, 206
Department of Energy, 58, 76, 168
Department of State, 40, 85, 122, 193
Department of the Navy, 209
Environmental Protection Agency, 168
Government Accountability Office, 186
Secretary of State, 78
Senate, 131, 137
Senate Armed Services Committee, 101
Senate Foreign Relations Committee, 185, 193
Strategic Command, 3, 219
University of Chicago, 13
University of Strasbourg, 17
uranium, 8, 9, 10, 14
enrichment, 2, 36, 183
uranium ore, 45, *See also* Yellowcake
uranium, enriched, 17
uranium-235, 2, 10, 12, 18, 20, 21, 22, 39
uranium-238, 10
Uruguay, 171
Use (of nuclear weapons), 52
in 1945, 52
Uzbekistan, 2, 58, 59, 153
V-1, 29
Vajpayee, Atal Bihari, 43
Van Allen belts, 100
Vanguard Class submarines, 37
Vanuatu, 171
Vanunu, Mordechai, 41
Vela (satellites), 41
Vela incident, 176
Vemork, 19
verification, 125, 130, 136, 148, 170, 174
international, 110
national technical means, 174
victim assistance, 166
Vienna Center for Disarmament and Non-proliferation (VCDNP), 114
Vienna Convention on the Law of Treaties, 93, 116
Viet Cong, 64
Viet Minh, 63
Vietnam, 63, 171
Vietnam War, 58, 63
The Virus House, 17
Volga River, 59
Von Braun, Werner, 61
von Weizsäcker, Carl Friedrich, 17, 20
Votkinsk Machine Building Plant, 191

W25 (warhead), 105
W47 (warhead), 75
W58 (warhead), 75
W76 (warhead), 37, 75
W87 (warhead), 32
W93 (warhead), 37, 76
Wallace, Ben, 76, 77, 91
War crime, 217, 220
of attacking civilians, 221
Warheads, 82
Washington Conference on Antarctica, 106
The Washington Post, 167
weapons of mass destruction, 143
Weinberger, Casper, 126
Weiss, Leonard, 176
Wells, H. G., 8
West Germany, 69, 71, 83, 189
Westmoreland, William, 63
Wheeler, John Archibald, 10
Whyte Gómez, Elayne, 157
Wilcox, Robert, 22
Wilson, Harold, 83, 108
withdrawal clause, 109
Wood, Lowell, 101
Woodliffe, John, 77
Woolf, Amy, 120
world without nuclear weapons, 48, 119
Wright, Christopher, 176

xenon
  poisoning, 14
Xinjiang province, 39
X-rays, 110, 176

Yalta, 25
Yamata, 56
Yellowcake, 41
Yellowknife, 178
Yeltsin, Boris, 137
Yom Kippur War (1973), 41, 61
Yongbyon, 46

Zaloga, Steven, 27
Zambia, 71
Zerbo, Lassina, 99, 114
Zinn, Walter, 10
Zumwalt, Elmo, 61